The Archaeologist's Field Handbook

The Archaeologist's Field Handbook

North American Edition

Heather Burke, Claire Smith,
and Larry J. Zimmerman

ALTAMIRA
PRESS

A Division of
ROWMAN & LITTLEFIELD PUBLISHERS, INC.
Lanham • New York • Toronto • Plymouth, UK

AltaMira Press
A division of Rowman & Littlefield Publishers, Inc.
A wholly owned subsidiary of The Rowman & Littlefield Publishing Group, Inc.
4501 Forbes Boulevard, Suite 200
Lanham, MD 20706
www.altamirapress.com

Estover Road
Plymouth PL6 7PY
United Kingdom

British Library Cataloguing in Publication Information Available

Library of Congress Cataloging-in-Publication Data

Burke, Heather, 1966–
  The archaeologist's field handbook / Heather Burke, Claire Smith, and Larry J. Zimmerman.—
North American ed.
    p. cm.
  Includes index.
  ISBN-13: 978-0-7591-0882-0 (cloth : alk. paper)
  ISBN-10: 0-7591-0882-X (cloth : alk. paper)
  ISBN-13: 978-0-7591-0883-7 (pbk. : alk. paper)
  ISBN-10: 0-7591-0883-8 (pbk. : alk. paper)
  eISBN-13: 978-0-7591-1227-8
  eISBN-10: 0-7591-1227-4
  1. Archaeology—Handbooks, manuals, etc. 2. Excavations (Archaeology)—Handbooks, manuals, etc.
I. Smith, Claire, 1957– II. Zimmerman, Larry J., 1947– III. Title.

CC76.B87 2009
930.1—dc22   2008014108

CONTENTS

PREFACE

This book began its existence in Australia with a similar title, authored by Heather Burke and Claire Smith and published by Allen and Unwin. After reading it, Mitch Allen, then of AltaMira Press, recognized that the book could have utility in the United States and encouraged Heather and Claire to turn the text into a version that could see use outside Australia. At the 2004 meeting of the Society for American Archaeology, Mitch, Heather, and Claire asked Larry Zimmerman to "Americanize" the volume, which he agreed to do. Larry, in turn, shifted the Australian terminology to American usage and rewrote those parts that were very specific to Australian archaeology. At the same time, none of the authors wished to entirely remove the Australian "flavour" of the book, so we hope that you will find it here and there. (Yes, except for the spelling of *flavor* in the last sentence and the occasional quotation from an Australian source, Larry did change spellings to the American version!) You'll certainly see this decision to retain the book's Australian influence in the references. Larry added pertinent American references but chose to leave many of the Australian ones, especially those that are reasonably accessible online or in libraries in North America. We believe it is very important to understand that archaeologists share many common experiences, no matter where they do their work. At the same time, however, we know from our experience working in various places around the world that one needs to adapt to local conditions and local standards of "best practice." We also need to mention that we have included Canadian materials as often as we reasonably could. Field methods are much like those in the United States, but governmental structures, agencies, and heritage laws differ, for example, in such basic matters as Canada having provinces and territories instead of states. We do realize that the materials here have a primary emphasis on the United States, so to those Canadians who may use this book, we ask your understanding.

The Archaeologist's Field Handbook is a hands-on field manual that provides a step-by-step guide to undertaking and successfully completing a wide variety of archaeological fieldwork projects, from simple site recording to professional consultancies. Our aim has been to combine clear and easy-to-understand information for undergraduate and postgraduate students on conducting fieldwork, with practical advice for successfully undertaking archaeological cultural resource/heritage management (CRM/CHM) projects. While this book is intended primarily for archaeologists, you don't need to be an archaeologist to use it. We expect that it will also be of value to interested members of the public, especially avocational archaeologists who want a greater understanding of professional approaches to fieldwork. In this respect, our intention is to make people aware of the legal and ethical obligations inherent in documenting and recording cultural heritage sites responsibly and well. To this end some methods have been omitted entirely from this manual because they should not be undertaken by amateurs. In particular, sampling rock art motifs for dating or any restoration or conservation work should be done only by trained professionals. Even most professional archaeologists don't have proper training to do some tasks, and wise professionals bring in specialists.

The main problem with writing a manual, particularly in archaeology, is that many cases must be dealt with on their own merits. There can be no hard and fast "recipes" for being a responsible archaeologist, although there is a clear need for guidelines and standards to guarantee high-quality work. The methods and guidelines presented in this book outline thresholds for professional practice rather than the *only* methods that can be used in a given situation. Every site is different, and to some extent, the field methods you employ in each situation will be different. The key is to be flexible: while there are basic principles and methods, each field project will have its own challenges and solutions. Moreover, while there is commonality in federal cultural preservation laws, there is a lot of variation in application of those laws by the states or provinces. This has led to considerable variation in the standards for professional conduct that are considered acceptable within each state or province. Through this book we are trying to promote some generally accepted standards and protocols and make this information available within one easy-to-carry volume. By firmly grounding essential practical techniques in an understanding of the contemporary ethical issues surrounding archaeology today, we hope that this combination will teach people how to conduct ethical archaeology at the same time that it provides much-needed hands-on practical advice.

ARCHAEOLOGY IN NORTH AMERICA

Archaeology is the study of past human behavior through material remains. In North America, this translates into a variety of interests: from Indigenous archaeology, which focuses on the Native American occupation of the hemisphere over the last 15,000 years or more, to historical archaeology, which deals with the last few hundred years since colonial contact. Another important branch of the field is maritime archaeology, which deals with underwater and coastal archaeology. Others might specialize in industrial archaeology, examining the growth and spread of industry as shown by its material remains and examining old mines, factories, and associated artifacts and features. While there may be areas of overlap between all of these, each has its specific challenges and opportunities.

Archaeologists work in a range of professional capacities. The main employment opportunities come from cultural resource management consulting, colleges and universities, museums, and government agencies. Archaeologists in colleges and universities work in either a teaching or research capacity, or both. Most university-based archaeologists teach undergraduate courses, supervise graduate students, and conduct independent research. These people normally possess a PhD in anthropology with an emphasis in archaeology. Some universities also have postdoctoral fellows, whose main task is to conduct research in their field of interest.

The task of most archaeologists working in museums is either that of a curator, who manages and cares for collections; a researcher; or an education specialist. Most curators need to have a minimum of a master's degree in archaeology, normally with additional museum training, but research positions usually are filled by people with PhDs. Archaeologists working in museums deal with various aspects of maintaining the museum's collections, such as liaising with other archaeologists who have conducted excavations and may wish to deposit material, or with researchers who wish to study the museum's collections. Some work directly with members of the public, researching exhibitions and providing educational programming around the exhibitions.

In the past 30 years, there has been dramatic increase in demand for archaeologists to mediate between the needs of development and the desire to preserve our cultural heritage. In fact, cultural resource management (CRM), or cultural heritage management (CHM) as it is starting to be called (and which we will use for the rest of this book, explaining why in chapter 8), is now the largest employer of archaeologists in the United States, and the vast majority of field projects are now conducted as CHM projects. Archaeologists with undergraduate degrees and archaeological field training and experience usually become crew members for CHM projects. They are affectionately known as "shovelbums" because they must be willing to move from project to project. Under federal regulation, a master's degree is the minimum education level for those who supervise CHM projects. There are actually more master's-level archaeologists in CHM than there are PhDs, although the number of the latter has been increasing. CHM is usually undertaken on a consultancy basis and is generically referred to as cultural heritage management in most of the world. Archaeologists can be involved in a variety of projects, ranging from recording and assessing the importance of sites and undertaking emergency excavations prior to development, to devising protection schemes for sites and artifacts, to creating interpretive materials. Because many development projects have some level of federal involvement, they are governed by cultural heritage legislation. Some CHM archaeologists work for government agencies at the state, provincial, or federal level, while others work for companies set up specifically to do CHM archaeology. Whether government or private, these consultants work very closely with each other to administer and execute heritage legislation. Government archaeologists are responsible for maintaining registers of sites, establishing guidelines for best practice, assessing consultants' reports, and working with developers and members of the public. Archaeologists employed in these agencies sometimes conduct research projects related to the management needs of their particular organization. Increasingly, Indigenous groups are employing archaeologists, and Indigenous people are starting to receive professional training as archaeologists. The kinds of work they undertake include research, managing cultural resources on tribal lands, developing cultural programs or community management programs, and developing interpretive materials for cultural centers.

All of these forms of archaeology involve a commitment to high ethical standards and good professional practice. Archaeologists employed in any of these jobs are likely to work in many different and interesting places and will need to call upon a diverse range of archaeological skills. This handbook has been designed to provide undergraduate and postgraduate students and first-time consultants with the basic tools needed to plan and undertake fieldwork in a wide range of field situations. The structure of this book (figure 0.1) follows the pattern of a typical archaeological field project: first a site has to be located, then recorded and interpreted, and the results properly documented. Each chapter deals with a segment of this process and covers the various methods that can be employed to achieve this on Indigenous and non-Indigenous sites. While each chapter can stand alone, the information is cross-referenced to help you locate related materials. In some places we repeat similar information to emphasize key points about best practice. Specialist terms are flagged throughout the text in bold and explained in the text rather than in a glossary.

Boxed texts outline the skills covered within each chapter, the fieldwork kit sections outline the basic equipment essential for undertaking each phase of fieldwork, and each chapter finishes with a list of further readings and useful resources. In order to teach some of the lessons of "real" archaeology, we have included handy hints from professional archaeologists from many countries who have developed their own personal ways to collect data in the field. The appendixes collate information about codes of ethics used by archaeologists today and provide lists of professional contacts and sample recording forms to make field preparation and recording simpler. These recording forms are not intended to apply to every archaeological excavation or survey; rather, they provide a guide to the kinds of information that should be recorded routinely. Inevitably, users will have to adapt them to suit their own particular purposes.

Some aspects of fieldwork require contact with relevant organizations and bodies. There are important kinds of information to be aware of, such as resource centers and government departments. Any relevant addresses and contact details are provided on the website that accompanies this book (http://nafieldarchaeology.com). For web URLs, the date the website was most recently examined is included in parentheses at the end of the entry. All web

FIGURE 0.1: The structure and contents of this book

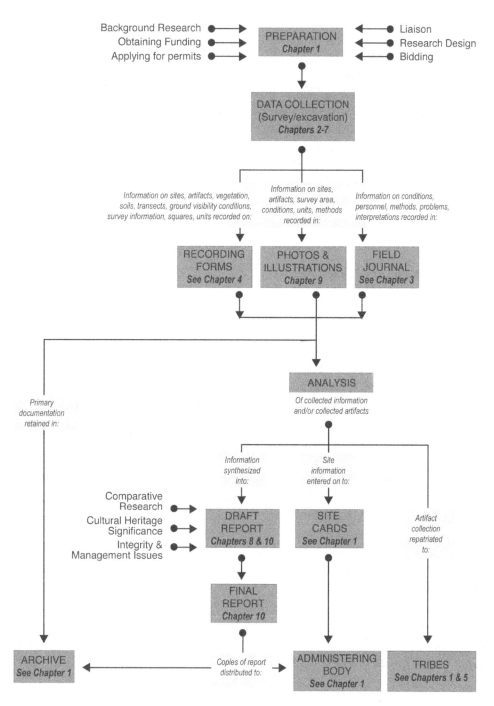

addresses were working as of that date. The fluidity of the web makes it difficult to keep track of all changes, particularly as this book will not appear in print for eight months to a year after the final check. If a website doesn't work, the problem may be that the server is not working temporarily. Check back after a time; if a website is not there within a day, it usually is gone. If it has changed URLs or been altered, try finding it by searching on key terms in a search engine such as Google (www.google.com). If a site is permanently gone, you will probably find links to sites with similar information, but be certain to evaluate their quality. Never accept information from any source—print or web—at face value!

While this book is intended as a basic field manual, it is not an exhaustive treatment of all techniques that are used in archaeology. In particular, because the postfield analysis of artifacts and sites has its own methods and problems, this book stops at the point where laboratory analysis begins. For information on this aspect of archaeology, we recommend Jane Balme and Alistair Paterson's *A Student Guide to Archaeological Analysis* (Blackwell 2006).

ACKNOWLEDGMENTS

This book, like any other archaeological project, could not have been completed without the help of many people. Many listed here contributed to the Australian version of the book, but others have been added for this version. We first would like to thank the people who gave us special advice or assistance. In particular, we thank Val Attenbrow for thoughtful comments on our original proposal, as well as Tessa Corkhill, Richard Fullagar, and Alice Gorman. Wendy Beck, Sandra Bowdler, Jay Hall, Matthew Kelly, Ian Lilley, Peter Veth, and Bruce Koenen all provided detailed comments on the manuscript. Their feedback has been invaluable. Second, thanks to all those who took the time to contribute field tips: Sonya Atalay, Val Attenbrow, Jane Balme, Fred Cooper, Aedeen Cremin, Bruno David, Steve Dasovich, Ines Domingo-Sanz, Richard Fullagar, Chris Glidden, Denis Gojak, Alice Gorman, David Gradwohl, Nicky Horsfall, Wayne Johnson, Liz Kryder-Reid, Lyn Leader-Elliott, Amy Lonetree, Chris Matthews, Robyn Najar, Jack Radley, Richard Robins, June Ross, Anita Smith, Mark Staniforth, Stephen Sutton, and Joe Watkins. Philip Bowman and Iain Davidson provided feedback on the Australian volume that has been incorporated into this edition. We would also like to thank Martin Rowney, Aidan Ash, Wayne Johnson, June Ross, Matt Schlitz, Mark Staniforth, and L. Adrien Hannus for kindly providing us with photographs and illustrations. All other photographs were taken by the authors. We would particularly like to thank the students of ARCH3302: Field Methods in Australian Archaeology, 2002 and 2003, photographs of many of whom appear in this book. Finally, we wish to thank Mitch Allen for his vision, not only for what this text might be but also for publishing in archaeology in general. We wish him nothing but the best for his new publishing venture.

IT'S NOT JUST ABOUT THE ARTIFACTS!

Archaeologists seek to learn about people in the past through the objects they made or used, then left behind. It is not just the objects (artifacts) themselves that are important, but also where they are found (the sites) and what other objects or traces of objects they are found with (their context). An artifact by itself can tell us only so much, and the context often is the most important factor for understanding the behavior or activities that put the artifact there in the first place. The most important thing to learn about archaeological fieldwork is to pay as much attention to the context as to the artifact. In writing this book we have tried not to privilege the artifact above the context, or the large or visually impressive site above the ordinary. When conducting archaeological fieldwork, it is important to remember that *all* traces of past human behavior are important. There is no substitute for field experience, but if you can keep this in mind, you are already behaving like a good field archaeologist.

CHAPTER ONE

PREPARING FOR FIELDWORK

What you will learn from this chapter:

What it means to be a responsible archaeologist
The legal requirements for conducting archaeological fieldwork
The importance of properly planning your research and fieldwork
Essential skills for finding funding
The importance of accurate record keeping
The ethical responsibilities of working with others

Archaeological fieldwork is not something that can be done *ad hoc*. Fieldwork has to be tailored to particular research questions and should be undertaken only with proper planning. Before going into the field you need to think through the aims of your field-work and what it is you want to know. What questions do you want to answer? What data do you need to address these questions? What methods will be required to collect it? Recording everything is rarely possible, and in most situations you will need to pri-oritize the information you collect. If you are looking for Indigenous sites in a large river valley, for instance, but have only one-and-a-half days to complete your survey, you are not going to be able to record the contents of every site in detail, but you will be able to plot all site locations and record some minimum information for each. On the other

The Basic Fieldwork Toolkit

Good boots
Hat and water bottle
Sunscreen and insect repellent
Prismatic compass
Global positioning system (GPS) (with spare batteries)
Relevant topographic maps for the area (preferably current editions at 1:24,000 scale)
Recording forms, field notebook, pens, and pencils
Scale ruler
Protractor (either a 360° full circle or a square Douglas protractor is best)
Clipboard
Photographic scales (at least one 50 cm and one small scale for artifact photography)
A 2 m ranging pole (preferably collapsible or telescopic for ease of carrying)
A roll of flagging tape (preferably the biodegradable kind) and/or individual artifact flags with colors distinct from natural landscape colors ("hot" colors usually work best)
Graph paper (metric)
Camera, digital or film, adequate memory or film, with spare batteries for either camera
A 30 m tape measure and a 3 or 5 m retractable tape measure
Ziploc plastic bags, in various sizes
Hand brush for cleaning off hard surfaces such as brickwork
Trowel (Marshalltown or other single-weld variety, preferably pointed)
Shovel, long-handled
Gardening gloves and pruning shears (sometimes called secateurs) for clearing away vegetation
Good first aid kit (see "The Basic Fieldwork First Aid Kit")
Pocketknife
Whistle (this can be used to locate a person who gets separated)

Optional:
Camping/general site equipment (backpack, camp cooking gear, chairs, folding tables, canvas or shade cover)

hand, if your fieldwork consists of recording a single building, you will probably be able to make a far more detailed and exhaustive record. Of course, even the most well thought out and carefully planned research must be flexible enough to cope with the changing conditions of fieldwork. Only in an ideal world could an archaeologist create a project based solely on the requirements of research alone. In reality, you will need to balance

The Basic Fieldwork First Aid Kit

A first aid kit can be purchased assembled, but add a few items.

Flashlight (with spare batteries) (a small one that tucks easily into a corner will do)
Tweezers for removing splinters, thorns, prickles, or ticks
Bandage tape and a small pair of scissors to cut it
One triangular and one roll bandage
Band-Aids or similar adhesive bandages
Cream for itches and bites
Thermometer (for fevers)
Burn ointment (especially important if you plan on cooking over an open fire)
Matches or a lighter
Anesthetic spray
Antiseptic ointment
Aspirin, acetaminophen, or similar pain reliever or anti-inflammatory
A small first aid handbook (these come in travel sizes and will provide instructions on
    what to do in most emergencies)

what you would like to do with the various constraints placed upon you and the project (Orser and Fagan 1995, 159). Routine constraints include time, not enough funding (there is never enough funding in archaeological research—see Black and Jolly 2003, 13–14), and not being able to access certain sites or areas. If you can think of any ways to narrow the focus of your project before you begin and make your time spent in the field more efficient, this can only result in a more manageable project.

DESIGNING YOUR RESEARCH

The most important thing to clarify at the beginning of any project is the purpose of your fieldwork. For what and whom are you doing fieldwork? What questions are you interested in investigating? What kinds of sites do you expect to find? What information will you need to collect to get the job done? Without some clear idea as to what you want to know and how best you will be able to get it, your project will be doomed from the start. For this reason, it is a good idea to work out your plan of attack in advance. This is not so urgent if you are working alone and will become less necessary as you gain more experience, but if you are working with a field crew it can be a very expensive (not to mention frustrating) exercise to keep them waiting while you work out what to do.

The most important first step in designing research is to outline the problem. This is essentially why you think your research is important and how you think it will contribute to the discipline of archaeology. Many projects, especially those associated with cultural resource/heritage management (CRM/CHM) **reconnaissance surveys** may be limited to locating potentially significant sites in a very limited area, but others may stem from research problems that might contribute new light on theories of human behavior in the past or contribute new methods for how we go about collecting or analyzing archaeological data. Not every study will be earth-shattering in its findings, but every research project should be well thought out enough so that it does not just reinvent the wheel. This means that you will have to do a literature search for reports and records relating to your research area to find out what other people have done in an area or in similar situations. You will also have to think through how you are going to operationalize your research problem: If I want to know this, what will I have to look for in the field to answer my problem? It is no use wanting to answer questions about the living conditions of 19th-century miners if you haven't collected any data from 19th-century miners' house sites. In fact, to answer this question properly, you probably would need to know what they were eating and drinking and how much of each product they consumed. In other words you probably would need to excavate a 19th-century miner's rubbish dump rather than collect data from a surface survey.

One way to develop the planning for your project is by writing a research design. In a **research design** you outline your research questions and how these were developed, the methods you intend to use to address these questions, and how your proposed work relates to existing research. This will help you to think through each step of the project and will allow others (colleagues, government agencies, clients) to understand your project clearly. All research designs must be logical and structured around a problem or question that is worthwhile answering and will contribute in some way to archaeological knowledge. Narrowing down your research to focus on a particular problem is the hardest part of writing a research design, although it is the core of any good research program (figure 1.1). Writing a formal research design is not something you would undertake before every trip into the field, but it is necessary if you are planning an academic research project or applying for an excavation permit. Applications for excavation or survey permits required by some states and agencies usually demand a research design of some kind, so it is well worth knowing how to write an acceptable one. In a sense the worth of your project will be evaluated through your research design; it is both a statement of how you intend to go about things and an outline of why your research is important. When developing a research problem, keep these factors firmly in mind:

- You must establish that the problem addresses a question or a set of related questions whose answers will make a contribution to archaeological knowledge. The archaeology should also be able to provide insights that no other discipline can. If the research proposes to answer questions that are marginal, or outside the range of current discussion in the discipline, you will need to show even more clearly that the answer to these questions will make a contribution. Adequately justifying your research problem is a necessary ingredient in any scientific research.

- You must define the nature and scope of the question. A research project should address a specific, clearly stated question and not just a general topic area or a set of data. Topical or data questions are rarely sufficient starting points for the design of scientific research.

- You must establish that the answer can in fact be solved. Trying to establish the site of the first use of specific Indigenous artifact types, for example, probably is unanswerable. This is part of thinking through your research and narrowing down the focus of your project to make it practical.

FIGURE 1.1: Thinking through your research problem. Your problem will condition nearly all aspects of fieldwork, and the more carefully it is conceived, the more efficient and productive your field program will be.

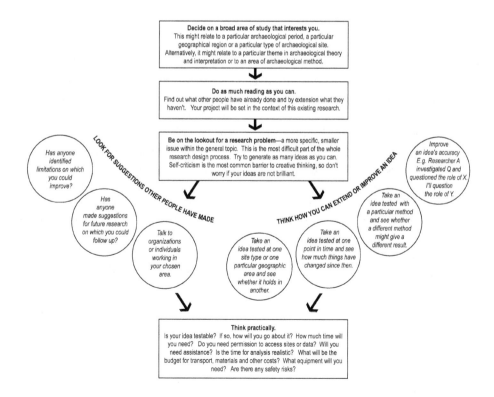

Archaeological List Servers

ARCH-L: A List Server Dedicated to Archaeology

Starting as a small electronic mailing list in 1986, ARCH-L grew rapidly into its present form in 1992 and now has more than 1,200 subscribers in more than 40 countries. ARCH-L has developed into a major source of information and a place for discussion of ideas. It is essentially a digital "mail room" where you can exchange information with others, and its purpose is to facilitate discussion about all aspects of archaeology. Messages regularly include questions to other subscribers, presentations of information, or discussions of results, a useful way of searching for information on archaeology that might not otherwise be available from published sources. To subscribe to the list, go to http://listserv.tamu.edu/archives/arch-l.html (accessed December 24, 2006), and click on the link "Join or leave the list (or change settings)." Fill out and submit the subscription form there, and you'll soon get an e-mail confirming your subscription. On that same page you'll find a real treasure, the searchable ARCH-L archives back to 1992.

The World Archaeological Congress List Server

For those who want to take a global perspective, we recommend the WAC list server, which was established as a service to the members and friends of the World Archaeological Congress (WAC). This is a multilingual list server, with 1,500 subscribers from almost 100 countries. The purpose of the list server is to facilitate global communication in archaeology and to act as a forum for disseminating information in line with the aims and agendas of WAC, which include addressing global inequities in archaeology and the decolonization of archaeological practice (see www.worldarchaeologicalcongress.org). To join this list you should visit the site http://listserver.flinders.edu.au/mailman/listinfo/wac. To send a message to the list as a whole you can send an e-mail to wac@flinders.edu.au.

Be aware that there are many other excellent list servers for archaeology, many of them for specific topics or places that might be of use to you. You can find a very thorough list with descriptions and links at http://archaeology.about.com/od/discussiongroups (accessed December 24, 2006). Most work in the same way ARCH-L does. Many list servers now are being replaced with web-based forums or discussion rooms, so you might look into some of those as well.

Steps for Developing a Research Design

In your research design you will need to include information on:

- The research objectives. What are you trying to do? Make sure that you lay these out clearly, so readers do not have to guess.
- Previous research in the study area or on the project's research questions. What have other people done that is relevant?
- Background environmental or other relevant information on the study area.
- The methods you intend to use. You should go into as much detail as possible here and think beyond the fieldwork itself. What methods will you need for fieldwork, analysis, and other data collection (e.g., oral histories)?
- The time frame you envisage for the project, including the time you will need to analyze your results and write up the report.
- If you are intending to excavate or collect material, you will need to outline relevant conservation techniques and short- and long-term measures for the appropriate curation and storage of the material.
- If you are intending to work with Indigenous communities, you should indicate their attitudes about the project and the extent of community involvement and support for the project. You may need to provide specific documents or permissions from some communities proving that your project is acceptable to the community.
- Finally you should outline the benefits of the project. What will this contribute to the discipline? What will associated interest groups get out of it? How will you return the results to the archaeological and wider community?

FINDING FUNDING

Archaeology can be expensive! Finding funding for your project is important and is hard work in itself. Many projects cannot be undertaken without funds to cover fuel and travel costs, to pay for staff, or to buy essential equipment. More important, funding also presents you with many ways to increase the quality of your work, for example, by allowing you to pay specialists to undertake highly skilled technical tasks. The first step in the process is to locate an appropriate funding body. Most universities have research offices to help you find funding sources. Once you find a possible source, read the job/funding description of your proposed funding agency to see if you fulfill their essential criteria. If you don't, then applying is just a waste of time. The essentials when applying for funding are having a product to sell, a good track record, and, in the case of CHM projects, often the lowest bid for work that still meets the project's specifications.

Two main factors will determine whether or not you will obtain financial support for your project. The first is the quality of your application. Whenever you apply for funding, submitting the best possible application is crucial. For any funding body you will need to demonstrate what you are going to do, how you are going to do it, and why the project is important. The second factor is whether the funding body has a mandate to fund the type of project for which you are seeking support. Bear in mind that all funding programs have particular purposes. If the purpose of the program is to support Indigenous archaeology, for instance, it is probably pointless to apply for a maritime archaeology project unless there is some clear overlap (i.e., the Indigenous sites are underwater). The point to remember is that funding is always targeted at achieving specific outcomes. If you are going to apply for funding from a particular body, then you will need to show that your project will help them to fulfill those outcomes. No matter how worthwhile the project or how well written the application, if the project falls outside of the organization's objectives, it will be eliminated immediately.

There are three main sources of funding for research or CHM fieldwork: government programs, industry partners, and foundations. While all three sources share things in common, there are also some specific strategies you can use for each.

Obtaining Government Funding

State, provincial, and federal governments have a range of funding programs that support archaeological research. One of the most important things to bear in mind about applying for government funding is that your application will be assessed by professionals. This means that you have to be particularly careful to show how your work relates to that of others. You will have to refer to the work of people who have done fieldwork in your project's geographic area, as well as to any previous research that has used a similar theoretical approach or dealt with a similar range of artifacts and sites. For example, if you are doing a CHM project along the Missouri River in South Dakota, you will need to refer to previous research in the specific area, as well as to any work that has focused on the archaeological or cultural heritage management issues germane to your project.

The other thing to remember is to check current priority areas for granting agencies. These can change from year to year, and it will strengthen your application if you are able to key into one. Finally, some government programs will ask you to justify your budget. The normal process is for an assessment panel to decide which projects it would like to fund and then to look closely at the budgets to see if they can be cut back. It is not enough to say that you need film or a research assistant and assume that the assessment panel will agree with you. You need to explain what you plan to photograph and how these photographs are essential to the completion of the project, or outline what tasks the research assistant will undertake and why the project cannot be completed without them. Remember, any item that is not justified properly will be the first to be cut if the panel decides to trim your budget.

Obtaining Industry Funding

Finding industry money requires slightly different skills. Some government programs—such as the National Science Foundation in the United States or the Social Sciences and Humanities Research Council (SSHRC) of Canada—primarily exist to further knowledge. This is rarely the case with industry funding, however. Industry bodies have specific purposes that are usually related to making money. Therefore, getting an industry partner to support your project will involve working out ways in which your research can help the partner to make money. This does not have to be a direct link—it might be through enhancing its profile or bonding with target groups, such as with the corporate sponsorship of conferences, or through providing the research that can be used in interpretive centers or cultural tourism. In short, industry sponsors usually do not fund projects for the warm and fuzzy feelings they will get out of it. Their job is to achieve specific outcomes that are at least partly economic, and they usually do not have the flexibility to give money away to good causes. The main question the industry sponsor will ask is, "What am I going to get out of this?" If you bear this in mind, you can develop your proposal so that you are able to meet both its needs and yours. For example, a local Chamber of Commerce might need archaeological sites identified to develop some cultural tourism programs. At the time you first approach them they may be thinking of cultural tourism as food, wine, and the arts. Your task becomes getting them to extend their thinking to recognize heritage as part of cultural tourism and identifying some specific ways in which your fieldwork will help them. This could be as simple as providing information for interpretive pamphlets or signs. Remember, you probably will have to draw the link for them—do not expect them to see this by themselves.

Obtaining Foundation Funding

Getting funding from foundations follows the same general rules. As with government programs, foundations are established for specific purposes, and it is important to show how your project will help them to fulfill their aims. Remember two special things about getting foundation money. The first is that your application will be assessed by a board of people who are unlikely to be archaeologists. This means that you will need to be especially clear in your explanation of the project and its significance so that it can be understood by a lay audience. Don't use lots of archaeological jargon!

The second thing to remember is that foundations, as with industry partners, need to be seen to be conducting good work. You can help foundations, not only by working with them to advance their agendas but also by giving them public recognition. For example, if the Ford Foundation funds an overseas speaker for your conference, then you probably will have to refer to that person as the "Ford Foundation Keynote Speaker." You also should remember to recognize all your sponsors, but particularly foundations, in all publications and reports that arise from your project. You need to be especially vigilant when submitting reports to foundations. Often, the reports will be presented to the same board that assesses your applications, giving you a good opportunity to show the high quality of your work. This helps you to establish a track record for excellence and will strengthen future applications to that foundation.

Getting the budget for your project right is one of the hardest parts of any funding application. The most important thing is to make sure that it is realistic—there is no point in getting only a small amount of funding for what is really a very large job. One of the worst outcomes for any project is when there is enough money to undertake the fieldwork but not enough to analyze or write up the results—this is not only bad ethical practice, but could have been avoided from the beginning. In short, don't undertake a project if you cannot finish it. Make sure your budget:

- Allows for preliminary research, fieldwork, analysis, and write-up time (as a guide you can usually allow for three days in the lab or office for every one day you spend in the field) and, if necessary, curation of the artifacts in the long term
- Includes fees for Indigenous consultants as needed (both for their time in providing you with information and their labor if they have acted as fieldwork assistants)
- Includes any necessary specialists' fees (e.g., surveyors, geomorphologists, conservators, or historians)
- Includes only items that are related to the part of the project for which you are seeking funding and that each item is fully justified

ARCHAEOLOGISTS AND ETHICS

Unless your project involves work on your own personal or family history, you will inevitably be working with other people's cultural heritage. Many different groups can have an interest in archaeology, including:

- Indigenous people
- Descendent communities (non-Indigenous)

Things to Bear in Mind When Applying for Funding

- *Take your funding application seriously.* In many ways applying for funding is like applying for a job—treat it as a major project.
- *Identify an appropriate funding body* and make sure that your proposal is consistent with its objectives.
- *Read the guidelines for applicants carefully* and make sure your application falls within them.
- *If forms are provided or if an application guideline spells out key questions to be answered, be certain that you fill them out completely and answer all questions thoroughly.* Forms or key questions allow proposal reviewers to have consistency in all the proposals they read, for fairness as much as for easing their task. Failure to use their form properly or to address all questions may disqualify you.
- *If at all possible, visit or telephone the people involved in the allocation of funding to explain your project.* This gives them the opportunity to ask any questions and to clarify any confusion. In addition, it gives them the opportunity to make personal judgments of your ability and reliability. Their knowledge may allow them to advocate for your proposal if they need to choose between proposals of equal merit. This is especially important for students and new professionals, as you cannot expect organizations routinely to fund unknown researchers.
- *Submit the best possible application,* and get colleagues to comment on it to help you refine it. Some funding agencies ask for or will allow "pre-proposals," which allows them to see if your research fits their guidelines or agendas.
- *Refine your application to highlight how it fits within the organization's program objectives.* Every organization will favor projects that relate to their priority areas.
- *Choose your referees carefully.* Some funding agencies allow you to suggest specialists to review your proposal. Make sure you choose people who can comment knowledgeably on the project and on your capacity to achieve a successful outcome. Most importantly, make sure they will produce the reference on time. This is your responsibility, not theirs, because you are the one who will receive the funding. The best approach is to choose referees who know either you or the project well and then remind them about four or five days in advance that the submission deadline is approaching. Once the deadline has passed, you should check with the funding agency to make certain that all references have been received and, if any are outstanding, go back to the referees, politely pointing out that the reference is overdue.
- *Aim to establish a reputation for producing results.* This means that the funding body can be more certain you will use the funding granted to you to complete a project.

(continues)

Things to Bear in Mind When Applying for Funding (*continued*)

- *Take great care with all reports that you submit.* Interim reports are often an institution's principal method for evaluating exactly how your work is progressing. It is up to you to satisfy the funding body that its money is being spent correctly. Take even greater care with final reports, showing that you have completed the project as planned and fulfilled all of your responsibilities. After all, you may wish to apply to this funding body again.
- *Don't confine yourself to one funding organization per project.* Apply wherever your project fulfills the criteria, but let each funding body know of any other sources you have approached. If you have more than one successful application, you could try to renegotiate the terms of the funding. For example, "I have money from Foundation X for this aspect of the project. May I use the funding from you for this complementary aspect?"

- Government agencies (see "Working with the Legislation")
- Developers or other CHM clients (see chapter 8, "Managing Cultural Heritage")
- Local community groups and organizations
- Landowners and tenants
- Other members of the heritage profession

As a heritage practitioner you have ethical responsibilities to each of these interest groups. When conducting fieldwork, you need to think about how your work is likely to affect them. Do you need to ask any of them for permission? Will your work promote positive change? Is it collaborative? Are there measures you can take to make sure that the people you are working with will get some benefit from the research? Thinking through and acting on these kinds of questions can make the difference between ethical and unethical research. The Society for American Archaeology, the Society for Historical Archaeology, and the Register of Professional Archaeologists all have their own codes of ethics that clearly set out the ethical behaviors expected of heritage professionals. Other professional groups, such as the World Archaeological Congress, have similar codes of ethics of which you should be aware.

Contacting Indigenous Communities

Correct and adequate consultation with Indigenous communities is one of the main ethical responsibilities of anyone working with Indigenous cultural heritage. You should do proper consultation because it is the "right thing to do," not because it is legally required,

A Checklist for Funding Applications

Have you demonstrated:

❏ The inherent value of the project?

❏ How the project will further the aims of the funding body?

❏ The extent of community support (especially that of Indigenous people who may be involved) for the project?

❏ Your ability to carry out the aims and objectives of the project?

❏ Your previous track record? If you are applying for funding for the first time it may be best to start out by applying for reasonably small amounts. You have not yet established your ability and dependability. Every funding body has a responsibility to fund projects that will be completed, and until you have established that you can be relied upon you cannot expect to be granted substantial funding.

❏ The tangible outcomes of the project (e.g., a report, a video, photos, tapes, the physical protection of sites, a thank-you letter in the newspaper)?

Does your application:

❏ Fulfill each of the eligibility criteria?

❏ Have methods that are consistent with achieving the aims of the study?

❏ Have a budget that is sufficient to produce the promised outcomes, but not inflated?

❏ Have a structure that is logical and well organized?

❏ Have a time frame that is realistic and "doable"?

which it is in many countries. Be certain that you understand what your legal obligations are before you do work on Indigenous lands or with Indigenous people. In the case of work on tribal or reservation lands in the United States, American Indian tribes for most legal purposes are sovereign nations with control over what happens on their lands. The federal government deals with tribes on a nation-to-nation basis, as do several states. This sometimes makes for complex interactions between tribal, federal, and state governments. Although the federal Bureau of Indian Affairs under the Department of the Interior has some authority and responsibility for tribally held lands, most tribes increasingly have moved toward sovereignty over tribal heritage matters. Several tribes have taken complete responsibility for cultural resources on their lands, using a tribal historic preservation officer (THPO) instead of relying on the state historic preservation officer (SHPO) for assessment of cultural properties on their reservations. All of this means that if you intend to work on any American Indian tribal lands you are obliged to have permission from the proper authorities of the tribe to do that work. If you have a contract or grant from a federal agency, you will need to get written permission from the tribal council or other legally constituted group or office authorized to speak for the tribe. Tribal practices vary. Some have a well-developed permit system while others have few, if any, research protocols. Having a system does not necessarily mean that the process will be less difficult.

Tribes normally will not grant permission to work on their lands unless you have consulted with them, as many heritage-focused laws demand. *Notification is not the same as consultation.* Consultation requires that you find out who the relevant authorities are, discuss your research with them, address any concerns or questions they might have, then readjust your research design to take their needs into account. *Consultation involves a shared shaping of project outcomes.* There can be lots of complexities to consultation. For example, your research may require work with elders or traditionally oriented people, individuals whom many tribes try to protect from outsiders. Being able to speak with these people is considered a great privilege, one to be earned, not just granted because you asked.

Because this can sometimes be a long and complex process, and may involve changes in your original aims and/or methods, you should start consultation as soon as possible and not leave it to the last minute. Indigenous people will not necessarily wish to work to your time schedule, and you may need to alter your plans to accommodate their wishes. Wherever possible you should also try to include Indigenous people as part of the fieldwork team—even if it is only to invite tribal council members, elders, and community members to visit and observe what you are doing in the field. Bear in mind that any such involvement of Indigenous people beyond cursory site visits will require appropriate payments for their time, even if they have only participated in an interview. If you hire individuals to work with your crews, they should be paid the same rate as your crew members. Although the recommended fee for consultation will vary from organization to organization, you can budget for at least $25/hour or $300 per day. These might seem high, but remember that these individuals are experts in their cultures and deserve to be compensated as you would any highly qualified consultant. Also, remember that working with you is only one part of their lives, and they will have other things they need to do and other obligations they have to fulfill. Be prepared to work around these as you would with most consultants.

Access to nonconfidential Indigenous material (whether photographic, artifactual, or documentary) held in government collections (such as the Smithsonian Institution or the National Archives) usually can be examined without tribal permission unless the tribe has asked for restrictions, usually where materials document sacred information. While most government agencies and some private companies have similar policies, if you are affiliated with a university, any research design that involves collecting oral traditions or that might have an impact on the tribe (which potentially is just about all archaeological research) should be sent through your university's **Human Subjects Committee** or **Institutional Research Board (IRB)**, a process that is federally mandated in the United States, Canada, and elsewhere. Although running archaeology projects by an IRB might seem restrictive, board members often raise issues you just haven't thought about that may impact the lives of those whose past you are planning to study. The thinking behind this procedure is that all research on Indigenous peoples will have an impact upon them, even if the non-Indigenous people conducting the research cannot foresee that impact themselves. Many archaeologists believe that Indigenous people should have control of, or at the very least involvement in, all research related to them, a sentiment that is reflected in the First Code of Ethics of the World Archaeological Congress (1990) and various other documents such as the United Nations (2006) Declaration on the Rights of Indigenous Peoples, which states in Article 18 that "Indigenous peoples have the right to participate in decision-making in matters which would affect their rights," supporting statements in Articles 11 through 15 that relate directly to rights associated with their cultural heritage. The codes of ethics of the World Archaeological Congress, the Canadian Archaeological Association, and the Australian Archaeological Association recognize that much archaeology deals with the living heritage of Indigenous people and encourage archaeologists to work in close collaboration with Indigenous people at all times. If you are undertaking a project that involves Indigenous sites, it is essential that you contact local Indigenous people during the early stages while there is still room to shape the research so that it fulfills both your needs and theirs. Consultation may be a matter of law, but it is definitely a matter of ethics.

Working with Indigenous Peoples

The main foundation for good ethical practice in archaeology is a respect for other people's cultural traditions. This means that your opinions and attitudes may need to be tempered by other worldviews that are not necessarily compatible with the scientific dictates of archaeology. While this does not mean that you must subject yourself to unreasonable demands, working with Indigenous communities routinely will require that you behave appropriately. This can take a number of forms, from not appearing in clothing that may be deemed offensive, to not visiting restricted areas or sites, to not pressuring people to accept your opinion or to answer your questions.

One of the main areas of ethical responsibility concerns the use of information provided by Indigenous consultants. In Indigenous systems, knowledge is not "open" in the sense that all people have an equal right to it. Indigenous knowledge is rarely definitive (in the sense that there is only one "right" answer), and it is often restricted. Because access to this knowledge is a source of power, it must be controlled by people with the appropriate qualifications (usually based on age seniority or some form of special training). In terms of archaeological fieldwork, this means it is essential that you obtain your information from the correct people (i.e., the people who hold the appropriate knowledge of sites). Bear in mind that, even if you are working on historical sites, you still may need to consult with elders or other tribal officials on whose land the sites are located.

Good ethical practice also means that you have a commensurate responsibility to ensure that the information is used correctly. What a scientist may view dispassionately as "data," a Native elder may view as highly sensitive, secret, or sacred information. Sometimes Indigenous people will impart restricted information to you, and it then becomes your continuing responsibility to ensure it is not seen or heard by an inappropriate audience. Maintaining continuing consultation is a long-term (but often unforeseen) aspect of a working relationship, particularly when it comes to the publication of your results. If you intend to publish your fieldwork, you should return to the community to show them what you wish to publish and how you will present the information. It is your duty to make sure that the publication does not contain information or images that elders or holy people wish to be kept restricted. Permission is not given forever, and you will probably need to get separate permission each time you wish to publish. If your fieldwork involves artifact collection or excavation, you also may be required to return the material to the Indigenous community after the completion of fieldwork.

Working with Other Community Groups

Consultation is not limited solely to Indigenous groups. Particularly if you are conducting historical heritage fieldwork, you may need to consult with local community groups, such as members of the local historical society or avocational archaeologists from the area. While it is not usually considered mandatory to consult with local communities in the same way it is for Indigenous groups, such consultation may have many benefits. It can help facilitate access to sites or information and may suggest fruitful directions for your research. "Community" incorporates all the people who live in the area in which an archaeological project is being undertaken and includes a range of interest groups, each of which might bring particular desires or skills to a project.

Approaching landowners or tenants for permission to access their land is a mandatory aspect of consultation, however, both as a matter of courtesy and privacy, as well as good ethical practice. In most cases it is actually a legal requirement before you set foot onto private land. On some CHM projects the contracting agency already may have blanket permission from landowners for people associated with the project to enter their property, but even if that is the case, asking permission is still the appropriate thing to do.

The simple rule of thumb is "If in doubt, consult"—certainly the more consultation you undertake, the less likely you are to alienate anyone, and the fewer problems you should encounter in the course of your project. It is both good manners and good judgment to consult with the community with which you are working and to make sure that the community benefits from the research you are undertaking.

This, in turn, raises another ethical responsibility: communicating your results to the wider community. Public excavations and site tours; school talks; public lectures; a project website; and popular publications, guidebooks, and interpretive materials are all excellent means to make your project and its findings accessible (see chapter 10, "Getting Your Results Out There: Writing, Publication, and Interpretation"). While this seems easy in theory, in fact it can take a great deal of time and commitment. Although many academic archaeologists have stressed the importance of communicating the results of archaeological research to the wider public, few do this in practice. It is important to remember that the public is interested, not only in the results but also in the process. Site tours and public excavations are popular because they teach people about what has been found and, in the process, about how we "do" archaeology.

Archaeologists and Their Profession

Archaeologists also have responsibilities to others in their profession. This relates mainly to the way in which data are collected, recorded, and archived and the potential for your results to be comparable with other projects. One of the main problems with many CHM projects is that their survey methods and the results of their recording and analysis are not clearly presented or use unclear or idiosyncratic descriptive terms. If no one understands what you mean by a "convex flake tool" or if you just refer to an artifact as "unusual," this will prevent anyone from drawing comparisons between their data and yours. This means that your results cannot be compared to similar projects elsewhere and therefore do not contribute to the pool of current knowledge.

Similarly, reports from your fieldwork should be available for reference by others. This is not always possible, of course, particularly if your report contains secret/sacred or otherwise confidential information, but ideally you should supply one copy to the client or funding body, one copy to the appropriate state (usually the SHPO) or federal heritage authority, copies to any interest groups who participated in the project, one copy to accompany the finds (if your project involved collection or excavation), and one copy to the nearest appropriate public archive or library (Sullivan and Childs 2003, 89). Be aware that some CHM reports are considered to be proprietary by the funding agency and may be a matter of legal contract. Before you distribute *any* copies, check with the organization with which you have a contract.

At a very basic level it is important to make detailed recordings of all fieldwork and to make certain that you retain and archive your field journal (see "Keeping a Field Journal" in chapter 3), notes, recording forms, and photographs. An archive should contain all the primary information relating to the collection and analysis of the data, including electronic versions where feasible, including:

- Your field notebook(s)
- Originals of your site recording forms
- Originals of your artifact analysis forms
- Originals of any other form of data collection
- Complete photographic archive
- The originals of any site plans, sketches, maps, or other drawings
- Copies of any oral history tapes or transcriptions made as part of the project
- Copies of any historical documents collected as part of the project
- An original copy of your report
- All relevant correspondence and permissions you sent or received as part of the project

If part of your project uses a computer database, *don't* just store this on disk—computer programs can be completely outdated within a few years, rendering your database inaccessible. If you have given your archive to a client, government repository, or museum you probably will have no control over updating the database or its software; if so, make sure paper copies of your database are available. Sometimes these agencies will come back to you years later for clarification on some of the information you have submitted. Many archaeologists routinely use computerized data collection, especially for photographs, but you will need to have hard-copy backups of essential files for the long term (for more advice on digital archiving, see "Storing Photographs and Illustrations" in chapter 9).

If you are working on a CHM project, it is the client funding the research who technically owns this archive, and you therefore have some responsibility to turn the contents of the archive over to them. This raises two thorny problems: (1) Who owns the intellectual property generated by your project? (2) What are the ethical responsibilities for keeping project archives accessible? In general it is unethical for you to retain exclusive rights to information that you have been paid to collect as part of a project, unless this clearly has been identified as a necessary part of the process (e.g., when Indigenous people request that information be protected as sensitive). This does not mean that any subsequent academic papers or publications written by you from your data are "owned" by anyone else.

Tips for Making Your Archive Last

It is not enough to create an archive simply by putting all your materials together. You must also ensure that you have used the correct media so that the recordings last and that everything is properly labeled and cross-referenced, so that if anything becomes separated from the rest of the archive, it can be replaced correctly.

- Never take field notes or fill in recording forms with a felt-tipped pen, unless you are certain it is permanent ink, because this may run if dampened.
- Highlighter pens, all water-based markers, and soft-lead pencils are also unacceptable.
- Instead use a ballpoint pen, a hard-lead pencil, permanent pens, or ink-filled technical drawing pens.
- Avoid recycled paper for your notes and forms, as this usually is less chemically stable. Also avoid color-stock paper, sticky tape, and Post-it notes, as these will all deteriorate over time.
- Because an archive needs to last for a long time, don't use metal staples or paperclips to fasten papers, or spiral bound notebooks for your field notes (they will rust).
- Never include carbon copies of documents, blueprints, dyeline prints, or other light- or heat-sensitive papers, such as thermal fax paper.
- Never split up or mix your records or cull what seems to be irrelevant material.

In general, the information you collect while in the field is technically the property of whoever funded the project, while what you do with that material (i.e., your interpretations, synthesis, or publications) is controlled by you. In addition, while it is very easy to say that you should turn the contents of your archive over to the funding body, this may not always be the best outcome. If you are working for small clients, for example, they may not wish to be burdened with a whole lot of extra paperwork, or they may have no facilities for storing this appropriately, and by turning it over to them, you actually may run the risk of preventing any future researchers from ever having access to those data again (even yourself!). Unfortunately there are few central repositories for this kind of primary information, and you will have to judge for yourself what is best for the long-term storage of your archive. If you are working for government departments, such as the National Park Service, there may be an expectation that you will turn the archive over to them, but they will usually make this clear in their contract specifications. Intellectual property is a very gray area, and before undertaking any fieldwork you should investigate the requirements and expectations of all concerned.

Write It Down and Put Your Name on It—Aedeen Cremin's Tips for Creating a Proper Archaeological Archive

It is amazing how many records get lost or become useless over time because they are not properly labeled. It is said that when professor R. J. C. Atkinson died, a box full of notebooks was discovered among his things. The notebooks contained meticulous measurements of stones from megalithic monuments, including probably Stonehenge, which he had excavated in the 1950s. None of the notebooks was labeled, and therefore all of that work went to waste. Don't let that happen to you. Here is a checklist for you to think about:

- Label every piece of paper you handle, explaining what it is, and put your name and the date on it.
- Acquire a notebook for each job—and label it, with a title, your name, and the date of use. The small stitched books are best, as you are not tempted to tear pages out. Yes, you'll end up with a box of half-empty notebooks, but at least you'll be able to find them when you need to. An obsolete disk or inadequate boilerplate will not give you the information you need in six months', let alone six years', time.
- Never "lend" your notebooks to anyone. They will never be returned, published, or acknowledged. If somebody wants them that badly, they can pay to photocopy them.
- Put a copyright sign on any original documents you produce. Although copyright laws protect you without it, the copyright symbol informs people that you care. Of course, put your name and contact details on the document—people can't acknowledge your work if they don't know who you are.
- Fully label any sketches you make (e.g., not "W" but "timber-framed double-hung sash window" or "rock-cut well"). Put a north arrow, scale, the date, and your name on the sketch. If the drawing is not to scale, say so. Label descriptions and measurements on the sketch if you can; if not, list them as a caption.
- Keep a full photographic record, with as many details as you can fit in (e.g., not "stamper battery from S" but "1915 stamper battery viewed from the 1930s mine shaft. Distance from shaft 15 m. Engine base is on right, stamper base on left; remains of amalgamation trays at center. From SSE"). Carry a compass and always check; *don't* guesstimate.
- Any photographs you produce should carry as full a caption as possible—written on the back of a print or incorporated onto the image on disk. Put your name in full (e.g., "Indiana Jones," not "Indy") and the date (this is often crucial for excavation records).
- Anything that involves other people also needs to have their names in full. An image labeled "Jo, Alex, and Rob on site" is not going to be very useful to anybody else.

- If you must use initials, use three or four. You would be amazed how many people have the same two initials as you and your colleagues.
- On a long-term project, survey, or excavation keep an ongoing field diary (yes, in the same notebook). There will be things you notice that may not be allowed for on forms, and it is good to have these on record, however casually. The sequence of work is also useful to know about later on.
- Remember that nothing is published on time, which is why you need to keep proper records. In the 1960s I worked on an excavation where the first director had died unexpectedly, leaving the work unfinished. His successor finished the excavation but never published it, as he had other work in train. He too died unexpectedly. Forty years later, a third person finally was commissioned to publish the full excavation report. Whether he did or not I don't know—I just hope our record keeping was OK. I certainly have no record of any sort, not even a souvenir snapshot. This sort of thing happens.
- The notebooks are your archive. If you have a career in archaeology they will be of interest to other people later, so don't throw them away even when you think they're past their use-by date.

PLANNING YOUR FIELD KIT

Possibly one of the most important tasks in planning for fieldwork is ensuring that you have the right equipment to complete the job (figure 1.2). Much archaeological fieldwork will not take place in the cozy confines of a city, but in rural, often rough areas, where you may not have easy access to tools or other field essentials you forgot to take. Before you go into the field, however, you will need to consider what equipment will be essential for you to collect your data, what other equipment might be necessary given where you are going, and anything else you might need. Obvious essentials should form the basics of any fieldwork kit:

- A pocketknife
- Sunscreen
- Insect repellent
- A good hat and boots
- A first aid kit
- A water bottle

Other items to consider are lightweight long-sleeved shirts that wick away moisture from perspiration, are sun sensible, and minimize exposure to insects or irritating plants.

FIGURE 1.2: A typical archaeologist on fieldwork. In a group of field workers, the archaeologist is always the one wearing all the gear!

Other suggestions will depend on where you are working: In some areas you may find that mosquito netting worn over your hat will protect you from mosquitoes and black flies and save your sanity. In areas with cactus, leather high-top boots and thick jeans that protect your feet and lower legs will be a godsend. Don't embark on any fieldwork without making sure you have all the right equipment and without preparing sufficiently—there is nothing worse than reaching a difficult and isolated site only to realize that there is no film for the camera or that you forgot to bring the site recording forms.

WORKING WITH THE LEGISLATION

All archaeology is governed by some form of heritage legislation. This is not intended to make your job more difficult; it is to protect sites and their contents from unwelcome interference or damage. All states and many provinces have some form of heritage legislation that needs to be followed. Unfortunately this varies widely and is not necessarily equally effective. Some are much stricter in their requirements than others, even down to the preferred format in which you should present your report. In general most states require you to apply for a permit before you excavate, collect, or otherwise disturb a site.

Mark Staniforth's Tips for Protecting Your Field Gear

Buy a Pelican or similar case. These are high-impact-resistant plastic cases designed to protect underwater cameras but make very suitable protection for any delicate field gear. I have a Pelican case set up with the following gear in it: a digital still camera, a digital movie camera, a standard Olympus SLR camera (for taking color slides), a GPS, a drawing board, photo scales, a minirod, a north arrow, a hand bearing compass, a 30 m fiberglass tape, an 8 m steel tape, two trowels, 12 trench corner pegs, plastic bags, string, and a line level plus assorted bits and pieces. This is enough gear to conduct basic survey work and to string out and excavate a test trench. The Pelican case is waterproof and airtight, you can stand on it, and it can be locked with a padlock. Perfect for throwing on a boat or in the back of a 4WD.

Before administering authorities will approve such a permit, however, they will require you to demonstrate that you have carefully thought through your fieldwork. They will ask you to submit a research design as part of your permit application, outlining your research questions, excavation/collection methods, and recommendations for the conservation and curation of any artifacts removed from the site. This last is very important and often more difficult than it might seem. Materials recovered from private property belong to the landowner, who has the right to request their return. You may need to negotiate with the landowner and try to convince the person to donate the items to a public repository. The same applies to tribal lands; the materials are owned by the tribe. They may wish to keep them under their control. More often than not, however, most groups have no interest in

In general, it is both illegal and unethical knowingly to damage a heritage site. Any form of unsanctioned alteration, removal, addition, or interference with the fabric of a site may be deemed damaging. Be aware that even ostensibly "useful" activities have the potential to cause damage, such as removing invasive vegetation overgrowth from an abandoned building (its removal may physically damage parts of the building), "tidying up" a historic site (what you perceive to be "old junk" may in fact be important archaeological artifacts), reerecting a collapsed official sign in a rockshelter (this may damage the subsurface archaeological deposits in the shelter), or cleaning graffiti from a rock art surface (this may remove traces of the art). Even though it may seem counterintuitive, sometimes the apparent "messiness" or physical degeneration of a site is actually part of its significance. Even if it is not, *you must have permission from the relevant state, provincial, or federal authority before you interfere in any way with a heritage site.*

most kinds of materials archaeologists collect. So, just ask if they wish for you to arrange for curation. As for artifacts on state or federal property, these are considered public property. Curation in a state or federal repository may be required, but at very least you should arrange for curation in a repository that meets federal curation standards (36CFR79; see www.cr.nps.gov/aad/tools/36cfr79.htm [accessed December 24, 2006]). Be certain to allow for processing and curation costs in your budget! These may be more than $400 per cubic foot for perpetual curation.

All government agencies require that you provide a written report on your fieldwork and that you submit recording forms for any new sites you find to the administering body. Most states and provinces maintain some form of database or register of heritage sites. Just as it may help your fieldwork to know what other sites have already been recorded in your area (but be aware that access to site databases or records may be restricted in some circumstances), so too, other researchers may want to know about your sites. As each state or province has its own set of standardized site recording forms, make sure you obtain copies of these before you go into the field and that you fill them in completely and accurately before you submit them. Because the precise requirements of legislation vary, make sure that you are aware of the relevant cultural heritage legislation and the requirements of the administering body in your state or province *before* you begin fieldwork.

State, Provincial, and National Heritage Legislation

In general in the United States and Canada, each state or province has its own laws to protect heritage sites on land owned by the state or province (see chapter 8, "Managing Cultural Heritage"). Native American/First Nations tribes also may have regulations to protect sites on their lands. Similarly, the federal governments have laws that protect sites on federal property. In the United States, heritage preservation efforts at all the governmental levels intersect in the National Historic Preservation Act (NHPA) of 1966 as amended several times thereafter. The NHPA set up a procedure for nomination of sites to the National Register of Historic Places. The law mandates a state historic preservation officer to oversee the process. Now tribes are able to request their own tribal historic preservation officer to work in place of the SHPO. Section 106 of the NHPA mandates that any federal undertaking, such as land modification or construction, as well as any use of federal funds or permitting, follow a process that identifies sites in the area of potential effect, determines whether the sites are eligible for the National Register of Historic Places, and, if they are eligible, then mitigates their loss by avoidance or excavation. Section 106 is the foundation of most cultural resource management archaeological surveys and excavations in the United States.

Federal laws in Canada are not as precise as provincial or territorial laws and primarily cover laws on federal property. However, it is implied that all government agencies and the private sector should be diligent in protecting archaeological and other heritage sites. Any activity that would prompt an environmental assessment under the Canadian Environmental Assessment Act is to prompt an archaeological assessment. Provincial and territorial laws are more specific, but there is variation in how archaeological resources are defined.

ARCHAEOLOGY IS COMPLICATED AND TIME CONSUMING

What all of this tells you is that archaeology is probably not as simple and straightforward an activity as you might have imagined. All that is described in this chapter needs to be considered and done *before* you head to the field. Everything discussed, however time consuming you think it might be, ultimately will expedite your fieldwork and allow you to practice it in an ethical way that will contribute to archaeological knowledge. In the next chapter you will find out that there is still more to deal with in terms of understanding the importance of locating sites you find on a landscape, which essentially is a matter of knowing how to read maps and sometimes even how to make them.

REFERENCES AND FURTHER READING

Australian Archaeological Association. 1994. Code of ethics. *Australian Archaeology* 39:129.

Australian Heritage Commission. 2002. Ask first: A guide to respecting Indigenous heritage places and values. www.ahc.gov.au/publications/ask-first.html (accessed December 24 2006).

Black, S., and K. Jolly. 2003. *Archaeology by design*. Walnut Creek, CA: AltaMira Press.

Langford, R. 1983. Our heritage—your playground. *Australian Archaeology* 16:1–6.

McBryde, I. 1986. *Who owns the past?* Melbourne: Oxford University Press.

Orser, C., and B. Fagan. 1995. *Historical archaeology*. New York: HarperCollins College.

Sullivan, L. P., and S. T. Childs. 2003. *Curating archaeological collections: From the field to the repository*. Walnut Creek, CA: AltaMira Press.

United Nations. 2006. Declaration on the rights of Indigenous peoples. www.ohchr.org/english/issues/indigenous/docs/declaration.doc (accessed December 24, 2006).

Vitelli, K. D., ed. 1996. *Archaeological ethics*. Walnut Creek, CA: AltaMira Press.

World Archaeological Congress. 1990. First Code of Ethics. http://worldarchaeologicalcongress.org/site/about_ethi.php (accessed December 24, 2006).

Zimmerman, L. J., K. Vitelli, and J. Hollowell-Zimmer, eds. 2003. *Ethical issues in archaeology*. Walnut Creek, CA: AltaMira Press.

For a range of other useful information, see the website accompanying the text.

CHAPTER TWO

NAVIGATION, MAPPING, AND LIFE IN THE FIELD

What you will learn from this chapter:

How to use maps to navigate to sites
How to understand scale
How to calculate a locational reference from a map
The uses of different kinds of maps
How to read bearings from a compass
How to use a GPS
Basic field survival skills
Basic field camping skills

Navigation and mapping are probably two of the most important skills in archaeological fieldwork. You will need these skills to get to and from sites, to avoid getting lost, to be able to record the location of sites accurately, and to create your own maps. The fundamental components of these skills are being able to understand a map, to extrapolate from that map to the physical features you can see around you, and to know how to read a compass. With these skills mastered, you will be able to perform most of the basic surveying processes you will ever need in the field.

USING MAPS

Maps are representations whose purpose is to help locate places in real space. Maps can range from simple sketch or "mud maps" to geographic information systems maps containing multiple layers of information. For sketch maps, precise information is of little importance; their main function is to get you someplace or to show the general relationships of objects or features to each other and the surrounding landscape. More complex maps containing precise information often are necessary for finding archaeological and other sites, letting proper authorities know their locations, relocating sites, protecting sites from ground-disturbing activities, and even analyzing sites in relation to each other in a cultural landscape.

Complex maps have some system for transforming points on the curved surface of the Earth into a flat, two-dimensional plan. These transformations are called **projections**, and there are various methods for creating them. For example, across the world, the most common projection is the **Universal Transverse Mercator (UTM)** grid system, which is a grid system that divides the world into 60 equal zones from west to east. Each zone spans 6 degrees of longitude and has its own central meridian. North America covers 28 zones of this system, from 2 through to 28, from the Aleutian Islands to Greenland. Because the system is so commonly used, many map types include ways to calculate UTM coordinates.

Because maps drawn at different times and for different purposes may have used different mathematical models of the Earth to flatten its curved surface, you should pay close attention to the specific system used to generate each map (most maps will explain the system they use in a legend at the bottom or some other location on the map itself). Because these systems do not necessarily match, carefully note which system you are using to calculate a location, as the same information under differing systems will not necessarily refer to the same point in space. Likewise, if you intend to use a GPS unit, determine the mapping system your GPS unit uses or has been set to (see "Using a Global Positioning System") to make the location references accurate.

You will need to become familiar with several different types of maps in the course of archaeological fieldwork. The most common of these are topographic maps, geological maps, and orthophoto maps. Most of them use similar locational reference systems—they just plot different kinds of information. **Topographic maps** depict all the visible natural and built surface features, whereas **geological maps** depict rock formations, geological zones, and soil types. **Orthophoto maps** combine aerial photography with topographic information. Each type can be very useful, but their coverage and scale can differ. The maritime equivalents of maps are **charts**, which depict the depth of the ocean rather than the height of the land.

Metric Measurements

If you don't know how to do so, learn to use the metric system. Most of the world and all of the scientific community use it, including archaeology. The English system (inches, feet, and so on, which few people in England use much any more) is useful primarily in historical archaeology for the study of structures that may have been built using feet and inches as the primary measurements. The metric system is simple, with all measurements divisible by 10. People have worried about having to learn conversion factors, which is probably the most confusing approach to dealing with metric. Just try to start thinking in centimeters, meters, and other metric system measures. The problem comes when you are reading an old map or archaeological report done in the English system and need to make conversions to metric. The Web has many sites that do conversions for you. To find one, type "metric English conversion" into a search engine such as Google, and you'll find lots of them. Type the numbers in the proper boxes, and the results are almost instantaneous. With maps, the major problem in the United States is that the USGS topographic 1:24,000 series maps that most archaeologists use are English, with the exception of the 1:25,000 and 1:100,000 series, which are metric.

Maps, including sketch maps, have a number of conventions. Most maps are oriented with north to the top, south to the bottom, east to the right, and west to the left. At the bottom of each map is a scale, a legend to explain the mapping conventions used to depict features, and in complex maps, a small boxed section telling you how to read the map's system for referencing locations. Most maps use some kind of grid system, so most maps also specify the grid zone designation for the map, which you will need to know when calculating a grid reference (see "Locational Reference Systems"). Maps also come in a range of scales (although not all scales are available in all areas) and vary from country to country, from very small-scale maps that cover enormous areas (such as 1:250,000 maps in the United States covering as many as 8,669 square miles) to large-scale maps covering much smaller areas in greater detail (such as 1:24,000 scale maps covering only 71 square miles). Scale is the ratio of the size of a feature as it is drawn on the map to its actual size. This ratio is given as a representative fraction, so that 1:100 means that 1 unit of measurement on the map (whether 1 mm, 1 cm, or 1 m) represents 100 of the same units when measured on the ground. Thus 1 mm on the map equals 100 mm on the ground, 1 cm equals 100 cm, and so on (table 2.1). To make things even easier, the representative fraction is also converted into a linear bar scale at the bottom of the map to show you this relationship graphically.

TABLE 2.1: The relationship between the scale at which a plan or map is drawn and the real distance this represents on the ground. In this table you can see that, at scales of 1:250 or larger, something that is 50 cm long is far too small to plot accurately onto a plan. Minor variations are due to rounding.

Scale of plan	Real measurement	Scaled measurement
	50 cm on the ground	2 cm on the plan
	1 m on the ground	4 cm on the plan
1:25	2 m on the ground	8 cm on the plan
(1 cm on the plan =	3 m on the ground	12 cm on the plan
25 cm on the ground)	5 m on the ground	20 cm on the plan
	10 m on the ground	40 cm on the plan
	50 m on the ground	2 m on the plan
	50 cm on the ground	1 cm on the plan
	1 m on the ground	2 cm on the plan
1:50	2 m on the ground	4 cm on the plan
(1 cm on the plan =	3 m on the ground	6 cm on the plan
50 cm on the ground)	5 m on the ground	10 cm on the plan
	10 m on the ground	20 cm on the plan
	50 m on the ground	1 m on the plan
	50 cm on the ground	0.67 cm on the plan
	1 m on the ground	1.33 cm on the plan
1:75	2 m on the ground	2.67 cm on the plan
(1 cm on the plan =	3 m on the ground	4 cm on the plan
75 cm on the ground)	5 m on the ground	6.67 cm on the plan
	10 m on the ground	13.3 cm on the plan
	50 m on the ground	66.67 cm on the plan
	50 cm on the ground	0.5 cm on the plan
	1 m on the ground	1 cm on the plan
1:100	2 m on the ground	2 cm on the plan
(1 cm on the plan =	3 m on the ground	3 cm on the plan
100 cm on the ground)	5 m on the ground	5 cm on the plan
	10 m on the ground	10 cm on the plan
	50 m on the ground	50 cm on the plan
	50 cm on the ground	0.4 cm on the plan
	1 m on the ground	0.8 cm on the plan
1:125	2 m on the ground	1.6 cm on the plan
(1 cm on the plan =	3 m on the ground	2.4 cm on the plan
125 cm on the ground)	5 m on the ground	4 cm on the plan
	10 m on the ground	8 cm on the plan
	50 m on the ground	40 cm on the plan

Scale of plan	Real measurement	Scaled measurement
	50 cm on the ground	0.2 cm on the plan
	1 m on the ground	0.4 cm on the plan
1:250	2 m on the ground	0.8 cm on the plan
(1 cm on the plan =	3 m on the ground	1.2 cm on the plan
250 cm on the ground)	5 m on the ground	2 cm on the plan
	10 m on the ground	4 cm on the plan
	50 m on the ground	20 cm on the plan
	1 m on the ground	0.2 cm on the plan
1:500	2 m on the ground	0.4 cm on the plan
(1 cm on the plan =	3 m on the ground	0.6 cm on the plan
500 cm on the ground)	5 m on the ground	1 cm on the plan
	10 m on the ground	2 cm on the plan
	50 m on the ground	10 cm on the plan
	1 m on the ground	0.13 cm on the plan
1:750	2 m on the ground	0.27 cm on the plan
(1 cm on the plan =	3 m on the ground	0.4 cm on the plan
750 cm on the ground)	5 m on the ground	0.67 cm on the plan
	10 m on the ground	1.33 cm on the plan
	50 m on the ground	6.67 cm on the plan
	1 m on the ground	0.1 cm on the plan
1:1,000	2 m on the ground	0.2 cm on the plan
(1 cm on the plan =	3 m on the ground	0.3 cm on the plan
1,000 cm on the ground)	5 m on the ground	0.5 cm on the plan
	10 m on the ground	1 cm on the plan
	50 m on the ground	5 cm on the plan

   Scale will make a difference in how finely you can plot features onto a map or how accurate you need to be when measuring an area for a site plan (see "Drawing Horizontal Surfaces" in chapter 9). To illustrate the difference scale can make, imagine you are plotting the location of a site by placing a 1 mm dot on a map from the ballpoint pen in your pocket. On a 1:24,000 scale map, the diameter of your dot will be something like 24 m; on a 1:100,000 scale map its diameter will have increased to 100 m; and on a 1:1,000,000 scale map the same dot will now be covering an area of some 1,000 km. If you were then to assign that dot a grid reference, so that the location of the site was permanently recorded, obviously the grid reference determined from the 1:24,000 scale map would provide a much more accurate fix. Generally speaking, for survey purposes a larger-scale map is better, as it will have a better resolution of surface features, making it easier and

FIGURE 2.1: The Crow Creek site (39BF11) is on a small peninsula on the Missouri River, shown on these topographic maps from central South Dakota. The differences in scale are apparent. The peninsula is clearly visible on (a) the 1:24,000 scale, much less so on (b) the 1:100,000 scale, and nearly gone on (c) the 1:250,000 scale.

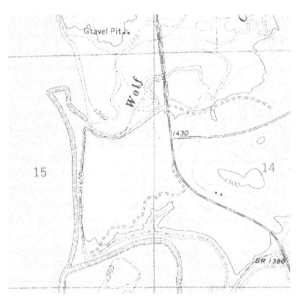

a

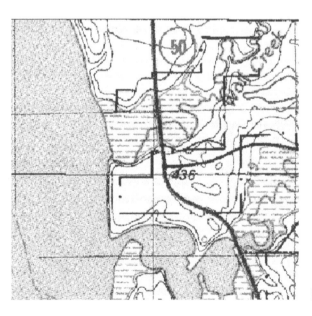

b

FIGURE 2.1: (*continued*)

more accurate to plot sites. While most surveys can get away with plotting sites on a 1:100,000 scale map, 1:24,000 is far more accurate (figure 2.1).

Geological Maps

Geological maps record the distribution of rocks and soil at or just under the land's surface. Having been made since the late 1700s, they have helped to provide information useful in everything from mining to water management and environmental stewardship. They can be of particular use to archaeologists in finding key resources such as stone outcroppings where quarry sites might exist. They also can be used to predict locations of sites in relation to certain landforms. The maps are based on a wide range of information, but most of it is "**ground-truthed**" by geologists in the field. However, a great deal of information can come from aerial photography, satellite imagery, global positioning system technology, and geographic information system (GIS)-based cartography. The main goal for geologists now is not to produce a single geological map but to develop a large, multilayered database of a wide range of geological features. Some of these data layers are available in many areas of the world, and their sophistication will only increase. At the moment, however, most archaeologists can make do with geological maps of their research areas.

One striking feature of geological maps is that they use vivid multicoloring, but if you look carefully, you can see that there is a **base map** printed in lighter colors that shows you political boundaries and major features so that you know where you are. Some may have contour lines. Many are available in the same scales as the topographic maps for an

FIGURE 2.2: Segment of a geological map from South Dakota along the Missouri River, including part of the key to geological units on the right. The landforms on which the Crow Creek site (39BF11) is located appear in the upper left corner of the map.

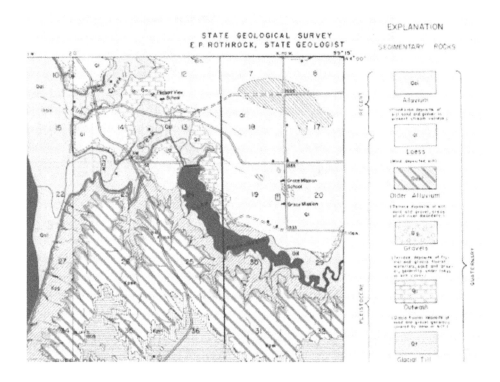

area (figure 2.2). The brighter colors represent a particular geological unit with certain kinds of rock or soil of a certain age. You may also see terms for some geological features named after where they were first observed or studied, much as archaeologists do with cultural complexes that are observed in a number of areas. Black letters indicate the time and nature of the unit, and different kinds of lines indicate a range of features from contacts between geological units to fault lines. The detail contained in geological maps is substantial, and as with topographic maps they take some skill to read. These maps often are now available online, with printed copies available at most state geological survey offices.

Topographic Maps

Being able to read topographic maps is a real skill and worth learning well. For most fieldwork, archaeologists in the United States use topographic maps issued by the United States

Geological Survey (USGS); many of them are now freely available online. Digital forms also are available. Print copies can be purchased in many places. "Topo" maps come in four different scales today, but over time there have been a number of others. The smallest current scale is 1:250,000, which covers the largest area. One inch on the map is the rough equivalent of 4 miles on the ground. The 1:100,000 metric series uses 1 cm to represent 1 km on the ground, a scale that is primarily useful for archaeology in large surveys. The USGS also publishes some 1:63,000 maps that cover as many as 282 square miles with a scale where 1 inch equals an equivalent of 1 mile, which means that 1 square inch on the map is about 1 square mile on the ground, still not useful for plotting small sites. The most useful topographic map for archaeologists in the United States is the 7.5-minute 1:24,000 scale quadrangle, covering no more than about 71 square miles. One inch on the map is about 2,000 feet on the ground. This series is available for the entire United States. In all, the USGS publishes about 57,000 7.5-minute maps plus many at other scales.

USGS topographic maps are useful because they contain a vast amount of information that is useful when you do an archaeological survey, including buildings, vegetation, terrain, standing water and streams, roads, and political boundaries. Each quadrangle, as the 1:24,000 scale maps are called, usually is named for a place that appears on a particular map; often this is a city or town. The name is printed in the top and bottom margins in the right-hand corners. Names of adjoining quadrangles are found in small, slanted letters at each corner and along each side of the map, or the position of the "quad" will be shown in the center of a cluster of adjacent quads in a small diagram (figure 2.3). Index maps are available that tell you which quadrangles cover the areas in which you are interested.

FIGURE 2.3: Topographic maps contain many kinds of information from grid references to scales, much of it along the sides, especially the bottom.

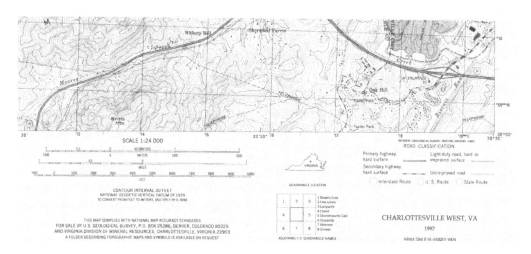

In Canada, the Centre for Topographic Information produces topographic maps at 1:50,000 scale. Provincial topographic quadrangle maps are available, with 1:20,000 scale standard for the north and 1:10,000 for the south.

The symbols used on the map are standard and conventional representations of cultural and natural features on the landscape. Standard colors represent features, such as blue for water or brown for contours. A complete list of colors and symbols is available on the back of some quadrangles but is more accessible online. One warning applies to the scale of some items on the maps. Sometimes buildings appear to be larger on maps than they are in reality, and the size of roads can be similarly misrepresented. This is one distortion that can get you into real trouble doing surveys, as roads can often appear to be much wider than they are in reality. A logging road that appears to be 10 m wide on the map actually may be only 2 m in reality.

Understanding Contour Lines

Topographic maps derive their name from the fact that they reflect the topography of the land (i.e., the changes in elevation across the landscape), which makes them especially useful for planning and executing archaeological surveys or for understanding locations of particular kinds of sites (figure 2.4). They also can give clues to how the landscape formed and what the possibility might be for deeply buried sites.

The usual way to show this on a flat map surface is by using **contour lines** (isolines) that represent places of equal height. If you walk around the side of a hill, for example, and stay at the same elevation, you would be following one of these imaginary contour lines. These are the thick and thin wavy lines you can see all over the map. Every fifth line is thick and will have small numbers attached to it at various intervals. Each line represents an interval of feet or change in elevation. The most common **contour intervals** on 1:24,000 maps are 5, 10, and 20 feet. The interval used can be found on the bottom of each map just under the graphic scale. On the map each contour line represents a particular height above sea level, and the numbers will tell you how many feet above sea level each contour line is. If the contour interval is 20 feet (the most commonly used), the elevation changes by 20 feet between each line. What that means is that when you see lots of lines in a small space, the change in elevation is large and the area steep. Contour lines that are farther apart indicate flatter ground. You can even tell which direction a stream is flowing because the contour lines form a V-shape with the tip of the V pointing upstream. The most important things to remember about contour lines are:

- When they are close together on the map they indicate steep slopes.
- When they are far apart on the map they indicate gentle slopes.

FIGURE 2.4: Contour lines and slope

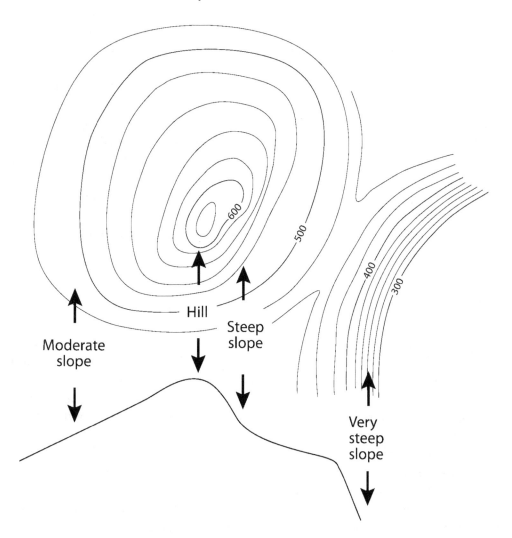

- When they are uniformly spaced on the map they indicate uniform slopes.
- When they decrease in spacing (when read from high to low), the slope is convex (outward sloping, like a hill).
- When they increase in spacing (when read from high to low), the slope is concave (inward sloping, like a valley).

Understanding contour lines will help to plan your surveys. In the initial decision making, particularly if you have to estimate how much time and money the survey is likely to cost (see "How to Prepare a Proposal or Bid" in chapter 8), it will be very useful to know whether you are going to be walking up the side of a mountain, or surveying around a gorge, as opposed to walking on relatively flat ground. Each of these terrains has specific features and challenges, as well as different potential for containing sites, and being aware of the rise and fall of the land is important for planning the amount of time it will take to conduct a survey. At the beginning, contour lines can seem confusing, but after you've studied the maps and taken them into the field with you over different types of terrain, you can assess the nature of the landform quickly just by looking at a topographic map.

Digitized topographic images of an area, or **digital elevation models** (DEMs), are readily available online for many areas and can be used with GIS software to visualize the topography of an area. DEMs can be rotated and even used to produce a three-dimensional "fly-through" of an area you wish to survey, providing you with an extraordinary planning tool (figure 2.5). These features may help you to understand the information on topographic maps. The best way to reach real understanding, however, is to take a map to the field.

USING LOCATIONAL REFERENCE SYSTEMS

Topographic maps allow you to use a range of systems to locate sites. The one with which most people have at least some familiarity is the **latitude** and **longitude** system (**geographic coordinate system**). The idea behind latitude and longitude is that the Earth is assumed to be a perfect sphere and rotates on a 24-hour basis (actually the Earth is more egg-shaped, and the rotation is not exactly 24 hours). The North and South Poles are fixed points. Lines are drawn at regular intervals "vertically" between them, with lines converging at the poles. Each arc is a meridian or longitude line. For convention, most countries agree that the prime meridian, or 0° longitude, passes through Greenwich, England, with a meridian at every degree around the 360º of the circle about 111 km apart at the equator. They go east and west 180º where they meet at the international date line, thus you label them east and west longitude. Latitude is similar, with lines running parallel to the equator at every degree, also about 111 km apart. Starting at the equator, they go north and south, so the reading includes a north or south latitude designation. Each latitude and longitude degree is divided into 60 minutes, and each minute into 60 seconds, with further subdivisions possible. The United States Capitol, for example, is located at 38°53'23"N, 77°00'27"W (38 degrees, 53 minutes, and 23 seconds north of the equator and 77 degrees, no minutes, and 27 seconds west of the meridian passing through Greenwich, England).

FIGURE 2.5: (a) A three-dimensional digital elevation model (DEM) shows the topography of the Crow Creek site (39BF11) area along the Missouri River in South Dakota from a high altitude. (b) An aerial photograph of the site from a lower altitude shows detail of the site. Compare this with a low altitude three-dimensional DEM from approximately the same angle and elevation. Data can be exaggerated to make the changes in elevation more distinct. They are remarkably similar.

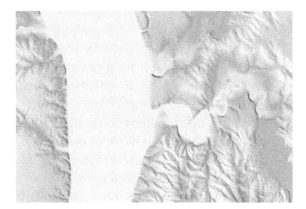

a

b

Latitude and longitude form a very precise system of location that is at the core of the global positioning system. With a handheld GPS unit, the latitude and longitude determined by the unit allow you to locate a site to within about 10 m of its true position. USGS topographic maps also include latitude and longitude designations along the margins of the quadrangle (figure 2.3). In fact, quadrangle maps are actually trapezoidal to reflect the convergence of the longitudinal lines toward the poles (i.e., in North America the top of each quadrangle would be slightly narrower than the bottom).

Universal Transverse Mercator (UTM)

The UTM system briefly discussed earlier in the chapter is one of the most common locational reference systems and is used extensively in National Register of Historic Places nominations (see "National Register of Historic Places Criteria" in chapter 8). UTM also is based on latitude and longitude but uses a metric grid system that covers the Earth with parallel latitudinal zones from the equator to 80 degrees north latitude for the northern hemisphere and from 80 degrees south latitude to the equator in the southern hemisphere (a different system is used for the polar regions, called the Universal Polar Stereographic projection). A series of 60 north-south longitudinal **zones**, each 6 degrees wide, provides the complementary axis. These zones are flattened in the UTM system with a grid of imaginary squares overlaying each, with lines 100,000 m apart.

Thinking of UTM as an x-y coordinate system may be useful, except that UTM readings always start at a **false origin** outside the zone to the southwest. This keeps all readings in the x-y system positive. All readings are made to the east, known as **eastings**, and to the north, known as **northings**. Eastings represent the distance that a unit or point is east of the start of the map zone. Northings represent the distance the unit or point is above the equator. By using eastings and northings it is possible to describe the location of any point on a map, by specifying the number of meters a point is east of the nearest vertical grid line and the number of meters it is north of the nearest horizontal grid line. This is called a **grid reference**, and depending on the degree of accuracy you want to achieve, it is possible to assign a grid reference that specifies a unique point on the surface of the Earth. Under the UTM system, the reading for the U.S. Capitol is 325755 m E, 4306467 m N; zone 18 N. Here the leading numbers define the easting and northing coordinates, indexed to zone 18 (north). UTM grid lines or blue tick marks, numbered progressively, are printed on the margins of USGS quadrangles (figure 2.3). You can buy or make UTM readers or coordinate templates to lay over the maps. Reading UTMs is not hard, but you need to be systematic, and there are several good sources to assist you. To read or assign a UTM grid reference you must follow three rules:

1 Because of the false point of origin, always read from the bottom left-hand (south-western) corner of the relevant grid square.
2 Always read the easting (the vertical line) before the northing (the horizontal line).
3 Always read eastings from left to right and northings from bottom to top. This means that when you are reading a grid reference for a site from a map, you need to read the closest easting to the left of the site (because eastings are always read from left to right) and the closest northing below the site (because northings are always read from bottom to top). Because this is the convention, if you wrote down the easting incorrectly as being the closest line to the *right* of the site, for example, you would actually be indicating to the reader that the site was to the right of that line and giving a grid reference that placed the site too far to the east. To remember the correct way to read UTMs, learn this simple mnemonic device: **read-right-up**.

If UTMs seem difficult, to a degree, they are, but after a few attempts to use them, they do become easier. However, if you don't use them frequently, you may need to refresh your memory about how to calculate them. To ease these difficulties, many handheld GPS units include calculation of UTMs. The error factors are similar to other GPS determinations, with errors from about 10–100 m, and GPS units work only where adequate satellite signals can be received, which means that in areas of very rugged topography, or near lots of tall buildings or in dense trees, their accuracy is limited. When using either hand-calculated or GPS UTMs, don't forget that what you are calculating is point data. To adequately locate a large site, you may need a number of points around the margins of the site, not necessarily your estimate of the **centrum** (the center of the site). Many state site forms and National Register nominations require more information than that. In the future, UTMs are more likely to be used for site locational information, not less, so understanding them is important.

United States Public Land Survey System (USPLSS)

For lands west and north of the Ohio River in the United States, the USPLSS is a coordinate system that uses large land segments divided into principal meridians that run vertically toward true north, with a horizontal baseline that runs perpendicular to it. The continental United States has 31 named and numbered meridians and baselines (Alaska has 5). Where baselines and meridians meet is an initial point of survey and is carefully plotted by latitude and longitude so that all measurements can have their origin at a known place. A system of townships, ranges, and sections derives from the initial point (figure 2.6). Strips of **townships** 6 miles wide run parallel to the baseline. The first strip

FIGURE 2.6: The system of township, range, and section layout

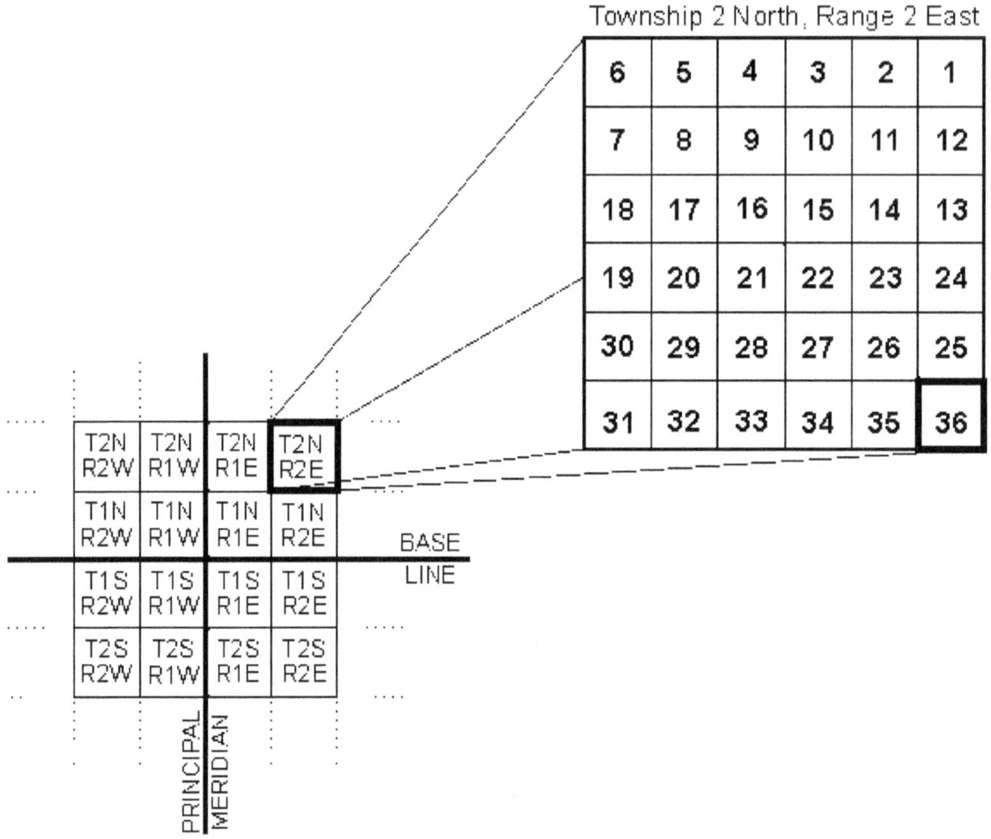

Township 2 North, Range 2 East

6	5	4	3	2	1
7	8	9	10	11	12
18	17	16	15	14	13
19	20	21	22	23	24
30	29	28	27	26	25
31	32	33	34	35	36

T2N R2W	T2N R1W	T2N R1E	T2N R2E
T1N R2W	T1N R1W	T1N R1E	T1N R2E
T1S R2W	T1S R1W	T1S R1E	T1S R2E
T2S R2W	T2S R1W	T2S R1E	T2S R2E

BASE LINE

PRINCIPAL MERIDIAN

north is designated T1N, T2N for the next, and so on. Similarly, if you go south, the first row is T1S, then T2S, and so forth. Six-mile-wide strips run parallel to the principal meridian and are designated **ranges**. Those east of the principal meridian are labeled R1E, R2E, and so on, while those west receive R1W, then R2W, and so forth. Thus each township has a unique township and range designation. Each is 6 by 6 miles square, so each square mile gets a section number as well. Sections are numbered from the northeast corner of the township going west from 1 to 6, then drop down a row and move from west to east with sections 7 to 12, alternating until section 36 is in the far southeastern corner. The major black grid lines on USGS topographic maps are townships and ranges, and the number in the center of each unit of the grid is the section number. Similar systems are used in Canada and in Texas except that section numbering proceeds differently. When it

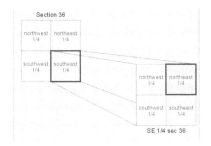

FIGURE 2.7: Labeling locations using the 1/4, 1/4 system within a section

comes to locating sites, sections are broken up into quarter-sections designated by their directional quadrant (i.e., NE, NW, SW, and SE; figure 2.6).

Similarly each quarter-section can be broken into quarters, as far as one reasonably wishes to take it. However, what is crucial to remember is that the designation is from the smallest quarter to the largest, so that a location might read something like NE1/4, SE1/4 of Sec 36, T2N, R2E, followed by the meridian designation. This would be read "the NE1/4 of the SE1/4 of Section 36, Township 2 North, Range 2 West," where the largest quarter is on the right and the smallest on the left (figure 2.7). A common problem is that people often reverse this order.

With latitude/longitude and UTM, the lines are imaginary, but with USPLSS these lines are literally surveyed onto the ground. This is particularly evident flying over the Midwestern farmlands, where section roads mark the section lines, and smaller roads mark quarter sections. Fencelines often mark smaller units. In many areas surveyors literally have marked section corners with brass-cap monuments, which is usually a metal disk about 3 inches in diameter on a concrete pipe with information about location engraved onto the disk. Where they have been found, these monuments are noted on USGS topographic maps. Each section is assumed to be 640 acres, but there is variation, or "slippage," in some areas essentially because a flat system is being imposed onto the curved surface of the Earth. The system is actually relatively simple and easy to understand with a bit of experience and practice.

East and south of the Ohio River, the old system of **metes** (lengths) and **bounds** (boundaries) is used to survey lands. This system is based mostly on land grants or private properties, which often followed natural features such as rivers or ridgelines and were irregular parcels of land. These require accurate surveying equipment.

Whatever the locational reference system, you can learn to locate archaeological sites efficiently and with reasonable accuracy for most scientific or heritage management purposes. A bit of study and experience will bring understanding of each system, and accuracies improve with practice.

MAKING SKETCH MAPS

One other kind of map that you may see referred to in reports and field notes is a sketch or "mud" map. Strictly speaking these are not maps but rough sketches of an area that usually are not drawn to scale (i.e., they are not measured accurately). Sketch maps are made in two main situations:

- To record the route you traveled to a site, so that you or someone else can find the site again (figure 2.8); and
- To give a general idea of the shape and context of a site if you don't have enough time to record it properly but need to know the basic layout of the site (figure 2.9).

Traveling sketch maps are an important and relatively easy way of making sure you can relocate a site. They are made fairly quickly and need to contain only the information that is essential to finding your way back to a site. Often, you will make these maps as you are driving to a site, so they are best done by a passenger. Traveling sketch maps are something that may be used by other researchers at some time in the future, and although inexpensive GPS units can easily record and provide waypoints, a sketch map may be better over the long term. Future researchers will not have access to any local information that you may have in your head, so it is best if you are as explicit in your directions as possible. Jotting down the precise GPS waypoint data on the sketch map may be an ideal approach. Some fundamental rules for making traveling sketch maps are:

- Make sure that the core information relates to the decisions you make at turning points on the route. Every decision to turn should be recorded.
- While sketch maps are not made to scale, some indication of distance traveled between waypoints is essential. You can do this by noting the odometer reading in the car, or if walking, by counting the number of paces.
- Major features of the landscape should be recorded to indicate waypoints on the route. These features should be permanent, such as a house, rather than ephemeral, such as "Cows in a field" or "Beer bottle in fork of tree."
- If you are using buildings as waypoints, don't just identify them in terms of their owners. The house that is currently owned by C. Orser will in all likelihood be owned by somebody else in the future.

Sketch maps of sites also are made to give a general overview of what the site looks like. They are made when you don't have time to record the site properly but still need some basic information. They can turn abstract phrases such as "a large scatter of stone artifacts"

FIGURE 2.8: A traveling sketch map

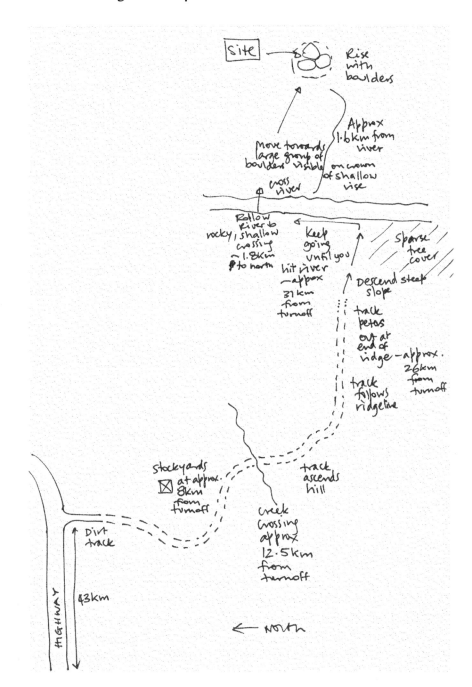

FIGURE 2.9: A sketch map of a site

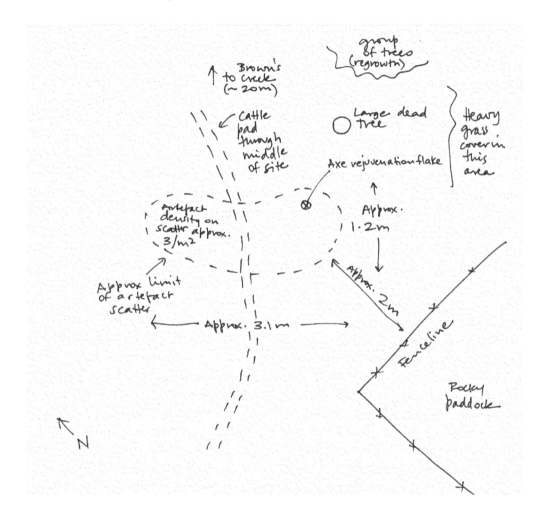

into a concrete image of the site itself. Again, these maps are made quickly and contain only the most significant information. They will not be useful for in-depth research or for making critical management decisions (such as how close a road can be built to the site). For either of these purposes you will have to return to the site and make an accurate map, drawn to scale (see chapter 4, "Site Survey and Mapping"). If you are working by your-self, you probably will be establishing the dimensions of the site through pacing (see "Us-ing the Compass and Pacing Technique" in chapter 4). Some fundamental rules for mak-ing sketch maps of sites are:

- Include at least one permanent feature in the map and all of the major features.
- Show the approximate location of all archaeological materials, their areal extent, and any areas of damage.
- Include basic information, such as a north arrow, your name, and the date on which you made the map.
- Dimensions can be included in approximate terms (e.g., approximately 20 m × 8 m), but it is best if you pace them out.
- As soon as possible, augment the sketch map with a UTM or other locational reference, photos, and notes, and *never* rely on a sketch map as the only recording of a site's location or its contents.

OTHER KINDS OF MAPS THAT MAY BE USEFUL

You may find a number of other types of maps useful in your fieldwork. One extremely useful map for doing surveys is the **plat** map (figure 2.10). Usually compiled into books on a county-by-county basis, plat maps are based on the U.S. Public Land Survey System discussed previously (i.e., they are divided into townships, ranges, and sections, with smaller divisions of each section according to property ownership). Updated every few years, often by commercial mapmakers but sometimes by county governments, they show representations of planimetric features such as streams, roads, and railroads. They are not necessarily to scale. Traditional maps are simple black-and-white line drawings, in some ways like a sketch map, but a recent trend is to use color to show different kinds of properties, such as parks or government lands. What is more useful is that the map carries names of the owner of the land, starting with the most recent owner based on deed records. These maps can be useful for driving on country roads and locating particular properties, but more important, if you need landowner permission, you usually can find out the landowner's name from the map. Many of these maps are now appearing online in digital form.

Sanborn insurance maps also can prove useful, especially on historical archaeology projects in municipalities. Produced by the Sanborn Map Company, these are uniform, color-coded, large-scale maps, dating from 1866 to the present, updated roughly every five years, meticulously detailing commercial and residential sections of some 12,000 cities and towns in the United States, Canada, and Mexico (figure 2.11). They were used by fire insurance agents to show the fire hazard risk for each property, and in doing so they denote property boundaries, doors and windows, roof types, water mains and hydrants, and a number of other hazard-associated factors. Many are now available digitally for numerous locations.

FIGURE 2.10: Plat maps show land ownership based on subdivisions of sections and some features such as streams or railroads. This map segment is from an early plat of St. Mary's Township, T27N, R15E, in Adams County, Indiana. Printed on inexpensive paper, plats are often updated every year.

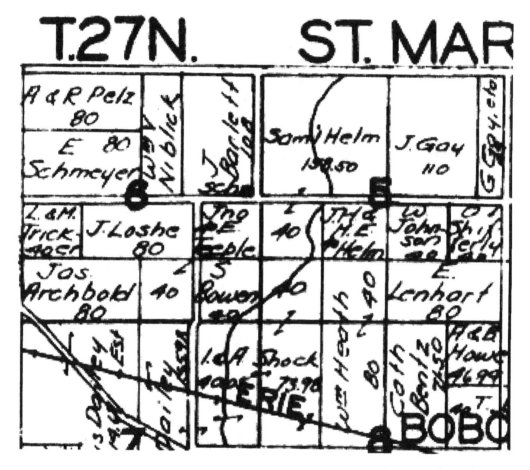

A good place to search for potentially useful maps is online, especially in map collections in university libraries and other archives. Many have now scanned and digitized old maps of their region and make them available to the public.

USING AERIAL PHOTOGRAPHS

Aerial photographs, as their name suggests, are literally photographs of a section of the Earth's surface taken from the air. While aerial photographs were originally taken in order

FIGURE 2.11: This section of an early Sanborn map of Indianapolis, Indiana, shows streets, businesses, and residences

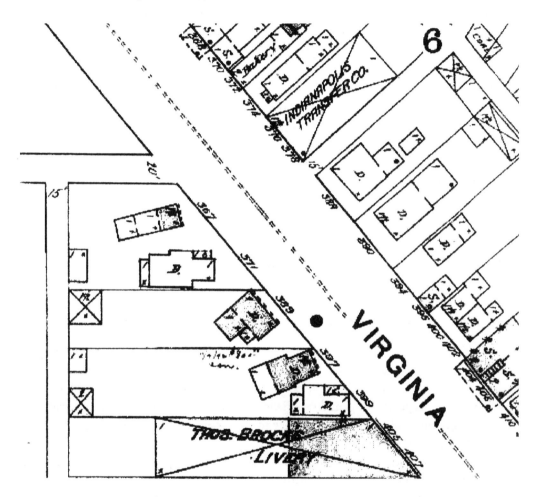

to map major environmental features, they also form a good basis for archaeological research and interpretation. An aerial perspective can be helpful in understanding past environments, as features such as recessional beachlines and dunes are much easier to identify from a distant perspective than close up. These data can be integral to understanding relationships between environments and people in the past, especially if you are researching Indigenous settlement patterns. For the historic period, aerial photographs can provide valuable snapshots of changing demographic and settlement patterns. In the same way that a larger-scale map is better for identifying particular sites or features, the lower the altitude of the aerial photograph (i.e., the lower the plane was flying when the photograph was taken), the greater the level of detail it will provide. The first systematic regional aerial photographs were taken in the 1930s, and in many regions have been taken at regular intervals since then. If you can obtain a sequence of photographs for the same area taken at different times, you literally may be able to see the major changes over the last 70 years. Aerial photographs provide the information base from which USGS topographic maps are made. Unfortunately aerial photographs are limited in their ability to show the spatial layout of sites because only large archaeological features will be visible from the air, but they are very useful for identifying general areas that may contain sites and that might be useful to survey. In North America many aerial photographs can be found online through local, state or provincial, and national government agencies. On some websites you can find all the aerial photograph series taken at intervals over a period of years.

Aerial photography can be used to:

- Key into a surveying strategy for a region
- Compare regional settlement patterns over time
- Detect specific sites, such as the faint outlines of old settlements, buildings, or roads
- Relate your site to the surrounding environment
- Assess relationships between sites within a region
- Assist in regional environmental analysis
- Assess a region's potential for significant sites

At a practical level, the best approach to aerial photography is to learn how to interpret photographs taken by others instead of taking on the costs and time to do your own. The amount and kinds of information you can deduce from an aerial photograph will depend upon your knowledge, training, and experience. While you don't need to be a specialist in geology or geomorphology, some experience in these fields can be helpful.

The World Wide Web is providing access to a wide range of aerial photographs. The web program Google Earth now provides some aerial photograph coverage of much of the Earth's surface and allows both high-altitude and low-altitude views with relatively good resolution (the more densely populated areas tend to have higher-quality images from a range of altitudes). Google Earth and a few similar programs are improving both coverage and quality almost daily. The ability to zoom and to tilt allows assessment of landscapes that can be extremely useful in planning surveys or doing landscape analysis.

USING A COMPASS

A compass uses a magnetized needle to indicate north. Following the principle that magnetic force is supplied by the molten iron at the Earth's core, the colored end of the needle (or the end with the letter N on it) will point toward the north pole of the Earth's magnetic field. To align a compass to north, turn the compass dial so that north (0°) on the dial matches the direction of the north end of the compass needle. Unfortunately the Earth's poles are constantly moving, and the North Pole indicated by the compass needle ("magnetic north") is not the same as the real North Pole ("true north"). This compass error is called **declination**, and depending where on the Earth you are, it can result in a difference of anything from a few degrees to up to 20–30° away from true north. Fortunately, on all topographic maps there is a simple chart that indicates the yearly degree of declination away from true north in any area (figure 2.12). You should bear in mind, however, that because the poles are constantly moving, this declination is also constantly changing and may be inaccurate on older maps.

FIGURE 2.12: Using a topographic map to calculate the difference between true and magnetic north. True north (TN) is the direction toward the Earth's geographic north pole, magnetic north (MN) is the direction in which the compass needle points, and grid north (GN) is simply the direction of all the vertical grid lines on a map. Grid north is always used as the reference point for bearings and grid references.

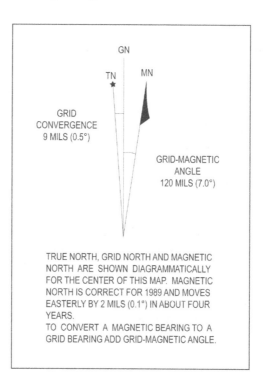

GN

TN   MN

GRID
CONVERGENCE
9 MILS (0.5°)

GRID-MAGNETIC
ANGLE
120 MILS (7.0°)

TRUE NORTH, GRID NORTH AND MAGNETIC
NORTH ARE SHOWN DIAGRAMMATICALLY
FOR THE CENTER OF THIS MAP. MAGNETIC
NORTH IS CORRECT FOR 1989 AND MOVES
EASTERLY BY 2 MILS (0.1°) IN ABOUT FOUR
YEARS.
TO CONVERT A MAGNETIC BEARING TO A
GRID BEARING ADD GRID-MAGNETIC ANGLE.

Remember that a compass will point to *anything* metallic or magnetic that is made of iron. This means that it cannot be used accurately if you are standing beside wire fence-lines or scrap metal, inside cars, or under or beside electrical power lines. Even metal objects on your person can affect your compass reading.

Taking Bearings

The direction in which you want to travel to get to your destination is called a **bearing**. Because there are 360° in a circle, compass bearings are referred to by the number of degrees they are away from north, always counting in a clockwise direction. For example, east is one-quarter of the circle away from north (which translates to 90°); south is directly opposite to north, or halfway around the circle (at 180°); and west is three-quarters of the circle away from north, or at 270°. The numbers on the movable compass dial are these degrees.

If you are using a compass to navigate your way across country, particularly if you are moving through dense vegetation, make continuous checks to ensure you have not moved

How to Read a Compass Bearing

- Point the compass toward your destination. If you are using the compass to make a plan of a site, this will be the point to which you want to measure; otherwise it will be the direction in which you want to travel.
- Keeping the compass fixed on your destination, move the dial so that 0° is aligned to the magnetic compass needle (which will be pointing toward magnetic north).
- The bearing of the point, or the distance it is away from north, can now be read off the compass dial (remembering always to read the numbers on the dial clockwise from 0°). This will be slightly different depending on the type of compass you are using (figure 2.13).
- For greater accuracy, use your arm to extend the directional arrow, or sight the compass on a ranging rod, or other highly visible feature, held at your destination.
- When you reach your destination, you should always take a **back-bearing** to your original location. This is a check on the accuracy of your original bearing. The difference between your original bearing and your back-bearing should always equal 180°, although an error of plus or minus 2° is often unavoidable. Taking and recording accurate bearings and back-bearings with a compass should allow you to plot your movements accurately and will be invaluable if you are navigating across country.

FIGURE 2.13: Taking a compass bearing. Using a prismatic compass (top), you must look through the compass to sight on your destination; using a protractor-type compass (bottom), you must sight along the compass using the arrow at the tip as a guide.

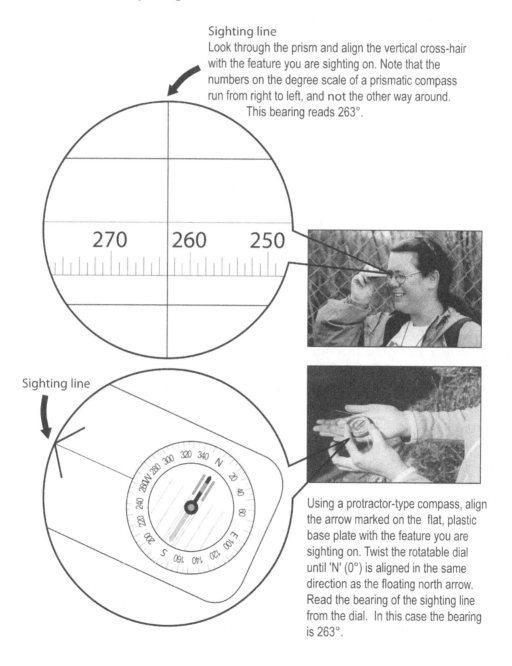

Sighting line
Look through the prism and align the vertical cross-hair with the feature you are sighting on. Note that the numbers on the degree scale of a prismatic compass run from right to left, and not the other way around. This bearing reads 263°.

270   260   250

Sighting line

Using a protractor-type compass, align the arrow marked on the flat, plastic base plate with the feature you are sighting on. Twist the rotatable dial until 'N' (0°) is aligned in the same direction as the floating north arrow. Read the bearing of the sighting line from the dial. In this case the bearing is 263°.

away from your bearing. One way to do this is by continually checking your compass, but by far the best way to maintain a bearing is to select a clearly visible object that lies along your path (such as a tree or a rock outcrop) and move toward it. If you can't find any obvious natural features, then send someone on ahead to act as a marker. Continue to do this for each leg of your journey. This process is called **point-to-point bearing**.

If you are using a map and a compass in conjunction to navigate toward a site, you will need to compensate for the declination. In other words, compass bearings taken on the ground must be converted into grid bearings before they can be plotted onto a map. Likewise grid bearings taken from a map must be converted into compass bearings before they can be used with a compass on the ground. To convert between bearings you either add or subtract the degrees of magnetic variation shown on the declination chart at the bottom of the map. For example, using the chart in figure 2.6, imagine that you have just taken a magnetic bearing from your compass toward a large rock outcrop. The bearing reads 50°. To convert this to a grid bearing that you could then plot onto your map, you would add 7° (because, over time, magnetic north has moved so that it is currently 7° east of grid north). Conversely, if you had taken a grid bearing of 50° from the map and wished to use it to navigate toward the outcrop, you would first have to convert the grid bearing to a magnetic bearing. To do this you would subtract 7°, thus giving you a magnetic bearing of 43° to follow on your compass. If you are using a GPS you can set your GPS to give you directions in magnetic degrees, thus eliminating the need to worry about compensating for declination (see "Using a Global Positioning System").

Once you have converted your compass reading to a grid bearing, you can use a protractor to measure this bearing directly onto a map. Like a compass, the outer rim of a protractor has degrees marked around its edge (either from 0–180° if the compass is a half circle, or from 0–360° if the compass is a full circle or a square). To measure a bearing, draw a light pencil line from the point where you are standing to the point to which you are navigating. Place the protractor on the map so that the center point or hole is directly over where you are standing and the north line (or 0°) is pointing to grid north on the map (i.e., the top), parallel to the eastings. Read the degrees off the edge of the protractor where it meets your pencil line.

USING A GLOBAL POSITIONING SYSTEM (GPS)

Global positioning systems have greatly simplified the process of navigating to and from sites and of recording site locations. A GPS unit can be used either on land or on water. It calculates a grid reference for your position from orbiting satellites, and they operate on the same map projection systems as official, published maps. When using a GPS on land, make

How to Orient a Map

Whenever you use a map in the field for navigation make sure you have the map correctly oriented to start with. This means ensuring that the directions on the map correspond to the directions of the same features on the ground. The easiest way to do this is to look for any readily identifiable features around you and turn the map so that it and you are facing in the same direction relative to those features. If you cannot identify any surrounding features, and are still unsure how to orient the map, you can use a compass:

- Lay the map flat.
- Place your compass on the map, and adjust the vertical lines on the map (grid north) to match up with magnetic north on the compass (the swiveling arrow needle).
- Check the declination in the legend at the bottom of the map, and make an adjustment to take into account the variation between magnetic north and grid north. For example, if the declination on your map is specified as 5°, you would need to shift the compass slightly so that its north arrow is pointing to a spot that is 5° east of grid north.
- The map will now be oriented correctly.

sure that you set the map system to match that of your maps. If your GPS readings are taken using a map system different from your printed maps, then your grid references will not plot accurately. Because the Earth is not a uniform sphere, mathematical models or **datums** were developed to make mapping accurate in world regions. The NAD-27 is the North American Datum (NAD) on which many topographic maps were based, and some state archaeologists' offices require site locations using this datum. NAD-83 was used to generate more recent topographic maps and the WGS84 (World Geodetic System) for the most recent maps. If you are having persistent problems in plotting your GPS readings, this is one of the first things to check. When using your GPS on water you will have to use latitude and longitude to plot location as this is the system employed on all charts.

Garmin, Trimble, and Magellan all provide high-quality models, accurate to within 10–15 m, that are easily affordable. They are also water and shock resistant and light and easy to carry. Because the degree of accuracy of which your GPS is capable will depend in part on the brand, make sure you always note down the make and model of your GPS in your field notes and report.

GPS units are simple to use and can be a great asset in the field, provided you keep some basic factors in mind. Most can be set to either magnetic north (good if you are navigating using a compass) or true north (good if you are navigating using a map). Make

Tips for Using Your GPS Efficiently

- Hold the unit away from your body, so that your body doesn't interfere with the satellite signal.
- Carrying your GPS unit in your hand all the time is not the best approach, nor is carrying it in a pocket. You can drop it or fall on it, damaging the unit. A padded carrying case, with places for extra batteries or even a map, attached to a sturdy strap across your chest works best, protecting the unit but making it readily accessible.
- When using a GPS to navigate to a known grid reference, walk along until you have correctly located yourself along either the easting or the northing, and then follow that until you reach the correct position.
- When you first turn on your GPS receiver it will "lock on" to all available satellites, provided the receiver has a clear and uninterrupted view. It is often worth leaving the GPS on for a few minutes before using it for serious work, as sometimes the initial readings can be misleading.

sure you know which one you are using. Because GPS units can be used all over the world, they also have to be set to the relevant map zone to give an accurate grid reference.

Because it is possible for errors to creep into any GPS reading (as a result of factors such as the number of satellites that are accessible, their geometry, atmospheric conditions, or signal reflection), it is always wise to check every reading against a topographic map to be certain of your location. Because GPS units are prone to running out of battery power at the most inopportune times, or may be unable to get a fix on a sufficient number of satellites for an accurate reading (particularly if you are surveying under dense tree cover or in rugged terrain), it is always wise to know how to calculate a locational reference manually (see "Using a Map to Calculate a Locational Reference"). If you plan to use a GPS under heavy tree cover you should investigate buying one with an external aerial.

FINDING NORTH USING YOUR WATCH

In case you are ever stuck in the field without either a compass or a GPS, you can use any analog watch to find north. This is not accurate enough to be able to map a site (see "Using the Compass and Pacing Technique" in chapter 4) or to navigate to a site, but it might be enough in a pinch to prevent you from being lost. To find north using your watch, point the number 12 on your watch toward the sun. North will always lie midway between the hour hand and the number 12 (figure 2.14). If you have only a digital watch,

Stephen Sutton's Tips for Successful Fieldwork

- Always have a good pair of boots. I recall a report at a conference in which the presenter admitted that part of the study area hadn't been surveyed "because we didn't have any boots."
- Take good care of your field assistants. It's essential to the success of fieldwork that your assistants are well fed and that their health and safety are assured.
- Plan your fieldwork. You need to be aware that the only data you have are what you collect. By this I mean that when you get back to the lab, and are working up your notes or collection to find something missing—too bad. It's almost always impossible to reconstruct from memory (either yours or your colleagues') or to find surrogates for the missing data. The only way to do it is to return to the scene, and this is expensive and time consuming.
- There is no "one way" to do anything. While careful attention to data collection is fundamental, it should also be appropriate. Work should be structured to ensure that the final product, the reason you're in the field in the first place, can be achieved, but after that there is a capacity to waste resources collecting data that will never be used.
- Don't rely on technology. There are digital machines for everything these days: GPS, laptop computers, EDMs, data loggers, digital cameras, and so on. They all have an amazing capacity to fail at the critical moment. There is no substitute for traditional skills such as map reading and surveying and the use of backup materials such as paper survey notebooks.

make a sketch of an analog watch and draw the correct time on it, leaving off the minute hand. Use the sketch in the same manner as a real watch to locate north.

SAFETY AND MAYBE EVEN SURVIVAL IN THE FIELD

Archaeologists often travel in remote areas on tracks, on dirt roads, and off-road. This can be highly dangerous, particularly if you are not prepared or if you are not being sufficiently careful. Never go into the field unprepared—archaeology is not worth dying for. The best advice for working in the field is to use common sense. Make sure you take enough water, particularly if you are going to be surveying large areas and doing lots of physical activity, even on cool days (you should always aim to drink the equivalent of 8–10 glasses of water a day). If you are going to a remote area, ensure that you have spare tires for your vehicle, emergency food rations, and some means of reliable communication

FIGURE 2.14: Making a watch compass

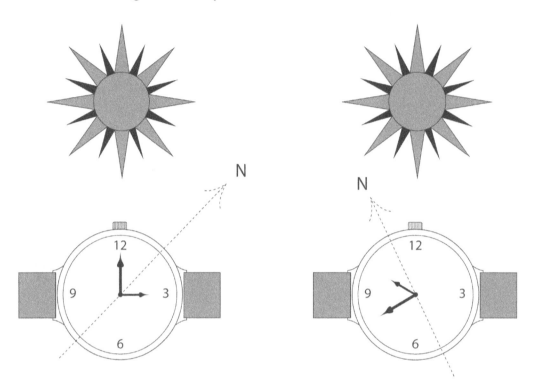

(such as a UHF radio or satellite phone, *not* just a mobile phone). Make sure that you tell someone exactly where you are going and when you expect to return.

Venomous snakes can be a wildlife risk in many areas of North America. Learning to identify them is useful. When walking in the field, wear sturdy boots that come at least as high as your ankles. Keep your eyes on where you are walking. If you see a snake, stop and remain still. If the snake is curled up and quiet you can usually detour around it, giving it a very wide berth. If the snake is moving or looks as if it intends to move, stay put. Keep quiet and do not move. Most snakes aren't aggressive and would rather flee than fight. When the snake has moved a safe distance away, move off slowly and quietly. Killing a snake unnecessarily, even venomous species, is unacceptable! Know what the primary habitats are for certain snakes, and pay special attention in those areas.

Other potentially nasty creatures are also a risk during fieldwork. When walking in the bush wear long-sleeved shirts and long pants, tuck your pant legs into your socks or boots, and tuck your shirt in as well—this will help to prevent ticks and other insects from traveling up your body inside your clothing. Check yourself carefully for ticks. Some, such as deer ticks, are extremely small but carry Lyme disease. If you get a tick, remove it by levering it out carefully with a pair of tweezers. Do not squeeze or pull the tick, and do not try to cut it out.

There are relatively few venomous spiders in North America, and scorpions are present in warmer and drier climates. They are rarely deadly, but bites or stings can be painful. Stumbling into a wasp nest or beehive can be very painful but rarely deadly (unless you are allergic), and some ants can cause problems. The best advice is to recognize possible habitats and to pay attention to your surroundings.

Although they are not numerous, North America has a range of plants whose leaves or other parts can provoke a nasty rash on exposed skin. Know how to identify such plants and how to treat the symptoms. Poison ivy is especially bad; find out how to identify it and how to deal with it. All parts of the plant can cause problems, even smoke from burning it in a fire.

Drinking plenty of fluids during and after strenuous fieldwork is essential, particularly if you're working in a hot environment. Heat exhaustion is a potentially serious condition that can arise if the body's heat regulation system becomes overwhelmed. If someone loses too much fluid through sweating, this decreases blood volume and blood flow to the vital organs. The person develops mild shock, which if not treated promptly can progress to heat stroke—an extremely serious and life-threatening condition. The symptoms and warning signs of heat exhaustion include:

- Normal or below-normal skin temperature
- Cool, moist, pale skin, progressing to red skin
- Headache
- Nausea
- Dizziness and weakness
- Exhaustion
- Sweating
- Rapid, weak pulse

If you think that you, or someone doing fieldwork with you, might be suffering from heat exhaustion, treat it promptly. Encourage the person to rest lying down in the shade, with legs slightly raised. Loosen any tight clothing, and remove clothing soaked with perspiration. If the person is fully conscious, give frequent small drinks of cool water. Often people suffering from heat exhaustion will feel better after resting in a cool place and drinking cool water or a sport drink (not iced!). To prevent heat exhaustion from becoming heat stroke, persuade them to stop all activity, as they may quickly go beyond the stage of making a rational decision for themselves. If they are nauseated or vomiting and unable to take any fluids, seek urgent medical attention.

Be sure that most of your crew know some basic first aid, and carry an extensive first aid kit in your vehicle and a small one in a pack. Before going to the field, having your crew receive basic first aid training, including CPR, is entirely worth the time and cost. The life they save may be yours!

RESPONSIBLE BEHAVIOR IN THE BUSH

- Don't walk onto or through private property without permission.
- Use a portable butane stove for cooking rather than deadwood, which is part of the natural ecosystem and can provide a home for animals. Stoves decrease the risk of forest or brush fires.
- Minimize the use of soaps, shampoos, and detergents. If you must use them, do so well away from streams or rivers.
- If toilets are not available, dig a small hole well away from any water source.
- Carry out everything you carry in, so that it can be recycled or disposed of properly.
- Leave the surroundings as they are as much as possible. Picking wildflowers reduces the chances of new plants and is illegal in many local, state, provincial, and national parks. Moving rocks can disturb animal habitats.
- Don't feed native animals, as this may cause them to become reliant on humans and unable to fend for themselves.
- If you're looking for somewhere to camp, check the area carefully for sites and artifacts first. There is nothing worse than waking up in the morning to find that you have pitched your tent and cooked your meals in the middle of an archaeological site.
- If you're making a campfire near a historical site, don't use any historical artifacts (e.g., bricks or stones from fallen structures) to make your fire.

CAMPFIRE COOKING

This can be either a highlight or lowlight of archaeological fieldwork. Cooking over an open fire is a challenge and requires techniques slightly different from using a normal kitchen. A camp oven is the standard cooking utensil and is extremely versatile. It can be used as a saucepan, a frying pan, or an oven, to cook anything from roast chicken, soups,

Joe Watkins's and Jane Balme's Tips for Surviving a Group Field Season

- Be aware of the climatic conditions where you'll be working, and make sure you're properly equipped for them.
- Make an effort to find out about the place you're going. Check out the local history.
- Be considerate of other people's privacy. In camp life there is rarely anything that people don't know about, but recognize that sometimes people need space.
- If you have any special medical needs (i.e., prescriptions), make sure you have a good supply.
- If you wear glasses bring an extra pair.
- Find out about the living conditions well in advance. Often toilet facilities are primitive, to say the least. If you need a private bathroom, bring it with you.
- If you're worried about poisonous insects or animals, find out where they live and avoid them as much as possible.
- Find out what phobias you have—and get over them.
- Be sensitive to the values of the culture you are working with. The kind of dress and appearance that may be suitable for young people in the city may not be suitable for rural communities. For example, short shorts, makeup, or long hair can be inappropriate in a field situation.
- Know how to use a compass. If nothing else, practice in your own backyard.
- If you can't follow any of these tips, stick to one-person projects.

and stews to cakes and biscuits. When using it as an oven, the most difficult task is to regulate the heat so that you don't burn the food. If you can, build your fire early and wait for it to die down before you begin to cook, using coals rather than direct flame. Don't place the camp oven directly over the fire: this will provide too much heat and burn the food. Instead, place it near the fire on a bed of hot coals and ash, and put three times as many coals on top of the lid as underneath the oven. This will ensure even distribution of

TABLE 2.2: Assessing coal temperatures

Seconds[a]	Heat	Temperature
6–8	Slow	250°F–350°F
4–5	Moderate	350°F–400°F
2–3	Hot	400°F–450°F
1 or less	Very Hot	450°F–500°F

[a]Number of seconds that hand can be held over hot coals.

the heat and won't burn the bottom. Dutch, camp, or Bedourie (the Australian version, which is lighter and made of steel instead of cast iron) ovens in particular were designed for this task. Use a wooden spoon to stir a camp oven, and always cook with the lid on. Unless you like ashes in your food, don't tilt the lid when you remove it. When trying to assess the temperature of coals, count the number of seconds you can hold your flat hand above them (table 2.2).

Before use, a camp oven will need to be "seasoned" with oil. This means heating it slightly, rubbing in a light coating of edible oil, and then heating it to a high temperature for around 30 minutes. Once it has been seasoned it should never be scrubbed with soap. A camp oven won't rust if you season it correctly, clean it properly, and keep it dry. Store the oven in a warm, dry place with the lid cracked so that air can circulate inside. A camp oven seems indestructible, but it will shatter if you drop it onto a hard surface or crack if you pour cold water into it while it's hot.

Jane Balme's and Joe Watkins's Tips for Successful Campfire Cooking

- Be aware that you are part of a team that doesn't include your mother. Don't expect others to clean up after you.
- Know how to cook at least three different meals on a campfire made from five basic ingredients (potatoes, onions, roadkill, and two others of your choosing).
- For instant popularity within the group, learn how to cook one great meal. You only have to cook on rotation, so you may only cook once or twice during the field trip. One great meal can establish your culinary skill—and you may never have to prove it again!
- If you have any special dietary needs make sure you have a good supply of what you need.
- Let the organizers know if you have any special allergies.

Basic Aussie Damper (or Camp Bread)

Damper is a traditional Australian bread made with no yeast. Along with tea and meat, it provided basic sustenance for stockmen and swagmen and was easily cooked on the coals of an open fire.

3 large cups of plain flour
2 teaspoons cream of tartar
1 teaspoon baking soda
1 teaspoon salt
1 dessert spoon (bigger than a teaspoon, but smaller than a tablespoon) sugar
Sufficient liquid to make a loaf (you can use water, milk, milk and cream mixed, or but-
  termilk)

Mix dry ingredients. Add enough liquid and mix with a knife until it forms a firm but soft dough. Place in lightly greased camp oven, cover lid of camp oven with coals, and leave for about 30 minutes. Eat hot, spread with butter and honey, syrup, or jam.

Beer Damper

3 cups self-rising flour
Pinch of salt
3 tablespoons powdered milk
3 tablespoons sugar
Enough beer to make a firm dough

Mix all dry ingredients; add enough beer to make a firm dough. Place in camp oven and cook with hot coals for around half an hour. Eat hot, spread with butter and honey, syrup, or jam.

Thai Green Curry

This can be made with chicken, with vegetables, or a combination of the two and should be served with steamed or boiled rice. These quantities should feed 8-10 people.

2 packets green curry paste (this should be about 6 tablespoons)
2 tins coconut cream (you can add about 1 cup of water if you need more liquid)
6 tablespoons fish sauce
6 tablespoons brown sugar
Chilies (amount will vary depending on how hot you like your curries—1, deseeded, for mild; 2 or more for hot). If you don't have fresh, use dried, but lessen the amount.
Basil—this recipe is best with fresh basil, but if you can't get it, use the chopped basil that comes in a tube in preference to dried basil.

Cook curry paste in 1-2 tablespoons oil for 2-3 minutes, add chopped chicken, and cook until browned. If using vegetables, stir-fry in paste 5-8 minutes (add the hardest vegetables first so they cook the longest). Add coconut milk, fish sauce, brown sugar, and chilies. Simmer, stirring regularly, for 20 minutes, or until chicken or vegetables are cooked. Add basil, stir, and serve.

Larry Z's Really Easy Cowboy Beans

Before leaving home, prepare by watching *Blazing Saddles*.

1 large can baked beans
1 regular can northern, pinto, or other beans (rinsed/drained)
½ pound hamburger
1 small bottle BBQ sauce
½ cup ketchup
½ cup brown sugar
Bottle of beer (drink what you don't use)

Cook, drain, and crumble hamburger. Season to taste with BBQ sauce. Add all other ingredients and heat. Add beer to bring it to the consistency you like.

Sing "Beans, Beans, the Musical Fruit" while heating. Serves four.

Pineapple Upside-Down Cake

1 plain cake mix, including ingredients listed on package (egg, water, butter)
½ cup brown sugar
1 small can sliced pineapple
About ½ cup butter or margarine
1 packet maraschino cherries (optional)

Melt butter or margarine in the bottom of the camp oven. Mix in brown sugar and spread evenly across the base of the oven. Save pineapple juice for the cake mix, and place pineapple rings in bottom of oven on top of the brown sugar. If you are using maraschino cherries, place one inside each pineapple ring. Substitute the pineapple juice for some or all of the water to be added to the cake mix. Add egg, and mix as per instructions. Pour cake mix over the brown sugar and pineapple. Bake until cake is browned and a knife comes out clean.

REFERENCES AND FURTHER READING

Australian Red Cross. 1995. *First aid: Responding to emergencies.* Carlton, Victoria: Australian Red Cross.

Biddle, D. S., A. K. Milne, and D. A. Shortle. 1974. *The language of topographic maps.* Milton, Queensland: Jacaranda Press.

Geoscience Australia. 2003. Coordinates, datums and ellipsoids. www.ga.gov.au/geodesy/datums/history.jsp (accessed February 6 2007).

For a range of other useful information, see the website accompanying the text.

CHAPTER THREE

FINDING SITES

What you will learn from this chapter:

The advantages of a systematic surface survey

Strategies for surveying a sample of your field area

How your choice of strategy is likely to affect your results

The basics of recording slope, geology, soils, transects, ground-surface visibility, and
  vegetation

The importance of assessing effective survey coverage

Why you need to define a site's boundary

The essential information to record when you find a site

Regardless of whether you are undertaking a research or contract archaeology project, the
initial part of most archaeological fieldwork will be directed toward finding sites. Unfortunately there is no foolproof way to do this, because the likelihood of finding sites depends
on a number of factors. The ground-surface visibility conditions you encounter in the field,
how much time is available, how large an area you have to survey, the number of surveyors you have, and even the nature of the sites themselves will all affect the potential for locating sites. In some places, such as on American Indian tribal lands, you may not be free
to conduct a survey at all, because Indigenous people may wish to control your movements
around the landscape so that you do not inadvertently encounter sites to which access is restricted. In any event, it is highly unlikely that you will ever be able to find *all* of the

archaeological sites that exist in an area, but in general you should ensure both that your surveying strategy is appropriate for the goals of your study (see "Designing Your Research" in chapter 1) and that you try to discover the widest possible range of sites.

WHAT IS A SITE?

A **site** is a place that represents a particular focus of past human activity. This activity may be related to past events, practices, or beliefs and may or may not have left behind actual physical traces. The various landing places of Lewis and Clark in their 1804–1806 expedition along the Missouri River, for example, have become important sites, even though they contain almost no physical evidence of these events. Likewise many purely natural elements of the landscape are important Indigenous sites because they are the embodiment of creation stories. If you are working with Indigenous groups you will need to take such sites into account. While these sites may not be accompanied by any physical evidence of past human behavior, knowing their location can be essential to understanding the use of the landscape in the past. An absence of material evidence is not necessarily evidence for the absence of human behavior—such a place may be providing information about what people chose *not* to do. People in the past actively avoided some areas, but such places nonetheless are still part of how they used and understood the landscape around them.

By contrast, an **archaeological site** is any place that still contains physical evidence of past human activity. This evidence can take an enormous variety of forms depending on the nature of the site and who created it, from actual objects or traces of objects (e.g., posts or postholes) to the physical by-products of a past activity (such as plow furrows or scarred trees). Almost anything can be an artifact because what we might regard as insignificant today may have had all sorts of meanings for people in the past.

There are some standard "types" of site that archaeologists commonly encounter. The two broadest categories reflect a general division into precontact and postcontact history: **Indigenous sites** (sometimes called prehistoric, Native American, or aboriginal sites) and non-Indigenous sites (usually referred to as Euro-American or **historical sites**). Of course, there is often considerable overlap between the two. The Inuit, an Indigenous people of Greenland and Canada, for example, had well-documented contact with non-Indigenous Norse sailors, colonists, and traders between the 10th and 15th centuries, and postcontact Indigenous sites, such as fur trade posts and forts, are an important part of recent Indigenous history, although they may contain predominantly Euro-American artifacts. Likewise, using the term "Euro-American sites" to refer to all non-Indigenous sites ignores the contributions of other groups to the settlement of the Americas. For simplicity's sake we use "Indigenous sites" to refer to all American Indian sites, whether pre- or postcontact, and "historical sites" to refer to all non-Indigenous sites (for some idea of the range of site types in each of these categories, see chapters 6 and 7).

The site is the basic operating unit of any field survey. Generally speaking, a survey is geared toward locating and recording as many sites as possible, although there are sometimes problems with focusing exclusively on the site as the sole unit of human behavior. Bear in mind that sites are just the concentrated physical remains of past human behavior and that, when created, none would have existed in isolation. Think of your own day-to-day behavior: you might perform many different activities in many places, but each place, or "site," is connected through the web of your movements and decision making. In addition, many of your movements will leave no physical traces, and your memories of the events of the day, the places you visited, and the ways that you used them are as much a part of your interactions with the landscape around you as the physical substance of the places and activities themselves. This is part of being *of* a place, rather than merely *in* it. People continually construct a social landscape around them at the same time that they interact with a physical one, and the archaeological sites that are left behind are simply the physical by-products of this ongoing process.

As an archaeologist, when you record a site, you are, in effect, only recording one "moment" of human behavior in space and time, so it is worth bearing in mind how each site might be part of wider patterns of human behavior on a larger scale (either across space or through time). Many of these patterns may be intangible in purely archaeological terms, although you may be able to access some of the ways in which people relate socially to the landscape around them through oral history (see "Recording Oral Histories" in chapter 6). These wider patterns create the **cultural landscape**, or the totality of human physical and social activity in an area. In theory, the cultural landscape could be analyzed at any scale, but in practice, it is usually viewed at a manageable level, such as within drainage basins or other well-defined geographic regions. This is mainly an administrative decision, taken to limit the potentially limitless idea of a cultural landscape.

Most sites are found through systematic surface survey, walking over an area of ground in such a way that you locate as many sites as possible (if doing a CHM survey) or representative sites (if you are seeking to understand the whole cultural landscape). During a survey you will need to record a wide range of complementary information. Because people use the landscape in a variety of ways, the location of sites usually will relate closely to their environment. For this reason it is essential to describe the topography, vegetation, water and stone resources, ground-surface visibility conditions, and survey strategy, as well as basic information about any sites you find. You may not always be able to record the maximum amount of information, but you must ensure that, whatever the other limitations of the project, you always record a basic minimum of information (see "What to Do When You Find a Site").

SYSTEMATIC SURFACE SURVEY

Without a doubt the most effective archaeological surveys are those carried out systematically on foot, sometimes called **pedestrian surveys**, moving slowly across the ground, using subsurface testing at regular intervals. A surface survey usually is conducted by walking lines or corridors (**transects**) across the study area. These may be straight lines between two points or sinuous lines following the contours of the ground. The width of a transect and its spacing in relation to other transects will depend on the time available, the number of people involved, and the nature of the terrain. Obviously the more transects you walk through an area, and the closer together they are, the better your survey coverage will be. In practice, a single field-walker can effectively scan 1 m to either side; thus if you are one of 10 field-walkers it should be possible to survey a transect that is 20 m wide in total. If, however, you are walking a transect alone, then the total width will be reduced to 2 m (figure 3.1).

Walking systematic transects is really only possible when the area you are surveying is relatively small, or if you have ample amounts of time in which to complete the survey. In reality, surveying for sites can be approached in a variety of ways, depending on the goals of the project and how much time and money are available. If a systematic surface survey on foot is not practical (e.g., you are surveying a very large area) or if there is limited time

FIGURE 3.1: The width of a survey transect is largely determined by the number of people who are available to walk it

Richard Fullagar's Tip for Successful Surveying

Always be prepared to get your boots wet. Even new ones. On a field trip to Papua New Guinea I was surveying obsidian quarries with Jim Specht. I was worried about getting my new boots wet, and so I walked over a ridge on Garua Island instead of around on the reef. Jim got wet on the reef and discovered a fabulous obsidian source that he refused to tell me about for over a year. Just kept it a secret. A suitable punishment I guess for putting clothing ahead of archaeology (which I haven't done since).

or resources to devote to the task, it is possible to conduct a survey by looking for artifacts out of a slowly moving vehicle. By doing this there is a much greater risk of sites being missed, however, and it is not recommended. Many CHM archaeologists consider such "windshield" surveys to be unethical.

SAMPLING

In preference, if it is not possible to undertake a complete surface survey, then you will have to limit your survey to certain parts of the landscape, a strategy known as **sampling**. Often, archaeologists are able to examine only a portion, or sample, of the total archaeological record (either from an excavated site or the landscape) upon which they base their interpretations. This is perfectly legitimate provided the sample is **representative** and not skewed by sampling bias in any way. This is where a sampling strategy becomes essential. Sampling strategies can be approached in a number of ways, and choosing which parts of the landscape to survey is not a trivial task. Because you can't know where sites will be located before you go into the field, the decisions you make as to which parts of the area to sample will directly affect the likelihood of your finding any sites.

Developing a Suitable Sampling Strategy

The distribution of archaeological material across the landscape depends on a number of related factors, such as the preservation conditions over time, the degree to which sites are exposed through erosion or the lack of vegetation, and the actual decisions of the people creating the sites and depositing the materials in the first place. The decision about which sampling strategy to adopt will therefore center around these kinds of factors, as well as more practical decisions based on the number of people conducting the survey and the funds and time available for the project. On CHM projects, some agencies might even require a sample size that is a certain percentage of the land to be surveyed. A similar principle can be applied to the excavation process, because the decision about where to excavate in a site is also a sampling decision. Samples can be either **judgment**, **random**, or **systematic** (figure 3.2).

Judgment Samples

This is a sample in which the researchers exercise their own judgment as to which areas will be most productive to survey, sometimes referred to as a "stratified" sample. This

FIGURE 3.2: The advantages and disadvantages of different sampling strategies

A. Judgement sample	B. Simple random sample	C. Stratified random sample	D. Systematic random sample	E. Systematic unaligned sample
Study area divided into geographic zones (creeklines, hill slopes, ridges, etc).	Random locations on the landscape are selected for survey.	Study area divided into geographic zones (creeklines, hill slopes, ridges etc).	First survey area is selected at random, and then all other areas are chosen in relation to this.	One survey area within each larger block is chosen at random.
Survey areas within each zone selected according to those areas the researcher considers will be most productive.	Advantages: Takes into account the geography of the area and recognizes there might be factors which affected the location of sites in the past.	Survey areas then selected randomly within each zone.	Advantages: Ensures that a portion of every area is sampled.	Advantages: Maintains a random element in the selection process.
Advantages: Those areas highly likely to contain sites (such as close to reliable water sources) can be given preference.	Eliminates potential sources of bias. All areas have an equal chance of being selected.	Advantages: Takes into account the geography of the area and recognizes there might be factors that affected the location of sites in the past.	Designed to give more even survey coverage.	Gives relatively even coverage across the total survey area.
Areas where it is unlikely sites will be found can be avoided.	Disadvantages: Sites unlikely to be literally randomly scattered about the landscape.	Disadvantages: Still a risk of personal bias.	Disadvantages: Sites may still be missed.	Disadvantages: Sites may still be missed.
Disadvantages: Will always be based on the researcher's preconceived notions of what the archaeology should be like.	In a truly random sample some areas or sites may be over-represented or missed entirely.			

judgment is usually based on past experience of where sites are likely to be located and ethnohistoric research into how the survey area might have been used in the past (see "Undertaking Ethnohistoric Research" in chapter 7). In a typical judgment survey the area would be divided into its various geographic zones (hill, creek, plain, gully, ridge, and so on) and the zones most likely to contain sites targeted for survey. In theory, while all zones might have an equal chance of containing sites, in practice we know that water, food, and raw material sources are all important for how people used the land and therefore where people might have camped or worked. Look at just about any contemporary map, and you'll see that people locate their villages, towns, and cities near key resources such as rivers and lakes and transportation lines.

The advantage of a judgment sample is that those areas that have a high likelihood of containing sites (such as close to reliable water sources) can be given preference, and areas where it is highly unlikely that sites will be found (such as on extremely steep slopes) can be avoided. This allows time and resources to be focused on the most productive areas and also takes into consideration the geography of the study area. Of course this has its disadvantages too. Such a survey cannot help but be biased by the researcher's preconceived notions of what the archaeology *should be* and runs the risk of creating a self-fulfilling study (Redman 1975, 149).

Predictive models sometimes can be used to give you the probability of sites being present in certain locations. In some ways, predictive models are like judgment samples, but done in very precise ways. When areas are relatively well known in terms of the usual locations of certain types of sites, you can bring together all the known factors about such sites and statistically calculate what the chances are of finding a site in a specific location. For example, you may know that in southwestern Iowa, you find 80% of the Central Plains tradition earthlodges on south-, southwest-, and west-facing slopes of 2–18°, with a slightly higher probability of upland versus bottomland locations, less than 300 m from a water source. This knowledge allows you to structure your sample or survey more efficiently. One good example is the Mn/Model Statewide Archaeological Predictive Model, developed and used by archaeologists with the Minnesota Department of Transportation (see www.mnmodel.dot.state .mn.us for a detailed description). Use predictive models cautiously, however, especially if they have not been **ground-truthed** (i.e., checked in the field for accuracy). A prediction of low site probability doesn't necessarily mean that there aren't any sites there, just that there is a low probability of their presence. You should always do at least some survey in such areas. Landforms often change through time, so buried sites also might be present.

Random Samples

Some studies attempt to remedy this bias by using a random sampling strategy, in which survey areas are selected by chance rather than by design. By using this strategy, no one area is given preference over any other, and all areas have an equal chance of being selected. A random sample can be **simple** (where random spots on the landscape are selected for survey, usually by imposing an imaginary grid over the study area and then selecting areas to survey within that grid based on random numbers generated from a table or computer program) or **stratified** (where the study area is divided into its geographic zones and then sampled randomly within each zone, as you would for a simple random sample survey). Like a judgment sample, a stratified random sample takes into account the geography of the study area and recognizes that there might be certain factors that affected the location of sites in the past. In reality, sites are unlikely to be randomly scattered about the landscape: people tend to follow behavioral patterns that relate to specific needs within the environment, such as water or shelter, and a stratified random sample recognizes that they tended to use the landscape in particular ways.

Systematic Samples

One of the problems with a truly random sample is that some areas or sites are likely to be overrepresented or missed entirely. The goal of systematic samples is to remedy this by ensuring that a portion of every area is sampled. You can do this either by **systematic random** sampling, where the first sample unit or area is selected at random, and all other areas are chosen in relation to this (e.g., if you decide to place a survey square every 10 km from the first, randomly chosen survey square), or **systematic unaligned** sampling, where the total area is divided into large blocks and then one smaller block within each larger block is chosen at random (Hester et al. 1997, 30). This still maintains a random element in the selection process but also gives relatively even coverage across the survey area.

Regardless of which strategy you consider to be ideal, the reality is that in some situations your survey area may be decided for you. Landowners may refuse access to their property, Indigenous people may not want you walking in particular areas, or some places might just be inaccessible. In any case, even if you are able to survey every centimeter of ground, you will still, in all likelihood, be able to see only a portion of the total archaeology of the area (Drewett 1999, 44). Sites might be covered by vegetation, soil, or leaf litter; the area might not be actively eroding so that no sites are visible; or poor light from heavily overcast conditions may cause you to miss small artifacts. The important thing is to recognize and record these and any other such limitations in your field journal so that others can recognize this bias and not assume a more thorough coverage of the landscape than you have been able to achieve. All of this, however, concerns only what might be visible on the surface, not what might exist beneath it.

SUBSURFACE TESTING

One big fear in carrying out a CHM contract is that you will miss a buried site only to have it discovered during a construction project. This might result in lots of "downtime" for expensive construction equipment and crews, not to mention that it might suggest that you didn't do your survey thoroughly. The fact is that in many areas, most sites are buried, with little or no indication on the surface. You don't have "X-ray vision," and you may not be able to afford the time or money to carry out a remote sensing project using ground-penetrating radar or some other technique. How do you locate sites not visible on the surface?

There is no foolproof way, so you can never be sure—a risk you just have to live with. You can increase your odds of finding such sites by doing some form of subsurface testing. In fact, some agencies require it as part of their survey standards for CHM projects. One of the first things you can do is to learn the basic geomorphology of the area in which you plan to work.

Geomorphology is the study of landforms and the processes that created them. Knowing these will allow you to predict where old buried surfaces might exist, such as alluvial fans along rivers, or landscapes people may have utilized or lived upon and on which sites might have formed. In such places, you probably should plan to do some kind of subsurface testing. Most states have organizations called geological surveys that sometimes can provide information on buried landforms that they generate from soil coring, prospecting, mining, construction, or other enterprises.

If there is a possibility of deeply buried sites that might be disturbed by a development project, you will need to find a way to do some deep testing. Usually this involves either coring or mechanical trenching. **Coring** can be done with a Giddings Rig or similar coring device. A Giddings Rig can be mounted on a pickup truck, tractor, or all-terrain vehicle and can be used in difficult terrain. The auger and soil tube can sample to a depth of about 10 m and take a core with a diameter of approximately 10 cm. As cores are removed, you examine them for buried **soils** that contain organic matter, indicating that they formed when the land was on the surface and plants grew in it. People might have lived on that surface. You also examine the cores for cultural materials, of course, such as stone tool debris, pottery, or modified bone.

Another approach is to use **mechanical trenching**, such as a backhoe. **Backhoes** use a clawlike device to dig a trench about 75 cm wide and can also trench about 10 m deep, depending on the size of the backhoe. A good backhoe operator can remove a few centimeters at a time, allowing you to see the surface as the trench goes deeper and to examine the backdirt for artifacts. As the trench gets deeper you can actually get into it and look at the profile it creates to see if there are buried soils, features, or artifacts. BEWARE! Getting into a trench that has not been properly shored up is very dangerous. If the walls collapse, you may be buried, which can cause very serious injury or death. Do not—under any circumstance—get into such a trench unless you are certain it has been made safe! Whatever the approach you use for deep testing, interpreting geomorphology and soils can be difficult; hiring a specialist is often the best practice.

Most of what you will do on a survey does not involve deep testing. When you can't see the surface very well due to vegetation, you need to do some shovel tests. **Shovel tests** are usually about a meter or so deep and roughly 50 cm in diameter, dug with your shovel. The idea is to uncover any cultural materials that are relatively near the surface and to get an idea of what the subsurface conditions are like. Some archaeologists believe that the idea is just to detect the presence or absence of cultural materials and thus don't worry too much about the size or precise depth of the test. Others wish to be much more precise and dig a 50 cm × 50 cm test with square corners and vertical profiles. Using either technique, you need to screen all materials coming from the shovel test, and you may wish to sketch the subsurface **stratigraphic profiles** (i.e., the layering you see in sidewalls of the excavation). How you approach it depends on the needs of the project, your own concerns with precision, and for whom you are working. Shovel tests can also be done with hand-operated bucket augers or small soil-coring tools such as Oakfield Soil Samplers. These provide a great deal of control but don't allow much visibility of subsurface conditions and certainly don't allow you to detect features, which shovel tests can sometimes reveal. Some archaeologists use mechanical augers. These are efficient but can reach speeds that tend to throw the soil some distance from the hole. Use them only if you can control the speed enough to allow you to examine the earth that comes from the test.

Some agencies require that shovel tests be taken at regular intervals across the survey area. This can be done by stretching out a tape and putting the tests at selected intervals. Most archaeologists map and number all shovel tests so that they can later understand what the tests are telling them about subsurface conditions and artifact densities. Some take detailed notes on each shovel test, which is highly recommended but takes additional time. The general rule is that all shovel tests are backfilled upon completion; open holes may injure people or animals that walk across the survey area.

Combining surface survey and subsurface testing to adopt a four-step approach to archaeological survey might allow you to overcome the problem of missing sites. Although it will not be foolproof, it will give you the best chance of finding a range of sites.

- *Step 1:* Familiarize yourself with all maps, aerial photographs, or any other sources of information that will give you an idea of the landscape and what you might find. From those sources, consider possible approaches to surveying the area.
- *Step 2:* Perform an initial reconnaissance survey of the study area to see whether there are any obvious site types or areas of disturbance and to get a feel for where within the study area it might be most productive to survey more intensively. During this phase you would record any obvious site types you come across (e.g., habitations, procurement areas, rockshelters, or quarries).
- *Step 3:* Using these findings, choose a sample of the area for intensive survey, in which you will record all visible sites, particularly those types that were difficult to see during the reconnaissance survey (such as stone artifact scatters).
- *Step 4:* Using these findings, choose a subsample of the study area where buried artifacts or sites might occur. In this phase you would undertake some form of subsurface testing to see whether soil or vegetation is currently covering sites.

RECORDING INFORMATION IN THE FIELD

Of course there is more to fieldwork than just looking for and finding sites. The archaeologist's job is also to record a wide variety of complementary information that is essential for

Larry Zimmerman's Faith in Archaeological "Intuition"

A few years ago, I went to the Yankton Sioux Reservation with two historian colleagues who had been examining records and looking for evidence of Euro-American–Yankton Sioux contact sites. In an earlier conversation, I had told them that archaeologists had pretty good intuition about where sites are located. Just before we drove down into the Missouri River valley, they challenged me. One of them said: "There's a village site as we come down into the valley not too far from where Choteau Creek goes into the Missouri. Tell us exactly where it is!" As we came over the hill, I glanced out the car window, noticed a little terrace remnant, pointed, and said, "Right on that little rise on the field about 50 feet from the creek." I was right—much to their chagrin—and they wondered how I knew. The secret is that when you've worked in an area for a long time, a predictive model for site locations is more or less in your head. In truth, it's just experience, not intuition, but it's always fun to flummox a historian who thinks historical documents are the best way to find sites.

understanding the context in which the research was undertaken, the physical and geographical context of any sites that were found, and the limitations of the research. This might enable the archaeologist, for instance, to make sense of why sites might be located in certain places and not others, or why no sites were found at all despite the best surveying strategy. Making all facets of the fieldwork process transparent is the only way in which archaeologists can ensure that their results will be able to be compared to those of other projects and therefore will contribute to the pool of current knowledge (see "Archaeologists and Their Profession" in chapter 1). There are a number of complementary strands of contextual information that you should record in your field journal or on specialized recording forms that you create. Record:

- Background information on the conduct of the fieldwork, the strategies that you adopted, the day-to-day operation of the project, and any problems that arose.
- Information on the survey transects, which indicates how well covered the survey area was.
- Information on the landforms, vegetation, soil, and geological formations encountered in the study area.
- Information on the water sources encountered in the study area.
- Information on the general ground-surface visibility of the survey area.

Excavation requires a different set of recording forms and is dealt with in detail in chapter 5. Some examples of survey forms to use for recording landforms, vegetation, water sources, and visibility have been included in appendix A.

KEEPING A FIELD JOURNAL

One of the most important aspects of any archaeological fieldwork is keeping a field journal (figure 3.3). This is essentially a diary in which you record the day-to-day details of your

Denis Gojak's Tip for All-Weather Site Recording

Surveyors' and miners' supply firms sell waterproof paper. This weighs in at about 80 gsm and can be used in a photocopier to provide recording forms that let you work in the least hospitable conditions imaginable! Team it up with a Fisher Space Pen, which writes upside down and on greasy surfaces and only costs a few bucks for a refill, and you will have no excuses left for not recording in any weather.

FIGURE 3.3: A page from archaeologist Robert Stone's field journal. A good field journal will contain enough information for you to make some basic interpretations of what you are seeing, which can be expanded upon later when you come to write up your report.

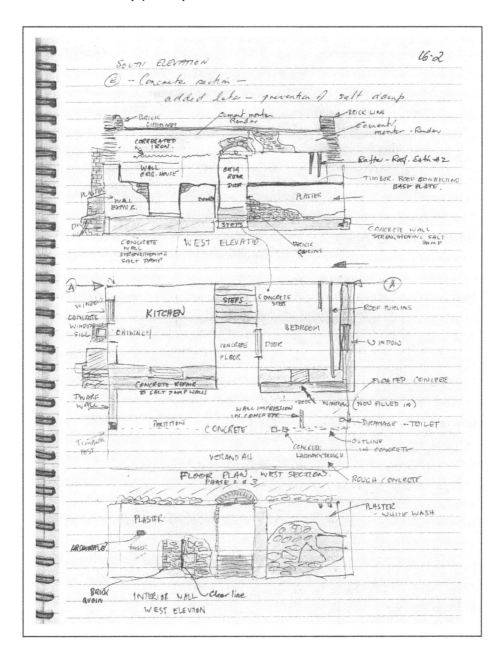

fieldwork, from the sites you record or the features you excavate, right down to the weather and light conditions (which, believe it or not, can affect your ability to locate sites or identify artifacts, particularly stone artifacts), the names of the people who participate each day, and any problems you encounter. It is also the place where you can record any impressions or interpretations of sites and features as they occur to you. This will be particularly important if you are one of many fieldworkers on a large project and your results are to be analyzed or written up by someone else, but it will also help to jog your memory later when you write your report. Your field journal will form an invaluable record of your fieldwork, and because you cannot predict what questions may interest future researchers, one day it may even provide new and unforeseen "data." A journal is a formal record of your fieldwork, and another archaeologist should be able to reconstruct your field program and understand the reasoning behind your decisions just by reading your notes. Remember, the more information you record in your field journal, the easier it will be for you or someone else to write up your results in the end. Don't trust your memory—write everything down.

RECORDING TRANSECTS

So that someone else reading or assessing your report can reconstruct your survey strategy, you need to be clear about the details of your survey transects. You will need to outline:

• Where your transects were located (this is best done by plotting your transects onto a map so that the area you have covered, and by extension the area that you ignored, is immediately apparent to the reader).

Important Things to Note in Your Field Journal

- The date, weather, light conditions, and personnel
- A summary of activities for the day, including details of the methods you used
- Progress made on the project during the course of the day
- Any problems you encountered and the solutions you adopted
- Any new research questions generated during the course of fieldwork, or interesting ideas to follow up
- Any interpretations of sites or features that occur to you during the course of fieldwork
- The reasoning behind any changes made to your methods or behind any decisions that affected the course of fieldwork and its possible outcomes
- Your own attitudes or moods, which might have had an impact on fieldwork

Nicky Horsfall's Tip for Keeping Good Field Notes

Take a portable [voice]-recorder with you. I find it very difficult to write good notes while doing field surveys. Either I can't read my own writing, I've written the same thing several times, or I've been too lazy to write down things that in retrospect I realize are key matters (rain doesn't help). So I started taking a [voice] recorder and just chatted away at that. Each evening I would replay the tape, with the hindsight of knowing all the events of the day, and just write down what was needed, expanding earlier comments if necessary in the light of later discoveries. I'm sure many fieldworkers do this. Problems arise on windy days (microphone noise) and you can feel a right fool talking to yourself, but it worked for me.

- How many transects you walked.
- How long each transect was.
- How wide each transect was (i.e., how many people were involved, and roughly how far apart each person walked).
- The vegetation and soil conditions that you noticed within each transect. This last set of information will be crucial for determining the effectiveness of your survey strategy (i.e., how likely it is that you could have missed or not been able to locate sites) (see "Determining Effective Survey Coverage: What Reveals, What Conceals").

RECORDING LANDFORMS, VEGETATION, AND SLOPE

Landforms are the topographic units of the landscape, such as creeklines, hill slopes, ridgelines, plains, or river valleys. Be careful to note the various landforms across which your survey transects pass, because different landforms will be associated with different erosional or depositional processes and different types of vegetation, ground cover, and water sources, not to mention different uses in the past. For this reason, in theory you should assess the length of your transects within each landform unit (i.e., when you enter a new landform unit, you should end one transect and begin another) and then assess the percentages of ground-surface exposure and ground-surface visibility that occur within each, although this may not always be possible (see "Determining Effective Survey Coverage: What Reveals, What Conceals").

Archaeologists commonly assess **vegetation** in terms of two factors: as a guide to the range of plant resources that would have been available to Indigenous peoples in the past; and for what it implies about current and past land use, which has the potential both to indicate the possible existence of historical archaeological sites and to affect survey conditions such as ground-surface visibility, access, and disturbance. Both Indigenous peoples and early postcontact settlers used plant resources for food and medicine, as well as to manufacture objects such as nets, baskets, and canoes. When recording vegetation, you should take note of:

- The vegetational structure (how tall the tallest trees are, what constitutes the understory, and the ground cover)
- The dominant species
- Other prominent species you can see, including native and nonnative species, because the presence or absence of nonnative species may be an indication of how intensively the land has been modified by Euro-Americans
- The approximate size of the largest trees, which is principally a guide to how old and well established they might be

Because the distribution of different vegetation types depends on other environmental factors, such as soil type, aspect, microclimate, and the availability of water and nutrients, you also will need to record these complementary sets of information (see "Recording Water Sources" and "Recording Soils and Geological Formations").

Archaeologists record **slope**, the degree of upward or downward slant of the ground, as a guide to the **integrity**, or the degree of intactness of a site. Any artifact that is still in the same position as when it was discarded is called *in situ*. Archaeologists look specifically for *in situ* artifacts, because these have the most potential for revealing unambiguous information about human behavior in the past. This is why assessing the integrity of a site is so important. If a site is largely undisturbed (if its integrity is good), then the artifacts within it are likely to be *in situ* (in the same positions as when they were last used). If a site has been damaged or disturbed in any way (if its integrity is poor), however, then there is less likelihood of the same high level of reliable information being retrievable.

In terms of recording slope, artifacts on a steep slope are more likely to have been disturbed as a result of gravity than are artifacts on a flat area. This can be a useful guide when assessing the boundaries of the site. Take the example of a stone artifact scatter extending several hundred meters with, say, 30 artifacts distributed randomly along it. If the site is located on flat ground, or on only a slight slope, you might conclude that the artifacts are part of one long, continuous site. If the site has a steep slope, however, it might be reasonable to conclude that the artifacts could be the result of a number of events, and that they should therefore be recorded as individual sites. In making such interpretations, slope should be used only in conjunction with other evidence, and in this scenario, it would be important to assess whether the artifacts occurred in discrete clusters or if they had a relatively continuous distribution. Lots of conditions may affect artifacts on a slope. Among the most important is the amount of rainfall and its intensity, which can cause a great deal of **slope wash**. Heavy or intense rain can easily move smaller artifacts downslope, with the rate of movement affected by ground cover and the frequency of the rainfall. Pay attention to and record evidence of erosion for any site on a slope.

Slope is recorded in degrees, either using a **clinometer** or estimated according to eye (figure 3.4). Using a clinometer is similar to taking a bearing with a compass. You sight through the clinometer along the angle of the slope, and depending on whether you are sighting uphill or downhill, you can read the degrees of elevation or depression. Sighting along flat ground (a horizontal plane), for example, will give you a reading in the 0–2° range. Tilting your head (and thus the clinometer) above the horizontal plane will give you a reading in degrees of elevation. The higher the number, the greater the slope. A midslope is in the 5–10° range, and steep areas will have a value of greater than 10°. Conversely, if you are standing at the top of the slope looking down, then tilting your head and the clinometer below the horizontal plane will give you a reading in degrees of depression.

If you are searching for archaeological sites, the most fruitful areas will be those with a slope of 10° or less. You are unlikely to find sites on slopes greater than 10°, mainly because people in the past will have preferred level or gently sloping ground for pathways and campsites, or because gravity may have caused the material to move to lower ground.

FIGURE 3.4: A guide to estimating slope by eye. If you are going to estimate slope, you must bear in mind that the eye tends to exaggerate slope.

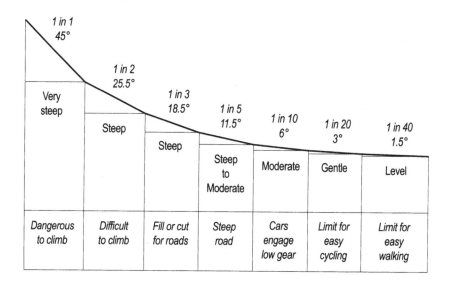

RECORDING WATER SOURCES

One of the major environmental factors affecting human behavior is water. People need to drink often and usually will not range far from reliable water sources. In those circumstances where they do, this is in itself an indication of a particular behavior (such as obtaining rare or prized resources). This is less true for historic sites than for Indigenous sites, but still holds as a general rule. The main types of water sources are:

- Permanent water, such as rivers
- Semipermanent water sources, such as large streams, some swamps, and ponds
- Ephemeral water sources, such as small streams or creeks
- Underground (artesian) water sources

Proximity to water influences not only the number of sites likely to be found but also the artifact density at those sites. Though sites can be located quite a distance from water sources, most are located in reasonably close proximity. In fact, the vast majority of Indigenous archaeological sites are likely to occur within 500 m of a water source, and many archaeological site forms ask you to record the distance of the site from a water source and the type of source. In general, sites located a long way from water will tend to be smaller and contain relatively few artifacts because they were probably short-term usage areas to which water would need to be carried. Sites that are located immediately near a water source are often situated on ground that is reasonably elevated above that source rather than on the flats or floodplains immediately adjoining it, because these are likely to have been subject to periodic flooding. Water sources also provide potential access to specific site types that will not exist anywhere else, such as rock walls and crevices used for rock art on many of the lakes on the Canadian Shield (Molyneaux 1981).

When assessing the relationships between sites and water sources it is important to remember that most continents have undergone massive environmental changes and that **Pleistocene** sites (i.e., sites that are older than 10,000 years) would have been located in relation to Pleistocene water sources, such as glacial lakes, which may not necessarily still exist today. For example, the beach ridgelines along Glacial Lake Aggasiz in contemporary Manitoba, Ontario, Saskatchewan, Minnesota, and North Dakota often contain evidence of early habitation, but today water may be nowhere near. Knowing how to recognize the ancient landforms associated with water may be as important as noting present-day water sources.

When conducting a survey for Indigenous sites, you must record the location of all water sources in proximity. As part of all site recordings make sure that you note:

- The distance to the nearest available water source (which may be an ephemeral creek)
- Any evidence of ancient water sources
- The distance to the nearest *reliable* water source, modern or ancient
- The type of source in all cases

RECORDING SOILS AND GEOLOGICAL FORMATIONS

The geological makeup of a region will affect the patterning of archaeological evidence in two ways (see "Geological Maps" in chapter 2). The availability of particular types and quantities of clay and stone resources will have affected Indigenous people's access to the raw materials needed to make ceramics (pottery) and stone artifacts, and local soil types and conditions may have influenced the availability of particular plants and animals in the past, as well as the ultimate preservation of archaeological sites in the present.

Most **clays** used by Indigenous peoples to make pottery are common gray, tan, or red clays and usually are sedimentary in origin, making them visible in beds that may be exposed along streams. The red color normally comes from iron oxide, but colors vary due to the mineral composition of the clay and may be gray, greenish, or brown. Clays are very plastic and "sticky," allowing them to be formed into shapes. When fired at relatively low heat, they become tight and hard due to the iron and other mineral impurities. Clay beds utilized by Indigenous people often are difficult to see or interpret, because many are along ever-changing stream banks and are relatively common in many areas. Postcontact, people also used red clays for making earthenware. These areas tend to be more visible because clays were often dug out in large quantities to make brick and tiles. Record the locations of all possible clay sources so that later, if you find pottery, you can try to trace it back to a particular clay bed.

Knowing the location of rock outcrops suitable for making stone artifacts is invaluable to the field archaeologist, as it is likely that Indigenous quarry sites, and the production of stone artifacts associated with them, will occur in the immediate vicinity. As a general rule Indigenous people tended to make stone artifacts from very fine-grained types of stone, as these produced the sharpest edge. **Chert** and many other forms of **siliceous** (high in silica content) stone are common materials for stone artifacts throughout the world, although not all stone artifacts were intended for cutting. Sandstone was a common material for making grindstones, and granite, a hard igneous rock, was a common material for pecking and grinding stone axes and adzes. When recording sites in the field, you always should record the location and nature of any available stone artifact raw material sources in the area.

Sometimes on a survey you will encounter large areas of natural rock outcrop, which may well be the kind of stone that Indigenous people favored for stone artifacts, but which may not actually have been used for this purpose. In some cases this background material may be sufficiently similar to real artifacts to be confusing. Silcrete, for example, can be fractured by the heat of the sun or by fire to resemble artifacts that have been heated in a campfire. While the spalling on the surface of the stone may be identical to that on deliberately heat-fractured stone, it is a natural product. This also can happen when cherty materials in limestone are crushed along with the limestone for gravel on roads. The crushing can mimic manufactured stone artifacts, and if a piece happens to be thrown from a road into a field by a vehicle tire, you might be deceived into believing it to be an artifact. Such confusing material often is referred to as **background "noise"** and is one of the many things that can interfere with your ability to identify artifacts correctly.

Soil type is important to archaeological fieldwork in two ways. First, the ability of a particular type of soil to support plant and animal resources that may have been used by Indigenous peoples or non-Indigenous settlers is crucial to the potential for finding archaeological sites. Second, the local soil conditions, in particular whether soils are **aggrading**

Recognizing Stone Artifacts in the Field

The trick to recognizing stone artifacts in the field is "getting your eye in," or training yourself to recognize things that are out of place. Don't just look for complete artifacts, but for evidence of stone tool manufacture. These may be flakes, both large and small; partially finished artifacts; and "shatter"—materials knocked off larger pieces to create rough forms for finer work. Because stone for tools usually is chosen for its particularly fine grain, most stone artifact raw materials are visually distinctive and stand out from the local soil and other natural stones around them. When you are surveying, keep a lookout for anything that is of an unusual color compared to the background material, or anything that is particularly smooth or **cryptocrystalline** (i.e., the grain of the stone is too fine to see with the naked eye). For example, many cherts turn a pink-to-red color when they are heated as part of stone tool making. If you find something that is suspiciously artifact-like, but it is not something you can be completely sure about, examine the surrounding areas very carefully. Always pay particular attention to areas close to water.

If you think you have found a stone artifact, look carefully for any of the telltale signs that mean it is a deliberate, humanly made product, rather than an accidentally or naturally fractured piece of stone (see "How to Identify a Stone Artifact" in chapter 7).

(i.e., accumulating, such as when a river valley silts up) or **eroding** (i.e., being removed), have a great bearing on archaeological visibility. For example, small artifacts may be covered by redeposited soils in an aggrading environment but exposed in an eroding environment. Another problem can occur in areas with light soils than can be easily windblown. Light soils, for example, can blow away, leaving only heavier objects such as stone tools. This **deflation** makes objects stand out but can also collapse objects from several thousand years into the space of a few centimeters. Similarly, windblown soils easily can bury sites.

Unfortunately, geological maps usually cannot provide this crucial information, although topographic maps will give some general guides, such as whether areas are likely to be flat (and therefore possibly aggrading) or steep (and possibly eroding). Study available geomorphological information from your survey area, which may give you clues. Don't be deceived: erosion and deposition by water or wind can happen very quickly, with many feet of soil removed or deposited in just a few years. The only way to record this information accurately is to take constant note of the conditions you can see around you during the survey, paying particular attention to the size, frequency, and cause of eroded areas (see "Determining Effective Survey Coverage: What Reveals, What Conceals").

RECORDING DISTURBANCE

Many different factors can disturb an archaeological site over time, from accidental or deliberate human activity (plowing, construction, demolition, removal, scavenging) to the activities of animals (grazing, trampling, burrowing, digging), insects (nesting, burrowing, eating), and plants (tree roots, vegetation overgrowth). Even the elements can disturb a site's integrity through erosion, deposition, scouring, or natural collapse. In reality, no site is likely to remain totally unaffected by some type of disturbance. The collective name archaeologists give to these activities is **taphonomic processes**; any source of such a process is a **taphonomic agent**. An assessment of the range of taphonomic processes that might have affected a site through time is principally your assessment of the integrity of a site, not only in terms of how disturbed you think it may be but also in terms of what might have caused, or be causing, this disturbance. It is for this reason that you need to record any potential sources of damage to a site and assess whether you think the site is in excellent, good, fair, or poor condition.

A good understanding of taphonomic processes and their effects also will be essential for interpreting the results from any surface survey or excavation, because one of the principal aims of the analysis will be to try to isolate which artifactual patterns are a result of human behavior and which are simply reflecting the results of various taphonomic agents.

DETERMINING EFFECTIVE SURVEY COVERAGE: WHAT REVEALS, WHAT CONCEALS

Effective survey coverage concerns not just how much of the survey area you have physically covered but also how favorable the conditions were for you to locate artifacts and sites (figure 3.5). Some sites are highly visible (such as buildings or rockshelters), while others (such as isolated artifacts) can be more difficult to locate and may even go unrecorded if vegetation or soil obscures them. As a result, two closely related factors can skew the results of any archaeological survey:

- Ground-surface visibility (i.e., how much of the surface is visible to you and what other factors—such as vegetation, introduced gravel, or leaf litter—might limit the detection of artifacts across this surface)
- Ground-surface exposure (i.e., what are the prevailing sedimentation conditions? Is the ground surface aggrading, eroding, or stable, and what kind of exposures are apparent as a result?)

FIGURE 3.5: The relationship between visibility, surface conditions, and the likelihood of finding archaeological sites

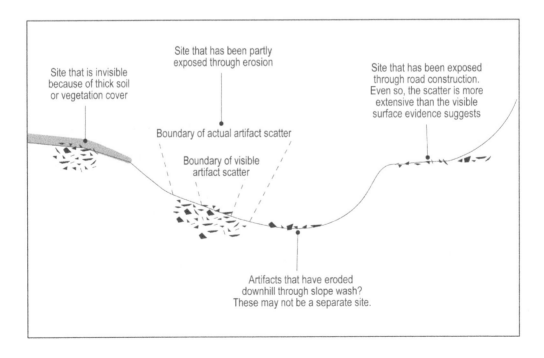

If you are surveying in an actively eroding area such as a creek gully, there is a greater likelihood that artifacts will be exposed, but if you are walking through a relatively stable and heavily grassed field, there may well be artifacts present that you cannot see. This is why you need to make careful note of the changing vegetation conditions and degree of ground cover across the survey area, as well as the type and size of any exposed areas that you encounter. Information about what has caused or contributed to the disturbance will also allow you to estimate how well preserved the site is or how seriously it has been affected.

To do this you need to take note of the approximate percentage of the survey area that is visible as bare ground and the approximate percentage that is exposed through erosion (table 3.1). This does not mean that you should focus your survey only on exposed areas and ignore anything with less visibility. Provided the artifacts are conspicuous enough, finding sites in areas with nearly 0% visibility is perfectly possible. These measures are usually represented as a percentage—either of the total survey area if it is small or within each transect or landform unit if the survey area is large. In general it is accepted that the outcomes of any archaeological surface survey can be representative only of the *visible*, rather than the *existing*, archaeological record.

TABLE 3.1: Recording visibility and exposure: two critical factors in being able to locate archaeological sites

Recording what reveals (exposure areas)	*Recording what conceals (visibility)*
Note the types of exposures that you can see (e.g., gully erosion, vehicle tracks, animal pads, areas of patchy grass cover)	Note the type of ground cover that is evident (grass, shrubs, leaf litter, gravel)
Note the causes contributing to this disturbance (e.g., recent rains, grazing animals, uprooted trees, anthills)	Note the approximate percentage of ground cover*
Note the approximate percentage of the ground surface that is exposed*	Note the presence of any distracting effects, such as gravel or naturally heat-fractured stones, which may make the identification of artifacts more difficult
Note the approximate dimensions of the exposed areas	Note any other factors that may prevent you from seeing artifacts (such as dumped soil or gravel, soil slumping)
You should also note the sedimentation conditions across the study area— which parts are actively eroding? Which aggrading? Which are stable?	

*You could assess this for the survey area as a whole, but it is more meaningful if you estimate it for each transect that you walk, or for each landform unit through which your transect passes.

WHAT TO DO WHEN YOU FIND A SITE

Recording a site is a selective process. On some fieldwork projects you will have ample opportunity to record every last detail, while on others, you will have limited time and a lot of work to get through. Regardless of which situation you find yourself in, there are minimum requirements for recording any Indigenous or historical site. Recording *at least* these aspects will ensure that, even if no further research is ever done on that site, or, in a worst-case scenario, if it is destroyed before further research can be undertaken, at least there will be a sufficient record of it.

Basic locational information:

- A locational reference for the site, either taken using a GPS or plotted by hand onto a topographic map (of at least 1:100,000 scale, but 1:24,000 is best) (see "Using Locational Reference Systems" in chapter 2).
- A description of how to get to the site. Imagine someone else trying to relocate the site from your instructions—how would you tell them to find it again?
- A sketch/mud map of how to get to the site that can complement your written description. Include major landmarks or features and approximate distances along the route.

Basic descriptive information:

- A brief description of the nature of the site, including its type, size, and environmental context.
- A brief list of the major features of the site and its contents, including an assessment of whether further research at the site is warranted.
- A brief assessment of the condition of the site and its contents (Is it well preserved? Has it been damaged in any way? How much has been damaged? Is it in danger of being damaged in the future?).
- A sketch plan of the site. This does not have to be measured accurately, but on the plan you should include an arrow indicating the direction of north and some idea of the scale (otherwise the plan will be meaningless) (see "Making Sketch Maps" in chapter 2).
- Photographs of the site and its contents illustrating significant features (see chapter 9, "Photography and Illustration").

For management purposes (see Pearson and Sullivan 1999, 116) you also should try to make note of:

- The name of the landowner.
- The landowner's attitudes toward the site.

- The ownership status of the land (if you know it). Is it individually owned? State or federally owned? Rented?

Once you have found a site, there are various obligations to notify the relevant heritage authority within a certain time frame (see "Working with the Legislation" in chapter 1). You may also have to fill out a recording form for your site and submit this to the same authority. Check with the relevant agency to find this out. In the United States, this is usually the State Historic Preservation Office or the state archaeologist.

In addition to this basic information you also may need to collect specific information relating to your research questions. A formalized recording form is the most efficient way of gathering your information consistently, particularly if you are recording the same variables at many different sites. A good form can serve as a checklist, standardize terms and parameters, and greatly speed the recording process. Most states have particular forms. They contain similar information but may have items in slightly different order or place differing emphases on them. Be certain to pay attention to particular instructions so that you don't have to go back to the field to get the pertinent information! Some examples of recording forms are included in appendix A. Other examples can be found in Feder 1997 and Flood, Johnson, and Sullivan 1989.

DEFINING A SITE BOUNDARY

Obviously some sites, such as a rockshelter or a stone alignment, will have clearly defined physical boundaries, while others will be much harder to determine unless the visibility is excellent. One definition of an open "site," in fact, is that it is only a unit of current human observation and not necessarily a unit of past human behavior. This means that a "site" may be only a small "window" in the landscape where artifacts are exposed on the ground surface—as a result of erosion, for instance—and not necessarily an accurate reflection of the full extent of the site (see "Defining the Boundaries of an Open Artifact Scatter" in chapter 7).

If you find a site just because of better ground visibility in a particular place, the site actually may be more extensive than you can see (i.e., there may be more artifacts in the soil beneath those you can see or hidden by the ground cover around those you can see). Open sites in particular often tend to be larger in size than what is visible on the surface. This often can make it difficult to decide on the site's boundary: Is it only the limit of visible artifacts? Is it the limit of the eroded area (if this is what has allowed you to see the artifacts in the first place)? If you have defined a site as a concentration of artifacts that is noticeably greater than the background scatter, do you draw the boundary at the limit of the concentration? You may even decide to use an arbitrary boundary, such as a fenceline or vehicle track to define a site. How you define a site's boundary is really up to you; just make sure that you note clearly what criteria you used to reach this decision and record them in your field journal and report.

The information from your survey always must be interpreted with care. Remember, the absence of artifacts does not necessarily mean the absence of archaeology on that spot (only that you cannot see it), just as the presence of artifacts does not necessarily imply that the human activity from which they arose occurred precisely on that spot (they may have been moved there as a result of erosion, downslope movement, or plowing, for example). You need to record as much information about the context of sites or artifacts as possible when you are in the field and take this into account when you draw your conclusions.

WHAT NOT TO DO AT A SITE

If you find a site, there are some simple rules to follow. Most of the advice about what not to do at a site is not only good ethical practice but also common sense.

- Don't interfere with the site in any way. Signing your name, chalking in petroglyphs, or digging or collecting artifacts without permission are not only irresponsible but also may be illegal.
- Don't collect "souvenirs," even to verify to state authorities that you have found a site. There might be some exceptional circumstances in which you should collect material from a site—such as when it is at risk of imminent destruction—but this would be highly unusual.
- Don't leave rubbish behind—take it with you when you go.
- Don't make details of the site public without obtaining the proper permissions first. Indigenous people in particular may wish to protect sites by keeping their details secret. Most state and federal authorities normally do not publicize information about site locations to protect them from looters.

A NOTE ON SITE NUMBERING AND NAMING SYSTEMS

When you locate a site or record a series of sites, you will have to label these sites with some temporary title to be able to refer to them in a meaningful way. Sites eventually receive an official **site number**, but that number usually is given when you prepare your survey report. You should devise a system to give the site a temporary designation separating it from all other sites you locate.

In the United States, sites are numbered according to a **trinomial system** (sometimes also called the Smithsonian system), as in 13ML121. The first number is the number of the state in its alphabetic sequence. Alaska and Hawaii come at the end because they became states after the system had been in use for many years. The second part of the trinomial is two letters, a designation for the county within the state, and the third is a number indicating the sequence in which the site was recorded in the county. Thus 13ML121 is in Iowa, in Mills County, and is the 121st site recorded in the county. However, while you are in the field, you'll need something else to refer to the site because most state officials wish to control the numbering of sites carefully. Their concern is understandable because there might be several surveys going on in one county at the same time. In some cases, particular labs or universities were given blocks of site numbers and could assign them as they wished. This caused problems because it left gaps between the blocks and caused a great deal of confusion about the number of recorded sites in some counties.

The "long narrow site in the bend of the river closest to the homestead" may be a good physical description, but it will be an unwieldy mouthful if you need to refer to it constantly in your field notes. Likewise, "Site 1" may seem a logical description at the time but does little to tie the site into your particular research program or its geographic area. Many archaeologists label sites with a meaningful alphabetical prefix (such as the first letter of the name of the property on which it is found or the CHM project that generated the survey) and then with a sequential number for each site found. Designations such as "LzBe1," although unpronounceable, ensure that each site name is unique to that research program. Sometimes sites are named after landowners, particular individuals associated with projects, events, or something equally memorable. This name often is recognized by archaeologists even after the official number is recorded, but the official number always should be used in written reports. Although how you code your sites is entirely up to you, try to make your site designations meaningful, and always think in the long term, particularly if your data are going to end up in a computer database.

David Gradwohl has become well known in the Great Plains and Midwest for his playful approach at naming archaeological sites. Working primarily in Iowa, the names he chose often reflected the agricultural emphasis of the state in combination with a landowner's name. Cribb's Crib site and Milo's Silo site are two of the more memorable names. Inventing clever and unique names like these probably are better than naming sites after individuals because many family names are relatively common. For example, there are at least three Zimmerman sites in the Midwestern U.S. alone!

REFERENCES AND FURTHER READING

Byrne, D., ed. 1997. *Standards manual for archaeological practice in Aboriginal heritage management.* Sydney: NSW NPWS.

Byrne, D., H. Brayshaw, and T. Ireland. 2001. *Social significance: A discussion paper.* Sydney: NSW NPWS.

Davies, M., and K. Buckley. 1987. Archaeological procedures manual. Port Arthur Conservation and Development Project. Occasional Paper No. 13, Department of Lands, Parks and Wildlife, Hobart.

Drewett, P. 1999. *Field archaeology: An introduction.* London: UCL Press.

Feder, K. L. 1997. Site survey. In *Field methods in archaeology*, ed. T. R. Hester, H. J. Shafer, and K. L. Feder, 41–68. Mountain View, CA: Mayfield.

Flood, J., I. Johnson, and S. Sullivan, eds. 1989. *Sites and bytes: Recording Aboriginal places in Australia.* Canberra: Australian Government Publishing Service.

Hester, T. R., H. J. Shafer, and K. L. Feder. 1997. *Field methods in archaeology.* 7th ed. Mountain View, CA: Mayfield.

Molyneaux, B. 1981. Landscape images: Rock paintings in the Canadian Shield. *Ottawa Archaeologist* 10(7): 2–8.

Pearson, M., and S. Sullivan. 1999. *Looking after heritage places: The basics of heritage planning for managers, landowners and administrators.* Melbourne: Melbourne University Press.

Redman, C. L. 1975. Productive sampling strategies for archaeological sites. In *Sampling in archaeology*, ed. J. W. Mueller, 147–154. Tucson: University of Arizona Press.

For a range of other useful information, see the website accompanying the text.

CHAPTER FOUR
SITE SURVEY AND MAPPING

> **What you will learn from this chapter:**
>
> The basic principles of surveying and mapping a site
> How to produce quick and accurate site plans
> How to keep your errors to a minimum
> How to set up and use an automatic ("dumpy") level
> How to record survey information in your field notebook and on recording forms

THE BASICS

Making maps is one of the most important tasks you will do as an archaeologist and one at which you should become comfortable and reasonably skilled. There are lots of types of maps and lots of ways to map a site. A site plan is the simplest and most effective way to record spatial information about a site. Even if there is only enough time to draw a sketch map, you still can use this to convey the basics of the extent, form, and main features of the site. A clear and accurate site plan is an essential part of any site recording (see "What to Do When You Find a Site" in chapter 3).

Doing survey work and making most kinds of maps involve the use of geometric principles, but don't let this frighten you. Most of it is really very straightforward for most of the work archaeologists need to do. Essentially you are working with distances and angles, whether you use simple triangulation or complex surveying instruments.

The Basic Surveying Toolkit

At least two 25 m, 30 m, or 50 m tape measures (larger sizes are best)
At least two 5 m, 8 m, or 10 m retractable tape measures (larger sizes are best)
Compass
Nylon builder's line/string
Plastic clothespins (for fixing a tape measure to a string baseline)
Tent pegs or wooden stakes (for fixing the ends of a baseline)
Mallet
Plumb bob
Ranging rod
Drawing equipment (see chapter 9, "Photography and Illustration")

Optional:
Leveling/surveying instrument (automatic level, EDM, theodolite, total station)
Tripod
Stadia rod or prism staff
Walkie-talkies

Making Your Map as Accurate as Possible

Although archaeology is a science, not much of what archaeologists do requires extreme accuracy, so when you survey a site and make a map of it, minor errors are not usually a big problem. How accurately you survey and map depends on the level of skill of the surveyor, the types of equipment available, time, and money. Do remember, however, that context in archaeology is extremely important. If you can't tell with reasonable certainty the relationships of objects to each other in vertical and horizontal space, your ability to interpret what you find will suffer. So why not strive to make your survey and your maps as accurate as conditions will allow?

The concept of relationships is crucial from the beginning. Obviously you can't just make a series of totally unconnected measurements at a site and then expect to be able to use them to draw up a coherent site plan. It is no use knowing that the barn is 5.8 m from the fence if you have no idea where the fence is in relation to anything else; or knowing that the fence and the barn are 5.8 m apart if you didn't measure how long the fence was or where, along its length, the barn was located precisely. Even if you made sure to measure the position and dimensions of every feature by moving systematically around the site ("the house is 12 m × 8 m, the fence is 3 m from the southeast corner of the house and is 25 m long, the barn is 5.8 m from the ninth fencepost from the northern end"), if you have made one mistake at any point in this sequence that puts a feature out of position, then every other subsequent feature will also be out of position. At the end of the exercise you will still not be able to create an accurate site plan, and all your time will have been wasted. *The most important element in an accurate survey is to ensure that the location of all features can be tied together in such a way that there are no "floating" measurements and the sources of error can be kept to a minimum.* This can be done only through the use of fixed reference points from which features are measured, and therefore to which the location of each feature can be tied securely. Usually you have one main reference point on a site, usually called a **site datum** or **datum point**. The datum may be a wooden stake that you hammer into the ground or some other fixed feature of the site. This datum often is related to an arbitrary line that you establish through your site for the purposes of survey. Such an arbitrary line is called a **baseline**, and if possible, one end of this baseline should be fixed to the datum point. Any measurement from a baseline to a feature is called an **offset**.

Your baseline may be a long tape measure (this is certainly simplest, because the distance along the baseline is easy to read off the tape) or a string-line of known length, which you have fixed to stakes in the ground. Where you place the baseline will depend on the size and shape of your site. Because it is an arbitrary line that you are using for convenience, it doesn't matter where in the site the line is located, as long as you can plot most or all of the features from it. If you are recording a stone arrangement, for example, you might choose to fix the baseline through the center of the arrangement so that you could conveniently plot all of the stones on either side of it. Similarly, if you are recording a historic collection of farm buildings, you may be able to use a fixed fenceline (provided you have measured it first) as your baseline.

If your site is particularly large or spread out, you may need to establish more than one baseline to be able to reach all features. In this case you could use the position of the first baseline to establish the position of the second and so on, but bear in mind that if you have made any errors in establishing the position of the second baseline, then any subsequent baselines will also be out. There is a real likelihood that your errors will be compounded.

To control this process of cumulative error, the most reliable means of surveying an area is to set up a series of baselines around the perimeter to form a **framework** that encases the site (figure 4.1). This uses all the same principles of measurement as a single baseline, repeated around each side of the framework until all the details have been plotted in.

When establishing a framework you need to keep a few basic rules in mind:

- Use as few lines as possible to keep your errors to a minimum (any form of quadrilateral is ideal).

FIGURE 4.1: A framework of baselines, the essential elements of any site plan

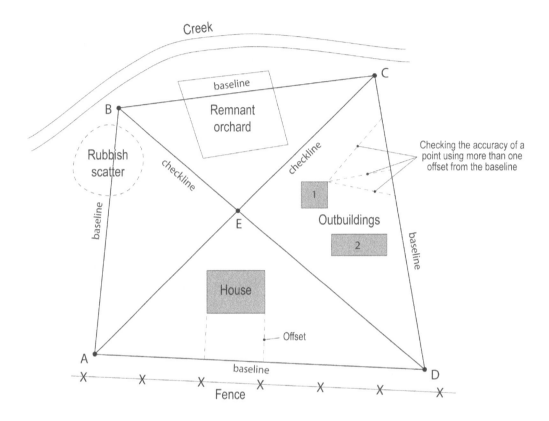

- Make sure that the framework is "rigid" (in other words, that your starting point is also your end point).
- Make sure that you check the accuracy of your framework before you begin detailed measurement, by measuring not only the length of the outside perimeter but also the diagonals between points. This is why surveyors commonly divide the area to be surveyed into triangles, then measure all of the sides (Hobbs 1983, 44–45). These diagonals are essential **checklines**, which will help to keep your framework rigid.
- Try to keep the angles of the triangles in your framework between 30° and 120°. If your angles are greater than 120° it is easy for errors to creep in.

By establishing a framework first, you give yourself a method for keeping a constant check on the accuracy of your plan without running the risk of getting bogged down in the details. A good framework will use the key elements of a site to establish the main spatial relationships between features. Once you have established this you easily will be able to check how accurately you have positioned the details in relation to these features, and in this way your errors should be kept to a minimum. This is what surveyors mean when they use the maxim *Always survey from the whole to the part.* This means establishing your baseline or framework first and only then measuring in the detail of particular features (see figure 4.1).

When establishing any baseline, either alone or in a framework, bear in mind several rules:

- All measurements along a baseline should begin from the same point (i.e., the same end of the baseline). This will be less problematic if you use a tape measure as a baseline, because all measurements will begin at 0.
- Always measure along the baseline first and only then to the feature.
- Always record your measurements in the same order.
- Do not move or disturb the baseline until all measurements from it are complete, including any last-minute checks you need for accuracy.

Keeping Your Errors to a Minimum

The biggest problem with all forms of survey is the potential for error to creep into even the most careful measurements. When you are making a series of measurements, it is very easy for one measurement to be slightly out, thus making the next slightly out and so on. If these errors are allowed to accumulate you could end up with serious problems. This is why the other basic premise of all surveying is to be constantly on the alert for potential errors and to keep these to a minimum wherever possible. This may be something as simple as making sure that all sides of your framework can be placed in areas that are free of excessive vegetation or other obstacles, making sure that everyone is familiar with the tape measures you will be using so that no mistakes will be made in calling out measurements, or making sure that all measurements are recorded consistently in a logbook. You will have to accept that some margin of error will be inevitable in all surveys (unless you are lucky enough to be using state-of-the-art electronic surveying equipment), but always aim to keep this within acceptable limits (see table 4.1). The only way to achieve this is to *make independent checks on your measurements as often as possible.* Remembering the tendency of surveyors to divide their survey areas into triangles, the simplest way to make an independent check on your framework is to not only measure the sides of your framework but also measure and plot the diagonal checklines between corner points (figure 4.1). Obviously this will not always be possible (particularly if there is vegetation in the way, or if

TABLE 4.1: Acceptable levels of accuracy for site plans

Scale of final plan	Acceptable error
1:5	2 mm
1:10	5 mm
1:25	10 mm
1:50	20 mm
1:100	50 mm
1:250	100 mm
1:500	200 mm
1:1,000	500 mm

you are plotting a site from a central baseline only) (see "Using the Baseline and Offset Technique"). In this case you can make independent checks on the position of key features by plotting them from more than one point along the baseline (figure 4.1). You should do this for all major features of your site anyway and for any features that are particularly important to your research goals and need to be plotted accurately.

TECHNIQUES FOR CONSTRUCTING A SITE PLAN

The simpler forms of site plan use basic orienteering skills that anyone can master; the more complex require particular items of equipment that may not always be available. The three simplest and least technical methods for constructing a site plan are:

- Triangulation
- Compass and pacing
- Baseline and offset

The advantage of these techniques is that they require little in the way of equipment and can be used in any situation. If you have to carry your equipment a long way to reach a site, there are obvious advantages in using simple techniques requiring basic equipment. There are disadvantages, too, in that these methods will not give the same accuracy as more sophisticated survey equipment, such as an automatic level or a total station/EDM.

The choice of which method to use will come down to time and resources. Probably the best way to deal with this dilemma is to decide how detailed your plan needs to be. If you are mapping a site that is going to be destroyed, you would want to record everything in minute detail, because this may well be the only recording that will ever be made of this site. In this case it would be best to use some form of electronic distance measurement device, such as a total station, because this will give you a highly accurate and detailed result. If, on the other hand, you just want to produce a plan showing the main physical features of a site as part of public record or for publication (bearing in mind that most plans are greatly reduced in size for publication and that, as the scale becomes smaller, the ability to depict finer units of measurement decreases), then it is probably more effective to use a simpler and less time-consuming technique (for more information, see "Drawing Horizontal Surfaces" in chapter 9). Whichever method you choose, make sure that you include an accurate description of it when writing up the methods in your report (for more information, see chapter 10, "Getting Your Results Out There: Writing, Publication, and Interpretation").

If at all possible, plot your results into a site plan while you are in the field (i.e., at the same time that you are taking measurements). This way you will be able to catch any mistakes as they arise and will be able to check on compass readings or particular measurements immediately. If you leave the site and then wait for a few days before you turn your measurements into a site plan, you run the risk of being unable to correct mistakes. Of course, this may not always be practical (particularly if you are recording a site by yourself), but try to draw up your plan as soon as possible while it is still fresh in your memory.

USING THE COMPASS AND PACING TECHNIQUE

This technique uses the length of your own stride to measure distance and a compass to plot direction. Its great advantage is that it enables one person to create a reasonably accurate plan of a small area relatively quickly. Before you can employ this technique in the field, however, you need to calculate the length of your stride, or your **pacing unit**. This is the average length of a single step and varies from person to person. It also varies for the same individual depending on whether you are walking uphill (when your pace will be shorter) or downhill (when your pace will be longer). It may even vary at the beginning and the end of each day according to how tired you are.

The compass and pacing technique is really only accurate for small areas, although the basic principles (i.e., taking a bearing with a compass to give direction and then pacing the distance to give a measurement in meters) also can be useful when navigating (to keep track of where and how far you have walked) or to give you the rough dimensions and spatial relationships of a site when drawing a sketch map. Your pacing unit will be useful any time you need to make quick approximate measurements.

How to Calculate Your Pacing Unit

You will need an area of relatively flat ground. Using a tape, measure out a length of 25 m, 50 m, or 100 m (you are actually going to calculate your pacing unit as an average of 100 m, but if you can't find that much room, pull out a smaller length and multiply it accordingly later), and walk this distance at least 10 times. Note the number of paces it takes you to walk this distance each time. Add these, and divide by the number of times you walked the distance to average the number (if you have used a smaller measured length of 25 m or 50 m, you will need to then multiply the average by 4 or 2 to arrive at a figure per 100 m). Divide 100 by this average to give you your pacing unit. For example, if you've walked a length of 100 m 20 times and the sum of your paces came to 2,500, then, divided by 20, this would give you an average of 125 paces per 100 m. One hundred divided by this average would equal a pacing unit of 0.80, or 80 cm. To use your pace as a unit of measurement, pace out the dimensions of whatever you are measuring and multiply by your pacing unit to arrive at a figure in meters. If your pacing unit was 0.80, for example, then a feature that you measured to be 6.5 paces in length would be in reality 5.2 m long.

Remember to maintain a comfortable walking pace as you pace out your measured length and whenever you use your pacing unit to measure features at a site. Try not to be overly conscious of your steps except for counting. If you exaggerate your steps you will never obtain an accurate or replicable measure of your pace. You should also perform this exercise on sloping ground (on around a 15–20% slope) to give you a unit for measuring up or down hills.

How to Plot an Area Using the Compass and Pacing Technique

- Work out a framework for your survey, such as the outer boundaries of the site, so that you can plot in all of the detailed features from this framework. Use as few lines as possible, but make sure that your framework is rigid—in other words that the starting and end point are the same. If you leave your framework open you will have no way to check the accuracy of your measurements. Each side of this framework is called a **traverse**.
- Beginning at the starting point (Point A), take a compass bearing (see "Taking Bearings" in chapter 2) to the second point (Point B) on the framework by aligning the compass either on a feature (if this is what you have used as a point) or on a ranging rod held at the point. In surveying terms such a bearing is often referred to as a **foresight**. Write down the bearing and count the number of paces it takes you to walk to that point. Make sure you walk in a straight line, noting the distance along the line of any features that cross it and the nature of these features. When you reach the second

point you need to take a back-bearing (in surveying terms, a **backsight**) to the starting point as an independent check. Remember that the difference between your foresight and your backsight should equal 180° (see "Using a Compass" in chapter 2), although an error of plus or minus 2° is perfectly acceptable. If the difference is greater or less than 180° you will have to check your bearings and possibly take them again. It is important that you do this correctly, otherwise your plan will not be accurate. If you are still having trouble, look around for any sources of magnetic interference that might be present, such as power lines or fences.

- Continue around the framework taking bearings to each new point, noting the distance and nature of features along each bearing and taking back-bearings (figure 4.2), until you arrive at your starting point (Point A again). This is called **closing** the traverse. Once you have completed your traverse you can take bearings and measurements to any additional features located inside or outside the framework from any of the points on the framework.

- Plot your plan onto graph paper. Using a scale rule, work out a suitable scale so that you can fit all of the features onto the paper (you may need to sketch in the dimensions and shape of your framework by hand to make sure that it fits on the page), aligning magnetic north to the vertical lines on the graph paper.

- Beginning at your starting point (Point A), use a protractor to plot your first compass bearing onto the graph paper (see "Taking Bearings" in chapter 2). Convert the number of paces to meters by multiplying the number of paces by your pacing unit, and measure this distance onto the page along the protractor bearing. Continue this process for all of the points around the framework. Because inaccuracies are inevitable in both the compass readings and the pacing measurements, it is unlikely that your traverse will close (i.e., that your starting and end points will plot on to the graph paper in the same location). Because of this, we will call the end point (which is really the same as the starting point) Point A^1. The distance between your original starting point (Point A) and end point (Point A^1) is called the **error of closure** (figure 4.3).

The best level of accuracy that can be hoped for by a compass and pacing survey is approximately 1:300, or an error of 1 m in every 300 m. The error of closure should not exceed 1:100 (Davies and Buckley 1987, 141). This means that, if the total length of your survey framework was 500 m, an error of closure of 5 m is the maximum acceptable error. Anything less than this is better of course, though it is unlikely that your error of closure would be less than 1.6 m.

- Before you can correct this error, much less start plotting details onto your survey plan, you need to make sure that the error of closure for your traverse is within the acceptable limit. Add up the total length of your traverse (i.e., add the distances for each leg

FIGURE 4.2: When recording the information from a compass and pacing survey, it is standard practice to start at the foot of the page and proceed upward, making sure that the figures for bearings and distances cannot be confused. A line is drawn across the page to signify the end of each leg, and details of features on either side of the route are entered to the right or left of the central column of measurements depending on their location.

Bearings and back bearings	Features visible to the left	Paces walked & features encountered	Features visible to the right
301° (BB)	Open paddock	800 back to point A	Open paddock
	Clump of trees extends	200 (clump of trees)	Shed
121° (B)	Grazing land	D (0 paces)	Grazing land
30° (BB)		600 to point D	
	Grazing land		House and grazing land
	Creek	350 (crossing creek again)	Creek
208° (B)		C (0 paces)	
152° (BB)		1000 to point C	
	Creek	400 (crossing creek)	Creek
330° (B)	Open paddock	B (0 paces)	Open paddock
252° (BB)		500 to point B	
	Open paddock	300 (following fenceline)	Large fig tree
70° (B)		A (0 paces)	

FIGURE 4.3: Plotting a compass and pacing survey

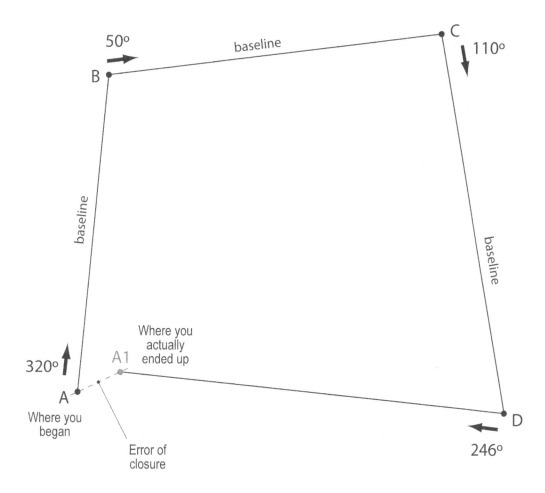

of your framework). Divide this number by your error of closure distance (i.e., the distance between Point A and Point A¹ as plotted on the graph paper). If you arrive at a figure between 100 and 300 you are within the acceptable limits.

- To correct for an error of closure, first draw a line on your plan between Point A and Point A¹ (remembering that they should actually be the same point) and measure the distance between the two. Using a set square (sometimes called a triangle), draw lines parallel to this line through each point on your framework (you will need these lines later to correct the positions for each point) (see figure 4.3).
- Now you need to construct a special linear scale to illustrate the error of closure between your starting point and your end point. To do this, draw a straight line that is

equal to the total length of your traverse. Obviously, because you are drawing this onto a sheet of graph paper you will have to use a suitable scale to fit this line on the paper. The scale will have to be much smaller than that used for plotting the framework and will really have to be smaller than 1:1,500 to work properly. A total traverse length of 300 m, for example, could be drawn at a scale of 1:1,000 (or 1 cm = 10 m) as a line that is 30 cm in length. The left-hand end of this line represents your starting point (Point A), the right-hand end your end point (Point A¹) (figure 4.4). Make sure you mark off the position of each point in your traverse along this line.

FIGURE 4.4: Correcting the error of closure

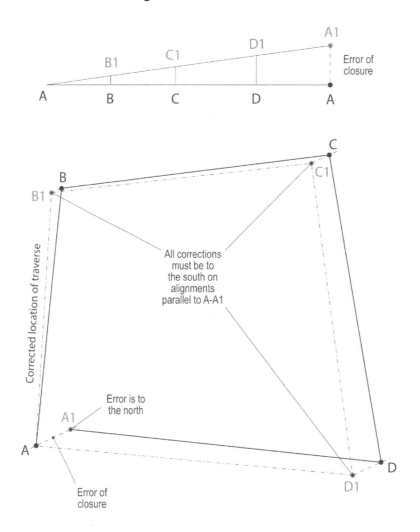

- On the right-hand side of this line, draw a perpendicular line equal to the length of your error of closure distance (remember to reduce it to the same scale you used to represent the total traverse length). In the example just given, for instance, say the error of closure distance was 5 m. To equal this distance at a scale of 1:1,000 you would draw a perpendicular line 5 mm long at the right-hand end of your scale.
- Join the top of this vertical line back to the starting point (so that you have a triangle), and working from the left-hand side, draw vertical lines marking off the position of each point in your traverse. The top of these lines will become points B^1, C^1, D^1, and so on. These distances represent the corrections necessary to adjust the error of closure at each of these points.
- You will notice that the length of the vertical lines increases as you move toward the right-hand end of the scale; this is because they indicate the cumulative error, which increases for each leg of your survey. The length of these lines also indicates the distance of each plotted framework point from its correct location; just use the length of each line to measure the correct location for each point on your plan. On the traverse map, draw lines through B, C, D, and so on that are parallel to the line you have already drawn through AA^1. Use the previously established corrections to determine the positions of B^1, C^1, D^1. Remember always to plot the corrected position for each point in the same relationship as that for your starting point and end point. In other words, if your end point plotted to the southwest of your starting point (meaning that the correct location is really to the northeast), also make sure that you plot the corrected position for every other point to the northeast. Join A to B^1, C^1, D^1, and then back again to A. Your traverse should now close (see figure 4.4). If not, you have serious problems and may have to start again.
- You can now plot in the details of your plan, remembering always to include the names of the people who made the map, the date, site, a scale, a north arrow, and a legend if you have used symbols (such as shading or cross-hatching) to depict detail. Because your compass readings will indicate magnetic north only, you should also use the degree of declination from a topographic map (see "Using a Compass" in chapter 2) to indicate true north.

USING THE BASELINE AND OFFSET TECHNIQUE

This technique uses the same principles as a compass and pacing survey (i.e., measuring the location of features from an established baseline) and requires little more in the way of equipment than a couple of long and short tape measures. Because it requires measuring to and from the baseline, however, it requires the labor of more than one person.

- First lay out a baseline. A long tape measure is best for this, as the distance along the baseline can easily be read off the tape as the survey progresses. Give careful consideration to where you lay out your baseline—it should be aligned in such a way that most (if not all) of the features can be measured from it without having to lay out another one. If you are plotting the ruins of a building, for instance, the baseline would be best laid out through the center and running down the long axis of the building, so that walls and other features on both sides can be measured from it. You can lay out the baseline on or above the ground (i.e., fixed to free-standing stakes for instance), but it must be kept straight and as horizontal as possible. Laying the baseline flat on the ground is simplest, because raised baselines tend to stretch and sag, although a perfectly horizontal baseline is rarely possible. Once again, the decision of precisely how much variation from the horizontal is permissible comes down to how accurate you need your survey plan to be—obviously every deviation from the horizontal introduces an element of error, so try to keep this to a minimum. If you are drawing a plan of a rockshelter, for example, the floor may be quite undulating and you may need to locate the baseline some way from the floor of the shelter to keep it horizontal.
- Remember, once the baseline is fixed, don't move it until all your measurements are complete.
- Take a compass reading along your baseline (it doesn't matter in which direction, but for consistency's sake from the 0 m point on the baseline is best) and note down the reading in your field notes. This will allow you to indicate the direction of magnetic north on the finished plan.
- You can now begin to measure offsets from the baseline to the various features of the site.

The most important thing to remember about a baseline/offset survey is that all features must be measured at right angles to the baseline. You must keep all offsets at 90° to the baseline to ensure that you are measuring the shortest distance between the baseline and the feature. If your angle varies above or below 90°, then the distance you are measuring will also increase or decrease, giving you an inaccurate measurement.

- Because the baseline is extending to either side of the person standing at the baseline, this person is the one most able to judge accurately when an offset is at the correct angle (figure 4.5). For anything over 3 m, you will have to use a different technique. There are three ways you can do this, all of which use basic principles of geometry to establish a right angle:

  1 Bisecting an arc
  2 3–4–5 triangle
  3 Triangulation

FIGURE 4.5: Over a short distance (anything less than 3 m) you can estimate a right angle for an offset reasonably accurately by eye, but *only* from the position of the baseline

It is much easier to draw a baseline and offset survey as you go along. In other words, have two people measuring (one always at the baseline and one always at the features) while a third person simultaneously plots the position of each feature onto graph paper and constructs the plan. Obviously the draftsperson will need to work out a suitable scale for the plan before any measuring begins and also will be the person responsible for literally "connecting the dots" or making the plan come together. As the draftsperson, you have the responsibility of keeping a sharp eye on how the plan is progressing—you are in the best position to notice if distances seem wrong or if features don't plot where they should. *Don't just blindly trust the measurements being given to you.* The measurers have no overall scheme in front of them to see the relationships between each point, but *you do*. Evaluate each measurement in the context of the plan as it is progressing on paper, and don't be afraid to ask for measurements to be repeated or for extra measurements to be taken. In this sense it is really the draftsperson who directs the survey, not the other way around.

If your site is large or very complex and can't be measured using a single baseline, you may need to establish a survey framework that is, in effect, a series of four baselines with the diagonals measured in to make the framework rigid (see "The Basics").

Methods for Measuring Right-Angled Offsets 1: Bisecting an Arc

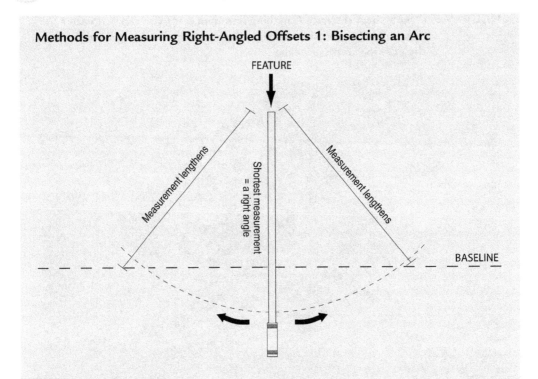

FEATURE

Measurement lengthens

Measurement lengthens

Shortest measurement = a right angle

BASELINE

To use this method, get one person to hold the end of a tape measure firmly on the point that is being measured, while you stand at the baseline and swing the other end of the tape measure over it in a short arc. As you swing the tape measure over the baseline you will notice that the distance increases as the tape reaches either end of the arc but lessens toward the center of the arc. It is this shortest distance that you are looking for, because this will indicate when the tape measure is at a right angle to the baseline. If you are not confident that you can work this out by eye, then mark each end of the arc where it crosses the baseline, measure the length of this distance on the baseline, and then divide it in half. This halfway point marks the corner of the right angle.

The baseline and offset technique is most accurate on level ground, but if there is any slope you will need to take care to keep your baselines horizontal. You also will have to take care with your offset measurements, because if any features are located considerably above or below the horizontal plane of the baseline (i.e., if they are on parts of the site that slope away from the baseline), you will not be able to measure along the ground to these points easily. If you did you would be measuring up or down the length of the slope, which would give you a longer measurement than would a properly horizontal offset. In

Methods for Measuring Right-Angled Offsets 2: 3–4–5 Triangle

This method relies on the 3–4–5 ratio of a right-angled triangle. In theory, if the measurements for each side of a triangle are always kept in units of 3, 4, and 5, or any multiple of these (e.g., 30 cm–40 cm–50 cm, 60 cm–80 cm–100 cm), then the angle between the two perpendicular sides of the triangle will always be 90°. In practice, however, you need to ensure that the dimensions of the triangle are large enough to give you an accurate right angle. In the building industry, for instance, anything less than a 3 m × 4 m × 5 m triangle would be considered unacceptable. This is one potential source of error to watch out for: if you are having trouble, then increase the dimensions of your triangle. For example, you want to lay out a second baseline perpendicular to your first. At the offset point on the first baseline (where the second baseline will begin), you fix the end of one tape measure. You measure along the first baseline for a distance of 3 m. This will be the base of the right-angled triangle. Holding the end of a second tape measure over this point, you give the ends of both tape measures to another person, who moves away from the baseline until standing at roughly 90° to the offset point. You already know that for the triangle to be a right angle these two measurements must equal 4 m and 5 m respectively, so keep adjusting both tape measures until you have them at the correct length. The point where they cross at the correct lengths is the other end of your right-angled offset.

this case you will need to hold the offset tape measure above the baseline so that it is roughly horizontal with the location of the feature being measured and use a plumb bob dropped below the tape to find your exact position on the baseline (figure 4.6).

USING THE BASELINE AND OFFSET TECHNIQUE TO RECORD VERTICAL SURFACES

The baseline and offset technique also is useful if you are recording standing structures or other vertical archaeological features, or if you need to create a cross section through a site

Methods for Measuring Right-Angled Offsets 3: Triangulation

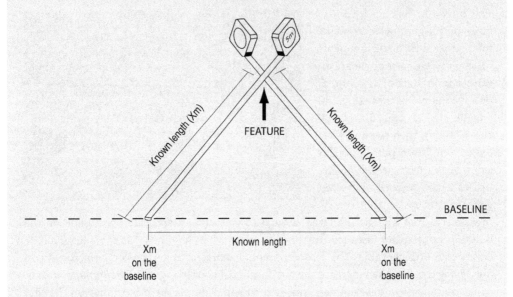

As its name suggests, this method uses triangles to plot the location of features. This is best done using two tape measures. Measure a known length on the baseline and hold or pin a tape measure at each point. Cross the other ends of the tape measures over the point you are measuring to and note down the length of all three sides of the triangle, as well as its position on the baseline. Because you know the length of all three sides, as well as its precise location along the baseline, you will be able to plot this triangle accurately onto your survey plan. This method is best used to plot features that are a long way off the baseline, but ideally the angle at the apex of the triangle (i.e., at the measured point) should be kept as close as possible to 90°. It should definitely be no smaller than 40° and no larger than 140° (Hobbs 1983, 46).

You may, of course, use more than one of these methods at the same site (for instance, for short measurements you might estimate by eye; for longer measurements you might prefer to use triangulation). It doesn't matter; just make sure that you record each measurement in your field notes. Make absolutely sure that you always record your measurements in the same order (i.e., reading along the baseline first, and then along the offset to the feature). *If you confuse the order of these readings at any time, you will not be plotting features in their correct locations.*

FIGURE 4.6: Using a plumb bob to establish your position on the baseline

such as a rockshelter (see "Recording Rockshelters" in chapter 7). In these cases, instead of your offsets being measured from a baseline across to a feature, your offsets will be measured above or below the baseline. Once again you will need to give careful thought as to where you place your baseline to ensure that all of the major measurements can be made from it. You also need to make sure that your baseline is kept horizontal and that all measurements above or below it are kept as close to vertical as possible.

Using Surveying Instruments

All surveying instruments are built around a way to read angles and to measure distances. In their simplest form they are little more than a compass with sights. They require that a person take readings of angles and distance, are reasonably accurate, and tend to be relatively inexpensive. In their most complex form, they use lasers and computers to do much of the work and can be extremely accurate (but also expensive). Some of the equipment is delicate and needs regular calibration for accuracy. You can find many types of survey equipment in archaeology, but because the expense of some instruments is great and extreme accuracy usually is not required, archaeologists tend to use cheaper equipment. In fact, archaeologists tend to gravitate toward surplus equipment and may use instruments decades behind the currently available equipment. Count yourself fortunate if your organization uses the latest equipment!

You will need to learn the equipment your organization has available. Fortunately, the principles of surveying behind the equipment are pretty much the same. If you learn the principles, the skills you use on one kind of instrument will be transferable to equipment you will use in the future. Mostly, the trend in equipment has been toward automation of the surveying process in an effort to increase accuracy and especially to decrease human error. If you want to be valuable on a project, learn surveying principles and learn to use a variety of equipment.

A Case Study in Recording a Cross Section through a Rockshelter

The aim here was to produce a cross section through the shelter to show the changes in the height of the ceiling and the slope of the floor of the rockshelter from front to back. This is important for looking at how people have used the spaces within the shelter and will help to make sense of the features recorded in the site plan. First, a horizontal baseline was laid out from the front to the back of the shelter. The front of the shelter was about 35 cm below the level at the rear of the shelter, so the baseline needed to be fixed to a ranging rod located outside the shelter. Because there were artifacts scattered across the floor of the shelter, the ranging rod had to be placed well outside the front of the shelter so as not to disturb any potential subsurface deposits. The end of the tape measure at the rear of the shelter was weighted down with a large rock (checked out first to make sure it was not an artifact). A series of measurements was made above and below the baseline to record the changing levels in the roof and floor. For measurements of ceiling height, a retractable tape measure was used as a plumb bob (the end held up at the point on the ceiling being measured and the other end dropped down immediately beside the baseline to obtain a reading of height). The same technique was used to record the slope of the floor at the front of the shelter.

FIGURE 4.7: Hypothetical use of the baseline and offset technique to create a cross section of a rockshelter

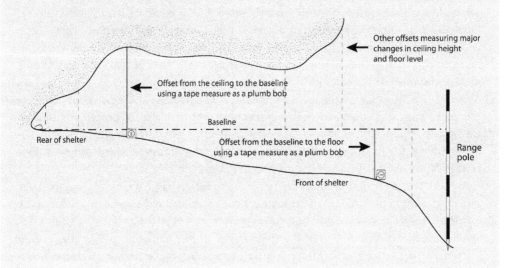

A Case Study in Recording the Wall of a Ruined Building

The aim here was to record the details of the construction techniques used in the wall and the extent of damage. A string baseline was established across the width of the wall about 80 cm above the level of the ground. Because the wall is only 1.5 m high, this was a convenient height from which to measure. The baseline was fixed to the wall using nails inserted firmly into the mortar (making sure not to damage the wall in the process), and a tape measure was pinned along the string. Measurements were made both above and below this baseline to the various features on the wall.

FIGURE 4.8: Hypothetical use of the baseline and offset technique to create a vertical "plan" (otherwise known as an elevation) of a wall

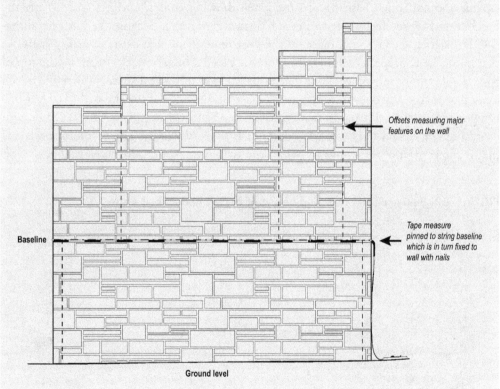

BASIC PRINCIPLES OF LEVELING

Using the baseline and offset technique to measure changes in the height of a rockshelter is a form of **leveling**, or surveying rise and fall. It is only useful over small areas, however, and indicates a major problem with the basic methods of site surveying. They can provide you only with a reasonably accurate plan of the horizontal layout of a site; none of them can give you an accurate indication of how the land rises or falls, or how steep or flat the area containing the site is. To document this you will need to be able to record levels: the changing height of the ground across the site (Drewett 1999, 66).

The principle of leveling is very simple. It involves projecting an imaginary horizontal plane across the site and measuring the height of the ground above or below this. Surveyors refer to this as the **line of collimation** (figure 4.9), and it is exactly the same in principle as the horizontal baseline you use when drawing vertical surfaces (see "Using the Baseline and Offset Technique to Record Vertical Surfaces"). Because the line of collimation is imaginary, you need a place on the horizontal plane that exists in reality (without that point the concept is useless). This point is called a **bench mark**. It can be the top of your site datum or any other point that actually exists in vertical space. Where the bench mark is located really doesn't matter, but a place off the edge of the site within a clear line of sight is best (after all, you don't want to put the bench mark in an area you'll later wish to excavate or behind trees or bushes that block your view of it). The best location is one that is above most of the things for which you will need to measure an elevation.

FIGURE 4.9: Surveying the changing height of the ground across a site

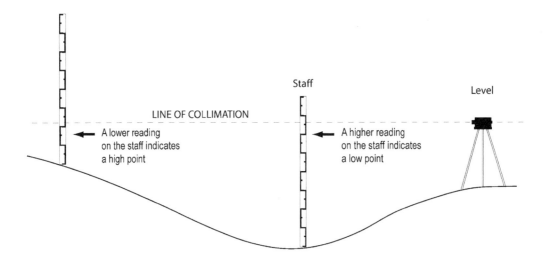

If you wish to go to the trouble, sometimes you can get a true altitude or elevation of your bench mark using a GPS unit or by finding a point of known elevation. For reservoirs such as those operated by the Corps of Engineers, the water level of the reservoir is measured daily as a distance above mean sea level. If you are close to the water and there is little wave action, you can measure the elevation of your bench mark in relation to the surface of the water. The U.S. Geological Survey also has placed bench marks at many locations. On a 1:24,000 topographic map you may see an X with an elevation marked next to it. This indicates the presence of a bench mark. Sometimes you also will find them near one corner of a bridge.

However, you really don't need to know the actual elevation of your bench mark; any point will do so long as it is a more or less stable point. Your site datum is not necessarily the best place if it is a stake pounded into the ground. These can be kicked out of position accidentally, and if you intend to come back to a site, you may wish to use the same bench mark so that your work can be correlated with earlier work.

The usual case is that you will not be able to measure the precise elevation of your bench mark above sea level. That you can't really doesn't matter because all you really need to be able to do is to measure the relationship of the ground surface and artifacts on this site, not their relationship to everything else in the world. Most people choose an arbitrary elevation, usually 100 m, as their bench mark.

The elevation of the ground surface, the height of your surveying instrument, or the position of artifacts in the ground can only be measured accurately with the proper equipment, such as an automatic level (often called a "dumpy" level) or surveyor's transit (both relatively inexpensive), a theodolite, or an electronic distance measurement (EDM) device. You will have seen surveyors using this and similar equipment—they are designed to be set level on a solid tripod, and the height at various points across the site are read off a stadia rod (a staff with units of height marked in alternate red and black segments) through the telescopic lens of the level. If you look through the telescope you will see one major vertical and one major horizontal crosshair. The horizontal crosshair represents the line of collimation, and by reading the changing height of the staff along this line you are reading whether the ground is rising or falling.

How to Set Up an Automatic or "Dumpy" Level or Transit

Step 1: Establish the location of the instrument. This is important, because ideally you want to be able to take as many readings as possible without having to move the instrument. Try to find a centralized spot from which all parts of the site are visible. Once you have decided on this, set up the level. First erect the **tripod** (the three legs that form the base). If you are working as part of a large group you should erect the tripod to the height of the shortest user. In any case make sure the tripod is at a comfortable height for constant use, and lightly but firmly tamp the legs into the ground. Don't make them immovable yet, however, because the next step will be to make sure that the instrument itself is perfectly level. Make sure that the head of the tripod (where you shortly will be attaching the instrument) is roughly level and doesn't have an obvious tilt in any direction.

Now attach the instrument. The level will have a base plate (figure 4.10) that can be screwed into the top of the tripod. Don't screw this in tightly yet, but make sure that the level is firmly fixed to the tripod and can't slide off. Now you have to level the instrument. As long as you have only lightly screwed the instrument in place, the slightly convex surface that is the head of the tripod will allow you to slide it around in a tight circle. Note the effect this has on the leveling bubble (figure 4.10), and see if you can get the instrument close to horizontal. All surveying equipment will have such a visual means for you to judge how level they are—usually a centrally located air bubble inside a marked ring on the circular base of the instrument or two bubble levels at a right angle to each other. You need to get the dumpy at least close to being level at this stage (i.e., the bubble needs to be almost within the circle if not completely inside it or the bubble in the center of both bubble levels), then tighten the screw holding the level in place. This probably will change the level of the instrument slightly, but don't worry; you can adjust this next. If

FIGURE 4.10: The major components of an automatic level

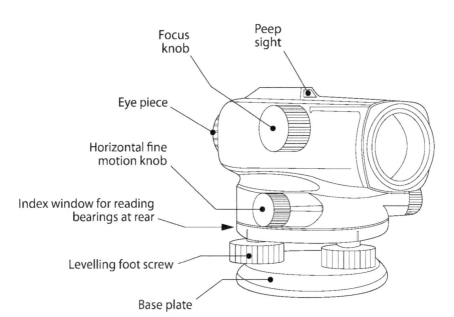

Focus knob

Peep sight

Eye piece

Horizontal fine motion knob

Index window for reading bearings at rear

Levelling foot screw

Base plate

you can't get the instrument anywhere near level at this stage you will have to rethink the positioning of the tripod legs and check whether any need lengthening or shortening. One of the ways to adjust the gross level of the instrument is to tamp the individual legs of the tripod more firmly into the ground. Keep an eye on the leveling bubble as you do this.

Most automatic levels use a combination of three (dumpy) or four (transit) large foot screws (figure 4.10) at the base of the instrument to make it perfectly level, although some may have an internal leveling mechanism. These foot screws are designed to be used in pairs (imagine a triangle for the dumpy or square for the transit underneath the instrument that can be raised or lowered slightly on each side). Align the telescope so that it lies parallel with one pair of foot screws, and using both hands, turn these two screws *outward* (i.e., in opposite directions toward the edges of the instrument). Note the movement of the bubble as you do so. If you had the instrument approximately level in the first stage, you will eventually succeed in getting the air bubble exactly in the center of the bull's-eye circle. Sometimes this process is deceptively quick and simple; sometimes it seems as if you'll never get it right, but you must persevere. Swing the telescope through 90° so that it lies directly over the third foot screw and make sure the bubble is still perfectly centered. Swing the telescope over each foot screw and check that the bubble remains centered. If the instrument has four foot screws, it will probably have two bubble levels at right angles to each other. Align one of the levels parallel to a set of foot screws, adjusting the screws until the bubble is in the middle of the level. Using that same level, turn the telescope to make it parallel to the other set of foot screws until the bubble is centered. Don't overtighten any of the screws. This should bring you into level, and you can make fine adjustments with relative ease.

Once you have figured out how to level one kind of surveying instrument, the skills are transferable to most other types. For a dumpy level the telescope is level when you level the instrument, but for a surveyor's transit, you also have to level the telescope. This is done with a single wheel and bubble level that is parallel to the telescope. Minor movements adjust the level, and the whole process is easy compared to leveling the instrument. Checking the level of the instrument and telescope between each reading is a good idea. Anything might jar the instrument out of alignment, and whatever you do, don't lean on the instrument or tripod!

Step 2: Once the instrument is steady and level, mark the location with a permanent fixture such as a wooden stake. This must be located directly beneath the instrument, so you will need to tie a plumb bob to the hook underneath the center of the tripod head and position the peg directly underneath it. Mark the top of this peg with an indelible cross. This is your first **survey station**.

Step 3: Measure the height of the instrument (HI or HOI) by using a tape measure from the ground surface to the middle of the telescope tube. Another method is to take a backsight to your benchmark. If you will not be moving the instrument because you will be completing *all* your work within a day (unusual!), you can just measure the HI above the ground with a tape measure, and record this in your field notes. However, be careful: if you want to come back to a site to do more work, either for mapping or excavation, put in a permanent bench mark. Also be aware that when you measure the height of the instrument, you are measuring to the middle of the telescope, not the top of the tripod!

Step 4: Begin taking readings. The first thing to do is to make sure the telescope is focused correctly. In most models the eyepiece will be surrounded by a rotatable dial that focuses the crosshairs (figure 4.10). Use this to make sure the crosshairs are sharply defined. Use the peep sight along the top of the telescope to align it approximately with the staff, and sight on the staff through the eyepiece. The horizontal fine motion control knob (or pair of knobs) on the telescope's circular base will allow you to shift the telescope incrementally left or right until it is perfectly aligned with the staff (figure 4.10). Use the focusing knob on the right-hand side of the telescope's body to bring both the crosshairs and the face of the staff into perfect focus (figure 4.10).

The first reading you will have to take *must* be a **backsight (BS)** to the bench mark to establish the HI as discussed in step 3. Reading elevations can be one of the most potentially confusing parts of mapping. One of the biggest problems is that people don't realize that they are really measuring between three parallel planes. The first is the plane of the line of collimation. The bench mark is on that plane, and it never varies. The second plane is the horizontal line that runs through the center of the level telescope on your instrument. The third is the plane that runs through the point on the ground surface or the surface on which an artifact rests.

The first thing you need to do is to establish the HI, usually only once every day, but certainly whenever the instrument gets moved. To do this, you level the telescope, then have someone hold the stadia rod on the bench mark and take a reading, which is a measurement of the height of the instrument—not above the ground, but above the bench mark. Add this reading to your 100 m arbitrary bench mark elevation. You might get a reading of something like 1.37, which added to 100 m means that the HI is 101.37 m. You then move the rod to a point on the surface or near to the artifact and take another reading. Subtract that reading from the HI and this gives you the elevation. Another problem has to do with the kind of instrument and the kind of rod you are using to read elevations. Telescopes invert the image you see, unless a correction is built in. Mostly you find this on transits, but you can get used to this very quickly. You may also find that the stadia rods you use also vary. Some rods are "self-reading" (i.e., the tape on them is adjustable). When the rod is placed on the bench mark, the tape is adjusted so that the instrument is "zeroed-out." This means that you will not have to do any adding or subtracting; the actual reading is your elevation plus 100 m. Just be aware of the type of rod you are using. Pay attention also to how the rod is divided in terms of units of measure.

How to set up
a level

Erect the tripod
* Unscrew the telescopic legs.
* Hold the top of the tripod at chin height and let the legs drop to the ground. Tighten the screws. The tripod must be at a comfortable height for constant use, so if you're working as part of a group, let the shortest person in the group do this.
* Lightly tamp the legs into the ground so that they form an equilateral triangle.
* Make sure the head of the tripod is roughly level.

Attach the instrument
* Carefully place the level on top of the tripod.
* Screw the large screw hanging beneath the head of the tripod partway into the base of the level. Don't make this tight yet, but make sure the level is firmly fixed and can't slide off.

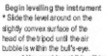

Begin levelling the instrument
* Slide the level around on the slightly convex surface of the head of the tripod until the air bubble is within the bull's-eye.
* You need to get this within the bull's-eye or very close to it at this stage. When you do, carefully tighten the screw holding the instrument in place.
* If you can't get it approximately level, rethink the positioning of the tripod legs. Check whether any need adjusting. One way to adjust the gross level is to tamp each leg more firmly into the ground. Keep an eye on the levelling bubble as you do this.

Make the instrument perfectly level
* Align the telescope so that it lies parallel with one pair of foot screws and, using both hands, turn these screws outwards (i.e. in opposite directions towards the edges of the instrument). Note the movement of the bubble as you do so.
* Make sure the air bubble is exactly centred.

Check the level
* Swing the telescope through 90° so that it lies directly over the third foot screw and make sure the bubble is still perfectly centred.
* Swing the telescope over each foot screw and check that the bubble remains perfectly centred.

Mark the position of the survey station
* Drop a plumb-bob from the hook suspended underneath the centre of the tripod head.
* Position a wooden stake or metal chain arrow directly beneath it.
* Mark the top of the peg with an indelible cross or flagging tape.
* Measure the height of the instrument above ground with a tape measure, and record this in your field notes.

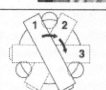

Focus the telescope
* Focus the cross-hairs using the dial surrounding the eye piece.
* Use the peep-sight on top of the telescope to align it with the staff.
* Use the horizontal fine motion control knob (or pair of knobs) on the telescope's circular base to shift the telescope incrementally until the vertical cross hair is perfectly aligned with the centre of the staff.
* Use the focus knob on the right hand side of the telescope's body to bring both the cross-hairs and the face of the staff into perfect focus.

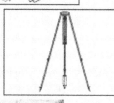

Many rods have what appear to be alternating 1 cm black-and-white squares. Many people get confused by not understanding that the line between the juncture of the black and white is what you are reading, not the square itself. All have some special way of denoting every 5 or 10 cm and will usually use a red number to the side to tell you what meter you are in. Most of the time, your readings will be in the 1–3 meter range.

Reading Angles and Distance

An automatic level also has the facility to read degrees from north so that each reading can be aligned to a particular compass bearing. As part of your first backsight and *before* you move the telescope for the next reading, take a compass reading on the staff along the same axis as the telescope to determine a bearing for the backsight. For example, this might be 270°. Rotate the large circular dial at the base of the instrument so that its reading in degrees aligns with your compass bearing (i.e., so that you can read 270° through the index window underneath the eyepiece) (figure 4.10). When you've realigned the telescope for the next reading you'll be able to read the bearing for that position directly by reading the degrees shown in the index window.

Once you have taken your backsight, all subsequent readings (to various features on the site) are called **intermediate sights**, or **inter-sights (IS)**. For each inter-sight, subtract the reading at the central crosshair from the height of the instrument to give you the **reduced level (RL)** for that spot. You can also use an automatic level to measure distance as well as height and so give you a plan of a site. Inside the dumpy's telescope you will see two smaller crosshairs above and below the major crosshair denoting the line of collimation. If you subtract the height of the staff at the lowest crosshair from the height at the highest crosshair and multiply by 100, this will give you the distance from the level to the staff in meters.

If you find that it is impossible to cover the entire site from one position (e.g., if there is heavy vegetation cover, or the site rises or falls too steeply for it all to be equally visible) then you will have to move the level to a new location. This follows the same setting-up principles as before, with one additional step. The last reading you were able to take from the present survey station will become your first **foresight (FS)**. *Don't move the staff from this location while the level is being moved.* The rule is that *the staff must remain stationary while the level is being moved* and *the level must remain stationary while the staff is being moved* (Casey 1972, 15).

Move the level to the new survey station (obviously you will have chosen this carefully so that you can see new parts of the site from the new location but are still within sight of the last foresight). Set it up again following steps 1 to 3 and then take a backsight to the location of the last foresight. If you don't take this reading you will be unable to tie the different parts of your survey together in the final plan. Calculate the new line of collimation for the second survey station by adding the reading for the backsight to the reduced level for that spot (which you calculated from the previous foresight reading). Continue your survey.

How to Fill in a Level Recording Sheet

This is relatively straightforward and lets you keep track of your readings as you go along. It is also the source data that you will use to plot your survey as a plan, so it is important that you do it correctly. A sample level recording sheet is included in appendix A. The first column on the sheet is a description of the location of the dumpy level (these are your survey stations). This assumes that you may have to move the instrument, so the various positions in which it is set up can be designated simply as 1-X or A-Z. Note the height above sea level of your bench mark (if you know it) in column 8. If you don't know this, choose an arbitrary level of 100 m (so you don't end up in negative numbers as the ground falls). This will be your first reduced level.

Remembering that the first reading after setting up a survey station will *always* be a backsight (either to the site datum or to the point of the last foresight), this is entered in column 2. There will only be one backsight per survey station, so *don't* enter any further readings in this column unless you have just moved the level. *Don't* make the common mistake of writing the foresights in this column—this will only confuse things later. The backsight will establish the line of collimation (i.e., how high the instrument is), which you calculate by adding it to the reduced level (in this case the site datum) to get a height in meters. Place this figure in column 7. Align the level to the correct compass bearing for the backsight (see "How to Set Up an Automatic or 'Dumpy' Level or Transit") and note the bearing in column 11.

The next readings you will take will all be inter-sights to the various features of the site you wish to plot. Place the staff on a feature and take a reading on the central (major) crosshair. Place this figure in column 3. The difference between this figure and the height of the instrument in column 5 will give you the reduced level for that location. Record this figure in column 8. Enter the value for the upper crosshair in column 4 and the lower crosshair in column 5. Enter the bearing in column 11.

Calculate the horizontal distance to that spot, so that you will be able to plot it onto your plan later (subtract the value of the lower crosshair from the value of the upper crosshair and multiply by 100). Place this figure in column 10. To check the accuracy of your survey, subtract the sum of the foresights from the sum of the backsights. Then subtract the last reduced level from the first. The answers should be the same. If you're taking many readings and using several pages of the booking form, you can check each page separately by making sure that each begins with a backsight and ends with a foresight. If an inter-sight comes at the end of a page, enter it as a foresight on that page and as a backsight on the next (Hobbs 1983, 53).

You can use the upper and lower crosshairs visible through the dumpy's telescope to check the accuracy of your survey readings. The difference between the value of the lower crosshair and the center crosshair should be the same as the difference between the value of the center crosshair and the upper crosshair. For example, if the reading at the center crosshair is 1.275, and the lower crosshair 1.240, then the reading at the upper crosshair should be 1.310. Each is 0.035 m distant from the center crosshair, and they need to agree to within 0.005 m or better. If you can't get your readings to agree, you'll have to take them again and check for potential sources of error. Is the staff vertical? Are you reading the staff correctly? If you are new to using a dumpy level you should check your readings regularly to minimize errors.

With the advent of more sophisticated forms of surveying equipment such as electronic distance measurement (EDM) instruments, it is possible to create extremely accurate site plans. An EDM uses a built-in transmitter to send out a laser beam toward a reflecting prism attached to a staff held at the position that is being plotted. The length of time taken for the beam to reach the prism and return to the EDM forms the basis for the calculation of distance. These measurements are recorded digitally for later download into a computer. A total station has both a theodolite (to measure levels) and an EDM (to measure distance) as parts of the one instrument. It can therefore give you both horizontal and vertical measurements as part of the same plan.

As a final word, no survey will ever be perfect. You will need to decide on the level of accuracy you require before you begin—a decision that will depend largely on why you are recording the site in the first place and what it is you want to know. For any site survey you should be aware that there are acceptable levels of error. For a plan plotted at a scale of 1:100, for instance, it is perfectly acceptable for measurements to be taken to only the nearest 50 mm; for a plan at 1:1,000, measurements need only be to the nearest 500 mm. As the scale becomes larger, the level of accuracy increases, so at 1:10 you should try to keep your measurements to the nearest 5 mm, for example.

These levels of accuracy also will have a bearing on the final scale at which you can draw your site plan. Remember, if you are recording a large site, the entire plan of which will end up being drawn on a single sheet, there is little point in recording things to the nearest millimeter. The relationship between the scale of your drawing and the smallest measurement you can literally draw is different from the standards for accurate measurement just given. Even though a plan drawn at 1:100 scale should be measured to the nearest 50 mm, anything that is this small will end up being only 0.5 mm on your final plan. Given the difficulty of drawing something that is half a millimeter long, the standards for plotting are somewhat broader (see "Drawing Horizontal Surfaces" in chapter 9 and table 9.1).

How to fill in a level booking sheet

1
Write down all preliminary information first
* Note the name of the site, the date and the names of the surveying team.
* Note the number of the survey station in *Column 1*, and a brief description of this point in *Column 12*.
* Note the height above sea level, or the arbitrary height of your survey datum. This will also be your first reduced level, so write the same figure in Column 8.

2
Take your first backsight
* Record the reading of the central cross-hair in *Column 2*, the value of the upper cross-hair in *Column 4*, and the value of the lower cross-hair in *Column 5*.
* Check the accuracy of your readings by calculating the difference between the value of the lower cross-hair and the central cross-hair, and of the central cross-hair and the upper cross-hair. Are they the same? If so, your readings are accurate. If not, check for potential sources of error.

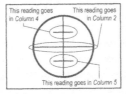

This reading goes in Column 4
This reading goes in Column 2
This reading goes in Column 5

3
When you know your readings are accurate
* Add *Column 2* to the datum height in *Column 8*. This is the height of the instrument and the line of collimation.
* Enter this figure in *Column 7*.
* Before you move the telescope take a compass bearing along the line of sight to the backsight. Adjust the moveable ring at the base of the instrument to the correct compass bearing.
* Enter the bearing in *Column 11*.

2. Backsight	8. Reduced Level (= HOI, Inter-sight)	7. Height of Instrument (HOI) (Line of Collimation) (= R.L. – Backsight)
1.85 +	100.00 =	101.85

4
Take your first intermediate sight (inter-sight)
* Record the reading of the central cross-hair in *Column 3* (*NOT* Column 2), the value of the upper cross-hair in *Column 4*, and the value of the lower cross-hair in *Column 5*.
* Enter a brief description of the point in *Column 12*.

5
Calculate the reduced level and the horizontal distance to this point
* Subtract the inter-sight from the height of the instrument (in *Column 7*) to give you the reduced level. Write this in *Column 8*.
* Subtract the value of the lower cross-hair (in *Column 5*) from the value of the upper cross-hair (in *Column 4*).
* Enter this figure in *Column 9*.
* Now multiply the value in *Column 9* by 100. This will give you the distance to the point in metres.
* Enter this figure in *Column 10*.

Upper X-hair = 1.275
Lower X-hair = 1.200
1.275 - 1.200 = 0.075
0.075 x 100 = 7.5 m

6
Continue to take inter-sights until you've either recorded all visible features or until you need to move the level to a new part of the site
* If you need to move the level, the last reading you can take from the old survey station becomes your foresight.
* Enter this reading in *Column 6*.
* Move the level to the new location and take a backsight to the location of the last reading. Do *not* move the staff while the level is being moved.
* Enter the backsight in *Column 2*.

2. Backsight	3. Inter-sight	4. Upper cross-hair	5. Lower cross-hair	6. Foresight
2.35				3.20

7
Calculate the new height of the instrument
* Add the backsight to the reduced level for that location (you've already calculated this, because the backsight was taken at the same position as the previous foresight).
* Enter the new height of the instrument in *Column 7*.
* Any new inter-sights or foresights taken from the new survey station will be converted to reduced levels by subtracting them from this new line of collimation.

This is the sum of the new backsight (2.35 m) & the reduced level (98.65 m)

Tips for Successful Leveling

- The most important point is to make sure that the instrument is properly level before you use it. If not, then none of your readings will be accurate.
- Once you have leveled the instrument, don't kick or disturb the tripod. If you do, you'll have to relevel the instrument before you continue, including taking a new backsight to the site datum and calculating a new line of collimation.
- If you are holding the staff then you have several responsibilities. You need to make sure that you are holding it upright. By looking through the telescope, the surveyor at the dumpy level will be able to see if you have tilted it to the right or left and can indicate to you in which direction you should move it. They won't know, however, whether you have tilted it forward or backward. To compensate for this (it can be very difficult to know whether the staff is truly upright when you are holding it), you can rock it slightly backward and forward so that the person at the dumpy can take the highest reading (which will be the horizontal). You also can use a small carpenter's line level, held against the back of the staff, to judge when it is upright (figure 4.11). Staffs for EDMs and total stations have a built-in air bubble so you can make sure they are level. If you have neither, a good approach is to stand with the staff in front of you and your feet spread a bit apart. Put the staff against your body halfway between your feet, and touch your nose to the back of the staff. Usually you'll come very close to vertical and with the staff facing the surveying instrument. You will have to ensure that you have not rotated the face of the staff away from the telescope. Watch the direction in which the staff is facing, and be prepared to adjust it if the surveyor can't read it clearly.
- If the surveyor can't see you or the staff at all (say if there is screening vegetation in the way), then you will have to move the staff slightly in one direction or the other until it becomes visible.

FIGURE 4.11: Using a carpenter's line level to check whether the stadia rod (leveling staff) is vertical

This is where walkie-talkies are invaluable. Sometimes only a slight adjustment will be necessary, but take care that as you move the staff you keep it upright and vertical. This is most easily done by moving the staff in small steps (sometimes only centimeters) in a given direction until the surveyor tells you to stop.

- To produce a contour plan you will need to take a series of spot heights across the site. Decide on a contour interval (the distance between contours), and join points of equal height across the site. One way to do this is to grid the site and take spot heights at each point on the grid. Another simpler way is to take spot heights at regular intervals (2–3 m works pretty well), but following a radius from your instrument. Change the radius by 10° (or some other interval you feel is adequate), and do spot heights on the next radius, continuing the process until you have gone around 360° or whatever portion of the area you wish to cover. Then connect points of equal elevation.

If you draw the plan by hand, remember that you should never ink-in original pencil drawings, because these are an essential element of the primary site archive (Drewett 1999, 177). Instead you should use drafting film (not tracing paper) to redraw the plan (for more information see chapter 9, "Photography and Illustration"), or scan it and redraw it using a computer graphics program.

REFERENCES AND FURTHER READING

Bettess, F. 1998. *Surveying for archaeologists.* 3rd ed. Durham, UK: University of Durham.

Casey, D. A. 1972. Elementary surveying for Australian archaeologists. In *Australian archaeology: A guide to field and laboratory techniques,* ed. D. J. Mulvaney, 5–21. Canberra: AIAS Press.

Davies, M., and K. Buckley. 1987. Archaeological procedures manual. Port Arthur Conservation and Development Project. Occasional Paper No. 13, Department of Lands, Parks and Wildlife, Hobart.

Drewett, P. 1999. *Field archaeology: An introduction.* London: UCL Press.

Eiteljorg, H., II, K. Fernie, J. Huggett, and D. Robinson. 2002. Archaeology data service. CAD: A guide to good practice. http://ads.ahds.ac.uk/project/goodguides/cad (accessed July 20, 2008).

Hobbs, D. R. 1983. Surveying techniques useful in archaeology. In *Australian Field Archaeology: A guide to techniques,* ed. G. Connah, 43–63. Canberra: AIAS Press.

Rick, J. 1996. Total stations in archaeology. *Society for American Archaeology Bulletin* 14(4). www.saa.org/publications/SAAbulletin/14-4/SAA16.html (accessed December 29 2006).

For a range of other useful information, see the website accompanying the text.

CHAPTER FIVE

BASIC EXCAVATION TECHNIQUES

What you will learn from this chapter:

How archaeologists excavate
Why careful control of the excavation process is important
How to dig
Standards for describing soil
How to use a Harris matrix to interpret stratification
Basic procedures for screening, recording, bagging, and labeling
Basic procedures for collecting on-site samples
Basic conservation measures for protecting excavated finds
Tips for surviving an excavation

THE BASICS

The aim of any archaeological excavation is to try to understand what may have happened at a site in the past by carefully excavating the various material remains that make up that site. Excavating requires both care and patience because, to be able to understand the sequence of activities at a site, archaeologists must slowly strip away each soil layer in succession. The basic principle on most excavations is that each new soil layer is removed completely before proceeding to the next—in other words, excavation proceeds horizontally first (i.e., by removing all traces of one soil layer first) and vertically second (when

The Basic Excavation Toolkit

10–12 cm drop-forged pointing trowel (make sure that the neck and blade are cast in one piece, otherwise it will break; Marshalltown trowels are legendary)

Hand shovel or dustpan

Plastic buckets

Clippers or pruning sheers for removing roots

Dental pick/plasterer's tool

Fine, soft paint brushes (in a range of sizes for cleaning large areas and for reaching into small cavities)

Hand brush or whisk broom (for cleaning hard surfaces and brushing up soil)

Spring balance (for weighing buckets)

Carpenter's string level (for making sure baselines are horizontal)

Screens with ¼-inch mesh hardware cloth (for screening soil from excavations)

Nested mesh sieves (in a range of sieve sizes—10 mm, 5 mm, and 2 mm are the most common)

Plastic sheeting, to cover the site or on which to lay out deposits

Knee pads (or foam squares), to make excavation more comfortable

Soil pH test kit

Munsell Soil Color Chart

Recording forms

Clipboard

Artifact tags (aluminum or polyethylene)

Nails (for securing tags to the walls of trenches if necessary)

String and line level (for marking the edges of excavation units and for establishing baselines for drawing sections)

Wooden stakes (for marking out the excavation units)

Mattock, pick, or shovel (for removing turf or for backfilling)

Drawing equipment (see chapter 9)

Photographic equipment (see chapter 9)

Tape measures, in a range of sizes

Ziploc plastic bags, in various sizes

Optional:

Wheelbarrows

A step ladder (you may need to stand on this to photograph trenches from above or to get in and out of deep excavation units)

A hand sprayer (you may want to wet the walls of the trenches to observe differences in soil color)

Artifact processing equipment (plastic basins, drying trays, toothbrushes)

General site equipment (chairs, folding tables, canvas or shade cover)

excavation of the next soil layer is begun). This kind of careful "layer-cake" excavation is called the **stratigraphic** or **context** system of excavation. Although not all excavations will adopt this process, it is the most common system followed by archaeologists (for more information see "The Principles of Excavation").

A **context** is any discrete archaeological entity on a site, such as a posthole, a depositional layer, a rubbish pit, or an erosion event (Drewett 1999, 107) and is the same thing as a "layer," a "feature," or a "stratigraphic unit." Under the context system the goal of any excavation is not to dig as deeply as possible as quickly as possible, but rather to be sure that all of the information from each soil layer, or stratum ("strata" is the plural), is kept together so that it may be analyzed later as a discrete entity. If you think of a site that has had many successive activities performed on it over hundreds of years, all of these activities may have left separate and distinct evidence behind them "trapped" in different layers of the soil. If archaeologists were to mix up all of these layers, they would be unable to separate the information from each activity, unable to date the sequence of activities, and unable to reconstruct exactly what had happened there in the past.

One of the most important things to realize is that, while all excavation aims to retrieve as much information as possible, in the process it literally destroys the site forever. No excavated site can ever be put back: once excavated it is gone forever and exists only in your recording forms, field notes, reports, photographs, publications, and archives. For this reason you must ensure that your excavations are always conducted according to the highest possible standards. As soon as you begin an excavation it is your ethical responsibility to ensure that it is done professionally, up to and including the standards you adopt for analysis, reporting, archiving, conservation, and curation. In the end it is better to go for less done well, rather than more done badly: "At the end of the day a well excavated, well recorded, fully published 1 × 1 m unit does considerably less harm than a huge, badly controlled, unpublished . . . excavation" (Drewett 1999, 97).

Professional recording standards require that an archaeologist control the excavation process as much as possible. Not all archaeological evidence is in the form of three-dimensional artifacts. Much evidence of past human behavior is subtle and perhaps not even instantly recognizable (such as stained soil from decomposed timber posts indicating the original location of buildings, or slightly darker layers of soil indicating the presence of charcoal from cooking fires). This evidence will be lost if care is not exercised during the excavation process, particularly with regard to changes in soil color, type, or texture as the excavation progresses (see "The Principles of Excavation"). Any change in the physical characteristics of the soil could be of great importance, so you should never underestimate what's happening under your trowel (see "Using a Trowel" and "Using a Brush").

The main aspect of this control is to enable the archaeologist to pinpoint where each and every piece of evidence comes from. Archaeologists must be sure of the exact location

Almost everyone recognizes an archaeologist as someone who excavates. All excavation or any other form of collecting artifacts, however, is inherently destructive and can never be repeated. This is why in most states and all federal agencies, an excavation permit *must* be obtained before excavation or collection can commence. The idea is to require quality work by being certain a proper research design is in place before work begins. Excavation should be a last resort—if you can get all the answers you want through nondestructive recording techniques, then *don't* excavate.

It is a primary ethical responsibility of all archaeologists that excavation is undertaken only by professionals (or under professional supervision) and never without proper research and planning. It is for this reason that excavation or the collection of artifacts is the one aspect of archaeology that is regulated in most states, provinces, territories, and tribal lands by legislation governing who may undertake such activities and how they should be conducted.

Removing artifacts from their location in a site or the landscape without the proper legal permissions is, in most cases, both unnecessary and harmful. While there may be some instances where it is unavoidable (such as when the place is in imminent danger of being destroyed, or when Native American nations insist on collecting items from sites on their lands), in general it is both illegal and unethical to remove artifacts. If you find a particularly interesting or unusual artifact, unless it is in danger of destruction or loss, by all means sketch it or photograph it (or both), but leave it where you found it.

of each artifact within the site (see "Recording in Three Dimensions"). The positioning of artifacts horizontally across the site can tell archaeologists how different parts of the site were used and what activities were performed there; the positioning of artifacts vertically through the site can tell archaeologists what happened when and the order of events in the past. This need to be absolutely sure of the **provenience** (sometimes also called **provenance**) of all artifacts is what drives archaeologists to keep all the evidence from a particular context together throughout the digging, screening, sorting, bagging, cleaning, and analysis process (figure 5.1). It is also why archaeologists tend to excavate carefully selected portions of a site in such a way that the boundaries of each excavation unit are very specific. Usually they do this by adopting a standard grid system and stringing out their excavation units to exact dimensions (See "Laying Out a Site Grid"). **Excavation units**, sometimes called **trenches**, usually are laid out in multiples of 1 m or 2 m and sometimes are divided into smaller squares of 25 cm or 50 cm within each meter square, called **quadrats**. A consistent and logical numbering system is also imperative for each trench and for each context or layer within each trench (see "Laying Out a Site Grid"), so that all the contents of a particular context can be recorded and labeled consistently. This num-

FIGURE 5.1: A flowchart to follow when recording an excavation unit, or context. This sequence should be repeated for all units.

bering system is like a library catalog: it is what ties the archaeological features and structures, the artifacts, their locations, and the physical descriptions of the various soil strata together, so that, in the end, the site may be analyzed in a meaningful way (see "Labeling Excavation Units" and "Labeling Finds and Samples"). You should give considerable thought to the numbering/labeling system of your site before you begin excavating to ensure that numbers are not repeated and that all units and contexts are numbered consistently and logically.

ON-SITE SAFETY

Public health and safety on an excavation, not to mention that of you and your crew, are also your responsibility. If you are excavating in a public place, you may have to erect mesh fencing or some other form of barricade to protect the public from any accidents, and for the same reason, backfilling the site after the completion of excavation is also your job. The location of your excavation units and their ultimate depth also may be a health and safety issue. For example, the **Occupational Safety and Health Administration** (OSHA), a United States government agency under the Department of Labor, has regulations requiring that any excavation over 5 feet in depth must be properly sloped, benched, or shored to prevent collapse. You will need to refer to the OSHA regulations when planning archaeological fieldwork. The **Canadian Centre for Occupational Health and Safety** (CCOHS) provides similar information for Canada. To avoid the dangers of deep, narrow trenches, you can cut the sides back in a series of steps, although this may create problems for recording. If you are going to be excavating on a deep or difficult site, you may need to consult a civil engineer.

BACKFILLING

You need to think about the end of your project even before you start it. Part of planning relates to safety, and backfilling is important for that reason, but also part of your professional obligation. In some cases, especially if an area will be destroyed by construction immediately after you are done, backfilling may not be needed. Usually you will be responsible for backfilling the excavations and returning the area to some semblance of its former appearance once the excavation is completed (i.e., ensuring that no open holes are left behind and removing your rubbish). Before you backfill, it is common practice to place plastic or weed mat on the bottom of the trench so that future archaeologists will know the mixed material put back into the trenches is the result of a past archaeological excavation and not some bizarre ritual practice of past people! Plastic or weed mat also will indicate clearly where your excavation ended, in case you or another archaeologist should decide to reopen your trenches. Archaeologists sometimes include readily datable items (such as coins with the current year) in the base of the trench before they backfill as a hint to future archaeologists. Be careful what you leave as a marker. Given currently available, inexpensive materials, there is no reason you can't leave markers with the date, name of the project, and other pertinent information in the excavation units.

As odd as it may sound, you need to overfill when you backfill. Excavation loosens the soil, and after you put it back, it settles. This means that you need to mound the soil over the excavations. You will find that in most cases, there will be more than enough soil to do this. If possible compact it either by walking or jumping on it or mechanically with soil compactors or heavy equipment. This is especially important if the land is used for agriculture. Farmers like nothing worse than driving their tractor into a hole that has settled into an excavation unit!

EXCAVATION PLANNING

All excavation requires careful planning (see "Designing Your Research" in chapter 1). Think about what aspects are important to the success of your project, and make sure you seek out and record those aspects during excavation. One of the key things to realize is the importance of maintaining flexibility in your methods. Every site is different, so you will need to weigh carefully the pros and cons and tailor the excavation methods to suit your particular research questions, the time available, and the individual nature of the site.

Once you have thought carefully through your research aims and how excavation can best serve them, all excavation follows a fairly standard process:

- Lay out a grid system of possible excavation units.
- Photograph the entire site before commencing (see "Photographing Excavations" in chapter 9).
- Excavate (this is in reality a complex series of steps in its own right; see figure 5.1).
- Photograph the entire site upon completion.
- Backfill and photograph it again.
- Perform an analysis.
- Write your report.
- Carry out conservation/curation of recovered artifacts.

THE PRINCIPLES OF EXCAVATION

Sites can be created over long or short periods of time—they even can be the remains of a single event—but excavation assumes that the order in which the different parts of the site have been laid down will reflect the sequence of events that occurred at that site in the past. This is known as the **principle (or law) of superposition**, which assumes that more recent deposits will be laid down on top of older ones. While this is not always straightforward, it is the fundamental basis for using **stratification**, or the way in which the structure of the soil is divided into different layers or **deposits**, to interpret what happened at a site. You should note the distinction between stratification (the process of sedimentary layering and its observed result) and **stratigraphy** (the archaeologist's interpretation of the stratified layers, in words or drawings).

There are often complicating factors to this, of course, such as when various natural processes deposit or remove material from a site (such as wind depositing silt, water eroding the site, or rodents churning and mixing up the soil in the **krotovina**, or filled-in burrows), or when later events remove or alter evidence of previous events. Three additional principles describe these possibilities:

- **The principle of association**, which presumes that items found together in the same deposit are of essentially the same age. This must be applied with caution because people may keep some items for a long time, as with a treasured tool or family heirloom, before they finally throw them away, making them much older than the other materials associated with them. Archaeologists sometimes call this **curatorial** or **archival behavior**.
- **The principle of reversal**, which allows for those rare cases when deposits have been removed from the site and redeposited in reverse order. This usually takes place as a result of major construction activity or digging, when large quantities of earth are removed and then redeposited upside down.
- **The principle of intrusion**, which states that an intrusion must be more recent than the deposits through which it cuts (Barber 1994, 85). An underground oven and a rubbish pit dug into the ground are examples of intrusions cutting into the older deposits around them.

All archaeological excavation is based around these four simple principles. Together they imply that, through the careful removal of the layers that make up a site, and a detailed description of their texture, color, and contents, an archaeologist can reconstruct the sequence of events (both human and natural) that took place at that site in the past. Put simply, by analyzing the stratification of a site it is possible to work out the whole story of human and natural processes that the site has to tell.

Because stratification is so important, most excavation proceeds by carefully stripping each stratigraphic layer from a site in turn. This is why, when you are excavating, it is important to describe and take note of any changes in soil color, texture, or appearance as you dig. It is also why you should not hurry. Stratigraphy is closely linked to the process of excavation itself, in that as you remove each layer, you form opinions about how the different strata in a site were laid down and how they relate to each other: "The archaeologist's golden rule is to excavate one layer at a time—and nothing in that layer should escape his or her detection. It isn't possible to read significance into a layer or level until you know how it lies, how it was formed, what its composition is, and what its relationship is to the layers above and below it" (Joukowsky 1980, 171–172). For this reason, excavation should proceed horizontally first and vertically second. In other words, you should finish excavating one unit or layer completely before you begin the next.

A site that has distinct layers or contexts is said to be stratified. Not all sites are like this, however, and therefore not all excavation proceeds according to the stratigraphic system. Some sites have no visible stratification, due perhaps to all the soil being uniformly dark; at others the more significant cultural layers might be covered by large quantities of later, less significant, debris, or the entire site may have resulted from a single event of a known date (such as a load of rubbish being dumped). In such cases, excavating according to stratigraphic levels would be fruitless. Even if you choose not to excavate the site according to stratigraphic layers you will still need to be able to control the removal of soil from the site if you want to draw any meaningful conclusions about the vertical or horizontal location of artifacts. In this case, sites often are dug in **arbitrary levels** that can still provide sufficient vertical and horizontal control. These arbitrary levels (occasionally referred to as **spits**, or stratigraphic units) can be any thickness you choose depending on the overall depth of the site and the degree of resolution you want to achieve in locating the artifacts. Ten centimeters is often a standard level. Keep in mind, however, that whatever arbitrary depth you choose as the standard for your levels, this will be the finest degree of resolution that you will be able to achieve in your analysis and results. If several different activities at a site have left behind them only 2 cm layers of deposit, which you choose to excavate in 10 cm levels, then any one of these levels is likely to contain information from several different activities. Because you have chosen to group them into one arbitrary level, you will not be able to separate them in your excavation or in your subsequent analysis or conclusions (there is an exception to this, so see the section on piece-plotting in "Recording in Three Dimensions"). Once again, flexibility is the key: some sites may require a combination of arbitrary and stratigraphic excavation, such as if you find thick, homogenous layers within an otherwise stratified site (generally at the beginning or end of the excavation) that can be removed by arbitrary levels.

APPROACHES TO EXCAVATION

Once you have decided on the most appropriate method of excavating your site, the next important decision to make is which parts of the site you are going to excavate. This is essentially a sampling decision, similar in principle to deciding how you are going to survey an area selectively (see "Developing a Suitable Sampling Strategy" in chapter 3). As with a surface survey, if you can't dig the entire site, you will have to make some meaningful decisions about which part or parts of the site are most likely to give you the information necessary to answer your research questions. There is an ethical element to this decision as well, of course, in that some archaeologists argue you always should leave some part of a site intact so that future generations of archaeologists, who may bring with them new and better methods, will still be able to retrieve some *in situ* information. There are two aspects to this decision:

- Deciding how much of the area to excavate
- Deciding where to place your excavation units

How Much?

There are two ways to approach the excavation of any site, which depend on how much of the site you wish to excavate: the **unit system** or the **open-area** (or **block**) **system**. The unit system is concerned with obtaining a cross section through the site and tends to excavate relatively small portions of the site to sufficient depth (it is often referred to disparagingly as the "telephone booth" approach). Because it aims to dig deeply, it is well suited to answering chronological questions, such as the sequence of dates, or the dates for earliest occupation, and for indicating the richness of the deposits and revealing the stratification of the site, because the walls of the unit preserve the stratigraphic profile of the excavation unit until the very end of the excavation. Because the unit system excavates narrow vertical slices through a site, however, it cannot expose spatial information across the site. The open-area system was developed in response to this need for horizontal information and exposes large expanses of the site but often to only a relatively shallow depth. It is thus quite successful at revealing information about activity areas or site structure, although it may not be so successful for establishing a sequence of dates (although it may be, if you dig deeply enough). Each system has pros and cons, and it is important to realize that each is designed to recover different types of information. They can, of course, be used in tandem to complement each other, or be combined with other methods such as mechanical excavation or surface stripping to answer many different kinds of questions. The choice of which to employ will depend on the time and resources available to you and the particular set of research questions you are asking.

Whether you are more concerned with chronological or spatial questions in large part will be determined by the type of site you are excavating. Historical sites, for example, usually are formed over a relatively short period of time and may be well documented. Therefore, detailed information about chronological change is not always important. The emphasis in these sites may be more on spatial questions—changes in patterning horizontally, across space—rather than chronological issues.

Where?

Intra-site sampling is the choice of where to excavate within a site. Remembering that vertical excavation units are designed to recover chronological information, and horizontal open-area excavations are designed to recover information about spatial activity areas, obviously the selection of excavation areas and the methods of excavation you adopt will influence the kind of data you can collect from a site. If you are investigating a rockshelter that has been inhabited by people for several thousand years, for example, you might want to know about the chronology of the site (i.e., the sequence of its occupation over time), or about the use of space within the site (i.e., were different people using different parts of the site for sleeping, eating, cooking, or some other activity?). Excavating the site through a system of vertical units is usually the best means of obtaining enough stratigraphic information to determine chronology, but it is utterly unable to tell you much that is meaningful about how space was used across the rockshelter because you haven't excavated enough of it. If you think of the rockshelter as analogous to your house, how representative would a shallow vertical "slice" through your house be for reconstructing all of your day-to-day activities? Similarly, a shallower open-area excavation will be better suited to recovering just this kind of spatial information but may not necessarily give you enough depth to obtain an adequate chronology. In reality, of course, obtaining information about chronology and the sequence of occupation is just as important as finding out about the patterning of activities across space, so in deciding where to place your excavations and how much of the area you are going to excavate you will need to think carefully about what it is you want to know and how best you will be able to find this out:

- What kind of data do you want to recover?
- What sampling approach best fits this goal?
- What sample size will best answer your questions (i.e., how much information will you need)?

In reality, you will be able to decide where to excavate only after you have completed an intensive surface survey of the area in question. Careful surface survey may reveal discrete activity areas or clusters of certain elements or features, or the patterning of artifacts across the ground surface may be able to tell you about differential erosional/depositional patterns across the site. Any indication that there might be more archaeological evidence below the ground surface will be a useful guide as to where to place your trenches. You also may wish to excavate a seemingly bare area of ground, however, to test whether what you observe on the ground surface is really a good indication of what exists below the surface. Examining the ground carefully before you dig also can tell you what kind of tools you will need to do the job properly (Joukowsky 1980, 172). Researching the recent history of your site also may give you some idea of what took place in the recent past at least, and therefore the kind of deposits you might encounter.

Subsurface Sampling

In making these decisions, the archaeologist is effectively trying to assess what might lie below the ground surface. There are more scientific ways of doing this than simply guessing, of course, all of which can be employed to help you decide on where it would be best to dig. This is called **subsurface sampling**. Sometimes small-scale subsurface sampling will be necessary to determine the horizontal extent of a site (see "Subsurface Testing" in chapter 3). Soil cores, auger holes, or shovel-test pits can be dug at intervals across the site to obtain broad stratigraphic or spatial information. Soil cores are commonly 3–5 cm in diameter, with auger holes slightly larger at 10–15 cm in diameter. Shovel-test pits are usually slightly larger than the width of a shovel blade (i.e., between 25–50 cm square) and have the distinct advantage of allowing you to examine the stratigraphy in the sides of the pit, something that is not possible for auger holes or cores. On large sites, you also can excavate long, narrow trenches, usually 50 cm or less wide and any selected length, at various locations through the site. Comparison between different methods of subsurface sampling suggests that shovel-test pits are the most effective means for "seeing" beneath the ground surface, although they are quite labor intensive (Hester, Schafer, and Feder 1997, 57–59). As with any form of sampling, the best results can be obtained only after careful forethought—you will have to consider not only where you are going to place your test pits but also how close together they should be and how deep they will be. Bear in mind, however, that any form of subsurface sampling will destroy a small portion of the site as it is dug, so it is always wise to limit the effects of this, particularly if you are going to conduct a larger-scale excavation later. Because all forms of subsurface testing will destroy a portion of the archaeological deposit, they should be part of your research design and may be considered to be part of any excavation permit or license.

Other forms of subsurface testing, such as magnetometry or the use of ground-penetrating radar, have the advantage of being noninvasive but can be conducted only by specialist operators with appropriate equipment.

LAYING OUT A SITE GRID

Once you have made your decision about where to excavate, the next step is to lay out your excavation units/trenches. The site grid is crucial in terms of being able to maintain control over the positioning of artifacts and features across the site. Archaeologists often use a grid that for convenience divides the site into 2 m grid units (often called "squares"). An excavation unit can be any multiple or fraction of these grid units, which are related to each other through a universal numbering system (figure 5.2). The two axes of the grid are labeled the X and the Y axis. Note that it is standard practice to begin numbering coordinates along these axes at a relatively high number, such as 10, to allow for the possibility of extending units if necessary but to avoid going into negative numbers when doing so.

You don't actually need to string out every grid unit across the site, although, to avoid having to measure them again, you should mark the ends of the X and Y axes with stable and relatively permanent stakes. If you want to excavate a trench that is larger than 1 m × 1 m but don't wish to string out the boundary of every 1 m grid unit within it, it is simplest to mark the corners of each unit along the edges of the unit with masking tape attached to the string.

You should formally string out each excavation unit within your site, however. The string outline of the square serves as a constant reference point for measuring depth and for ensuring that the sides of the square are kept straight. You must ensure that all of your excavation units are kept square (meaning horizontally rectilinear and vertically straight-walled), however, because this allows you to control the excavation process. As a first step, establish where the edge of your unit will be, measure its length, and then mark the two corner points with stakes hammered lightly but firmly into the ground.

FIGURE 5.2: A hypothetical grid across an excavated site. Any of the squares in between the already excavated units can be opened and assigned X and Y coordinates from the established grid.

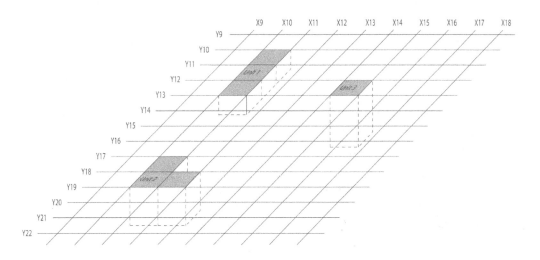

Because units are usually laid out in multiples of 1 m with 90° corners, the next step is to mark the opposite corners.

Establish a right angle from one established stake to a third corner stake using triangulation (see "Using the Baseline and Offset Technique" in chapter 4). Install a fourth corner stake by the same method and then measure all four sides *and* the diagonals to be sure that the unit is square. Table 5.1 provides diagonal measurements for excavation units up to 15 m × 15 m, on the principle that the diagonal of a square will always measure 1.414 times the length of the sides. This is related to Pythagoras' theorem, which states that in a right-angled triangle, the square of the hypotenuse is equal to the sum of the squares of the opposite sides. In practice, even though you have measured the first side of the trench carefully, and then triangulated the opposite two corners from this, a unit rarely will be perfectly square on the first attempt. Inevitably you will have to keep adjusting the positions of your stakes until the unit is actually square. The only way to do this is to keep measuring the sides and the diagonals until you have them right (figure 5.3).

Once you have strung out your squares, make sure you don't trip over the string or stakes during excavation. For this reason you may wish to tie flagging tape or some other brightly colored material to the stakes to make them easy to see (and avoid). Remember that the corners will be your permanent reference points for excavating and measuring, so it is very important not to disturb them.

LABELING EXCAVATION UNITS

All excavation units within the grid of your site must be numbered logically so that all finds and descriptions of deposits can be tied securely to their place of origin. There must be no confusion about this, and deciding on a logical labeling system is a first priority. Every artifact or sample that comes out of a square, and every description of a layer or a feature, must be able to be described so that you know precisely where it came from, otherwise it will be impossible to draw any meaningful conclusions about your site. Even though you have X and Y coordinates for every grid unit, these would be very time consuming to transcribe onto every bag or recording form, so you can simplify the system by assigning a number to each unit. At the very least a labeling system should contain a site prefix or code for the site (such as its trinomial system number; see "A Note on Site Numbering and Naming Systems" in chapter 3), a unique designation for each unit, and a consecutive and unique number for each context or layer. Individual artifacts or samples within each context also can be numbered if required. This string of letters and numbers will be the code that is written on every bag containing an artifact or sample (see "Labeling Finds and Samples") and on every recording form.

TABLE 5.1: Diagonal measurements for archaeological units

Width (m)	Length (m)														
	1	2	3	4	5	6	7	8	9	10	11	12	13	14	15
1	1.414	2.236	3.162	4.123	5.099	6.083	7.071	8.062	9.055	10.050	11.045	12.042	13.038	14.036	15.033
2		2.828	3.606	4.472	5.385	6.325	7.280	8.246	9.220	10.198	11.180	12.166	13.153	14.142	15.133
3			4.243	5.000	5.831	6.708	7.616	8.544	9.487	10.440	11.402	12.369	13.342	14.318	15.297
4				5.657	6.403	7.211	8.062	8.944	9.849	10.770	11.705	12.649	13.601	14.560	15.524
5					7.071	7.810	8.602	9.434	10.269	11.180	12.083	13.000	13.928	14.866	15.811
6						8.485	9.219	10.000	10.817	11.622	12.530	13.416	14.318	15.232	16.155
7							9.899	10.630	11.402	12.207	13.038	13.892	14.765	15.652	16.553
8								11.314	12.042	12.806	13.601	14.422	15.264	16.125	17.000
9									12.728	13.454	14.213	15.000	15.811	16.643	17.493
10										14.142	14.866	15.620	16.401	17.205	18.028
11											15.556	16.279	17.029	17.804	18.601
12												16.970	17.692	18.439	19.209
13													18.385	19.105	19.849
14														19.799	20.518
15															21.213

FIGURE 5.3: The sequence for laying out an excavation square

How to string out a trench

1 Decide where your first corner point will be and hammer a peg lightly but firmly into the ground. Measure the first side of your trench and hammer a second peg into the ground.

2 Establish the position of your third corner point
Measure the length of the second side and use the correct diagonal measurement to ensure it is at right angles to the first. Where the tapes cross at the correct points is the location of your third corner peg. Hammer the peg lightly but firmly into the ground.

3 Establish the position of your last corner point
Repeat Step 2 to locate the last corner point. Measure the length of the fourth side and use the length of the diagonal to test it. Hammer the last peg into the ground.

4 Check your accuracy
Measure the lengths of all sides again and check the length of both diagonals again. Adjust the position of any corner pegs necessary until you have the trench completely square.

5 Set up an outer framework of pegs
Place two pegs slightly behind each corner point along the same axes as the sides. These are the pegs that you will actually use to string out the trench.

6 String out the trench
Loop the string around each of the framework pegs to form a triangle at each corner. Make sure the string is tight and the pegs are all firmly hammered into the ground. Remove the initial corner pegs, which would otherwise collapse into the trench as you excavated.

7 Label each corner point
The convention is to place a label at each corner indicating its N–S and E–W coordinates. Because you may wish to extend a trench later, the convention is to arbitrarily begin these coordinates at 10 so that you don't go into negative numbers. List the N–S coordinate first, the E–W second.

Stephen Sutton's Tip for Stringing Out an Excavation Square

Even after you've strung out your unit it's possible for the string to move (or, more likely, for some unfortunate person to trip over it or kick the stakes out of alignment). To make it easier to reconstruct the precise location of your original corners, mark the place where the strings cross with a permanent, easily visible pen line. In this way, if the string is ever moved you'll be able to see its original position easily and replace it accordingly.

RECORDING IN THREE DIMENSIONS

Because archaeologists want to know the exact location of artifacts and features both horizontally and vertically, they record these things according to their position both along the length and the width of the excavation unit (their position on the X and Y axes of the site) and also according to their position through the depth of the deposit. This is called the Z axis (figure 5.4).

The most accurate and easy way to measure depth is to use a surveying instrument to do **piece-plotting** (i.e., to plot individual finds). If you don't have access to one you will have to use an old-fashioned tape measure. If you use this low-tech solution make sure that you always measure from a fixed horizontal baseline (the string of the unit is fine provided you use a carpenter's string level to make sure it really is horizontal and hasn't been disturbed at all during excavation). Any alteration of movement in this baseline will affect all your subsequent measurements. To measure the Z axis, it is sometimes prudent to pound a small nail carefully into the top of a stake in one corner of your unit. The top of the stake can be "shot in" with your surveying instrument to be sure it is at the actual elevation of the baseline. Tie a string, at least as long as the diagonal of your unit, around the base of the nail. Each time you need to measure the Z axis, extend the string, put a carpenter's string level on it, level it, and measure down from the level string to the point or object you wish to measure.

Piece-plotting each artifact and feature in every level can be extremely time consuming, so you need to think carefully before using it. Piece-plotting works best with a so-

FIGURE 5.4: Using X, Y, and Z coordinates to plot the location of an excavated artifact

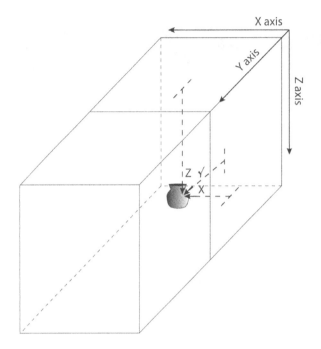

phisticated surveying instrument, such as a total station, that can quickly read and download the data into a data logger. Even with sophisticated equipment, you need to take lots of precautions, especially holding the rod and prism vertical. Consider several questions: How can you plot each piece when objects are in a jumble, as with flakes from stone tool manufacture? How many points on each artifact or feature do you measure? What if an artifact is on a slant into the ground? The better strategy is to plot only the most significant materials from each level unless your research questions demand greater precision.

On many sites, recording the precise position of every individual artifact in three dimensions is not always practical and is not necessarily going to provide you with more accurate or "better" archaeological information, unless there is good evidence that the artifacts are still in their area of primary use or discard (Drewett 1999, 143). Recent research (Balme and Beck 2002) suggests that plotting artifacts to within a 25 cm or 50 cm quadrat (e.g., an artifact was recovered from unit 1/context 10/quadrat a) will provide sufficient spatial resolution to answer most questions about activity areas at a site. Any special or unique finds can still be plotted individually if necessary. Thus, it is worth remembering that greater precision doesn't necessarily create greater understanding; in fact, striving for it may be a waste of time and money (see several papers in Lock and Molyneaux 2006).

RECORDING THE EXCAVATION PROCESS

Just as with a surface survey, there are several complementary aspects to an excavation that must be recorded consistently and in detail as the excavation progresses. These will be essential pieces of information in the final jigsaw puzzle that will be your archaeological analysis. The core aspects to record throughout any excavation are:

- The soil or deposits (for each context or level)
- Any features encountered
- The process of excavation itself

DESCRIBING DEPOSITS

The four main elements to record when describing soils are:

- Color
- Texture
- Consistency
- Coarse components or composition

It is important that you standardize such descriptive information as much as possible, so that other people reading your report will know precisely what you mean. If you let everyone describe a variable such as color in their own way, for example, you will end up with as many descriptions as there were workers. In reality, none of these attributes can be assessed in the field with any kind of scientific accuracy, and the standards employed by soil scientists and archaeologists vary considerably. Your goal should be to try to record as much descriptive information in as standard a fashion as possible.

Color should be recorded using a **Munsell Soil Color Chart**, which provides an internationally recognized standard against which to assess **soil color** and makes the process far more objective than would otherwise be possible.

The basic divisions of soil **texture** are sand, silt, and clay, defined in terms of the size of their mineral particles (sand = 0.06–2 mm; silt = 0.002–0.06 mm; clay = less than 0.022 mm). For on-site purposes, however, use a more general measure that can be estimated by hand-texturing, such as whether or not the soil will hold its shape when damp. The overall rule of thumb is that clay coheres, silt adheres, and sand does neither. Thus, clay will be sticky and plastic, silt will have particles that are invisible to the naked eye, and sand will have a visible gritty feel when moistened (Roskams 2001, 178). A general test that you can apply to all types of soil is to roll it into a ball and test its malleability (figure 5.5). If the soil can be rolled into a sausage shape that still holds its shape when bent into a ring, then it is largely clay; if it breaks when bent into a ring it is largely silt. Sand, of course, cannot be rolled into any shape.

Consistency measures the degree of compaction of the soil and whether or not it holds together. Variations in compaction across a deposit can be important, because different activities on the site will have affected the consistency of the soil in different ways. To assess consistency, take a slightly moist cube of soil and try to crush it between your thumb and forefinger:

- If it cannot be molded into a cube at all, it is a **loose** soil.
- If it crushes easily (if there is no resistance), it is a **weak** soil.
- If low pressure is required to crush it, it is a **friable** soil.
- If greater pressure is required to crush it, it is a **firm** soil.

FIGURE 5.5: Sediment composition flowchart (after Museum of London 1990)

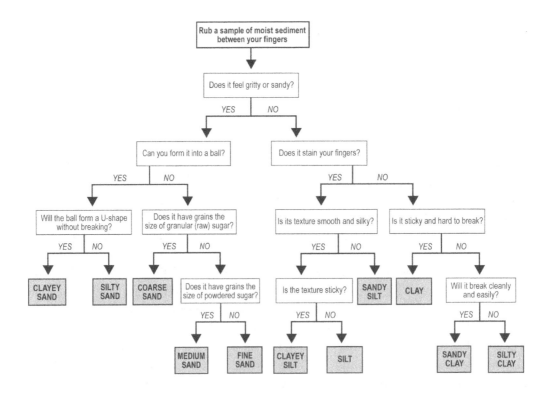

TABLE 5.2: A guide to estimating the size of visible particles

Description	Particle size
Clay/silt	Not visible to the naked eye
Fine sand	0.02 mm–0.06 mm
Medium sand	0.06 mm–0.20 mm
Coarse sand	0.20 mm–2.00 mm
Fine pebbles	2 mm–6 mm
Medium pebbles	6 mm–20 mm
Coarse pebbles	20 mm–60 mm
Cobbles	60 mm–100 mm

- If it cannot be crushed at all, it is a **compact**, or **hard**, soil.
- If it is bound together with a substance other than clay, it is a **cemented** soil (Roskams 2001, 180).

The assessment of the **coarse component** is an estimate of the size of visible particles within the soil and of the proportion of different grain sizes in the deposit. When assessing the size of the visible particles, use the general guide in table 5.2 (Museum of London 1990).

When assessing the proportion of different grain sizes (composition), you can estimate the percentage of inclusions and their approximate grade size using the chart in figure 5.6.

If possible, you should also estimate the degree of sorting that is visible in the deposit (figure 5.7). This is an assessment of the frequency with which particles of the same size

FIGURE 5.6: Estimating the percentage of inclusions (after Museum of London 1990)

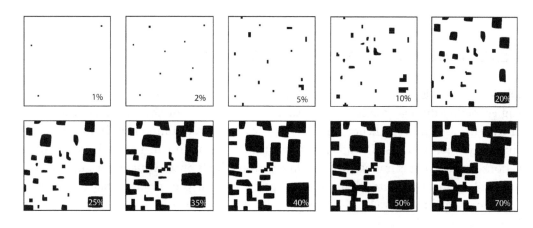

FIGURE 5.7: Estimating the degree of sorting (after Museum of London 1990)

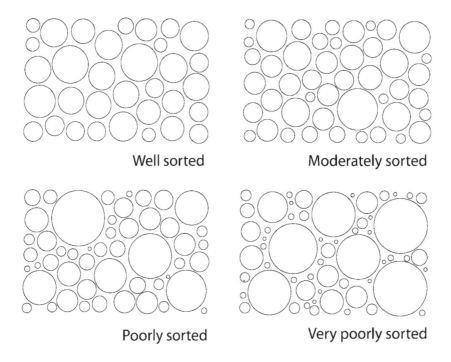

occur and will give you some idea of how the deposit was laid down. A deposit in which all of the particles are of very similar size, for example, indicates that it has been well sorted prior to deposition (by water or wind, for instance).

DESCRIBING CULTURAL FEATURES

Obviously you also have to record any cultural evidence (i.e., the artifacts and features) you encounter during excavation. For example, the presence or absence of stone artifacts or charcoal within a rockshelter deposit is clearly an essential component. In historical archaeology when you describe other features in the excavation (such as walls, timbers, or various materials), it is important to outline their methods of construction using standard terminology so that others will understand precisely what you mean. Detailed standards for describing timber, brick, and other remains are contained in "Describing Structural Components" in chapter 6.

DESCRIBING THE EXCAVATION PROCESS

An excavation is described essentially by the information you record in your field notes, detailing the day-to-day running of the dig and any problems or successes (see "Keeping a Field Journal" in chapter 3). Your details of the sequence of events for the day and the decision-making process can be invaluable for sorting out problems in later analysis, or for clearing up any unwitting mistakes made on recording forms or artifact bags. A general rule is that there can never be enough detail. The first time you learn the importance of notes is when you have the task of doing the analysis of an excavation using notes someone else has made!

RECORDING SECTIONS

One of other main ways in which archaeologists record stratigraphic information from a site is by drawing and photographing the vertical walls of their excavation units. These walls are called **sections** or **profiles**, and the aim is to represent both the visible soil layers and the discernible archaeological features as informatively as possible. Stratification is what allows the archaeologist to place events at a site into chronological order. Because the principle of superposition (see "The Principles of Excavation") rests on the assumption that the deposits at a site are laid down in sequence over time, it is also the basis for **relative dating**. This is the process of putting things into order from earliest to latest, but without assigning any specific dates to the things themselves. **Absolute dating**, on the other hand, uses a particular technique or process to assign a specific date to something (such as when radiocarbon dating is used to date a piece of bone). Both forms of dating are essential to archaeological research. Without some knowledge of when things happened, it is impossible to properly interpret a site. For this reason it is important that your photographs and section drawings represent the vertical sequence of layers or contexts visible in the wall of the trench as accurately as possible (see "Photographing Excavations" and "Drawing Vertical Surfaces" in chapter 9).

The principle of drawing a section is exactly the same as drawing a site plan: using baselines with offset measurements to plot features (see "Using the Baseline and Offset Technique" in chapter 4 and "Drawing Horizontal Surfaces" in chapter 9). Remember that the scale at which you draw the section will determine how much detail you can include in it. The hardest part of drawing a section is deciding where one layer or context ends and the next begins. Sometimes, lightly wetting the profile with water from a hand sprayer will bring out distinctions in soil color, but another way around this problem is to use different symbols to identify a distinct boundary as opposed to an indistinct or uncertain one.

Balks or No Balks?

Some archaeologists recommend leaving **balks** (i.e., part of the wall between all adjacent squares) as you excavate. Balks can be any width you desire so long as the balk is wide enough to remain stable, which depends almost entirely on the nature of the soils. Balks allow you to see the stratification on all sides of the square and to record the profile, and they may help in developing Harris matrices (described in "Interpreting Stratigraphy"). There are disadvantages. Any artifacts or features remain in the balk unless you excavate the balk after you draw the profile. If the balk is accidentally knocked down, you may lose the provenience on artifacts. Balks work well for stratigraphy but impede your ability to see patterning between squares. Use of balks depends on your research questions and your need for unit or open-area excavation.

You can draw a section either cumulatively (i.e., as each context is excavated) or at the end once all excavation is complete. If you draw your section cumulatively then make sure that you include all the necessary coordinates to allow the individual drawings to be fitted back together later. If you draw your sections at the end, you probably will have to refer back to your excavation notes to know which contexts you are seeing and drawing in the profiles. A certain amount of annotation will be necessary to make your section drawings intelligible to someone else, but try not to reproduce all of the information from the context or excavation recording sheets. For more information on how to draw a section, see "Drawing Vertical Surfaces" in chapter 9.

INTERPRETING STRATIGRAPHY

Current archaeological analysis does not rely solely on drawn sections for interpretation. A Harris matrix is probably the most commonly used means of making sense of archaeological stratigraphy, although there are debated alternatives. Harris matrices work best for the kind of deposits for which they were developed (i.e., complex historical archaeological sites with structures). They are not necessarily very useful for precontact Indigenous sites, as these tend not to have the same kinds of deposits.

A Harris matrix makes it possible to represent a complete three-dimensional stratigraphic sequence for a site in a single two-dimensional diagram. Its great virtue is that it enables all contexts excavated at a site to be shown simultaneously and not just those contexts that appear in the section (recent research has indicated that up to 40% of recorded contexts will not show up in any section [Bibby 1993, 108]). According to Harris, only three stratigraphic events are possible on a site (Harris, Brown, and Brown 1993, 10):

- Deposits (the context or layer, which can be either natural or cultural, horizontal, or vertical [i.e., a structure such as a wall]). This is the result of any event that acted to place evidence at a site, such as layers of debris or the construction of a wall.
- Interfaces between one layer and the next (i.e., the surface of the context).
- Cuts, such as pits, wells, or graves, that are dug through earlier layers and that can be defined as stratigraphic units in their own right. A "cut" is essentially something that has happened on the site to remove evidence, rather than to deposit it. It is therefore a "negative" feature, but it is important to record it in the same way as you would a "positive" feature.

At the time of excavation, a decision must be made as to the nature of each context: is it a cut or a cultural or natural deposit?

There is no room here to include all of the interpretive information that can be encoded into a Harris matrix, or to explore the various alternative schemas that have been developed in response to its perceived flaws. We have included only the basic principles of the Harris matrix as one means of attempting to define relationships between different strata on an archaeological site. A Harris matrix is best produced as excavation progresses, and each context must be added to the matrix at the time of its excavation. This is the **only** time that inconsistencies or unclear relationships between contexts can be sorted out through further excavation or investigation, if necessary. Interpreting stratigraphy is rarely straightforward, and you should never assume that you will be able to remember stratigraphic relationships between units. If you are working on a large site you may only be excavating a small part of the total sequence anyway, so your observations of how contexts relate to each other will be vital to the overall understanding of the site.

The essential basis of the matrix is very simple: a number, always written or drawn inside a consistent rectangular box, is assigned to each context or unit. Horizontal and vertical relationships between contexts are represented by horizontal or vertical lines drawn between boxes to represent the sequence. There are only three possible chronological relationships between any two contexts (see figure 5.8).

The elegance of the Harris matrix is that it reduces all possible forms of stratigraphic connections to one of these three relationships and then uses these relationships to build a complete chronological sequence for the site. You can combine these three stratigraphic relationships in a variety of ways (see figure 5.9).

Constructing a Harris matrix requires the excavator to think logically about the relationships between contexts and ensures that all contexts, regardless of size or supposed im-

FIGURE 5.8: The stratigraphic relationships of a Harris matrix

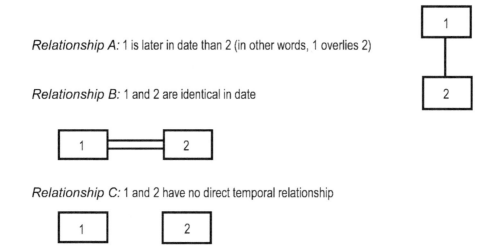

Relationship A: 1 is later in date than 2 (in other words, 1 overlies 2)

Relationship B: 1 and 2 are identical in date

Relationship C: 1 and 2 have no direct temporal relationship

portance, are included in the final analysis (Bibby 1993, 106–107). When establishing matrix sequences:

- First, look for correlations **across** the sequence (i.e., horizontal correlations). This means looking for deposits that are of the same date, or for deposits that may once have been part of a single continuous unit but that have since been cut by later intrusions (relationship B). This last is quite difficult to do, and direct correlations between units must be inferred with care. It is for this reason that Harris matrices can be produced only as excavation progresses, as decisions about where each context fits within the overall sequence will often be based on similarities or dissimilarities between physical characteristics (e.g., color, texture, inclusions), surface level, or the nature or date of re-covered artifacts. The physical characteristics of the units in question probably will be the best guide as to whether or not two units are linked. This is one of the key reasons that it is imperative to record all descriptive information about excavation units using consistent terminology (see "Describing Deposits").
- Second, decide on the associations of successive units (i.e., vertical correlations). This means deciding on the sequence of deposition for the site—what is above or below each context (relationship A)?

Where a stratigraphic sequence exists, it makes sense to interpret it from the earliest elements upward in the same order in which it has developed (Roskams 2001, 247).

FIGURE 5.9: Representing stratigraphic relationships in a Harris matrix (after Brown and Harris 1993)

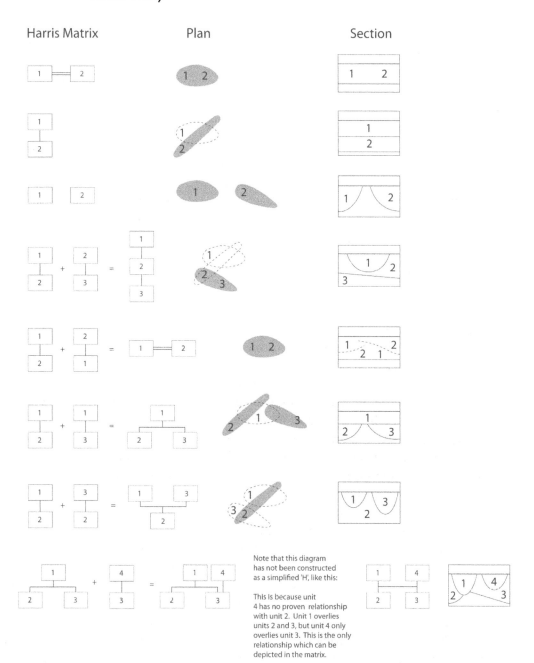

Note that this diagram has not been constructed as a simplified 'H', like this:

This Is because unit 4 has no proven relationship with unit 2. Unit 1 overlies units 2 and 3, but unit 4 only overlies unit 3. This is the only relationship which can be depicted in the matrix.

Constant use by archaeologists has amended the basic Harris matrix in many ways to depict a wide range of complementary information (figure 5.10). By altering the form of the lines between boxes, the shape of the boxes themselves, or their relative positions, a matrix can be made to depict the strengths of linkages between strata, different types of debris resulting from different activities, relative or absolute periods of time, even construction sequences for standing structures (see "Recording Standing Structures" in chapter 6).

USING A TROWEL

You use a trowel both to define the extent of a deposit and to remove it to expose the underlying layers. The nature of the deposit (its texture and consistency) will determine the most appropriate troweling techniques. The main decision you will have to make is whether to use the point of the trowel or the edge of the trowel to remove the soil. This will really depend on the depth of the layer, the compaction of the soil, and how large or fragile the artifacts contained within it are. If the deposit is loose or sandy, for example, then it is probably easier to scrape the soil away with the edge of the trowel; if it is hard and compacted then the only option available to you may be to try to break it up carefully with the point of the trowel. On the other hand, if you are excavating a site containing relatively large and fragile artifacts (such as mollusk shells), then removing the deposit in "chunks" rather than scraping it away and risking slicing through the fragile organics may be your best option.

If you're scraping, always use your trowel with the edge of the blade at a very low angle, almost parallel to the ground, and pull it toward you (figure 5.11). The idea is to remove a very thin layer of earth as you scrape. A higher angle (more slanted), will make the blade of the trowel go deeper, removing a thicker layer. You will probably need to keep your weight over the trowel to do this effectively, which may prevent you from sitting down as you dig. If you adopt this method you will have to work so that you pull the excavated material toward you onto the unexcavated portion in front of you, rather than pushing it away onto the already exposed surface. On some sites with fragile artifacts you may be better off to loosen a small area of soil in a corner of the square closest to you with the trowel first, and then use the vertical face of this pit to open up the remainder of the grid unit. In this case you can use the tip of the trowel both to loosen the dirt and at the same time to turn it over, and you will work away from you. This method, however, can make it more difficult to discern subtle stratigraphic changes in soil color or texture, so use it with caution if you are a novice. For either technique, remember to always keep your dustpan and bucket handy so that you can continually remove the excavated soil from your square as you dig. Once you have filled up your bucket you probably will have to screen the contents. The

FIGURE 5.10: The basic principles of the Harris matrix can be adapted to record a wide variety of complementary information (after Brown and Harris 1993)

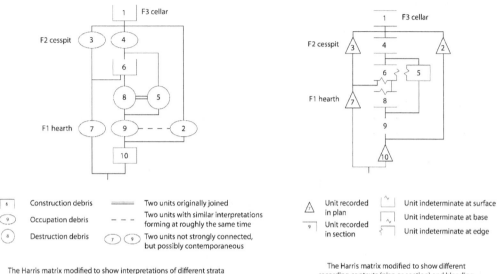

6	Construction debris	══════	Two units originally joined	
9	Occupation debris	– – –	Two units with similar interpretations forming at roughly the same time	
8	Destruction debris	7 9	Two units not strongly connected, but possibly contemporaneous	

The Harris matrix modified to show interpretations of different strata and the strength of relationships between them

⚠	Unit recorded in plan		Unit indeterminate at surface
9	Unit recorded in section		Unit indeterminate at base
			Unit indeterminate at edge

The Harris matrix modified to show different recording contexts (plan or section) and blending apparent at the interfaces of some strata

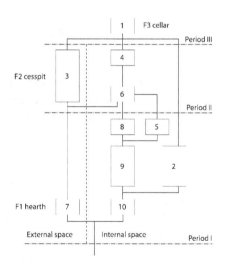

The Harris matrix 'stretched' to show relative time

Liz Kryder-Reid's Tips for Working in Hot Weather

In addition to the essentials of drinking lots of water and wearing sunscreen and a hat, here's some advice from a veteran of hot and humid summer field seasons:

- Put leaves—the broader the better—inside the crown of your hat. They create natural air conditioning!
- Put sulfur powder in your socks to ward off chiggers. Having feet that smell like rotten eggs seems a worse fate until you get that first ring of bites around your ankles (and if you do, try suffocating them out by putting dabs of nail polish over the bites).
- For biting insects, everyone has their favorite spray, but the Lower Mississippi survey swore by Avon Skin So Soft diluted in a spray bottle.
- Setting up awnings can bring the relief of shade, but try to avoid blue and green canvas that distorts the soil color.
- Same goes for sunglasses, which are important eye protection but should be taken off periodically to check for soil features and always when reading a Munsell chart.
- Frozen water bottles that thaw over the day are a welcome treat at lunch, and sports drink mix in the cooler can help ward off electrolyte loss.
- Keep a bee sting kit on-site at all times. Even if no one on the crew is allergic, you never know when a visitor might be.
- Food handling concerns are for real. I've seen field seasons ended early because the crew was wiped out by the effects of poorly refrigerated food. Blue ice only goes so far, and coolers can become their own germ fests. Disinfect them daily, and don't take chances on risky foods.
- If armadillos burrow in your backdirt piles overnight, shoo them out but don't touch them. They're the only animals other than humans that can carry leprosy!
- If all else fails, cave archaeology is always shady and cool!

screens may be located some distance from the actual excavation, so make sure that you do not make the buckets too heavy to carry (see "Screening and Sorting").

Learning how to trowel effectively is a bit of an art. As you first trowel, you tend to dig down too much. After a bit of experience, you can begin to "read" the earth through your trowel. You can feel the granularity or compaction of the earth in your square, which may indicate some kind of feature. You may be able to tell the compaction of soil as well by gently tapping the point of your trowel on the earth. If it makes a ringing sound, the earth is more compacted, again indicating a possible feature.

You also may need to learn to use a variety of small tools to aid excavation when a trowel won't do. Some of the most common tools on archaeological excavations are den-

FIGURE 5.11: Use the edge of the trowel to pull sediment toward you onto the dustpan. Any fragile or delicate artifacts will require careful brushing to avoid damage.

tal picks, the kind used to clean your teeth. Most archaeologists actually get these as discarded tools from dental offices. They have very tiny points and allow work with delicate artifacts or can be used to remove soil around their edges. Dental picks are sharp, so use them with care. Similarly, small knives also may work well. For extremely compacted or rocky soil, when using a trowel or shovel is impractical or impossible, a small pick mattock may be needed to break up the soil. They need to be used with extreme care both for safety reasons and because they can easily break artifacts. Another useful hand tool is pruning shears, especially when there are lots of small roots in your square. Don't try to pull the roots out; you will only damage your excavation by pulling up any soil or artifacts with the roots. Expose, then cut, the roots to remove them.

USING A SHOVEL

Trowels, dental picks, and picks are not the only tools used for excavating. As often as not, you will use a shovel. If you've never used a shovel before, it can actually be more difficult to use than a trowel and a lot more dangerous to the excavation, you, and the people around you. Why is it potentially more dangerous to the excavation? The main reason is that it moves a lot more dirt than a trowel, but you also may get careless and hit your shovel into the wall or knock out a stake. The danger to you comes from improper use. If you use the wrong kind of shovel or don't handle it properly you may injure your back, shoulders, arms, or hands. Most shovels require that you put weight on them to dig into the ground, then lift the material on the shovel out and deposit it elsewhere. To do this most effectively, put one hand on the end of the handle while holding the handle in the other. Lean into the shovel using your legs as much as your arms or back. Then when you lift, use your legs again, not just your back or arms, and don't lift the blade of the shovel any higher than your shoulder. Never hold the shaft or handle of the shovel with both hands around it and no hand on the end because you will have almost no control. As with trowels, shovels work best when they are sharpened, and that leads to other problems. Sharp things cut, and if you are careless when swinging a shovel or don't watch where you put the blade, someone may get seriously injured. To protect your feet always wear good boots when shoveling, and don't use a shovel in a square if fellow excavators aren't wearing proper footwear. If you aren't used to lots of work with your hands, you may also wish to wear gloves when you trowel or shovel. Constant use can give you painful blisters. Thin cotton or leather gloves seem to protect your skin and give you proper control or "feel" while you dig.

As with trowels, shovels come in different sizes and shapes of both handles and blades. Short D-handled spades with a long blade work well for shovel testing to dig small, deep holes but don't work well in an excavation. Long shovels with no handle and round, pointed blades work best in an excavation, especially when the point has been ground down so that the blade's end is almost straight across. Using this kind of shovel, a skilled user can **shovel-skim**, removing as thin a layer as a trowel and much more quickly. Shovel skimming also tends to give the soil a different texture and sometimes allows you to see soil discolorations more easily, which may indicate a feature. A straight-blade spade is terrific for cleaning sidewalls that are not vertical or for creating a smooth, flat surface on a stream bank where you might want to look at stratification. Most projects use several shovel types. As an excavator, you need to find out what types and lengths work best for you. Shoveling takes practice, so don't be embarrassed if your first uses make you look like a "klutz." If you haven't used a shovel before, don't be afraid to ask for instruction.

The University of Iowa Field School "Garf" Rule

If you "garf" someone—that is, cut the person and draw blood—at the next possible opportunity you must buy your victim all he or she can drink of his or her favorite libation in one "session." Garfing someone can be a costly mistake. The point of the rule is to be certain you suffer as much pain as the other person does. Be careful!

Caring for your equipment is important. Keep trowels and shovels sharpened. They don't need to be razor sharp, but you can put a good edge on them with mill bastard (yes, they really are called that!) flat or similar files. In some soils, you may need to do this frequently. With shovels, cleaning the blade daily with a wire brush is best. Keep metal equipment dry, and when storing it for a long time, coat the metal with a thin layer of oil to prevent rust. With long-handled shovels, always lay them blade-down so someone won't step on the blade and cut themselves, trip, or raise the handle quickly and hit someone with it. Trowels, as well as carpenter's string levels, tapes, pens, brushes, dental picks, and other small items, easily can become buried in backdirt and lost. Though they are small, these items are not cheap, and replacement costs quickly add up!

USING A BRUSH

Archaeologists use brushes to clean the soil from delicate or fragile finds and to tidy up the base of each soil layer after it has been excavated and before it is photographed (see "Photographing Excavations" in chapter 9). Small brushes and excavation tools (such as dental picks or plasterer's tools) are best for excavating in small cavities. If you come across a discoloration in the soil or other unusual feature, it may be best to brush this down with a handheld brush until you can determine what it might be, rather than to keep troweling and run the risk of damaging it. Soft hair-bristle brushes (like those used for typical household cleaning) or whisk brooms are best for sweeping up loose dirt.

PAYING ATTENTION!

Whatever tools or techniques you adopt, you must ensure that you always work slowly and carefully, and take careful note of any apparent changes in the texture, color, or nature of the deposit. The goal of all stratigraphic excavation is to define as far as possible the limits of each stratigraphic layer as it is being removed and to remove each separately and in its entirety before beginning work on the next. As the excavator it is your job to ensure that underlying strata are not cut into prematurely, thus destroying any opportunity for you or anyone else to observe vital relationships between layers. *In essence you are removing only the uppermost layer until something different appears.* This is simple to say but not always easy to do. Some differences between different stratigraphic contexts will be very subtle (such as when one area of soil has a different texture or particle size to other areas around it); others will be readily apparent (such as a layer of fill that is a different color from that underneath it). There is no easy answer here, and being able to distinguish between different layers will largely be a matter of experience. Sometimes you literally can "feel" the difference as you dig, when one area is harder or easier to dig than those around it. *As a general rule, whenever you encounter any noticeable change in the soil (color, texture, hardness, inclusions), stop and assess the situation carefully before you proceed.* If you find you've made a mistake (and cut too deeply, for example, or removed a layer that you thought was uppermost but that turned out to underlie another adjacent layer) the best response is to stop and record the situation fully (with drawings and notes) before you proceed. The most important thing to remember when excavating is always to work systematically. The best advice is to go slowly and methodically, and always ask for advice if you are unsure.

You should be aware by now of the necessity for archaeologists to control the excavation process. One of the many ways in which they do this is by trying to dig their excavation units as squarely as possible (i.e., by trying to remove the soil within their units in careful blocks). This is because they wish to know precisely where every artifact and feature come from within the site: obviously if the wall of a trench has been **undercut** (i.e., if it slopes away from the excavator, into the adjoining area) then any artifacts that are recovered from that undercut zone actually come from the next square. One of the main aims of good excavation, therefore, is to keep the sides of your unit vertical and the walls and floor square (unless you are digging according to the context system, in which case the base of each context will be following a stratigraphic layer, which is highly unlikely to be square). If you are excavating many small contexts, you don't need to be too rigid in keeping your walls absolutely vertical; they can be trimmed in a single operation before photographing the unit at the end of each context. Remember to keep the soil from the trimmings and any artifacts the trimmings contain separate from the other contexts. You have no way of knowing whether that soil and those artifacts come from the top of the trench, the middle, or the base—all you know is that it came from the trench wall.

An inevitable problem presents itself when an artifact appears in an upper level but crosses into one or more levels below it. This is more of a problem when using arbitrary levels, but it also can occur due to rodent activity or later human disturbance. In this case, the artifact should not be removed until you are certain you have reached its bottom. Do not dig down around the artifact into the next level! Wait to dig around it when you are removing the soil of the next level. You can create an earthen pedestal for the object as needed.

Chris Glidden's Cautions about Excavation Personalities

First-time archaeological workers have all sorts of misconceptions when going out on their first field experience, from dreams of cozy campfire talks to delusions of finding the Cross of Coronado. But there are more pitfalls on the site than there are excavation units! The site novice doesn't know what to expect or how to negotiate successfully through this "mind field." Some of the best people on the planet are archaeologists, but this little guide has been prepared in order to help the inexperienced excavator know what personality types to avoid:

- *The Don Juan and the Lovely Lolita*—Sexual liaisons are not uncommon in the field. Although most site romances don't last, it is best to avoid them, especially the physical relationships between site workers and "the locals." They are fraught with problems, the kind that could get you and the entire cadre of archaeologists thrown off the island. Remember that some will fall in love, some will fall in love more than once, and some who say they are in love will still be going home to their spouses.
- *The Suck-Up*—They sit at the right hand of the throne and are the first ones to agree with every edict coming out of the director's mouth. Suck-ups will report any infractions of the rules, will make them seem larger than they are, and will report you for peeing in the poop house or pooping in the pee palace. Don't get caught in the vacuum they create.
- *The Know-It-All*—These people have been everywhere, have seen it all, and have done everything. From digging for alien remains on the moon to gunning down insurgencies from their excavation unit, they will always "best" whatever story is being told by others. You can roll your eyes in disbelief, but don't confront them with their absurdities. Eventually they will hang themselves; just give them the rope.
- *The Nonbather*—Most sites will produce one or more people who declare on the third day that they will not be bathing or changing their clothes for the duration of the field experience. Perhaps they are just too lazy to wash and do their own laundry and are not able to smell themselves, but being in an excavation unit with them can tear the eyes up so quickly that you will not be able to see the feature that you are troweling through. One individual who tried this was thrown into the river by the second week, had his clothes set on fire while he slept, and after a month was eventually shipped home with body lice and scabies. Those little critters are hard to get rid of after a month of no bathing, so stay clear and "upwind" of the nonbather.
- *The Malcontent*—Someone is always unhappy, but if the same ones are unhappy every day, stay clear of them. These people are just generally miserable in their lives and

(continues)

Chris Glidden's Cautions about Excavation Personalities (*continued*)

bring their personal rain clouds wherever they go. If you associate too closely with them, they will succeed in changing your own perception. Don't let them metastasize into your being or into the group's body. If they get "surgically" removed, you do not want to be the adjoining tissue that is also cut out.

- *The Drinker*—Don't be alarmed at the amount of drinking that goes on in the evenings. Although most are not alcoholics, being away from home and out in the field seems to lend itself easily to drinking away most nights. The younger, inexperienced ones will fall into trees, water, excavation units, or whatever maladies are found on-site. The older ones just tell their stories and fall asleep early. If you cannot make it through a field experience without the aid of alcohol, perhaps you should rethink your choice of occupations. And if you find yourself situated in the same excavation unit with one of them the next morning, have some fun with the person. Talk loud and laugh often, bringing up all the times you got sick after eating certain foods like chili, burritos, or sauerkraut.

- *The Stoner*—Easily recognized after a week or so, they are the ones who are consistently going off alone and coming back a little later happier than when they left. Although more amusing than problematic, if caught, they will be gone quickly. You don't want to get caught in their smoke and kicked out too.

- *The Scapegoat*—Almost every project has a scapegoat, someone everyone else blames for anything that goes wrong. Any of the types already described easily can become the scapegoat. Don't become one!

- *Anyone carrying a notebook with a "NO WHINING" sticker on it*—These individuals are usually the directors or principal investigators of the site or their immediate staff. They have dirt to dig, artifacts to draw, and a thesis to prove. They are not concerned with your feelings or problems. If they display the sticker, they don't want to teach or mentor; they are only interested in the work you can help them accomplish. Stay low and inconspicuous, biding your time until the field experience is over. You cannot win in this situation; you can only endure until it is over and vow that when you are in a position of power on a site, you will be more tolerant to those who are having trouble adjusting—no matter how many times you hear the same inane complaints of food, sanitary conditions, and personality conflicts.

The 10 most common complaints heard on an archaeological work site:

1 Extreme drinking every night
2 People pairing off into couples
3 Bad food

4 Bugs

5 Personality conflicts

6 Unsanitary bathroom facilities

7 Too much or too little rain

8 Too much heat in the working hours

9 Too much cold in the nighttime hours

10 Despotic directors

If you can't deal with anything just listed, you probably shouldn't be an archaeologist, but just in case you wondered, out of your bed, archaeology is just about the best thing you can ever do!

In the end the degree of accuracy that is necessary in your excavation technique will depend on the research questions that are being asked: if your research absolutely depends on knowing exact stratigraphic divisions between layers (such as if you are investigating activity areas or precise changes in use over time), then you will have to proceed with great care; if you are interested only in broad divisions of use or chronology, then a less precise excavation strategy may be adopted, sometimes even extending to excavation of the site using arbitrary layers (see "The Principles of Excavation").

The best way to ensure that the sides of your trench are kept vertical is to stand or kneel directly above them and trim from the top down. It is easy to undercut the walls if you try to trim them with the wall in front of you because you can't see whether you truly are cutting vertically.

Excavation Etiquette

- Never undercut a trench wall, even if you can see an interesting artifact in the wall of the square.
- Never pull an artifact, stone, or other feature out of the wall of the square.
- Never pull an object out of the ground. Excavate around it until you have reached its base and then remove it in one piece after it is fully recorded.
- If an object or unusual feature is uncovered, a good rule is to leave it in place (*in situ*) until the area is completely excavated and the object can be removed carefully in its proper stratigraphic context.
- Don't walk on newly excavated areas (particularly someone else's!) unless it is absolutely unavoidable (e.g., if you need to clean up that area prior to photographing or drawing it).
- When working in a rockshelter avoid wearing boots with big tread, as the tread can disturb small artifacts and the fine silty deposits often built up in these places. Tennis shoes or some other sturdy footwear with fine tread is best. In other words, wear the appropriate shoes given site conditions, excavation techniques, and safety considerations.
- When you are excavating, always move backward across the unit to avoid kneeling on the freshly excavated surface.
- If weeds or roots are present, cut them with pruning shears, don't pull them.
- Don't trip over the string or the stakes or disturb them in any way during excavation.
- Never step too close to the edge of a trench as you may run the risk of collapsing the wall and becoming the most unpopular person on the dig. If you are excavating in a deep unit, get someone to help you in and out or use an appropriate ladder so that neither of you puts your full weight on the edge of the excavation.
- Never sit on the edge of a trench (for the same reason).
- Be willing to take your turn at a variety of tasks. Excavation requires screening, sorting, cleaning, and backfilling as well as actual digging, and no one wants to be restricted to one task all the time.
- Bear in mind that tempers get frazzled, particularly on long or arduous digs and in bad weather, and you may have to maintain goodwill even in the face of seemingly overwhelming obstacles. It does not help anyone if you sulk, and a temper tantrum can destroy everyone's morale for the whole day.
- Different people have different physical tolerances and may work at different paces, so be patient if someone works more slowly than you do or needs more guidance than you do.

- If you are a unit or site supervisor, be supportive in the way you provide advice to people who are learning to excavate. Try to remember that people aren't born with excavation skills and that some people will need more specific instructions than others.
- If you're supervising other workers make sure that you brief them as fully as possible before the dig begins. Make clear what your aims are and what you want to know. This will help them to understand the importance of following particular procedures and guide them in terms of what to look for. Update these briefings regularly so that no one feels lost.
- If you're camping with other workers during the dig, remember to be tolerant of others, particularly after a hard day's work. Don't hog the shower, and do your fair share of the household tasks (such as cooking or cleaning). Believe it or not, the main sources of irritation on archaeological fieldwork are who gets priority over the showers and who should be doing the cooking!
- Most important, fieldwork is a job, not a holiday, so make sure you are always on time and promptly back at work after breaks.

SCREENING AND SORTING

Most artifacts from sites are not recovered during the process of digging but in the subsequent process of **screening** (also called sifting or sieving) the excavated soil. In the interests of stratigraphic control, it is important to screen each excavated soil layer separately and to keep all artifacts and samples from each layer distinct through careful labeling and bagging. Never allow your bucket of excavated soil to become mixed with buckets from another grid unit or another layer—and never allow the artifacts you recover from your bucket to become mixed with others unless they all come from the same context and will be bagged together anyway.

Most screening is done by hand (i.e., by emptying your bucket into a handheld screen, shaking it to remove the loose soil, and then sorting through the material trapped in the screen for artifacts). This is one of the most time-consuming jobs on-site and is usually where a backlog will build up if there are not enough screens. For this reason make sure that you have enough screens (and enough people to use them!) to keep the process moving. On some large sites it may be possible to use mechanical screens to speed the screening process, although you will still need the same amount of time to sort through the screened material for artifacts. For the vast majority of sites, ¼-inch mesh hardware cloth will do for screening. Only the smallest flakes and bones will get through; however, you can make or buy screens that have a variety of mesh sizes. If you are looking for extremely

Val Attenbrow's Tips for Excavating Shell Middens

Identify Stratification and Excavate Accordingly

Shell middens vary widely in size, composition, and complexity. They range from deposits that are homogeneous throughout, to deposits that are finely stratified and that may contain, for example, hearths, lenses of specific shell species, and/or tool manufacturing events, as well as animal bones and stone artifacts. Excavation should proceed in a manner that ensures any stratification is identified so that excavation units can reflect stratigraphic boundaries.

Where a midden appears to be homogeneous, excavators still need to take account of how the deposits may have accumulated (i.e., whether there is a slope in the particular areas being excavated). If the surface of the midden (or an exposed face) suggests materials accumulated on a sloping surface, then the orientation of excavation units should not be horizontal but on a slope that approximates the way the deposits accumulated. This will prevent excavation units from crosscutting any "layers," even if they are not visible during excavation.

Choose the Most Appropriate Screen Mesh Size

If the midden is composed mostly of whole shells, then a 5 mm mesh may be sufficient, unless numerous small (<5 mm) species are also present. Where stone artifacts are present and fish bones are abundant, then nested 5 mm and 2 mm are recommended, although the shell analysis to identify species composition may be based on materials retained in only the 5 mm screen. In deposits where fish bone is present but sparse, the addition of a screen with 1 mm mesh may be necessary to recover the bones. Depending on the species, the addition of a 1 mm sieve where fish bones are abundant may enable more bone to be recovered (i.e., more fragments, greater weight), but it may not enable a greater number of species to be identified.

Look for Shell Tools and Manufacturing Debris

It is often the case that only samples of the shell component of middens are analyzed to determine the species composition; sometimes "excess" shell is discarded in the field. In such situations these deposits should be inspected prior to discard for any shells that may have been used as tools or for shell that is the debris from the manufacture of shell tools. Both bivalves and gastropods were used as scrapers and cutting implements, for example, in processing plant foods, as well as adzes to make wooden artifacts.

Make a Reference Collection

Make a collection of whole shells of all visible species, large and small, from the shoreline adjacent to the excavated midden. This can be used as a reference collection to aid in the identification of midden species. Collect several specimens of each species, particularly gastropods, so that some can be broken up to examine the internal surfaces and shape of the column. If an analysis of meat weights and so on is to be carried out, collect live specimens. Bivalves and gastropods will stay alive for some weeks, or put them in preservative to keep them longer.

small flakes, you can use small hand screens (2 mm, 3 mm, 4 mm, or 10 mm are all standard) that can be "nested" together (i.e., with one fitted over another) so that you can screens through two mesh sizes simultaneously. When using nested screens, always remember that the larger mesh size fits over the smaller one. The decision of which mesh sizes to use will depend on the nature of your site and what questions you want answered. A small mesh size will obviously make a big difference in excavating a shell midden that may contain many small and delicate fish bones but may be redundant on a historical site containing relatively large fragments of glass and ceramics. (See figure 5.12.)

FIGURE 5.12: Most screening on archaeological sites is done by shaker screens, but some is done by hand using screens with different mesh sizes

On sites with clay soils, wet screening may be the only way to retrieve artifacts. Immersing hand screens containing excavated material into large containers of water sometimes can be effective, although at some sites a pressurized stream of water may be necessary to break down the clay and reveal artifacts. Wet screening is a much more labor-intensive process than dry screening and can damage artifacts, particularly if you have to push the clay through the mesh to break it down. All artifacts removed during wet screening will have to be allowed to dry before they are bagged.

As with shoveling and troweling, learning how to use a screen properly requires some practice. Screens come in a variety of forms, from small handheld ones to larger rectangular screens suspended from a tripod used by two or more people. The most common form is a **shaker screen** that can be operated by one person who can screen through a relatively large amount of material quickly. The screen's box is rectangular with handles at one end and is held up with two legs near the middle of the box. The legs are bolted to the box so that the box can be moved back and forth with the handles (i.e., "shaken"). You need to learn how much soil you can put in the screen and still be able to shake it. Using shaker screens can be hard on shoulders, arms, and back, so learn your limits. Try to put your whole body into it, not just your arms. You may want to use gloves if you have to push soil through the screen because the mesh can abrade your skin. Your supervisor may allow you to use the flat bottom of a trowel to push soil through, especially clods that refuse to break or clay that balls up as it moves back and forth. Whether by hand or by trowel, pushing too hard may crush small objects such as pot sherds or bones.

Another major question in relation to screening is where to do it. This may sound trivial, but because all of the soil (often called **spoil**, or **backdirt**) that goes through the screens will ultimately have to be put back into the trenches, you should consider very carefully where to place it. Screen piles can become very large, very rapidly and have a habit of spreading widely at the base, particularly if people continually walk on them. When deciding where to place your spoil heaps:

- Use flat ground not too far from the excavations (think how far you can expect people regularly to carry heavy buckets full of soil). Making sure that the spoil piles are as near as possible also will help you when you have to backfill.
- Think about whether or not you will have to clear the ground surface of vegetation first to ensure that you don't lose any soil.
- Think carefully about where you are likely to excavate, particularly in terms of allowing yourself the option of extending excavation units. In other words, don't place your spoil heaps where you may later want to dig a unit. Moving the backdirt pile is no fun!
- Remember that sometimes, no matter what your decision, the place you choose for screening will be wrong.

Once you have removed all the artifacts from the screen they will have to be bagged and labeled to keep track of them. The precise system for tracking and labeling artifacts will depend on the preferences of the excavator or site supervisor, but as a general principle all artifacts will be grouped together by context/stratigraphic unit and placed in clearly labeled finds trays or bags. Any special finds that require immediate **conservation** should be bagged and labeled separately and treated immediately (see "Conserving Finds On-Site" and "Labeling Finds and Samples"). For detailed information on recommended conservation treatments for excavated materials see the Museum of London (1990) and Watkinson and Neal (1998).

Sometimes artifacts will be sorted into different classes on-site (e.g., glass, ceramics, bone, or metal) before being bagged, but the complexity of this process will depend on the size of the site and the preferences of the excavator. If you can, do as much as possible of the basic processing (cleaning, washing, gross sorting) on-site. Remember that for every day you spend in the field, whether surveying or excavating, you should ideally allow three days or longer in the lab or office to process or write up the results.

Mike Morwood's Tips for Protecting Rock Art When Excavating

[Note: Screening is called "sieving" in many countries, including Australia and Indonesia, where Mike Morwood does much of his work.]

Because dust is highly abrasive, it can be extremely damaging to painted rock art panels, particularly in the confined space of a rockshelter. To reduce dust during the excavation process:

- Place a screen or curtain (calico is suitable) between the excavation area and the art surface and leave a gap of at least 30 cm between the screen and the rock art surface to allow the air to circulate.
- "Carpet" the ground surface of the shelter or place wooden planks parallel to the edges of the excavation area to reduce dust stirred by traffic.
- Because sieving is the greatest generator of dust, place the sieves on plastic sheeting and contain the spoil heaps on this sheeting.
- Sieve downwind of the rock shelter, erect a screen between the sieving area and the general excavation area, and place calico "skirts" around the base of the sieves.
- During backfilling, place the spoil into Hessian [burlap] or plastic bags and stack the bags in the trenches [units]. Complete the backfilling by placing a layer of dirt over the bags.

From Morwood 1994, 10–12

Anita Smith's Tips for a Successful Excavation

- Carry your own little kit of the following essentials (and have your name on them!): tweezers, pencil, soft brush, photo scale, magnifying glass, compass, line level, clinometer, small flashlight, notepad—it all fits into a fanny pack.
- Sitting on the screens may not seem glamorous, but it's where you learn heaps from the more experienced people around you.
- If you are unsure—ask, ask, ask, and keep asking! There's nothing worse than realizing you've discarded the only fragment of nonlocal stone in the entire site because you didn't think it was important (which I nearly did).
- Fieldwork is part of the process, not simply a means to an end. It offers insights into the archaeological material that can never be known from lab analysis alone.
- Notes, notes, and more notes—everyone is diligent on the first day but after that they tend to taper off. Keep writing them regardless of the conditions; they are invaluable when you come to analyze material months or even years later.

Always clean artifacts gently. Ceramics, glass, and stone artifacts can be cleaned with a soft toothbrush and water (Drewett 1999, 145). Other materials, such as rusted metal, some pottery, bone, or shell are often highly friable and shouldn't be washed unless it's obvious they won't be damaged. Most metals are not stable and when exposed to air will deteriorate rapidly. You should use only a dry brush to clean these kinds of fragile materials. Bear in mind if you are excavating stone artifacts that washing will remove any potential residues from the surface of the artifact (See "Recovering Artifacts with Residues and Use Wear" in chapter 7) and may remove charred food residue on the inside of pots that can be used to assess what was being cooked. When cleaning, make sure that you keep the overall dig recording system intact. In other words, clean each bag of artifacts separately, and make sure that every artifact goes back into the labeled bag from which it came. Never separate the contents of any bag from its label or context identifier. If you wash artifacts, you may wish to make separate labels that duplicate bag information and place them with the materials as you lay them out to dry. This way you won't dampen or ruin the bag by getting it wet.

CONSERVING FINDS ON-SITE

You don't have to be specially trained as a conservator in order to follow some basic principles for caring for excavated finds. A general rule of thumb is that organic materials should be stored in an environment similar to the one in which they were found. For example, finds from a damp environment are best kept damp, those from a water-logged environment are best kept wet, and those from a desiccated environment are best kept dry. Even ordinary soils will hold some moisture content, however, which means that artifacts may have to be dried out before they can be bagged. For this reason avoid placing metal or fragile organic materials directly into sealed plastic bags because the moisture cannot escape and the resulting "sweat" may cause the finds to deteriorate. Instead, store them in hard polythene boxes with silica gel to keep the interior of the box dry (Drewett 1999, 146) or in perforated polythene bags to allow moisture to escape. Alternatively you can thoroughly air-dry objects before storage. If you are dealing with a compound object (one that is made up of more than one type of material, such as a shoe or a hafted tool) then do not separate the components. If you are trying to re-assemble broken artifacts (such as ceramic vessels), make sure that any chemical compounds used to hold the pieces together will not damage the artifacts and that the process is reversible. Basically, common sense will always be the best on-site guide—if an artifact is fragile or friable, don't wash it; handle and store it carefully. Seek professional curatorial advice before doing anything further and before doing anything you are unsure of (see "Managing Archaeological Collections").

LABELING FINDS AND SAMPLES

This may seem trivial, but the labels that you attach to artifacts or samples need to be durable and legible for a very long time: archaeological artifacts are of little value if there is no record of their origin. The most durable labels are made from plastic and aluminum. Because they deteriorate easily, paper and card labels are not usually recommended. When you write on these labels you should use permanent markers so that the writing is as durable as the labels themselves. You also can use basic black ballpoint pens, because, although their ink is less permanent, writing with the pen will make an indelible impression in the surface of the label that still can be read even if the ink has faded. When labeling a find or a sample, be sure to include on the label:

- The name of the site or the site number
- The excavation unit from which the object came
- The context, layer, or level from which the object came
- The date
- A basic description of the contents (e.g., glass, metal, soil sample)

Jane Balme's Tips for Excavating Bone

- Observing small differences in the appearance of bones during excavation can pay enormous dividends in the quality of information gathered during excavation. The presence of clusters and alignments of bones can tell you about postdepositional processes. Articulated bones indicate a lack of disturbance and hence provide information about the spatial distribution of activities.
- Observations aren't worth having unless you communicate them to other members of the team and write them down!
- A sample of animal bones is useless without labels containing information about their source. This includes their location within the site (excavation unit and level) as well as the mesh size of the screen from which they were taken. The best way to make sure that you don't forget some information is to be consistent in your labeling. Write down the information in the same order each time.
- Label the sample immediately, and never leave any samples lying around unlabeled.
- Condensation in plastic bags will cause paper labels to disintegrate. You can reduce condensation by putting a few pinpricks in the bag, but you will need other labels too. Permanent marker on the outside of the plastic bag is good, but because this can scratch off, make sure that you pack the bags in boxes to reduce this problem.
- Patience is definitely a virtue when dealing with archaeological bones. You will need patience to pick each bone individually from the samples and lots more when you do the identifications in the laboratory.

COLLECTING SAMPLES IN THE FIELD

Archaeologists often collect samples of materials found during excavation for analysis in the laboratory. This may include samples of charcoal, wood, or bone to use for radiocarbon dating; soil for extracting pollen or seed samples; or even small flakes of ocher from rock art for dating or determining the source of the ocher. It is not enough that you just collect anything that you like in any way that you like. The best samples are those that are found *in situ*, are properly described and recorded, and can be linked to archaeologically meaningful features (such as living floors, hearths, specific occupational periods, and so on) (Hester, Shafer, and Feder 1997, 323). When collecting samples you must follow certain procedures to ensure that your samples don't become useless for later analysis. In particular you must be aware of:

- The proper methods for collecting different kinds of samples to avoid contamination. You may need a specialist to do it correctly.
- The different quantities of each kind of material that will be sufficient for proper analysis.

Collecting to Avoid Contamination

The major kinds of samples collected by archaeologists are:

- Soils with a high proportion of silica, such as sands, or other suitable minerals, such as quartz, feldspar, or zircon, for **thermoluminescence (TL) dating**
- Artifacts, provided they have been kept from sunlight, for TL dating
- Charcoal, for **radiocarbon dating**
- Soils, for botanical analysis

Any organic material can be dated with radiocarbon techniques, including those found in table 5.3. When collecting samples to use for radiocarbon dating, take particular care with the handling and packaging of samples to avoid contamination. Because any form of modern carbon will contaminate an archaeological sample, don't use paper or cloth bags to hold samples, and don't use cotton wool or tissues as packing materials for samples (Gillespie 1986, 5). Certainly don't let anyone smoke near the site. The best storage containers are strong polythene bags, aluminum foil, and small glass vials. While you are still in the field, pick out all obvious foreign matter from your samples (stones, plant roots and leaves, loose soil or sand), and make sure that you have an adequate quantity for analysis (see table 5.4).

TABLE 5.3: Some of the range of organic materials that can be radiocarbon dated

Textile	Charcoal	Wood
Shell—marine, river, estuarine	Sediments/soils/peats	Ice cores
Plant material (e.g., seeds)	Bone	Antler
Leather	Coprolites (fossilized feces)	Paper
Pollen	Hair	Fish remains
Parchment	Coral	Insect remains
Avian eggshell	Horn	

Tips for Collecting Soil Samples for Thermoluminescence Dating

Samples that will be submitted for thermoluminescence dating need to be kept away from sunlight. Thermoluminescence is used to date sediments that have been long buried and will give you a date for when the mineral grains within the sediment were last exposed to sunlight.

- You can collect a sample by inserting plastic piping within the wall of the excavation, but you will need to ensure the sample is not contaminated by grains that fall as the piping is inserted.
- Only do this out of direct sunlight (i.e., collect the sample at night, or shade the collection area).
- Place your sample directly into an opaque or semi-opaque water-tight container, and put the container immediately into a black plastic bag or other light-tight storage.
- Make absolutely certain that your TL samples are not exposed to any sunlight at all once they have been collected, and keep their exposure to fluorescent light to a minimum (less than 10 minutes).
- If you must examine the sample use a torch or a bulb light.
- You should aim to collect two samples from each level, making sure they are not situated close together and that each is approximately 0.5 kg in weight. This would be roughly equivalent to a lump 10 cm across.
- It is best to collect samples for TL dating as far as possible away from the bedrock, as small grains of bedrock can work their way through the soil profile over time. This is especially important for friable soils, such as areas with sandstone outcrops.
- Make sure you collect only TL samples that are deeper than 20 cm below the ground surface. If they are any closer to the surface they are likely to be inaccurate.
- The laboratory that dates your TL samples will also need to know the moisture content of the surrounding soil. You will need to provide them with details of burial conditions, location of the samples, a description of the surrounding deposits, and a rough estimate of how the average water content of the soil relates to the probable content of the samples supplied.
- If there is any information about seasonal or long-term variations in rainfall, or evidence that the water table might have been anywhere near the context of your samples, the lab will want to know that too.

[Many of these tips come from Byrne 1997.]

TABLE 5.4: Suggested sample quantities

Material	Minimum weight (g) for standard dating	Optimum weight (g) for standard dating	Roughly equivalent to	Equivalent quantity for AMS dating
Charcoal (clean)	2–5	20–30	A handful	5 mg (min); 50 mg (recommended)
Charcoal (dirty)	3–5	20–50	Two handfuls	
Charcoal that is gray-brown, either hard (mineralized) or soft and smeary (leached), with no defined woodstructure	5–10	50–100	½ bag*–four handfuls or more	
Charcoal that is finely spread throughout the deposit (but that "smears" on excavation, rather than being seen as definite lumps)	1,000	5 full bags*		
Wood	5–7	30–100	A piece approx. 30 cm long × 2 cm wide × 2 cm thick	5 mg (min); 100 mg (recommended)

(continues)

TABLE 5.4: (*continued*)

Material	Minimum weight (g) for standard dating	Optimum weight (g) for standard dating	Roughly equivalent to	Equivalent quantity for AMS dating
Cloth or paper	3–5	30–100	A 30 cm × 30 cm piece	15 mg (min); 100 mg (recommended)
Shell	5–40	100–200	Varies with the type of shell	
Bone	20–100	100–200		1 mg (min); 30 mg (recommended)
Charred bone	200–500	1,500–3,000		
Collagen	100–300	800–3,000		
Organic sediment (soil)	500	1,500–2,000	2 medium-sized bags*	10 mg (recommended)
Seeds	7–10	100		
Grass/leaves	5	35–50		
Flesh, skin, or hair	5	45		
Peat	15	100	¼–½ bag*	
Dung	7	30		

*Bag = 15 cm × 30 cm plastic bag

Alice Gorman's Tips for Collecting Samples for Radiocarbon Dating

There are two types of radiocarbon (C14) dating: standard radiometric determinations and AMS (accelerator mass spectrometry), which can be used for samples too small for standard dating. AMS costs more than standard dating, however, so contact the lab for the latest prices before you begin. You will need approximately 500 mg for a standard radiocarbon date, but only 5–10 mg for an AMS radiocarbon date. When collecting samples:

- Handle them as little as possible.
- In preference, pick them up using the point of the trowel or a pair of tweezers. You can use gloves but be advised that some forms of disposable gloves contain a dusting of corn flour, which, as an organic powder, may contaminate your samples.
- Wrap each sample in aluminum foil, and clearly label it so that it can be easily distinguished. You can place your sample directly into a plastic bag, but make sure you tell the lab what you've done.
- Remember to exclude all modern carbon from your sample, so *never* include a cardboard or paper label in the bag with your carbon sample.
- If you must use a cardboard or paper label, double-bag the sample (put the sample inside one bag, seal it, then place the sample and the label inside another sealed plastic bag).
- For advice on sample collection and packaging, don't hesitate to contact the laboratory.

Sample treatment:

- Samples should be dry, as bacterial activity in wet samples can affect the final age determination. If you must dry out your sample, use a low-temperature oven that has never been used for radioisotope experiments. Cover the samples lightly with perforated foil and heat at a temperature of at least 40° until dry.
- Record details of any treatment, such as drying, to submit with the sample.

Documentation:

It is important to have full documentation for all samples. Much of this information is routinely recorded for any archaeological procedure; however, some laboratories have specific requirements, so check with them before collection. The kinds of information needed may include:

- Collection: date, sample weight, grid references, latitude and longitude, depth of sample and stratigraphic position, and stratigraphic relationship to other samples

(continues)

Alice Gorman's Tips for Collecting Samples for Radiocarbon Dating (*continued*)

submitted. Was the sample sealed in a recognizable horizon, or sealed in a localized feature such as a grave or pit? How secure is the stratigraphic context? Was the sample wet or dry when collected? Can any more material be collected? Did the sample come from a surface or excavated deposit?

- Treatment and storage: If the sample was wet, how was it dried? Did you use any chemical treatments or preservatives? Was the sample cleaned? Did you do anything else to it?
- Estimated age: This helps the lab to select the appropriate instrument for measurement as well as enabling them to contact you at an early stage if the estimated age seems to be significantly different from the measured age.
- Environment: Geological, archaeological, paleoenvironmental, associated cultural, paleobotanical, or other material; perhaps also site sketches and photographs.
- Taphonomy, or how the sample got to where you found it: The factors that are relevant here are other natural activities that may have affected the carbon content of your sample, such as visible root penetration in the collection area, evidence of leaching or humus penetration in the soil profile, and the like.
- Contamination: Any other carbonaceous material in the horizon, such as calcium carbonate ($CaCO_3$)-bearing rocks in the catchment, or potential sources of noncontemporaneous carbon.
- Nature of the sample: For example, note whether shells are marine or freshwater; note the family/genus/species if known for wood, charcoal, shells, seeds, and so on; note the type of bone (e.g., femur).

Submission:

- Most labs have web pages and submission forms online. If you are sending samples overseas, there may be customs regulations you have to follow.
- Make sure you keep copies of all of your submission forms in case anything is lost or needs to be checked.
- Turnaround times vary from 4–6 weeks to a few months, so check before you send your samples in.
- Some sample types require additional pretreatments to remove contamination, such as dilute acid/alkali treatment for decomposed wood and charcoal or for peat and lake sediments. Check the website and be aware that you may need to include the cost of pretreatments in your budget.

For other organic samples (such as bone or shell):

- When submitting shells, clean off all soil, sand, and debris, and air-dry the samples prior to packaging.
- Cleaning should be done only with a brass, steel, or nylon brush. *Never* use animal-bristle brushes or organic-fiber brushes.
- Make sure your shell sample consists of one species only, and preferably of large, single shells rather than fragments.
- When dating shell samples, make sure that you identify the shell species to the laboratory to avoid inaccurate dates. Shell species in the ocean will absorb less C14 from the atmosphere than lacustrine or riverine species and may return widely different carbon dates.
- Shell samples should also be tested for secondary recrystallization using X-ray diffraction (XRD) so that rogue carbons are not being dated.
- Try to avoid cleaning bone samples.

Samples that will be submitted for botanical analysis need to be protected from contamination by modern pollen that easily can blow into a site. Once the sample has been collected it is impossible to distinguish between contemporary pollen and aged pollen, as they look identical.

All samples must be properly recorded before collection—it is essential that basic information about possible associations, any evidence of disturbance, the method of collection, the handling and storage procedure you followed, the depth and position of the sample within the excavation unit, and the condition of the sample when collected all be noted at the time of collection. For example, if you handle a charcoal sample with your fingers, you will need to inform the laboratory of this, as the oil on your skin can contaminate the sample. You will need to give to the laboratory any details of all the collecting and bagging procedures followed when you submit your samples, as you may not get accurate dates without it.

Appropriate Quantities for Samples

This will vary according to how well preserved the material is and the particular technique that is going to be used to analyze it. The best rule is to collect as much of a sample as possible and to collect more than one sample of material from the same layer so that the results can be cross-checked for discrepancies or anomalies (table 5.4).

Field expedience implies finding a practical means to an end (i.e., you do what it takes to get the job done even if you don't have the precise tools you need or if you don't exactly follow the "rules"). If you left a tool back at camp and it's an hour hike back to get it, you can usually find a substitute. If one technique that you've been taught doesn't work in a particular circumstance, try something else. The idea is to get the job done as efficiently as possible without violating core excavation principles or ethics. In other words, when you are in the field, you sometimes just have to get creative!

MANAGING ARCHAEOLOGICAL COLLECTIONS

What happens once you have collected your artifacts or excavated your site, analyzed your results, and written your report? You are likely to be left with boxes of excavated material, some of which may be highly fragile or fragmentary, and a large paper and photographic archive. At this point you will have to make a decision about what to do with this material. As a professional it is your responsibility to make sure this collection is taken care of in the long term, either by turning it over to a recognized authority (a repository that meets federal standards or a state or local museum) or by repatriation to a tribe or other entity. Before you do anything with a collection, however, you will have to weigh your ethical responsibilities (see "Archaeologists and Their Profession" in chapter 1) and make sure that you are aware of your legal obligations under state legislation (which may require you to turn the collection over to a state repository) or as specified in your CHM contract. You also will have to consult with the relevant authorities and other interested parties. While it would be ideal to turn all excavated collections over to an official repository for permanent care, in reality no museum is likely to want a collection of broken glass, fragments of domestic ceramics, and miscellaneous rusted metal. You need to find out what the repository's collection policy is *before* you begin excavating, because if they agree to accept the collection, they probably will require you to follow particular methods when documenting and storing the archive. Be aware that there is a curation crisis in the United States and in many other places in the world. Your professional obligations don't end in the field; they extend to the laboratory and to the curation facility where artifacts are analyzed and then stored in a way that protects them and makes them accessible for future use.

Richard Robins's Tips on the Proper Care and Management of Excavated Collections

If you intend to collect and store any archaeological material, the management of the collection begins at the inception of your research project. As archaeological excavations or surface collections are essentially destructive activities, it is incumbent on you to ensure that the material is preserved in the best possible way. From a research perspective, these collections serve the important function of providing a check on the work of the original collector. From a site-management perspective, well-made and well-managed collections may reduce the necessity to undertake further collection or excavation on a site. There are three essential elements to proper collection management: organization, conservation, and storage.

Collection Planning (Organization)

As a first step, consult with staff at the repository where your collection will eventually be housed. Most state museums now have strict depositional requirements, and they will be able to tell you the necessary procedures and requirements for the deposition of material. If a museum has a computerized database, use it. It will be a useful tool to coordinate and track the collected material, including the paper archive, and if you use the museum's official registration system from the outset you will avoid unnecessary duplication and minimize handling of the artifacts. One of the golden rules of collection management is always to consult with museum staff and conservators *before* you begin fieldwork. The other is to make sure you obtain some preliminary estimates of the time and costs required to manage and store your collection so that the final figure doesn't come as a nasty shock.

Conservation

Conservation is the most underrated aspect of any archaeological excavation, so you should devise a plan to manage your archive prior to undertaking a collection or excavation. You will need to work out some preliminary costs for conservation, particularly in terms of estimating the time that will be needed to process the material. Prior to collecting any material you should consult with someone with conservation expertise. This person will give you an idea of what you can and can't do. The following are some of the basic rules that should be followed:

- Immediately following excavation, maintain an environment around the artifact as similar to its burial conditions as possible.
- The less done to an object the better, and keep handling to a minimum.

(continues)

Richard Robins's Tips on the Proper Care and Management of Excavated Collections (*continued*)

- Ensure that techniques, particularly those using chemicals, are reversible. It is also helpful to know in advance the kind of laboratory tests you might use and any implications these may have for the way in which you collect or store your samples. The wrong treatment during excavation may make your artifacts or samples useless for analysis.
- Document *everything* done to the artifacts.
- Anticipate field conditions and plan accordingly—prepare a field kit with the correct storage materials.

Storage

Storage is not only an organizational issue but also a conservation one. It is essential to use materials that will not decay or damage artifacts or aspects of them, such as blood residues or starch.

Do *not* use:
- Matchboxes
- Plastic bags with twist ties
- Colored plastic containers
- Plastics with PVC
- Acidic paper or cardboard
- High-acid tissue
- Paper towels
- Newspaper
- Glass containers
- Rubber bands
- Pressure-sensitive tapes

Do use:
- Clear Ziploc plastic bags
- Clear plastic containers
- Acid-free cardboard boxes
- Acid-free tissue paper
- Polythene or polyether foam
- Gore-Tex
- Unbleached muslin
- Bubble pack without PVC
- Silica gel and natural-fiber cloth bags

Martha Joukowsky's Tips for Excellent Excavating

- Don't hurry. Excavation requires a calm and purposeful approach.
- Remember that all excavation proceeds horizontally first and vertically second.
- Be systematic. When a new layer or anything unusual is encountered *stop*. Clean off the remaining soil so that none of the material from one layer will be mixed with the one below it.
- All grid units should be excavated in the same direction.
- Ideally excavation should proceed from the uphill side of the trench to the downhill side, so that newly excavated areas won't be trampled.
- For the same reasons, always clean higher surfaces before lower ones.
- Always keep the trench wall swept clean so that the area being excavated is not contaminated by falling dirt or debris.
- Always clean the top of the trench by moving the dirt back from its edges, so that the dirt doesn't fall into the trench and contaminate other layers.
- Always keep the trench walls vertical by cutting sharp right-angled corners at the bottom and by regularly trimming the walls as you go along to ensure they are kept straight.
- Don't wait until the earth dries out before you trim the walls, as there is greater risk of a cave-in when the earth is dry.
- Keep the wall trimmings separate to the material excavated from the body of the trench.
- Always be on the lookout for soil discolorations around features. This could be an important clue to interpreting those features.
- Make sure you record sterile layers in the same way as other layers.
- Make sure you record all descriptive information as objectively as possible.
- Don't swing tools (such as picks, mattocks, or shovels) higher than your shoulder. Don't cut too deeply with them either, as you may damage buried artifacts.
- Only fill buckets two-thirds full with soil. Soil, particularly if it has a high clay-content, can be very heavy.

From Joukowsky 1980, 172–175

REFERENCES AND FURTHER READING

Balme, J., and W. Beck. 2002. Starch and charcoal: Useful measures of activity areas in archaeological rock shelters. *Journal of Archaeological Science* 29:157–166.

Barber, R. 1994. *Doing historical archaeology: Exercises using documentary, oral and material evidence.* Englewood Cliffs, NJ: Prentice Hall.

Barker, P. 1998. *Techniques of archaeological excavation.* London: Routledge.

Bibby, D. I. 1993. Building stratigraphic sequences in excavations: An example from Konstanz, Germany. In *Practices of archaeological stratigraphy,* ed. E. C. Harris, M. R. Brown, and G. J. Brown, 104–121. New York: Academic Press.

Brown, M. R., and E. C. Harris. 1993. Interfaces in archaeological stratigraphy. In *Practices of archaeological stratigraphy,* E. C. Harris, M. R., Brown, and G. J. Brown, 7–22. London: Academic Press.

Byrne, D., ed. 1997. *Standards manual for archaeological practice in Aboriginal heritage management.* Sydney: NSW NPWS.

Carmichael, D., R. H. Lafferty, III, and B. L. Molyneaux. 2003. *Excavation.* Vol. 3 of *The archaeologist's toolkit.* Walnut Creek, CA: AltaMira Press.

Childs, S. T., ed. 2005. *Our collective responsibility: The ethics and practice of archaeological collections stewardship.* Washington, DC: Society for American Archaeology.

Davies, M., and K. Buckley. 1987. Archaeological procedures manual. Port Arthur Conservation and Development Project. Occasional Paper No. 13, Department of Lands, Parks and Wildlife, Hobart.

Drewett, P. 1999. *Field archaeology: An introduction.* London: UCL Press.

Ewen, C. R. 2003. *Artifacts.* Vol. 4 of *The archaeologist's toolkit.* Walnut Creek, CA: AltaMira Press.

Gillespie, R. 1986. *The radiocarbon users' handbook.* Oxford University Committee for Archaeology, Monograph No. 3, Oxford.

Harris, E. C., M. R. Brown, and G. J. Brown, eds. 1993. *Practices of archaeological stratigraphy.* London: Academic Press.

Hester, T. R., H. J. Shafer, and K. L. Feder. 1997. *Field methods in archaeology.* 7th ed. Mountain View, CA: Mayfield.

Joukowsky, M. 1980. *A complete manual of field archaeology.* Englewood Cliffs, NJ: Prentice Hall.

Lock, G., and B. L. Molyneaux, eds. 2006. *Confronting scale in archaeology: Issues in theory and practice.* New York: Springer.

Morwood, M. 1994. Handy household hints for archaeological excavations at rock art sites. *Rock Art Research* 11:10–12.

Museum of London. 1990. *Archaeological site manual.* 2nd ed. London: Museum of London, Department of Urban Archaeology.

Polach, H., J. Golson, and J. Head. 1983. Radiocarbon dating: A guide for archaeologists on the collection and submission of samples and age reporting practices. In *Australian field archaeology: A guide to techniques,* ed. G. Connah, 145–152. Canberra: AIAS.

Roskams, S. 2001. *Excavation.* Cambridge: Cambridge University Press.

Sobolik, K. D. 2003. *Archaeobiology.* Vol. 5 of *The archaeologist's toolkit.* Walnut Creek, CA: AltaMira Press.

Sullivan, L. P. and S. T. Childs. 2003. *Curating archaeological collections: From the field to the repository.* Vol. 6 of *The archaeologist's toolkit.* Walnut Creek, CA: AltaMira Press.

Watkinson, D., and V. Neal. 1998. *First aid for finds.* London: Rescue/UK Institute for Conservation Archaeology.

For a range of other useful information, see the website accompanying the text.

CHAPTER SIX
RECORDING HISTORICAL SITES

What you will learn from this chapter:

The diversity of historical archaeological sites found in North America
Basic documentary research techniques
The difference between primary and secondary sources
The essential questions to ask when recording standing structures
How to date standing structures from their components
The main classes of historical archaeological artifacts and how to record them
Oral history interviewing techniques

WHAT ARE HISTORICAL SITES?

Historical archaeology studies the colonial past of North America—the places and artifacts that have been left behind by over 500 years of non-Indigenous activity. While most of these sites are limited to within the last 500 years, at least one site is older than this: the site created by the Norse in 11th-century Newfoundland at L'Anse aux Meadows. Although most professional archaeologists don't accept the evidence, many nonarchaeologists believe that there is evidence of the Norse and many others traveling deep into the interior of North America well before Columbus (see Feder 2006; Williams 1991). Intense contact between Europe and North America certainly didn't happen before the Age of Exploration (1500s–1700s), but regular European efforts to settle North America

began in the late 1550s, with continuously occupied settlements starting with Spanish occupation in 1565 at St. Augustine, Florida. "Contact" sites (places where Indigenous and
non-Indigenous activities overlap, such as missions or fur trade posts) are also deemed to
be historical sites because they fall within the colonial time period.

Historical sites thus represent a great diversity of activities, all part of the many ways in
which Europeans and other settler groups have attempted to explore and exploit the North
American continent (figure 6.1). The main categories of historical site often reflect the different kinds of industries that have been established over the last five centuries, such as mining, pastoralism, agriculture, commerce, whaling, or lumbering. These kinds of explicitly
work-related categories, however, tend to exclude the historical contributions of those other
than adult males and ignore common site types such as houses, schools, hospitals, or cemeteries. In reality there are as many different types of historical site as there are different types
of human behavior in the past, and in a sense there is little point in trying to separate them
according to function. One distinction we have drawn in this chapter is between **standing
structures** (i.e., any built feature that exists substantially above the ground) and sites that
have been reduced to surface or subsurface traces only. This reflects the slightly different
recording methods necessary for each, rather than any hard-and-fast distinction in site use
(for more information see "Recording Standing Structures"). The other useful distinction
lies literally at the water's edge, between maritime (underwater) historical archaeological
sites and land-based sites. Although many of the techniques for recording and excavation
are the same, underwater archaeology has its own particular challenges.

THE BASICS

Investigating historical sites is similar to investigating any other type of archaeological site
in North America, in the sense that archaeologists still set out to answer a similar range of
questions: What activities were people doing here and why? When were they doing it? Did
they succeed? When and why did the activities cease? The chief difference between historical and other kinds of archaeology lies in the alternative sources of information about
past human behavior that historical archaeology can employ. Because historical archaeological sites have been created within the last few hundred years, they fall within the period of written records. This means that a wide variety of documentary records often can
be used to complement any archaeological study. Historical archaeology is therefore as
much about researching the documentary evidence for sites and artifacts as it is about
recording and analyzing the archaeological evidence (See "Using Historical Documents").

Despite having access to sometimes quite detailed written evidence of past events or
behaviors, historical archaeology still aims to be more than just "history with artifacts."

FIGURE 6.1: The range of historical sites in North America

Old houses and domestic sites. A site doesn't have to be below ground to be considered archaeological.

Cemeteries and burial sites

Urban sites. Many historical archaeological sites are located beneath the landscapes of present towns and cities.

Maritime sites. Whaling, shipping and related activities have left physical remains underwater and around the coastline.

Industrial sites. The dam at St. Anthony's Falls in Minneapolis was a key to 1800s mechanization of flour mills and lumber processing.

Historic gardens such as those at the James J. Hill Mansion in St. Paul provide clues about the lives of the wealthy.

Many old mines are only visible through their workings, the equipment long since having been taken away.

Military posts and battlefields such as Ft. Ridgely were prominent in hostilities between Native Americans and the government

One of the main reasons for consulting historical records before carrying out archaeological research is to make sure that what you want to know can't just be discovered from the archives. The primary emphasis of historical archaeology is always on relating the documents to material (archaeological) evidence and understanding just what the limitations of this process might be. Documents always are created for a purpose and are not necessarily objective, and all of them have their own inherent biases. They are also fragile things that often do not survive and are, in any case, not created around every facet of human life. Most of the ordinary people who settled the continent were either unable or disinclined to write down the daily details of their lives, leaving enormous gaps in our understanding of the past. The material (archaeological) record goes some way toward filling these gaps because it is far more durable and was created by all kinds of people. Historical archaeology is a search for the many aspects of human behavior that we never could know from the documents alone.

Most recording of historical sites follows the standard pattern for any site—for example, completing recording forms, compiling survey plans, and photographing the site and its contents—and no specialist skills or methods are required. The exceptions to this will be if you are recording underwater sites, or when you are required to record standing structures or to date historical artifacts, or when you need to use documentary or oral sources to complement the archaeology. Buildings, in particular, are a type of archaeological artifact that require their own system of recording.

FINDING HISTORICAL SITES

Although the methods used to find historical sites are identical to those used to find Indigenous sites (see chapter 3, "Finding Sites"), you can employ some strategies that are peculiar to historical archaeology. The first and most obvious is to look for telltale signs of old habitations or other site types, particularly remnant vegetation such as trees and garden plantings, many of which long outlast the garden itself. Disturbed areas (perhaps the site of a former building) may also have different patterns of regrowth and often include high densities of introduced weed species. Plants such as stinging nettles often invade such areas, providing a good indication of some form of past human activity. Remnant fencing is also an indication of Euro-American alteration of the landscape, although this does not necessarily mean that there is (or was) a habitation nearby.

Domestic artifact scatters are often easily visible as a result of the quantities of durable household debris (such as glass and ceramics) commonly discarded. You should always be on the lookout for trash pits or other potentially stratified deposits that may be useful for excavation purposes. Obviously if you want to excavate you need to find deposits with some depth to them. Pit toilets (also called outhouses or privies) and wells in particular usually are extremely rich sources of historical archaeological information because it was common to use them as convenient trash pits. They can thus contain all sorts of debris, from food remains to broken ceramic vessels and used glass bottles. If you can find such deposits they will provide the best chance of substantial and well-datable archaeological remains relating to the occupation of a site.

Old maps are particularly useful and can be a mine of information, quite literally showing you the locations of sites, although you may encounter problems with the scale of them (see "Other Kinds of Maps That May Be Useful" in chapter 2). Some maps note a scale in "chains"—the original steel bands used by surveyors to measure distance. For conversion purposes 1 chain is 66 feet, or 19.8 m. Maps of townships will show allotments and sometimes structures; parish maps will show land allocations and the name of the first buyer or grantee, as well as tracks and roads, but usually not much else. Surveyor's plans sometimes are quite detailed and may even contain notes describing the structures included on the plan. For mining sites, the original mine records often will contain surveyor's plans noting surface features, although the level of detail varied considerably from surveyor to surveyor. Particularly valuable in the United States, the General Land Office surveys began in 1785, with detailed instructions for the survey parties to record the environment, water sources, mines, camps, villages, roads, and even trails.

You also can try interviewing local landholders, especially if they maintain an interest in local history or if their families have lived in the area for a long time. Obviously, you cannot just barge in and demand to know where sites are located, but even an informal oral history interview can be a very rewarding and productive experience (see "Recording Oral Histories").

In any case you should always investigate the history of an area before you go into the field, because this will give you the best guide as to what to expect (see "Using Historical Documents"). Once you have found a site, there are three ways to collect information about it:

- Documentary research
- Field study
- Collecting oral histories and other community information

USING HISTORICAL DOCUMENTS

Historical documents are the first and most obvious place to start for historical archaeologists. You will need to look at libraries, archives, and museums for:

- Archival and other document collections
- Maps and plans

- Photos and pictures
- Books, articles, reports

Historical documents come in many forms, from company reports and accounts; birth, death, and marriage certificates; census records; wills and probate inventories; church and cemetery records; and maps and plans to diaries, letters, and photographs or newspaper articles and advertisements. It is not always possible to search exhaustively for every piece of documentation that relates to a site, and many documents may be of little use in answering archaeological questions. In practice you probably will have to target particular types of documents that are more likely to provide you with useful information.

One major distinction you need to be aware of is between **primary** and **secondary sources** and their respective uses. Primary sources are firsthand accounts prepared at the time of an event (such as surveyor's plans, newspaper reports, government correspondence, or diary entries), whereas secondary sources (such as regional histories) are usually compiled at a much later date. Although secondary sources may well be based on primary sources, they are an interpretation of selected parts of them and are therefore considered less reliable. They are often a good place to start, however, as they can provide overviews of places or events and may contain useful information that can then be cross-checked or followed up in more detail from primary sources. When researching an area or a site, start with the secondary sources to find out where the major industries were located, or where the original settlements were established, and follow this up with selected primary source research for more specific guidelines as to where to survey and what to look for.

Of course, it is equally possible for both primary and secondary sources to be wrong, and as a researcher you must keep an open mind when examining any historical document. Just as you should be aware of your own biases, so, too, should you be aware that all documents are prepared for a reason and that this reason is not necessarily objective. Whatever documentary material you are using, you need to question the source of the information and try to verify it by cross-checking with other sources wherever possible (Sagazio, Kellaway, and McWilliam 1992, 7). Remember also that the availability of different forms of documents will vary widely from place to place and from time period to time period.

Primary documents can be found in several major places:

- Federal and Commonwealth repositories contain a range of records, most of them from government agencies. These often are housed in major facilities in Washington or Ottawa, but many also are housed in regional records centers. These facilities often also have extensive collections of photographs, oral histories, and a range of other records.
- State and provincial repositories and archives hold official correspondence and records, but usually relating to government functions. Some government departments may

Just What Is a Historical Fact?

Don't put too much faith in the truth of historical documents. Even people who are firsthand witnesses of events tend to see things differently from other witnesses. Much is due to their physical location in relation to the event, but much also can be related to their social status, their emotional situation, and any number of other factors. Some historians feel that if you have substantial agreement from several primary sources, you have a historical fact. Documentary agreement may indicate higher probability of accuracy, but more than once, the physical evidence of archaeology has challenged the "historical facts."

even maintain their own special archives relating to their functions. Many of these still may cover a range of useful information including maps and plans, newspapers, government gazettes, official correspondence, reports, and census information. Some state or provincial historical facilities hold invaluable collections of material relating to their citizens, including personal correspondence, genealogy records, and extensive pictorial and photographic collections. Some may have large collections of artifacts, from pre-contact items to the contemporary.

- Private or university archives may hold special collections of information relating to specific areas, such as university or company histories.
- Special-purpose museums often contain detailed records about an area, family, or product and can be especially valuable in providing information about the history and production of artifacts you find in sites.
- Local repositories, such as city or county libraries, historical societies, or heritage centers, often contain a wealth of rare local information, although this is not always easily accessible. Because most historical archaeological studies tend to be local, time is well spent visiting the local resources to evaluate their materials.

Larger collections tend to maintain up-to-date catalogs of their precise contents, and search engines for many collections are now available online. The major national and state or provincial libraries also have searchable online databases of their collections. If you are unable to visit a collection, some repositories will conduct research for you for a fee, although the waiting period for such research can be lengthy.

An important factor to bear in mind when conducting primary documentary research is to ensure that you always cite primary resources adequately. This is not as easy as it sounds. How do you reference a probate inventory? A private letter? Or an undated and unattributed newspaper clipping? While there are no hard-and-fast rules, the key to citing a primary document is to make sure that you provide enough detail to enable another researcher to find the same item and to be consistent in the way you organize the information. To ensure this you must remember to include:

- A description of the document, including the author and the title (if there is one). If there is no formal title you can refer to it in terms of the type of document (e.g., "marriage certificate"). If the document is a letter it is usual to include the name of the recipient as well.
- The date of the document or document bundle (if known). If you don't know the precise date, a date range will suffice, usually indicated by the use of "ca." for "circa" written before the date, indicating that it falls within a range of 10 years either side. If you don't know this or can't work it out, you will have to note down "n.d." for "not dated" as part of your reference. In this way you signal to the reader that it is the document that is at fault, not your scholarship.
- The location of the document, including the name of the collection, the precise reference numbers allocated by the repository (if any), and the place where the document may be consulted. This will be a relatively simple task if the document is held in a formal collection but may be more challenging if it is held by a local historical society or a private individual.
- In order to be consistent, look in recent journal articles in historical archaeology journals or books to get an idea of the types of information and formats commonly used in the discipline.

RECORDING INDUSTRIAL SITES

As a specific class of historical archaeological site, industrial sites also require a particular approach to research and recording. An industrial site can be anything resulting from large- or small-scale extractive, manufacturing, or processing activities and will cover a gamut of sites from mining, whaling, shipping, and milling to factories or railways. The study of any industrial site requires some familiarity with the technology and processes used there. To record it adequately you will need to know how the site operated (i.e., what industrial processes went on there, what equipment may have been on-site, how different parts of the site may have been used for separate aspects of the overall process, or how the technology or the process changed over time). This will help you to understand both what occurred there in the past and the location and nature of the archaeological remains that you can see in the present. This information sometimes can be found by researching both the history and nature of the particular industry itself and the specific history of the site,

How Safe Is Your Soil? Wayne Johnson's Occupational Health and Safety Tips for Working on Historical Archaeological Sites

You should never assume that the soil on your site is nontoxic. Soil contamination can take many forms, from heavy metals and chemical residues to bacteria and other harmful residues. Many of these potential toxins are the result of chemical processes developed since the advent of the industrial revolution and are more common than you might think.

Industrial sites can be particularly toxic. For five millennia, industrial activities have involved the processing of metal ores, which usually leave residues in the soil. Arsenic and lead mines are in themselves hazardous owing to the nature of the material extracted, let alone processed. The secondary stage of metalworking, making alloys or using chemicals as flux, will also produce toxic residues, which may have been casually disposed of—usually buried as fill or in disposal pits on-site. Gold mining has long used arsenic as part of the process of separating the metal from quartz. The toxic residue was then washed away, to settle either in the surrounding soil or more usually down a waterway. In harbor cities many industries were clustered around harbor sites with ready port access. On such sites, oils, diesel, and other liquid fuel spills seep into the soil where they remain as residues. Remediation of such sites is expensive and may not necessarily have cleared the site of all hazardous substances. In addition, seemingly innocuous metalworking industries, such as blacksmiths and iron or brass foundries, may have used fuels such as coal with a high tar content containing toxic trace elements.

Potential health hazards can occur even on ordinary domestic sites. Sheets of asbestos insulation, or "lagging," were commonly wound around pipes leading from machinery such as steam boilers. Over the years this "lagging" degrades, releasing fibers into the air, which also settle on the ground in confined spaces. Between the 1910s and the end of the 20th century, asbestos fibrous-cement sheeting ("fibro") was used extensively in the domestic building industry. Although relatively stable in sheet form, if broken it too will release fibers into the air. Lead-based paints commonly were used on domestic houses throughout the 20th century. Wherever there has been a regime of scraping off flaking paint prior to repainting, there is a danger of high lead levels in the surrounding soils and building interiors. Likewise, for most of the 20th century, lead-based petroleum used to fuel cars was escaping into the atmosphere via exhaust systems. Since lead is relatively heavy it does not tend to spread far from the source of the emission, and tested levels are found to increase closer to busy roads or in the roof spaces of buildings located close to busy roads.

Pest control within domestic structures has attracted the use of chemical poisons for at least the past two centuries. Rodents were particularly targeted, with baits laid

(continues)

How Safe Is Your Soil? Wayne Johnson's Occupational Health and Safety Tips for Working on Historical Archaeological Sites (*continued*)

beneath floors in an attempt to eradicate the nuisance. Nineteenth-century city dwellings are often characterized by the extensive archaeological deposits that accumulate beneath floorboards, often attributed to the purposeful sweeping of refuse into the void beneath. Sampling of soil samples from some historical archaeological sites in Sydney, Australia, however, indicated high arsenic levels in these deposits. Owing to their porosity, animal bones were particularly susceptible to absorbing this poison. Because arsenic can be absorbed through the skin, rubber gloves had to be worn by archaeologists working with the artifacts recovered from these deposits. Even organic fertilizers can contribute to toxicity in the soil.

As an archaeologist you need to be aware of such health hazards and, if necessary, take steps to minimize direct contact or prolonged exposure. In particular you should be aware of the recent history of your site to minimize potential threats to your own and other people's health. Wherever possible make sure you investigate the history of your site in detail *before* you begin fieldwork to assess what potential toxins might be lurking in your soil.

although for smaller, less well known industries or sites there may be little or no specific documentation remaining.

When working on any industrial site you should make yourself aware of the potential occupational health and safety issues of contamination from industrial by-products and take the necessary steps to minimize exposure for you and others working for you. If in doubt, get your soil or other possible hazards tested before work begins.

Nineteenth- and early 20th-century technical manuals or engineering works written for the industry are another invaluable source of information, which are unparalleled for details of equipment and processes. If you can't find manuals about the industry, try comparing the industrial archaeology of your site to archaeological reports for similar sites elsewhere, although this may involve tracking down repositories of unpublished archaeological reports.

In addition, specialist journals were published for almost every major profession and trade throughout the 19th and 20th centuries. The range and type of specialist information you can extract from these is unparalleled, as even the advertisements may contain pertinent information. It is well worthwhile investigating what collections of these journals are available in your nearest major library.

RECORDING MARITIME SITES

Maritime archaeological sites are more than just shipwrecks; they also include many land-based activities associated with maritime industry and trade, such as whaling stations, docks, jetties, and shipyards. As such, the same basic techniques for site recording (e.g., surveying, mapping, photography, and drawing) are used on land-based maritime sites. As with any other kind of industrial activity, you need to be familiar with the way the industry operated to be able to record a land-based maritime site adequately. This means understanding how the whaling industry operated and how whales were processed after killing, for example, or how dry docks or slips worked, or how ships were built. The underwater component of maritime archaeology also uses the same basic techniques, albeit with certain modifications to cope with the underwater environment. Underwater surveys of shipwrecks use the grid system for recording and excavation, the baseline and offset technique for drawing site plans, and scales for all underwater photography.

In terms of historical documents, shipping records will give you information on ship movements that may be useful if you are tracing the voyages of a particular ship. Often these won't provide all the information you will be seeking: they may indicate only the date a ship left a particular port and the date it returned, so you will need to read between the lines to understand what this might mean. For example, if the ship was known as a whaling vessel, the time period that it was away from port may give you some indication of how far it went, and the season it was absent for may be a clue as to whether or not it was engaged in whaling.

RECORDING STANDING STRUCTURES

Not everything archaeologists do is necessarily related to excavation. Archaeologists usually have little training as architectural historians, but in CHM projects they often are required to document architectural remains. Many sites have no subsurface deposits to excavate or have only their surface remains recorded owing to time and money constraints. The study of standing structures is one example of how detailed archaeological information can be obtained without excavation. A standing structure may be anything from a building, such as a house, a barn, or a church, to a feature such as a kiln, a jetty, or a bridge; in short, anything originally created to serve some human need in a relatively permanent location that now exists substantially above the ground (cf. Davies and Buckley 1986, 86). When recording any standing structure your goal should be more than just describing it. A proper recording should provide enough information to re-create the

Steve Dasovich's "Worries to Ponder before Trying to Become an Underwater Archaeologist"

Humans are not meant to live or function in water, but a few of us have decided to perform surveys and excavations while fully submerged in it. Underwater archaeology is interesting, fun, exciting, challenging, and well, cool, but it's difficult and dangerous. Here are some things to consider before you "jump in."

- Don't smoke now or later. Smoking damages your lungs. Lungs are important for breathing. Breathing is important for staying alive. Breathing is physically more difficult underwater. Don't smoke!
- Know how to swim well. Most underwater archaeology gets done in or under water. Swimming is how you move in water. Tides, waves, and currents make it more difficult. The better you swim, the better you move.
- Don't get your C-card (certification card) from a three-day course taken on a whim while vacationing in the Caribbean. Although they are fun, you don't really learn what you need. The goal is actually to *study* about how to dive and how to be safe while diving. Remember, when you are underwater and breathing air, you are actually on life support.
- Be in shape. Equipment is heavy on land, and while underwater nasty things can happen. Scientific diving is not easy. Anyone who tells you otherwise either has not done it, has not done it properly, or is just a show-off and therefore dangerous to dive with.
- Get a physical from a physician who understands the effects of diving on your body. Ailments and nonnormal physical problems that cause little or no problem on land can be extremely dangerous while diving.
- Don't be claustrophobic (or get over it). Most underwater archaeology takes place with limited or no visibility.
- Fear dangerous animals (including some people). Such a fear is reasonable, but a crippling fear isn't. Don't take up underwater archaeology if you have a crippling fear of fish.
- If you don't like to have fun and like to have money, don't become an underwater archaeologist.

Despite these worries, there are no fewer dangers in your normal, everyday terrestrial lives. Just be sure you go into this ready to study diving and all its intricacies. Divers function in an environment that is inherently dangerous, so the more educated and trained you are, the safer you'll be.

sequence of construction and the history of the building's use and from this, to reconstruct in some measure the changing lives of the occupants.

Recording standing structures follows a process similar to recording any other type of archaeological "site," in that you need to ask the same range of questions. When and how was it constructed? What material was used and where did it come from? How may the structure have been altered through time? To do this you need to record four sets of complementary information:

- The nature of the individual elements that make up the structure (i.e., the walls, the floor, the roof)
- How the elements are put together (i.e., their construction and manufacture)
- Details of any surface treatments (on the walls, the floor, and so on)
- The overall condition of the structure and its individual parts

The two least altered parts of a building usually will be the space in the roof and under the floor, so make an effort to investigate these areas whenever possible. Details of how these areas have been constructed often will give you an excellent guide to the construction sequence of a building, even if all of the internal elements have been made to look contemporary (figure 6.2). Sometimes not all elements of a structure will remain *in situ*. In this case it may be equally important to know what *might* have been there (if there is any physical or documentary evidence of the element's existence) and what could have happened to it. Questions to ask of each set of information are included in table 6.1 (which is by no means an exhaustive list).

One of the main things to be continually aware of when you are recording a building is how much the structure and its components may have been affected by later activities. This is an assessment of the integrity of the place and will be particularly important if you are also assessing its cultural heritage significance (see "How to Assess Cultural Heritage Significance" in chapter 8). As you record the individual components of a building and how they have been put together, look for signs of how the structure might have evolved or been altered over time or for signs of the reuse of materials from older structures.

Describing Structural Components

As with all archaeological recording, consistency is the watchword when describing the physical components of a building. Always aim to use standard terminology, particularly when describing construction techniques and methods. We have included only the basics here (figures 6.3 through 6.6), drawn largely from the Museum of London's descriptive standards for timber and masonry construction. More detailed descriptions of architectural features can be found in Poppeliers, Chambers, and Schwartz (1983); McAlester and McAlester (1984); and Foster (2004).

FIGURE 6.2: Two roof timbers from the same building. The timber at the top is earlier in date and shows the characteristic irregular zigzag marks made by a hand-operated pit saw. The timber at the bottom is still in situ and shows the semicircular marks characteristic of a circular saw, indicating that it can only have been manufactured after the introduction of steam-driven saw milling technology.

Pit-sawn timber can be recognized by the irregular, but straight criss-cross marks made by the movement of the hand-held saw.

In contrast, the characteristic semi-circular saw marks on this ceiling joist indicate that it was cut with a circular saw. Such technology was only available after the introduction of steam powered saw mills to an area.

Both of these pieces of wood came from the same structure, and by virtue of their different manufacturing techniques, help us to understand the sequence in which the building was constructed.

TABLE 6.1: Elements to consider when recording a standing structure

Individual elements	How the elements are put together	Surface treatments	Condition
• What are the walls made from? The roof? The floor? The ceiling?	• What methods have been used in construction?	• Have the internal or external surfaces been treated in any way (e.g., with sealants, caulking, coverings)?	• Are any elements in particularly good condition?
• Are there any original fittings or evidence for them (e.g., windows, shutters, skirting boards, fire surrounds, rim locks)?	• What technology did these methods require?	• Have the internal or external surfaces been finished in any way (e.g., adzed, tuck pointed, scored)?	• Are any elements in particularly poor condition?
• Have there been any obvious alterations or additions?	• How successfully have the various elements been put together?	• Is there evidence for any decorative finishes (such as paint, wallpaper, mortar, or plaster)?	• Is there any evidence for use-wear patterns (i.e., physical evidence of function or the extent of use)?
• Were the various elements manufactured by machine or by hand?	• Is there evidence for any particularly skilled or unskilled craftsmanship in this?	• What decorative features are there (e.g., dados, curtains, cornices, ceiling roses)?	• Are all elements of the structure present?
• Is there evidence for any particularly skilled or unskilled craftsmanship in this?	• How well suited is the building or the parts of the building to its purpose?	• Is there evidence for any particularly skilled or unskilled craftsmanship in the finishes or the features?	• What is missing?
• Is there any evidence for elements having been altered or recycled from somewhere else?			• Have any attempts been made to repair the structure?
• Are there any trademarks or other manufacturing information, such as a patent or design number, even a brand name?			• Is there any evidence for what might have caused the deterioration of elements?
• Do the elements have any other distinctive attributes?			• Is there danger of further deterioration to the structure?
			• Is the structure under any immediate threats?

FIGURE 6.3: The basic elements of a building (after Coutts 1977)

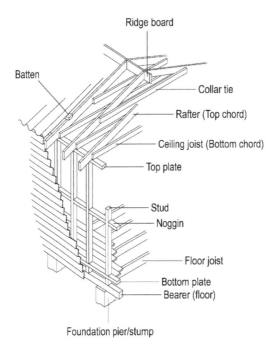

FIGURE 6.4: Common carpentry joints (after the Museum of London 1990)

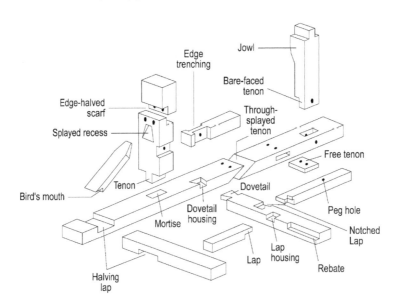

FIGURE 6.5: Brick bonds and forms (after the Museum of London 1990)

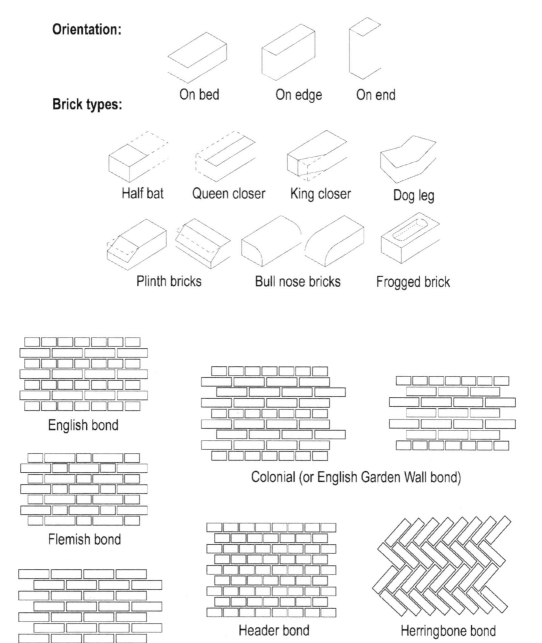

Orientation:

On bed   On edge   On end

Brick types:

Half bat   Queen closer   King closer   Dog leg

Plinth bricks   Bull nose bricks   Frogged brick

English bond

Flemish bond

Stretcher bond

Colonial (or English Garden Wall bond)

Header bond   Herringbone bond

FIGURE 6.6: Stone courses, finishes, and jointing (after the Museum of London 1990)

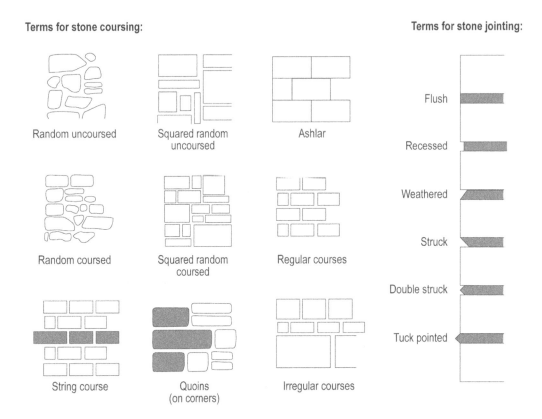

Dating Structures from Their Components

In general, dating a structure from its components alone is very difficult. Even if you can find evidence of a manufacturer's mark, trademark, or patent number (the most "datable" information), materials may have been stored for a considerable time before use, they may have been recycled from an older structure, or they may simply have been manufactured over a long period of time. At best, you will probably be able to narrow down construction only to a date range or to before or after a certain period.

If you do a great deal of documentation for a project you may wish to find or develop a rough guide to some major changes in building materials and construction techniques used in the area. The intent would be to provide a guide to those inventions or technical developments that may be useful for assigning a rough date range to a building. Bear in

Denis Gojak's Tips for Recording Standing Structures

- An orienteering compass provides a quick and easy way of drawing a complex, non-right-angled structure with all the walls correctly oriented. Lay the side of the compass along the wall or alignment to be measured, then turn the graduated compass circle so that the inscribed mapping lines correspond with the north arrow. Lay the compass on the drawing page with the same bearing relative to north at the top of the page (i.e., so that the north arrow again lines up with the inscribed mapping lines). If you want to be doubly clever, align the north arrow to an offset bearing that is equal to the difference between magnetic and true north.
- People surveying old buildings should arm themselves with an inexpensive flat metal 150 mm steel rule, with English/metric divisions. These are ideal for getting exact measurements of timber (the 3" × 4" that is really 68 mm × 110 mm) and for checking if floorboards are butt-boarded or tongue and groove. If a floor is butt-boarded, the ruler will slide straight through. If it stops about 5 mm in along a sample of boards, then they are tongue and groove. Also, a steel rule if properly sharpened is perfect for scraping paint, gouging divots from walls to examine what's underneath, cleaning fingernails, and lifting lino to read the old newspapers. Any more effective and it would outdo the K-tel Fishin' Magician or a Swiss Army knife.

mind that these dates won't be exact for all areas (innovations will have taken longer to reach regional areas, for example). If you can find them, trademarks or manufacturer's marks may provide a finer resolution of date.

Many construction materials are less helpful in this respect than you might think. For example there was no standardized size for bricks throughout the 19th century, so changes in brick dimensions are not particularly useful for dating purposes. After the introduction of the first machine for mass producing bricks in the mid-1800s, their shape became more regular and their size slightly larger until by the 1870s/1880s all bricks were machine made. Brick size also can vary considerably even between bricks made from the same mold, as a result of differential shrinkage in the kiln.

Once you have decided on the sequence of construction for a building, you can represent it using the concepts of the Harris matrix, by assigning a context number to each element and then plotting them into a matrix path (see "Interpreting Stratigraphy" in chapter 5). This is a sophisticated means to present both your data and your analysis together in a single diagram (figure 6.7).

FIGURE 6.7: Presenting data from a structural analysis in Harris matrix form (Davies 1993)

Applying the Harris Matrix to the elements of a standing structure
Either singly:

◯　　An element derived from subsurface fabric

▢　　An element derived from standing fabric

△　　An element derived from historical sources

Or in combination:

An element derived from both subsurface and standing fabric

An element derived from both subsurface and historical sources

An element derived from both standing fabric and historical sources

An element derived from all three

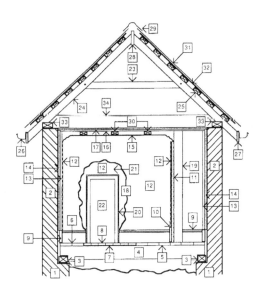
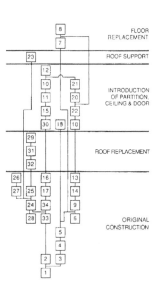

HABS/HAER/HALS/CRGIS

In the United States, you should be aware of the four federal projects that document important architectural, engineering, and industrial sites throughout the United States and its territories. Started in 1933, the Historic American Buildings Survey (HABS) documents America's architectural heritage and provides design and interpretation of historic resources. The Historic American Engineering Record (HAER) has been in existence since 1969 and seeks to document historic sites and structures related to engineering and industry. Historic American Landscapes Survey (HALS) strives to document historic landscapes through measured drawings and interpretive drawings, written histories, and large-format black-and-white and color photographs. The Library of Congress serves as a repository for sets of measured drawings, photographs, and written histories of more than 40,000 structures and landscapes. The National Park Service Cultural Resources Geographic Information Systems (CRGIS) facility's mission is to "institutionalize the use of GIS, global positioning systems (GPS), and remote sensing technologies in historic preservation within the National Park system as well as with State Historic Preservation Offices (SHPO) and Tribal Historic Preservation Offices (THPO)." All four programs have detailed sets of guidelines, and on some cultural heritage management projects you may be asked to provide documentation according to the guidelines of any of these programs. Detailed descriptions of each program and their guidelines can be found on the Heritage Documentation Programs website at www.cr.nps.gov/hdp. The records of the four programs also can serve as a valuable research tool, especially HABS.

RECORDING HISTORICAL ARTIFACTS

In all cases the recording of historical artifacts follows much the same process as recording any other type of artifact, asking a similar range of questions: What is it? What is it made from? How and when was it made? How was it used? To do this you must look for and record those particular aspects that can most clearly show how and when the artifact was made and for what it was used. These are called **diagnostic features** and are the most useful for identification and dating purposes. For many artifacts you may find this information lacking entirely—for example, a small 1 cm × 2 cm fragment of dark brown glass from the body of a bottle is unlikely to give you much information about the specific contents of the bottle or its date of manufacture. In this case you should not spend too much time recording this artifact, but instead focus on searching for and recording more informative pieces of evidence.

The context in which an artifact is found—in terms of whether or not the artifact has been disturbed since it was discarded—is particularly important to record. This is an assessment of the integrity of the site, which will be useful in your later analysis (see "Recording Landforms, Vegetation, and Slope" in chapter 3). If you think that an artifact is in its original location (*in situ*), you need to pay particular attention to where it was found and what was associated with it.

You also must make sure that you use consistent terms when describing any artifact so that other researchers can understand precisely what you mean. The following sections contain basic identification information and standard terminology for several common categories of historical artifact. Obviously the entire array of historical artifact types would be impossible to describe in a volume like this, but the discussion of the range of bottle, glass, and ceramic objects will give you an idea of the range and complexity of any single type of artifact. You can find detail in a wide range of specialist literature, old mail-order catalogs, and compendia on particular artifact forms.

RECORDING BOTTLES AND BOTTLE GLASS

As the most common containers used in colonial society, bottles are a ubiquitous find on historical archaeological sites. Indigenous people after contact also sometimes used bottles received in trade, so recording bottle glass can form a component of Indigenous site recording as well (see chapter 7, "Recording Precontact and Early Postcontact Sites"). The basic components of a bottle are the body, shoulder, neck, rim, finish, base, push-up, and heel (figure 6.8).

There is enormous variation in the shape and style of bottles, which can tell you when the bottle was manufactured and the purpose for which it was used. The diagnostic features to look for and record for bottle glass are:

- Shape
- Base
- Mold marks
- Mouth
- Seal/closure
- Trademark
- Decoration
- Color

FIGURE 6.8: The parts of a bottle

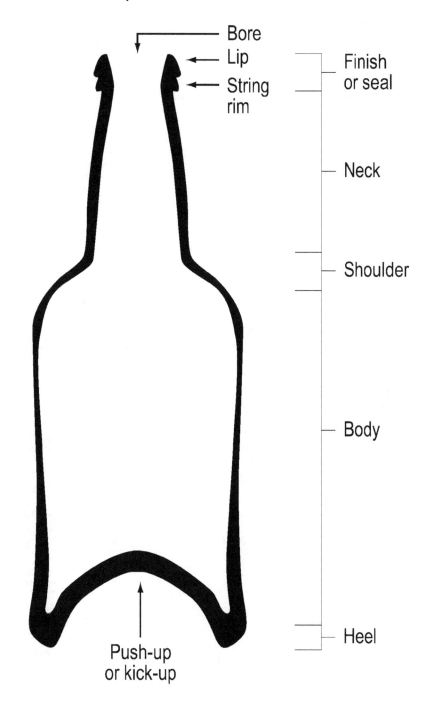

Recording Shape

The shape of some bottles will be relatively easy to describe; for others it can be very complex. To accurately convey the shape of the vessel you may have to describe it in three planes:

- As viewed with the body horizontal (i.e., a description of the cross section of the bottle if it were cut in half through its midsection) (figure 6.9).

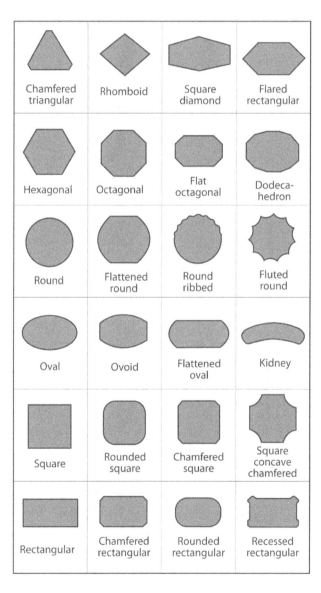

FIGURE 6.9: Describing the shape of a bottle in the horizontal plane

- As viewed with the body vertical (i.e., a description of the cross section of the bottle if it were cut in half down its length) (figure 6.10).
- Its three-dimensional body shape. "Cylindrical" may be a much simpler way of describing the general shape of a bottle, as opposed to straight/vertical, circular/horizontal.

FIGURE 6.10: Describing the shape of a bottle in the vertical plane

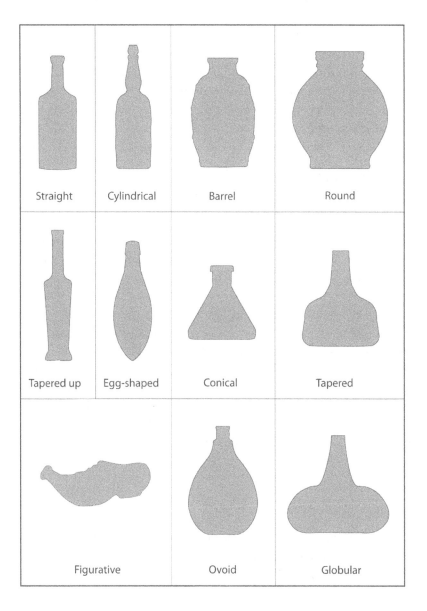

Straight	Cylindrical	Barrel	Round
Tapered up	Egg-shaped	Conical	Tapered
Figurative	Ovoid	Globular	

Recording Mold Marks

Changes in glass manufacturing technology have resulted in several distinctive criteria that can be used to date bottles. Machine-made bottles have very well-defined mold seams, so make sure you take note of the number of mold seams that are visible and their placement on the body of the bottle.

Recording Closures

Recording closure is essentially documenting the shape and form of the neck and mouth of the bottle. Methods for sealing in the contents of a bottle have changed over time, particularly since the rapid technological changes of the Industrial Revolution. Make sure you take note of the way the lip and string rim of the bottle are formed and any other evidence for how the bottle was originally sealed.

Recording Trademarks, Decoration, and Color

Make sure you record all trademarks and their placement. Even the most inconspicuous letters and numbers sometimes can be a guide to the company that made the bottle, the contents of the bottle, its date, or its place of manufacture. Embossed letters and numbers on a bottle base may refer to a mold number, the manufacturer, and sometimes also the place of manufacture. When recording such information, make sure you record both its form and placement on the bottle.

Color is another important aspect of bottle manufacture of which you should take note. When describing the color of a bottle, be careful to distinguish between "clear" bottle glass, which has an aqua tint, and completely colorless glass. So-called clear bottle glass naturally has an aqua tint and can be made completely colorless only by adding a bleaching agent, some of which are useful for dating purposes. The distinctive color of amethyst bottle glass, for instance, results from the use of manganese to produce clear glass, which, when exposed to sunlight, is apt to discolor to purple. Dark green bottle glass, commonly referred to as "black" glass because its color is so dark, was the most common material for alcohol bottles in the 19th century.

Recording Other Types of Glass

Not all glass on an archaeological site is bottle glass. Decorative glass bowls, cups, vases, and ornaments were also common on domestic sites, made from cut and pressed (or molded) glass. Cut glass is made by hand and has always been much more expensive than

TABLE 6.2: How to distinguish between cut glass and pressed glass (Boow 1991, 85–86)

Characteristics of cut glass	Characteristics of pressed or molded glass
Will not have any mold seams	Will have a mold seam at the upper, outer lip, although this was sometimes deliberately blended into the design, making it hard to see
Will be flat sided and appear to have sharp edges	Will have a smooth, internally tapered surface (i.e., it will flare outward at the top)
Its surface is often polished, smooth, and glossy	May have a "disturbed" surface texture sometimes disguised by an overall stippled design
Design edges will be sharp and distinct	Design edges will tend to be rounded (Jones and Sullivan 1989, 34–35)
Designs are usually geometric (mostly panels, flutes, and miters)	Designs will occur in a greater variety of patterns, including lacy, stippled, and naturalistic patterns

pressed glass. It is relatively easy to distinguish between pressed and cut glass because of their different manufacturing methods (table 6.2).

Window glass is another form of glass that occurs in many historical sites. Because of the limitations of glassblowing technology, it was impossible to make large, flat sheets of glass until the mid-1800s. Window panes made before this date were all made by hand and tend to be relatively small. The earliest were made using a technique called "crown glass" in which flat panes were literally spun from a molten bubble of blown glass and measured around 25 cm square. From the 1830s onward, window panes were made from a flattened glass cylinder and could measure anything from 60 cm × 45 cm up to 1.5 m × 90 cm (Freeland 1988, 6, 79). The introduction of machine technology finally resulted in glass panes that were of uniform thickness and size. When you find window glass at an archaeological site, you must always record its thickness (table 6.3) and whether or not it is hand or machine made.

TABLE 6.3: The changing thickness of window glass throughout the 19th century

Varying thickness of different types of glass pane		
Crown panes	To ca. 1870	Less than 2.8 mm
Cylinder panes	To ca. 1910	3–4 mm
Rolled sheet	After 1890	Greater than 4.5 mm
Drawn sheet	After 1920	Up to 6 mm

Source: Boow 1991, 111

RECORDING CERAMICS

Most of the ceramics found on historical sites in North America initially were imported from England or Europe, but eventually locally produced ceramics became the norm. Ceramics can be hand made (such as coil pots), thrown (on a potter's wheel), or molded (also sometimes referred to as "pressed"). Avoid using the meaningless word "china" to describe ceramics; this was simply a generic term used by 17-century European merchants to describe porcelain vessels exported from China. As with any kind of artifact make sure you use consistent terminology when you describe the various parts of a ceramic vessel (figure 6.11).

FIGURE 6.11: The parts of a ceramic vessel

Flat ware

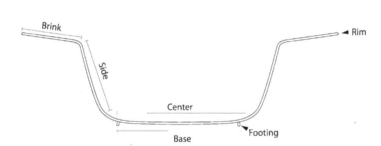

Hollow ware

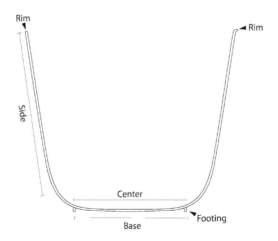

Historical archaeologists draw many distinctions between different types of ceramic vessels based on a whole range of features. The difference between flatware (plates, platters, saucers, and the like) and hollowware (bowls, cups, tureens, and similar vessels) refers to the shape of the vessel; other distinctions are drawn according to the purpose of the vessel or its method of manufacture. Archaeologists often will describe a ceramic vessel according to its use (i.e., vessels used to cook, mix, or store foodstuffs are called "kitchenware," while vessels used in serving and consuming meals or beverages are called "tableware.") All of these categories are more descriptive than classificatory—in other words they tell you something about the gross general categories to which a vessel might belong ("bowl" versus "plate," or "mixing bowl" versus "soup bowl") but tell you little about the specifics of that particular piece. When recording ceramics from an archaeological site it is better to distinguish between manufacturing methods—that is, are they porcelain, stoneware, or earthenware?—each of which had a different range of uses. Other important features to record are:

- The color of the paste (i.e., the color of the clay used to make the vessel). This characteristic is one that will allow you to distinguish between stoneware and earthenware, for example. Look at the edge of a broken ceramic fragment (you may have to clean it first to see the paste color).
- The decorative technique employed.
- The color of the decoration.
- Any visible trademarks.
- The vessel type (if you can tell).

Recording Ware Type

A piece of ceramic will be porcelain, stoneware, or earthenware, depending on how highly it was fired and what use it was intended for.

Porcelain is made from a mix of clay and stone fired to a very high temperature so that it becomes impervious to liquids. It is translucent, which means that if you hold it up to the light you will be able to see light through it. Porcelain was invented and perfected in China and initially was very expensive. Although its price decreased through time as manufacturers produced it locally, it was always more expensive than other wares. Hard-paste porcelain is distinguishable by virtue of an abrupt boundary between the body of the vessel and the glaze, while on soft-paste porcelain the glaze and the body blend together. Porcelain was used for all forms of tableware, as well as a variety of nontableware items, such as dolls, marbles, figurines, and buttons.

Bone china and **ironstone china** were developed by manufacturers trying to find a cheaper, more durable alternative to porcelain. Experiments with the extremely expensive hard-paste porcelain resulted in the development of bone china, which was manufactured by adding bone ash to the refined clay body. This produced a white ceramic of good translucency at reasonable cost. Other techniques added finely powdered stone and iron slag to the clay to produce "ironstone china," first patented in 1813. Like bone china, this new material was favored for its cheapness and durability and was variously referred to as "ironstone china," "stone china," or "opaque porcelain." Except for the highest-quality services, bone and ironstone china replaced porcelain in popularity during the 19th century.

Stoneware is halfway between porcelain and earthenware. It is made from coarse to refined clay and fired to a point where partial vitrification renders it impervious to liquids. Stoneware commonly has a grey, tan, or brown fabric (i.e., the color of the actual clay itself). Even though nonporous, it is always glazed, either with a self-glaze produced by salt glazing (literally throwing salt into the furnace to change the color of the outside of the pot) or with an applied glaze. Stoneware was very common during the early to mid-19th century and was used to make a number of specialized vessels, such as crocks, jam and pickle jars, ink bottles, and ginger beer and ale bottles. Its use for manufacturing tableware was limited to ca. 1720–1805.

Earthenware is not fired to the point where vitrification occurs and is therefore light and porous unless it has been glazed. Earthenware came in both common and refined forms. Common earthenware was of lower quality and was used to make a range of industrial products such as flowerpots, tiles, and sewage pipes, as well as tobacco smoking pipes. Only in the 17th and 18th centuries was it used to make tablewares. Refined earthenware was made from better-quality clay and, as a cheap alternative to porcelain, was used to make a range of different tablewares. It commonly has a white, buff, yellow, or brown fabric. Refined and decorated white earthenware tablewares were extremely popular from the 1870s/1880s until the turn of the century and are the most common domestic ceramics found on North American historic archaeology sites. Plain white refined earthenware often was used commercially and is sometimes called "hotel ware" because it was thick, durable, and inexpensive and therefore popular for hotel dinner settings. Marked hotel wares generally are dated to after the mid-1800s.

Recording Decorative Technique

Take note of the type of decoration and how it has been applied to the vessel. The main types of decoration are:

Embossing. This is a raised or molded decoration with no color. Typical examples are scalloped rims on the edge of plates. Molding was particularly popular between 1850 and 1890 on clear-glazed white ironstone vessels (Wetherbee 1985).

Glazing. A glaze is a glassy coating over the inside or outside of the vessel. A slip is a fine clay that has been diluted to a creamlike consistency with water. Vessels are dipped into this liquid clay to give them a smooth, glassy outer surface. If you find a sherd with a complex glaze or slip, record the exterior or primary glaze first, followed by the interior or secondary glaze. The most common forms of this technique are (AHAPN 1998):

Albany slip. A lustrous brown slip that coats the entire vessel.

Bristol slip. An opaque white slip containing zinc oxide. It is often found in combination with an Albany slip on stoneware bottles.

Clear glaze. This was usually applied to white earthenware vessels, although variations of it include *creamware*, which has a cream-colored tint to it, and *pearlware*, which has a bluish tint.

Rockingham. This is a dark brown mottled glaze that looks as if it has been "dripped" onto the vessel and was particularly popular between 1830 and 1870.

Salt glaze. This is a glaze used on stoneware that results from throwing handfuls of salt into the furnace during firing. The salt combines with the silica in the clay to form a shiny outer coating that often has a slightly pitted surface, like orange peel.

Color decoration. There are many ways of decorating a vessel with color, including transfer printing, hand painting, luster, edge banding, lithographic decals, hand stamping, hair lining, gilding, and colored pastes or glazes.

Transfer printing. This is produced from an inked design engraved onto a copper plate. Most transfer prints used only a single color and were common on tablewares in the 1820s. Intricate dark blue to purple transfer prints were especially common in the mid-19th century. A technique called flow blue, where chemicals added to the kiln during firing caused the transfer print color on the vessels to run or flow, was introduced to the transfer printing process in the 1820s. Flow blue was popular throughout the 19th century for everyday place settings. Reproduction transfer print designs were introduced after 1900 and are still marketed in limited quantities (AHAPN 1998).

Hand painting refers to colors that have been applied using a brush or the fingers.

Luster uses either a metallic oxide luster or an iridescent luster and was particularly popular in the 1920s.

When you record a transfer print, take note of whether it has been applied underneath or over the top of the clear glaze. The earliest transfer prints were applied over the top of the glaze, which means that they will scratch or wash off. These are called **overglaze** patterns. Later prints were applied underneath the glaze, which means they will not come off. They are called **underglaze**.

Edge banding is a thin band of color applied by brush to the rim of the vessel. The width of this band can vary from 2–6 mm.

Lithographic decals were supplied on paper-backed sheets and pressed onto the vessel over the top of the glaze after firing. Introduced in the 1860s, they were cheaper and faster to apply than transfer prints but not widely manufactured until the 1900s. Decals are usually polychrome (many colored), with the individual colors precise and distinct (AHAPN 1998).

Hair lining is a thin line of contrasting color printed over or under the glaze. It is usually only 1–1.5 mm in width and often placed inside the rim of a cup or around the rim of saucers and small bowls.

Gilding is the application of liquid gold or silver to the rim of a vessel with a fine brush. It was in use in the United States from 1894.

Colored pastes are when the clay itself is colored and then covered with a clear glaze. The color of a ceramic body, or paste, refers to the fired color of the clay. To determine a paste color you need to examine a clean or freshly broken edge, not just the exterior glaze.

Shell edging is a shell-edged design pressed into the rim of an earthenware vessel. After firing, the edge was often trimmed with blue or green (see also Sussman 2000). Inexpensive edge-decorated tableware was produced by British potteries from about 1770 to 1850 (Noel Hume 1969, 394).

Spongeware and *spatterware*: Spongeware was a distinctive form of decoration applied with a sponge. The result was a mottled blue, red, yellow, or green pattern. Spatterware was most popular between the 1830s and 1840s and was applied by tapping a paintbrush dipped in pigment as the vessel was turned on a wheel (AHAPN 1998; Robacker and Robacker 1978, 32).

RECORDING ORAL HISTORIES

> The very fact that . . . remembrances exist only in memory means that they are a nonrenewable resource. . . . When a generation dies, it is like burning down an archive full of unique and nonretrievable information. (Orser and Fagan 1995, 150)

Archaeology involves working with people. If you are working in the historic period or with Indigenous cultural material, interviewing people can give you many insights into how artifacts were used in the past, as well as the complexities of their social significance (see also "Recording Indigenous Histories" in chapter 7). Oral histories can be as valuable as written documents, particularly in relation to those aspects of daily life that don't translate directly into archaeological artifacts, such as personal beliefs, feelings, reactions, or kinship networks. The most important thing to bear in mind when recording an oral history is that it should be treated as a collaborative process between you as the interviewer and the interviewee. It is not a process of "extracting" information from an "informant," but building a shared understanding of what a site or artifact meant to the people who used it in the past and what it means to the people you are interviewing. You also should be aware that most university-based research involving oral histories will need clearance through a Human Subjects Committee (Institutional Research Board) before you can begin.

When recording an oral history don't just target important or historic events. These are singular occurrences that, while interesting, provide little information about ordinary people and their day-to-day life. The minutiae of many common daily activities (such as certain types of food preparation) would be lost to us without oral history. When conducting an interview you will have to strike a balance between letting people follow their own memory trails, which may provide you with information you haven't anticipated, and keeping them on track so that you get some minimum of information that is useful to you. For best results interview people in an environment where they feel comfortable, such as their own home, or take them into the field to visit a site to identify specific features and try to induce their memories with visual cues. If you cannot take people into the field, take some photographs of sites about which you seek information to show them during the interview and perhaps to prompt them that way.

Wherever possible, ask open questions (i.e., questions that require more than a simple "yes" or "no" answer) because these will elicit the most information. If you don't think your question has elicited enough information, try following up with exploratory queries such as "Tell me more about . . ."; "Explain what you mean by . . ."; "Give me an example of . . ."; or "What date/year did that happen?" For the same reason, avoid asking leading questions ("The house was painted red, wasn't it?"). These essentially tell people the answer or supply a potential answer for them rather than allowing them to explore their own memories of the event. Once you have asked a question, wait and listen to the response. Even if the urge to interrupt—either to clarify a point or to ask another question—is great, don't. Make a note of the point and follow it up later.

In all interview situations you will have to make some judgments about the reliability of the information and not accept everything at face value. People sometimes tend to repeat other (usually written) histories. Make sure the stories you are being told are not being rehashed from someone else's already published history or, if they are, that you trace them back to their original source.

The ethics of good practice are particularly important when conducting an oral history interview (see "Archaeologists and Ethics" in chapter 1). The interviewees are providing you with information, but you must be sensitive to the effects it may have on them or others.

If a memory is painful, or difficult to recall, or embarrassing, don't press the issue. Keep a close watch on the body language of the people being interviewed, which might tell you how comfortable they are with the whole process (be careful: if they are from a culture different from yours, body language may be deceiving!).

Before you start the formal interview, be certain any recording equipment you have works and that recording levels are appropriate for the situation. Run a quick test if it will not be distracting to the interviewee. Try for the best possible recording situation, eliminating background noise as much as possible. For example, a classroom or office is a more suitable environment than a beach, where you will have to deal with the background sound of surf, or places where there is a lot of wind. In most field situations the quality of recording is going to depend on ambient noise levels as much as on the quality, number, and positioning of microphones. When choosing a recorder you may need to consider whether it supports multiple inputs, if you think you may be interviewing groups of people. Apart from this, it is important to understand the characteristics of the sound a recorder can capture and how it can be copied to other media. A reasonable audio sampling rate is 44 kHz and a word length of 16 bit. Internal microphones will pick up machine noise, and minidisks and MP3s do not produce archive-quality recordings. Analog tapes are still okay, especially if you use chrome tape, which doesn't stretch as much as polyester tape does, but the tapes will have to be digitized in order that the content can be archived in the long term. Carry extra batteries as may be needed.

Use an external microphone if you want high-quality recordings, but remember that microphones can be intimidating for some people. The extent to which you and the interviewee are prepared to accept the recording process intruding into the interviews will be an important factor in your choice of recording equipment. Some people are uneasy about wearing wireless or wired microphones or are uncomfortable in front of a camera. Apart from this, you will have to consider how portable or inconspicuous you want your recorder to be. When it comes to the point of transcribing the interview, transcription with time alignment is a good way to index the content of a file. Free software such as Transcriber or Elan will allow you to type in your transcript while selecting corresponding chunks from a wave view of the audio track. The software creates a file that associates the transcript chunks and time codes. Recording technologies are rapidly improving.

At the beginning of the interview you must be very clear about the nature of the project, the purpose of the interview, and how you intend to use the information. Identify yourself and the interviewee by name at the beginning of the recording or at the beginning of your notes, and state the date and place that the interview is being produced. Note basic particulars about the people you are interviewing. How old are they? Where were they born? Without knowing at least how old they are, you will not be able to correlate information about events that happened to them at certain stages of their lives to calendar dates/years.

At either the start or the end of the interview you must ask the interviewee for permission before you reproduce any part of it or make it available in any kind of public document. This process is called "informed consent" and is particularly important when you are interviewing Indigenous people. When obtaining informed consent you need to give an outline of your project and make sure people understand that their participation is voluntary and that they can change their mind at any time about participating. Sometimes you may need to obtain a signed consent from your interviewees. This will be essential if you are seeking funding for Indigenous research from funding bodies or agencies. Some interviewees may be concerned about the "legalese" in the document or may not wish to sign it but may be willing to give consent orally, so you can get consent on your recording.

It is also important that you minimize any potential harm to participants. This includes physical harm, subjecting people to undue stress, and undermining their self-esteem. While archaeology seems pretty innocuous on the surface, our job is actually writing the story of other people's pasts, and some of these stories have the potential to hurt people. For example, in the past, some archaeological research has been used to support racist and hurtful stereotypes of particular ethnic groups or Indigenous people. You need to ask yourself what kinds of precautions have been taken to keep risk at a minimum: Does your study involve particularly vulnerable subjects who may require special consideration?

Finally, if you are interviewing people you will need to give them the option of being anonymous, and you may need to take special measures to ensure their privacy. This is particularly so if you are working with Indigenous people, who are often very cautious about how they will be portrayed by researchers. Some Indigenous groups will not consent to research being undertaken unless they have a certain amount of control over the process and the publications that will arise from the research.

REFERENCES AND FURTHER READING

Association of Historical Archaeologists of the Pacific Northwest (AHAPN). 1998. Draft historical archaeological materials cataloguing guidelines. www.mindspring.com/~larinc/ahapn/crm/laboratory/labmanual.htm (accessed August 18 2003).

Blumenson, J. J. G., and N. Pevsner. 1990. *Identifying American architecture: A pictorial guide to styles and terms: 1600–1945.* New York: Norton.

Boow, J. 1991. *Early Australian commercial glass: Manufacturing processes.* Sydney: Department of Planning and Heritage Council of NSW.

Chidley, G. A. 1994. *How to research the history of a house.* Trenton, NJ: Department of Environmental Protection, Division of Parks and Forestry, Bureau of Parks, Historic Preservation Office. www.state.nj.us/dep/hpo/4sustain/houseresearch.pdf (accessed March 18 2007).

Cossons, N., ed. 2002. *Perspectives on industrial archaeology.* East Lansing: Michigan State University Press.

Coutts, P. 1977. Old buildings tell tales. *World Archaeology* 9(2): 200–219.

Davies, M. 1993. The application of the Harris matrix to the recording of standing structures. In *Practices of archaeological stratigraphy*, eds. E. C. Harris, M. R. Brown, and G. J. Brown, 167–180. London: Academic Press.

Davies, M., and K. Buckley. 1987. Archaeological procedures manual: Port Arthur Conservation and Development Project. Occasional Paper No. 13, Department of Lands, Parks and Wildlife, Hobart.

Feder, K. 2006. *Frauds, myths, and mysteries: Science and pseudoscience in archaeology.* New York: McGraw Hill.

Foster, G. 2004. *American houses: A field guide to the architecture of the home.* Boston: Houghton Mifflin.

Freeland, J. M. 1988. *Architecture in Australia: A history.* Melbourne: Penguin.

Hudson, K. 1963. *Industrial archaeology: An introduction.* London: John Baker Publishers.

Jones, O., and C. Sullivan. 1989. *The Parks Canada glass glossary.* Ottawa, ON: National Historic Parks and Sites, Canadian Parks Service.

Lewis, M. 1992. Physical investigation of a building. In *The National Trust research manual: Investigating buildings, gardens and cultural landscapes*, ed. C. Sagazio, 37–53. Sydney: Allen and Unwin.

McAlester, V., and L. McAlester. 1984. *A field guide to American houses.* New York: Knopf.

Museum of London. 1990. *Archaeological site manual.* 2nd ed. London: Museum of London, Department of Urban Archaeology.

Noel Hume, I. 1969. *A guide to the artifacts of colonial America.* New York: Knopf.

Orser, C., and B. Fagan. 1995. *Historical archaeology.* New York: HarperCollins.

Poppeliers, J. C., A. Chambers, and N. Schwartz. 1983. *What style is it?* Washington, DC: National Trust for Historic Preservation Press.

Robacker, E. F., and A. F. Robacker. 1978. *Spatterware and sponge: Hardy perennials of ceramics.* New York: Barnes.

Sagazio, C., C. Kellaway, and G. McWilliam. 1992. Researching buildings. In *The National Trust research manual: Investigating buildings, gardens, and cultural landscapes*, ed. C. Sagazio, 5–26. Sydney: Allen and Unwin.

Sussman, L. 2000. Changes in pearlware dinnerware, 1780–1830. In *Approaches to material culture research for historical archaeologists*, ed. D. Braund, 37–43. Ann Arbor, MI: Society for Historical Archaeology.

Wetherbee, J. 1985. *A second look at white ironstone.* Lombard, IL: Wallace-Homestead.

Williams, S. 1991. *Fantastic archaeology: The wild side of North American prehistory.* Philadelphia: University of Pennsylvania Press.

For a range of other useful information, see the website accompanying the text.

CHAPTER SEVEN

RECORDING PRECONTACT AND EARLY POSTCONTACT SITES

THE BASICS

An **archaeological site** is a place where any human activity occurred and left some kind of evidence of the use of the place. The latter is important because archaeology is based on the analysis of material culture, the kinds of objects or artifacts people leave behind. There are, of course, sites where people did things and left no trace, but unless we have some way of detecting their use, archaeologists normally can't find them. Perhaps these sites were places for rituals or ceremonies that were fleeting, used little, and left nothing behind. Certainly these sites were important in people's lives, and without knowing about them, a more complete understanding of a people's behavior is impossible. We may, however, be able to detect their locations and nature by examining oral tradition or consulting with the descendants of people who used the sites.

This raises a common question about sites. How many artifacts or features does it take to qualify a place as an archaeological site? If a hunter shoots an arrow and misses, then can't find the arrow and projectile point, is that single point, found by an archaeologist centuries later, a site? Some archaeologists would argue that it is, but others would just mark it as a **findspot** where a single artifact or a small number of artifacts is found. The precise number of artifacts required to qualify as a site is ill defined and probably not all that important. What is important, however, is trying to understand and locate the many kinds of sites a people used across the landscape on which they lived.

In North America, archaeologists generally use the terms **prehistoric** and **historic** to classify sites temporally, but this usage is falling out of favor because of the erroneous implication that Native Americans were without a history until the coming of Europeans. A more contemporary usage is **precontact** and **postcontact**, looking at sites that were used just before contact with Europeans and after.

WHAT IS A PRECONTACT SITE?

Native Americans, the Indigenous inhabitants of North America, have occupied the land for at least 12,000 years and probably much longer. With minor, relatively recent exceptions, this happened mostly without cultural interaction with Europeans. Native Americans have interacted with the land in many different ways over this enormous time period and have left behind many physical traces. There are many different kinds of Indigenous or precontact sites, ranging from stone artifact scatters, shell middens, and rock art to urban complexes, ossuaries, and temple mounds. As Native Americans made contact with European and other cultures, their sites began to contain trade materials or to show these non-Indigenous influences, which archaeologists call postcontact sites. Be aware that site types often overlap and that terminology for sites can vary regionally. Only some of the main types can be discussed here.

RECORDING INFORMATION ABOUT SITES

The checklists for site recording in this section refer only to the specific elements peculiar to each type of site. All site recordings are conducted with two complementary purposes in mind: to record information about the contents, form, and spatial arrangement of the site; and to record information about preservation conditions and other management issues. For

FIGURE 7.1: The range of indigenous sites in North America

A shell midden in central Kansas provided environmental and dietary information.

Rock art like this petroglyph of a hand at Jeffers Petroglyphs can be found in many places.

Burial mounds such as Grand Mound on the Canada-US border reflect some Native American views about death and social structure.

Apartments and kivas at Bandelier National Monument are one of many types of sophisticated Pre-Contact architecture.

The large, fortified, Crow Creek village in Central South Dakota

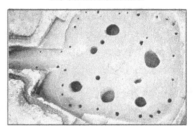

An excavated Plains Village earthlodge shows many structural elements.

Deeply buried and stratified sites such as this one from southwest Iowa can prove difficult to excavate

Bison remains from a procurement and processing site.

all sites you should always record a description and map of its physical location, the owner of the property on which it is found, and a plan of the site, and you should take photographs (see "What to Do When You Find a Site" in chapter 3). Normally you also should record the location of any nearby plant, stone, or other key resources and proximity of the site to the nearest water source and its type (e.g., a lake or river). If you do any test excavations of any type, you will need to record their placement on your site plan.

Most state historic preservation officers or state archaeologists have official site forms with required information, and some have specific forms for each major type of site (i.e., one form for rockshelters, one for stone arrangements, one for rock art sites, and others for the types considered important in the region). Take a supply of site forms with you into the field in the event that you locate any sites. Some of the main site types are discussed on the pages that follow.

Artifact Scatters

The most common type of site across North America may be debris from the manufacture of stone artifacts found scattered on the ground surface with little else; tools in various stages of manufacture may or may not be with them. **Lithic scatters** such as this are one kind of **artifact scatter**, which is one kind of **open site**, a site that is not in a protected or covered location such as in a cave or rockshelter. You should remember, however, that there are other types of open sites, such as middens or burial mounds, and artifact scatters may be associated with them. Indigenous people used different kinds of artifacts for many day-to-day purposes, and stone artifacts in particular were often numerous, used for skinning and butchering animals, grinding seeds and nuts, and manufacturing wooden artifacts, or for hafting as axes, adzes, knives, or spear points.

Lithic scatters can range in size from a few flakes, cores, and tools to a high-density scatter over a large area containing a wide range of different artifact types or perhaps nothing but flakes (for more information on defining a site and its boundaries, see "Defining the Boundaries of an Open Artifact Scatter"). Stone artifact scatters occur both as surface concentrations of material and as stratified deposits that may be datable, and they may or may not be associated with other cultural remains such as charcoal, shell, or bone. Archaeological information from open sites can be used to infer a wide range of behavior, such as population movement, customary exchange systems, and even activity areas if there is a sufficiently wide range of complementary material. An artifact scatter does not necessarily imply that people actually camped on a site but may indicate only that some type of activity was performed there (such as the manufacture of stone "tools") or that people passed through the region.

Quarries

Quarry sites are locations from which Indigenous people have extracted stone for making stone artifacts, ocher for use in painting, clay for making pottery, or some other substance important in their practices. Because people usually did not manufacture artifacts at quarries, finished tools rarely appear. Instead, larger fragments of stone and sometimes roughly formed artifacts can be found. Stone artifact quarry sources ranged from easily acquired loose river cobbles to large outcrops that had to be actively quarried.

Findspots

As the name implies, this refers to individual stones or other artifacts found by themselves in no obvious association with any other artifacts. Whether such artifacts were accidental or purposeful discards, they should still be recorded. Although an isolated artifact is not strictly a "site" (the definition for which varies from state to state and province to province), it is often what the archaeologist will encounter. Of course, it is possible that there were once other artifacts there that have since been removed or that the visibility conditions prevent you from seeing them (see "Determining Effective Survey Coverage: What Reveals, What Conceals" in chapter 3). If you find what seems to be an isolated artifact, make sure you search the area around it carefully to ensure that it is indeed isolated.

Middens or Midden Scatters

A **midden** is literally a deposit of trash where people have discarded materials in the same place for a relatively long period of time, usually ranging from months to decades. A **midden scatter** usually was created over a shorter period. and the remains are far less dense. A **shell midden** is a special kind of midden where marine or freshwater shells are the dominant component. A deposit with only a handful of scattered shells on its surface or an excavated deposit that contains only a few sparsely distributed shells normally does *not* count as a midden. Shell middens can occur along coastlines, around estuaries, along coastal and inland river floodplains, and around the shores of coastal or inland lakes. They also can occur as deposits within rockshelters and can range in size from a small, low-density surface scatter of shellfish remains to a high-density midden containing a variety of shellfish species, as well as animal bones, stone artifacts, and other archaeological remains. The presence of a shell midden or midden scatter does not necessarily imply that people actually camped at a place but may indicate only that they passed through the area.

Other forms of midden also are common. The debris from daily living often is discarded near or right on living surfaces and builds up over years, sometimes leaving deep deposits.

Because of the way middens are formed, stratigraphy within them is usually difficult to ascertain unless the wind or water deposits occasional layers of culturally sterile materials.

Stone Arrangements

These can range from cairns (piles of rocks) to extremely elaborate boulder alignments covering large areas. Some stone arrangements were used in ceremonial activities. Many of these are animal effigies such as turtles, snakes, or bison and may mark clan or totemic areas. Others were constructed for more secular purposes (such as to act as route markers, hut walls, or fish traps). For example, on the Great Plains, tepee rings are common, with the stones used to hold down the hide covering of the tepee.

Rock Art Sites

Rock art is divided into two basic types, pictographs and petroglyphs. **Pictographs** are made by painting, stenciling, or drawing, while **petroglyphs** are made by the removal of parts of the rock surface by pecking, grinding, abrading, or engraving (see table 7.1). Rock art is of great interest to archaeologists because it encodes many levels of social informa-

TABLE 7.1: How to recognize different rock art techniques (after Clegg 1983, 90)

Rock art technique (How it's made)	Distinguishing characteristics (What it looks like)
Rock art made by removing material from the rock surface (engravings, petroglyphs, carvings)	
A. Friction:	
A(i). Scratched (single stroke)	A U-shaped or V-shaped groove
A(ii). Abraded (repeated friction)	A U-shaped or V-shaped groove
A(iii). Rubbed (broad surface)	A rubbed area
B. Percussion:	
B(i). Pounded (direct percussion, e.g., hammering)	A pit (round, oval, deep, shallow, etc.)
B(ii). Pecked (indirect percussion, e.g., chiseling)	A pit (round, oval, deep, shallow, etc.)
C. Rotation:	
Drilled	A pit (round, oval, deep, shallow, etc.)
Rock art made by adding material to the rock surface (colored paintings, drawings)	
D. Mechanical:	
D(i). Stencil	Paint sprayed around the outline of an object (often a hand)
E. Delineated:	
E(i). Painting (materials applied when wet)	
E(ii). Drawing (materials applied when dry)	

The symbol "/" is the shorthand for denoting that one technique is applied on top of another (superimposition). Example: D(i)/E(ii), or stencil superimposed on drawing.

tion about the people who made it. It is also very useful for archaeological analyses because, unlike many other artifacts, it is securely tied to place. You can be fairly certain that the rock art was made for—and meant for—the place where you find it. The great weakness of rock art research is that it is very difficult to date. While there have been enormous developments in rock art dating over the last decade or so, it is still a job for specialists and requires expensive laboratory processes. The good news is that, should you need this expertise, there are a number of rock art specialists able to do both recording and dating.

Rock art is restricted in its distribution to regions where suitable rock surfaces occur, but almost any flat surface provided an excellent location for rock art. Pictographs tend to be found in sheltered locations such as rockshelters or caves, while petroglyphs tend to be in open or minimally sheltered areas. Large boulders might also be engraved or painted.

Motifs on rock art are extremely variable, from animal figures and hunting scenes to geometrics. In certain areas, the motifs can be used to provide a rough date for the art (Keyser and Klassen 2001; Whitley 2001). Rock art depicting scenes of what are obviously Europeans or Americans, or their associated material culture, such as guns or boats, shows that the art was made well into postcontact times.

Habitation Sites

Habitation sites are places where people chose to live. They can be open sites or closed sites. Most habitation sites had some sort of shelter that may have been temporary or permanent, large or small. They can be small villages with a few lodges or large centers with a variety of structures, but the key function was to provide a place of residence. Habitation sites can be part of even larger centers that might also have ritual or civic structures. Most habitation sites will be near a source of water and other key resources. **Activity areas**, where people tended to concentrate on doing single or only a few activities, such as cooking or hide processing, will show evidence of activities important for people's daily lives.

Because habitation sites are extremely variable, advising any single recording or excavation strategy is difficult. However, such sites tend to have a variety of activity areas, and if you wish to understand the full range of lifeways on the site, you will need to sample different areas and may need to use larger **block excavations**, which expose large areas of a site, to understand the nature and extent of the activities.

Rockshelters or Caves

Although living deep in caves was unusual, people sometimes did live near the mouth of a cave or more likely in a **rockshelter** where there was a sufficient overhang of rock to provide a roof and walls to protect people from the elements. Rockshelters offer unique excavation problems. Sometimes rock from the ceiling of the shelter falls onto the living surface. A large rockfall may preclude excavating anything below it without the use of heavy equipment to move the rock. In dry rockshelters excavators should wear breathing apparatuses to filter out the dust stirred up by excavations and screening. The dust can also cause various forms of mycosis (i.e., diseases caused by the spores of parasitic fungi) (Sledzik 2001).

Indigenous Special Places and Other Significant Sites

These can be either modified sites/features or natural features of the landscape (such as rock outcrops or water sources) that possess special significance because of their role in Indigenous belief systems. These sites may be part of creation stories or associated with important life events and ceremonies. Some may be unmodified features of the environment, in which case there may be few, if any, tangible features peculiar to these sites that indicate to non-Indigenous people the special significance of the place. Independent information from Indigenous communities is essential for the identification of all such places.

Burials, Ossuaries, and Mounds

Most cultures practice some form of treatment of the dead. During postcontact times, most burials took place in formal **cemeteries**, often following religious practices of the dominant society. Precontact disposal of the dead took a variety of forms. Individual burials sometimes involved **primary inhumation** where a single body, but sometimes more than one, was placed directly in the ground after death. Bodies could be **extended**, with legs straight out. Others might be in **flexed** position, with arms and legs drawn up to the chest in fetal position. **Secondary inhumation** involved removal of the flesh by purposeful defleshing or by natural methods, with bodies being put in trees or on scaffolds. After bodies were skeletalized, the bones were gathered into **bundles**, then placed into the ground. **Ossuaries** contain the remains of several individuals, often the product of secondary inhumation, and the bones are mixed or jumbled. Sometimes remains were **cremated** (i.e., burned). Any remaining fragmentary bones were put into bundles, then sometimes buried.

Mounds are piles of earth raised over remains and may contain primary or secondary inhumations, cremations, or a combination. Often a burial chamber can be found just below the surface of the ground with the mound raised above it, but sometimes remains are placed directly on the surface. Mounds might be built all at one time but often are built over a period of years and sometimes contain a number of bundle burials. Mounds may be low and in linear or conical forms, but they may also be very large, in excess of 10 m in height, length, or diameter. Mounds may be single or in groups, from 2 to more than 100. Be aware that not all mounds contain burials. Truncated pyramid mounds were often platforms for temples, while others, such as effigy mounds in the shape of animals, might have been clan or territorial markers. Burials often can occur in unexpected places such as under packed earthen floors of houses.

Unless done in close collaboration with the relevant Indigenous groups, deliberate excavation of human remains is best avoided. However, sometimes remains may be found in archaeological contexts exposed by erosion or development, or in unexpected places during normal excavations. Such sites and remains may hold great significance for Indigenous people, as well as for non-Indigenous people, and the disturbance of burials or burial places can be a very sensitive issue. There may be legal reporting obligations before the remains are further disturbed (for more information see "What to Do if You Encounter Human Remains").

Postcontact Sites

Postcontact sites are places with evidence for contact between Indigenous Native Americans and other groups of people. **Contact** should not be thought of as a precise date but as a complicated process that happens when people of different cultures meet. Contact happened at different times in different places, for example, with groups on the Florida coast first meeting Europeans in the early 1500s and people of the Great Plains not meeting them until the 1700s. Also important is a recognition that material culture from Europeans often was traded between Indigenous groups years, if not decades, ahead of actual physical contact. Equally important is that European items traded to Native Americans were not necesssarily the same in function or meaning as they were to Europeans. The diseases that so devastated Native American populations often spread from tribe to tribe well before some tribes made direct contact. To further complicate the matter, there is mostly controversial evidence that there may have been Native American contact with both non-European and European groups before Columbus (Kehoe 1998, 190–207). Postcontact site types range from trading posts to military installations, and even large cemeteries that contain victims of disease.

RECOGNIZING ARCHAEOLOGICAL MATERIALS FOUND AT SITES

The kinds of materials found on the surface or in test excavations sometimes give clues about the type of site you are recording. A very general rule is that the greater the number of *types* of materials and artifacts found, the greater the likelihood the site is some kind of habitation site. The reason for this is that people tend to make, use, and keep more items when they live someplace for a longer period of time. There are complicating factors, of course, such as length of occupation of a site and level of material culture complexity exhibited by a group. Precontact sites tend to have fewer artifact types than do postcontact sites, but certainly some of the near-urban cultures of the Mississippi River valley and the Southwest had a broad material culture. Detailed discussion of all materials and artifact types here would be impossible, but a general coverage can be useful, especially categories based on the materials from which artifacts were made, hints for recognizing them on a site, and some concerns about their treatment if they are found.

Artifacts Made from Relatively Perishable Materials: Fabric, Hide, Basketry, and Wood

Most cultures use a wide variety of organic materials that do not preserve well, yet they may be crucial for clothing, food processing, transportation, or shelter. In most North American locations you will not find these materials except in unusual preservation circumstances. Dry environments of caves or rockshelters of the West and Southwest or permafrost zones of the sub-Arctic and Arctic provide the most consistent preservation, but some extremely wet or muddy environments also may preserve organic materials. Some charred wood preserves reasonably well in most areas, as with the ends of posts used in house construction, purposely charred by the builders to keep them from rotting.

Organic materials found on or in sites should be treated with extreme care. The best advice is to consult with a conservator trained in dealing with organic materials; if that is impossible, try to keep the environment of the artifact the same as that in which you found it until a conservator can deal with it. Sometimes, even in environments where preservation is difficult, you can find clues of organic materials, such as impressions of fabric left on the wet clay of pottery before it was fired. If the material on which the clue is found is stable, you usually can treat it as you would similar artifacts of that material, though you may wish to provide special protection if it is a unique piece.

Artifacts Made from Bone, Antler, Teeth, and Shell

Bone, antler, teeth, and shell artifacts tend to preserve better than other organic materials, although acidic soils can destroy them quickly. These materials are relatively easy to recognize in the field, but whether they were altered by other taphonomic agents sometimes is difficult to determine. On tilled fields in the Midwest or East, the materials may blend with remains of last year's crops, such as cornstalks, and can be hard to see. Even if you do spot them, how did they get there? If you find a lot of shells by a water source, but not in the quantities of a shell midden, you might suspect that they are naturally deposited, but if you find them well away from water, something or someone had to bring them to the spot. Certain animals such as raccoons sometimes will take shellfish away from water and open them, but if the numbers are large, people may be responsible. Similarly with animal bone and teeth, animals die and their bones and teeth can be spread out by scavengers or other taphonomic factors, and one or two animals leave relatively few bones. If you find more bones or teeth than might be left by predators and scavengers, you again can suspect human intervention.

Artifacts made from shell are relatively common but sometimes are difficult to recognize. Larger shells may make good digging tools, but shells commonly are made into items for personal adornment, such as beads. Others were etched or engraved into ritual objects. In North America, certain shells often were traded long distances, so if you find a shell that is out of its normal range, you can suspect that humans transported it.

When humans hunt animals they tend to dismember them in fairly predictable ways. If animals are large and the people mobile, they may remove elements that have little meat or other uses, caching or abandoning them at the kill site. As part of butchering the animal, joints are chopped apart and muscles may be stripped from the bone, both actions leaving distinctive cut marks on the bone. Long bones of animals may be fractured to remove the marrow, which causes spiral fractures on the bone, almost certain evidence of human use. Bones also can be made into a wide range of tools for practices such as hide processing or planting, tending, and harvesting crops.

Antlers and teeth were used in more limited ways. Antler tines sometimes were used for pressure flaking in stone tool manufacture. Pieces of antler and the teeth of some animals were used for personal adornment. Horticultural peoples sometimes used the mandibles of deer with the teeth left in as sickles to harvest crops, or antler racks hafted to handles as rakes to work soil.

Artifacts Made from Metal

Because smelting was unknown in North America in precontact times, little metal appears in precontact sites. Meteoric iron was rarely used. The most common metal on precontact sites in the Great Lakes region is naturally occurring copper, part of the so-called Old Copper culture (ca. 5000 BP). Copper nuggets were cold-hammered into knives, projectile points, and other tools and adornments. Copper tends to corrode into a blue-green color, which usually makes it easily visible. Artifacts of iron and brass are present on many postcontact sites, usually as items of trade from Euro-Americans. Iron usually was made into knives or arrow points. Silver or gold trade ornaments or adornments are much rarer.

Artifacts Made from Fired Clay

The earliest pottery in North America appeared approximately 4,000 years ago and probably was made in imitation of either ground stone bowls or baskets. Pottery usually was made by mixing clay with a tempering agent such as plant fiber, grit, ground-up pottery, sand, or shell; forming it into a vessel or other object; letting it dry; then firing it. The pottery wheel came with contact, so precontact pottery was hand-formed using a number of different techniques. Precontact pottery also was open-air fired. Pottery could be plain but often was decorated by impressing, stamping, or incising designs in the wet clay. Painting was more limited. Vessel forms range from simple inverted cones, usually earlier in time, to globular and elaborate effigy forms, usually more recent in time. Generally, vessel walls were thicker on early pottery but became thinner through time.

Precontact pottery sometimes is very difficult to recognize on the ground surface. Made from soil, pottery tends to blend with the material around it. If pottery is painted or otherwise decorated, it may be easier to recognize. Pottery on a site tends to indicate that the site is a habitation site because pottery is both heavy and breakable. More mobile people rarely made it or carried it with them. Postcontact trade brought in a variety of ceramic and glass materials, and they were extremely important trade items. Crockery, stoneware, porcelain, and glassware—especially glass trade beads—also appeared. All are fairly certain markers of a postcontact site.

Artifacts Made from Stone

Stone certainly has been a material used everywhere, even by the earliest humans, and it has served many purposes. Some stone was used as part of routine daily activities, while other stones could be crafted into a wide variety of tools and objects for art, ritual, and other aspects of people's lives. Knowing more about stone and its uses is essential because stone has been employed everywhere and in North America is one of the most important markers of precontact sites.

Fire-Cracked Rock

People sometimes used stones for cooking. In stone boiling, hot stones were put into a basket or bag of water to bring the water to a boil. After a few uses, the stones would break apart and would be discarded. Other stones were used to line fire hearths, and after many uses, they too would break apart. Certainly some breakage occurs naturally, but **fire-cracked rock** (or **FCR** as it is sometimes designated) in quantity on the surface is a general indicator of a habitation site. In fact many avocational archaeologists call it "camp-rock," which to them indicates that an area contains a site.

The problem with fire-cracked rock is that quantities are often so large as to make for collecting and curation problems. At the very least, on the surface FCR should be mapped before being collected because its concentration may indicate an activity area. The literature on FCR is scant, but besides mapping it, many archaeologists weigh it and sort it into size categories. Many then discard it, but recent research suggests that stones were often selected for their ability to hold heat or resist breakage and could be brought in from some distance (Brink and Dawe 2003). Given the curation issues, however, a sampling procedure is well advised; you need to consider carefully your reasons for collecting FCR.

Ground and Flaked Stone Tools

People flaked some tools from larger pieces of stone, and in other cases they pecked, ground, or polished certain stones into tools. The difference in approach certainly was due at least as much to the type of stone as to the type of tool they wished to make. Flaked stone tools usually were fashioned from stone with a relatively high silica content that exhibits **conchoidal fracture** properties (i.e., when it breaks, the break is cone shaped). Understanding and controlling that breakage pattern allowed people to manufacture a wide variety of stone tools with sharp edges, ranging from projectile points to cutting, chopping, and scraping tools. Ground stone tools were made from coarse-grained stones that generally were unsuitable for flaking, such as granites or basalts (although some stones such as slate can be chipped into a rough shape before grinding and polishing). People made many kinds of ground stone tools including axes, adzes (a small curved-bit woodworking tool), celts (a small straight-bit chopping tool similar to a hatchet), bowls, pipes, and even some projectile points.

RECORDING FLAKED STONE ARTIFACTS

Flaked stone artifacts are made by **percussion** (i.e., by hitting one stone [called a **core**] with another [called a **hammerstone**] or with a wooden or antler billet) or by **pressure** (i.e., by applying pressure directly to the edge of a flake with the tip of an antler tine or similarly pointed tool). This process is called **knapping** (figure 7.2). Artifacts made by knapping have a number of things in common, and it is these things that an archaeologist looks for when identifying a piece of stone as a flaked artifact.

There are many systems for recording these stone artifacts in the field. Some attributes are more useful and easier to assess than others, and the recording system you choose may depend on the questions you wish to answer. In recognition of this we have not tried to establish a set of rules to follow. We have not tried to provide guidelines for detailed analyses either, as there are several debates surrounding which characteristics are considered the most useful to record and why. All we intend here is to outline some of the basic parameters that can provide you with quick and useful information in the field. For more detailed information on recording stone artifacts see Andrefsky (1998).

The obvious first step is to be able to recognize a flaked stone artifact when you see one. Doing so is not as easy as it might seem, and a question nonarchaeologists often ask is, "How do you know that rock is an artifact?"

FIGURE 7.2: Knapping, the process of making a flaked stone artifact

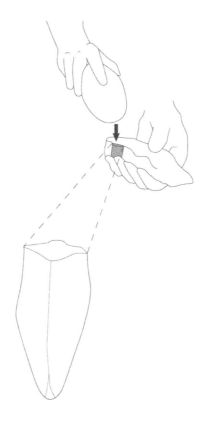

Archaeologists classify flaked artifacts according to four basic technological divisions:

- **Flakes**. The piece of stone that is removed by percussion or pressure from the core.
- **Cores**. The piece of stone from which flakes have been removed.
- **Retouched flakes**. Sometimes people will use a flake as a core and knap it to remove other, smaller flakes from along the edge. These twice-knapped artifacts are called retouched flakes. The appearance of retouch also may be created by using the flake.
- **Flaked pieces**. Artifacts that cannot clearly be identified as a flake, core, or retouched flake are just called flaked pieces. This is a category for artifacts that are clearly artifacts but that have lost their defining features or became detached because the core shattered in the process of knapping.

Knapping usually also produces a lot of smaller waste-material flakes that are not used but found scattered in quarries and in lithic production activity areas. **Shatter** is usually rough, blocky pieces, while **debitage** is usually smaller, flakelike, unused material.

How to Identify a Stone Artifact

How to Identify a Flake

Basic morphology:

- The "back" of the artifact (the side that was part of the outside of the core) is called the dorsal surface.
- The "front" of the artifact (the side that was once part of the interior of the core) is called the ventral surface.
- The "top" of the artifact (the part that the knapper hit to remove it from the core) is called the platform or proximal end.
- The "bottom" of the artifact (the end opposite the platform) is called the termination or distal end.

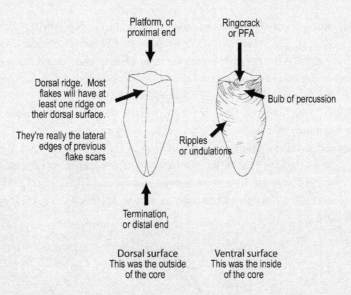

When trying to decide whether a piece of stone is a flake, look for these important features:

- When a flake is removed from a core there is often a distinctive circular mark where the hammerstone has hit the core. This is called a **ring crack**. Because the ring crack occurs in the precise spot where the hammerstone has hit the core, it sometimes also is called the **point of force application** (or **PFA**).
- The ventral surface may have a **bulb of percussion**, or a rounded bulge where the force from the hammerstone has radiated through the stone and split it from the core.
- The ventral surface also may have other features, such as concentric **ripple marks** or waves, which spread out from the ring crack.

(continues)

How to Identify a Stone Artifact (*continued*)

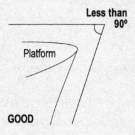

GOOD

To successfully remove a flake
the angle between the platform
and the ridge must be kept to less than 90°

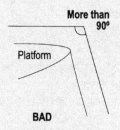

BAD

If not, no amount of force will be
sufficient to split a flake from the core
and the force of the hammerstone's
blow will simply dissipate

How to Identify a Core

The key to identifying a core is to look for the opposite but complementary characteristics to those you look for in a flake. One of the key characteristics of a flake is the rounded bulb of percussion on the ventral surface. One of the key characteristics of a core, therefore, is the negative imprint of this bulb—a rounded hollow where the flake was split off from the core. This is called a **negative flake scar**.

Even flakes may have negative flake scars—anything that has been removed from the core after the beginning of the knapping process is likely to carry away with it the negative imprint of earlier flakes. The crucial distinction in telling a flake from a core, however, is that *a flake must always have the positive attributes* of the knapping process (a bulb of percussion), whereas *a core will have only the negative attributes* (flake scars). The only exception to this will be if a flake has been used as a core, in which case you may see both kinds of attributes.

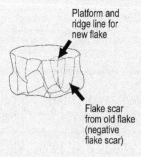

Platform and
ridge line for
new flake

Flake scar
from old flake
(negative
flake scar)

How to Identify a Flaked Piece

This actually is quite difficult, and your success at identifying them will depend to a large extent on your experience. Because this category was created explicitly for all those definite artifacts that have no defining attributes, if you are unsure about what is or is not a "definite" artifact, then this category will be highly problematic for you. Artifacts that are highly weathered or that have been shattered in a fire might fall into this category, but so might artifacts that were detached as part of the knapping process. This category is not meant to be a catchall "too hard" basket for all those things that you think might be artifacts—if you are unsure, seek a second opinion. Ask a colleague or supervisor for help. The easiest way to identify a flaked piece is to look for ventral or dorsal features. If you can define any of these, such as ring cracks, negative dorsal scars, or undulations, then the artifact is a broken flake. If you cannot but are sure the piece derives from knapping, then it is a flaked piece.

Recording Other Important Classes of Stone Artifacts

Manuports. This is a category for pieces of stone that obviously are not found locally in the area and therefore could only have been carried in by people. It doesn't necessarily have to be knapped (although it may be)—just exotic to the local area. You will be able to tell whether a piece of rock is exotic only by familiarizing yourself with the local geology and stone sources.

Grinding stones. Unlike flakes, which are customarily made from fine-grained, sharp-edged raw materials, grinding stones are made from coarse-grained and abrasive materials such as sandstone or basalt. They were used by Indigenous people to grind seeds, root tubers, or ocher and consist of two parts: a flattened "dish" in which the material rested and a rounded stone that was held in the hand and used as a pestle or muller. These are sometimes referred to using the Mesoamerican terms *metate* (the "dish") and *mano*. Look for relatively flat, dish-shaped (concave) stones and smaller rounded stones of the same material (but note that you might not find them together). One surface of each stone (and possibly more than one surface of the muller) is likely to be smoother and possibly polished as a result of repeated grinding.

Ground stone axes, adzes, celts, and mauls. These commonly were made of volcanic (igneous) raw materials such as basalt or granite, because they are extremely hard. To make an axe, a "blank" (an axe-shaped piece of stone) is knapped or pecked into the rough axe shape. One end is worked further to create a chopping angle, the **bit**. This edge of the axe was then ground smooth until it was sharp. Usually the remainder of the tool was pecked and ground until it was uniform to provide better balance and the look of a finished tool. Ground stone axes often were very stylized, with extreme care taken in creating the tool.

The end opposite the bit is called the **poll**, which, if well formed, could be used as a hammer or maul and sometimes shows battering from that kind of use. Some axes will have a groove partially or completely around the body of the axe to aid in attaching the axe to a wooden haft using a variety of techniques and materials. An entire axe will be easy to identify because it will have these ground edges and because it will be made from hard volcanic material. If, after use, the edge of an axe became dull, Indigenous people would often knap some further flakes from the axe's cutting edge and regrind it. These

(continues)

How to Identify a Stone Artifact (*continued*)

waste flakes are called "edge sharpening flakes" and will also be relatively easy to spot because of their distinctive raw material and because they may have polish on some margins. Adzes and celts usually were used for woodworking, were smaller in size, and show no evidence of hafting. Mauls usually were made for pounding and thus have no bit. They may have been grooved for easier hafting. Usually their form has a much cruder look than most ground axes, and there may be evidence of battering on the ends, just as you may find on the poll of an axe that was used for pounding.

To produce a particular kind of flaked stone tool a knapper will sometimes remove many flakes from a core. When a person sits down in a particular spot to knap an artifact, the place sometimes is called a **knapping floor**. At sites that were knapping floors, archaeologists can sometimes literally **retrofit** (i.e., put the flakes back together) to understand the process of making an artifact. In some cases this allows them to see the original shape of the core and to work out how the person went about reducing the core to make a particular collection of stone artifacts. Many of the artifacts an archaeologist finds in the field are the waste products from this process rather than the desired end product, which usually was taken away for use elsewhere. In recording such a group of stone artifacts, archaeologists try to distinguish between those flakes that were removed at the beginning of the process and those that were removed from the core toward the end of the process. One way of doing this is to measure the amount of **cortex**, or the original, weathered outside surface of the core that is visible on each flake. Cortex can be pebble cortex, from a water-rolled pebble, or outcrop, from an exposure of stone. Either way, it will appear on the dorsal surface only. If you can see cortex on the dorsal surface of the artifact this means it has come from the outside of the core and was removed at the beginning of the process. If, however, the artifact has no cortex, it obviously has come from the interior of the core and was removed nearer the end of the process. Archaeologists use the relative amount of cortex on an artifact to distinguish between three types of flake, according to when they were struck off the core:

- **Primary** (where the entire dorsal surface is covered with cortex; this means the flake was one of the first to be struck off the core)
- **Secondary** (with some cortex and some flake scars; this means the flake was not one of the first, but was still struck off early in the manufacturing process)
- **Tertiary** (an artifact with no cortex; these flakes must come from the last stages in the manufacturing process)

Be careful not to confuse cortex with weathering, which results from prolonged exposure to the elements. The thing to remember is that weathering can occur on all surfaces of the artifact (including dorsal and ventral), whereas cortex will be found only on the dorsal surface.

USEFUL INFORMATION TO RECORD WHEN YOU'VE FOUND AN ARTIFACT SCATTER

When you have found a scatter of artifacts in the field, you should record some basic data about the artifacts and the site (a recording form is included in appendix A). The standard aspects of the site that you need to record are:

- The types of artifacts that occur in the scatter. Can you recognize any correlation of one artifact type with others? Might this be a particular activity area? For example, FCR in association with pottery and charred bone might indicate a cooking area. This is mostly impressionistic; more precise assessment can be done later.
- For stone materials, what types of tools appear? Estimate how many flakes there are. How many cores? Flaked pieces? Retouched flakes? How many of the flakes appear to be primary, secondary, or tertiary? Is there stone material other than chipped stone?
- The size (an estimate, if not exact length, width, and any other appropriate attribute) of each artifact or of a representative sample of them if there are many, as well as other obvious characteristics (figure 7.3). You need to make sure that you estimate or measure all artifacts consistently and that you write in your field notes exactly how you did this.
- The density of artifacts across the site and how this changes. This is a basic assessment of how many artifacts there are and usually is measured in terms of the number of artifacts per square meter. This is often phrased as "X artifacts/square meter in the center of the site, dropping off to X artifacts/square meter on the margins of the site."
- Whether the extent of the site is defined by declining visibility or by a declining density of artifacts (see "Defining the Boundaries of an Open Artifact Scatter").
- The range of lithic raw materials. You need to be able to recognize how many different types of raw materials there are and what they are. You also need to take note of how many artifacts are made from each kind of raw material. What is the most common? What is the least common? If possible, you also should try to identify the sources of these raw materials. Other archaeological studies may be able to help you here, as could a knowledge of the local geology (see "Geological Maps" in chapter 2) or information provided by ethnographic sources. If you are unsure of what kinds of raw materials you can expect in your study area, research it thoroughly *before* you go into the field. You may wish to build a small comparative collection of raw materials known to

FIGURE 7.3: How to measure and record the key attributes of a stone artifact

How to record a flaked stone artifact:

1. Length:
On the ventral surface, measure the length in mm from the ring crack to the mid-point of the termination (this is called percussion length). NOTE THAT THIS NOT AUTOMATICALLY THE LONGEST POINT OF THE FLAKE (although it may be).

2. Width:
Measure the width in mm at right angles to the length, at the mid-point of the length (this is called percussion width)

NOTE THAT THIS NOT AUTOMATICALLY THE WIDEST POINT OF THE FLAKE (although it may be).

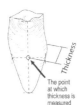

3. Thickness:
Measure the thickness in mm at right angles to the width at the midpoint of the length

The point at which thickness is measured

4. Platform width:
Measure the width of the platform in mm from one lateral edge to the other

If the platform is as wide or wider than the width of the flake this is called a broad platform

If the platform is narrower than the width of the flake this is called a focal platform

Platform thickness

5. Platform thickness:
Measure the platform thickness in mm at right angles to the platform width at the widest point of the platform

6. PFA diameter:
Measure the diameter of the point of force application (PFA) in mm from one side of the ring-crack to the other

PFA diameter

7. PFA/Dorsal ridge relationship:
Turn the flake over and describe the relationship between the PFA and the dorsal ridge.

It may be:

Directly behind a clear ridge   To one side of a clear ridge   Between two ridges   Behind a previous PFA (no ridge)   No relationship (this usually means the core has been rotated)

NOTE: If your flake doesn't fit into any of these categories, use 'Indeterminate'

8. Overhang removal:
Examine the platform carefully. Look for small negative flake scars on the dorsal ridge below the platform. These are designed to correct the angle of the flake or to remove previous ridges.

This is called overhang removal.

9. Core rotation:
Count the number of negative flake scars on the dorsal surface which are not aligned in the same direction as the flake.

This is a measure of core rotation, or how many times the core was turned during the knapping process.

10. Termination:
Describe the shape of the flake's termination.

It may be:

Bulb of percussion | Platform

A feather termination

A hinge termination

A step termination

A plunging termination (sometimes called an 'Outre-pass2')

The form of the termination reflects the way in which the force from the hammerstone traveled through the core. A feather termination is what the knapper is trying to achieve, because it increases the length of the useable edge. In a plunging termination the knapper hit the core too hard and actually broke off the bottom of the core along with the flake. In both step and hinge terminations the flakes have split off prematurely leaving behind an inwardly curved or right angled ledge. When the knapper tries to remove subsequent flakes, they, too, are likely to be step or hinge terminations, making the core more difficult to knap. Hinging sometimes leads to cores being abandoned completely.

11. Negative flake scars:
Count the number of negative flake scars on the flake's dorsal surface. Don't worry about those less than 5 mm long.

12. Describe the shape of the terminations for the negative flake scars on the dorsal surface. How many are feather, hinge, step or plunging terminations?

13. Breakage:
Note whether the flake has been broken since it was made. Flakes are often snapped in half or have their ends broken offÑ either transversely (across the flake) or longitudinally (along the flake).

Trampling (by either people or animals) is one of the main causes of broken flakes.

Note which piece of the flake you have, the proximal end, the distal end, one side (lateral) or the middle (medial).

Transverse snap | Longitundinal snap

Proximal ➡
Medial ➡
Distal ➡

Recording cores:

1. Measure the length in mm along the widest dimension of the core.

Length

2. Measure the width in mm at right angles to the mid-point of the length.

Width

3. Measure the thickness in mm at right angles to the width.

The point at which thickness is measured

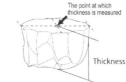

Thickness

4. Count the number of platforms from which flakes have been struck (all directions).

5. Note whether any of the platforms have been specially treated by the knapper as part of the process. Look for overhang removal or grinding on any of the platform edges.

6. Estimate the percentage of the core that still retains cortex.

7. Count the number of distinct cortical surfaces. Note that this will depend on being able to distinguish a change in plane. For a pebble there may be only one because the surface is round.

8. Count the number of negative feather terminations.

9. Count the number of negative step and hinge terminations.

be from sources in the area in which you are working. It can be carried easily if you use small samples or kept in your field camp. The collection may not provide information about all the materials you find, but it may help you to quickly recognize some materials as being from outside the area.

Obviously if you have found a large site with high artifact densities, it is unlikely that you will be able to record much of this information for every single artifact. In this case you will have to make some decisions about how to sample your site (see "Developing a Suitable Sampling Strategy" in chapter 3). Some archaeologists adopt a strategy of walking transects across the site and measuring all artifacts that occur at set points along that transect (e.g., by counting all artifacts within a square meter every five meters along the transect); others identify different zones within the site and sample evenly within each zone.

Once you have gathered this information for all or part of your site you can then begin to compare different attributes against each other—do different types of raw materials tend to occur in specific locations? Are there areas within the site with particularly high densities of artifacts? Are there changes in the relationships between the stone artifacts and other types of artifacts or archaeological features at the site (such as middens, mounds, hearths)? (See figure 7.4.)

RECOVERING ARTIFACTS WITH RESIDUES AND USE WEAR

Residues and use wear are the physical traces left on the edges and surfaces of artifacts as a result of their use in various tasks. **Residues** can include trace amounts of starch, blood, hair, or woody tissue still adhering to the artifact. Some residues will last much longer than others (resin, for example), particularly those that become compacted into tiny crevices in the stone. Pottery used in cooking might contain charred material that can be analyzed for food type by gas chromatography. **Use wear** is a description of the physical changes to the edges of an artifact as a result of its use: artifacts used to cut grasses, for example, develop highly polished edges; others used to saw bone develop particular forms of edge damage (for a full listing of a range of use-wear types see Fullagar 1989, 45).

A detailed recording or analysis of residues and use wear is not really practical in the field and is best undertaken by a specialist. If you are retrieving stone artifacts for later analysis in a laboratory, however, bear in mind that the best artifacts to examine for residues will be those that have been protected from the elements and that are retrieved through excavation (Fullagar 1989, 40). It *is* possible to recover residues from artifacts in surface scatters, although the most productive will be those that have been protected in

FIGURE 7.4: An example of how to work through the analysis of an artifact. You need to look at many different aspects of the artifact's life history in order to analyze it properly (after Wright 1983, 123).

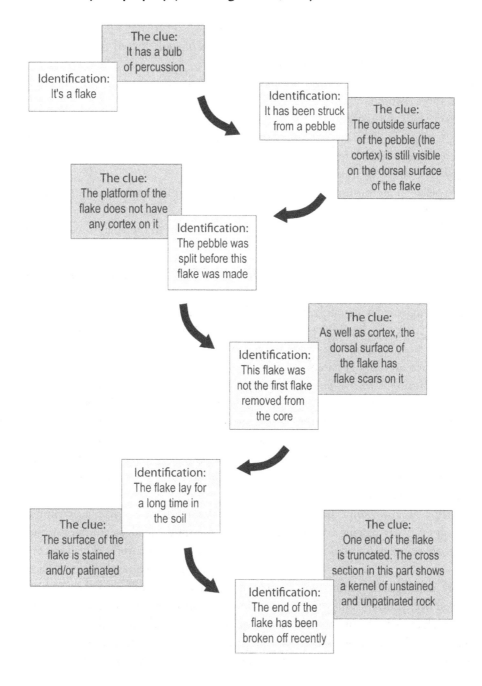

some way. When collecting artifacts for later analysis, follow these basic procedures to ensure that any residues are preserved (Fullagar 1989, 41):

- When you excavate the artifacts, try to leave as much of the adhering soil on them as possible.
- If you need to clean them, lightly brush them with a soft-haired paintbrush. If necessary you can rinse artifacts in water.
- Don't scrub artifacts. If soil is impacted and difficult to remove, gently rub the artifact with a wet cotton swab or a soft-haired paintbrush.
- Try to handle the artifacts as little as possible. It is not strictly necessary to wear gloves, and it may not even be desirable because many disposable types contain powdered starch that can leave a residue on the artifacts.
- Bag each artifact separately.
- *Don't* place an aluminum tag inside the bag (these will actually leave a residue on the artifact that might obscure other residues).
- *Do* submit a detailed history of excavation and handling to the analyst with the artifact.

DEFINING THE BOUNDARIES OF AN OPEN ARTIFACT SCATTER

While this might seem a straightforward task, it is actually one of the most difficult decisions of any survey. Indigenous people have lived in North America for so long that large parts of the landscape are absolutely littered with artifacts. If the artifacts visible on the ground surface are only apparent as a result of erosion or visibility conditions, however (see "Determining Effective Survey Coverage: What Reveals, What Conceals" in chapter 3), the question of where the site really begins and ends is not straightforward. In some places artifact scatters can be found across such extensive areas that the entire landscape could be defined as one large archaeological site. It would be impractical to record every artifact in such a situation. The reality is that people would have used different parts of the region in various ways and at different times, so no purpose would be served by defining the whole region as a single site.

In such a situation some archaeologists would define the boundaries according to artifact density (i.e., by placing an arbitrary boundary around the areas containing the highest numbers of artifacts and defining the rest as "background scatter"). This is an arbitrary decision as well as a pragmatic one and will be decided upon as a result of the aims of your fieldwork and what questions you are trying to answer, as well as the environment in which you find yourself (Sullivan 1983, 6) (for more information see "Designing Your Research" in chapter 1). Most archaeologists would accept that if you find yourself in an area literally covered with artifacts then you are more likely to define sites in terms of those places that contain the greatest density or variety of artifacts. On the other hand, if you have been surveying for six hours before you find your first isolated artifact, then that artifact probably assumes great significance.

Likewise, if the artifacts you are recording are only visible as a result of erosion you will need to consider whether the boundary of your site is the extent of the eroded area, the limit of visible artifacts (which may or may not coincide), or some other arbitrary feature (such as a fenceline or land boundary). As a general rule the most important thing to remember is to clearly state your definitions and assumptions in your journal and report so that whatever definition you adopt, it will be clear to others how this might have influenced your results. In most cases the boundary will have to be defined according to the extent of visible artifacts, even though you may well suspect that there could be more artifacts underneath the surface. One of the major decisions you will have to make in this case is whether or not you think there are **potential archaeological deposits** (**PADs**) at the site. You should note that, because of visibility problems, some administering authorities may require subsurface investigation to determine the full extent of a site as a matter of course. Even though it is common knowledge that open sites tend to be more extensive than they appear on the surface, you should not attempt to guess at the hidden component. If you have a strong suspicion that the site is greater in area than what is visible, write these suspicions in your field notes, always explaining why you think this might be so.

Checklist for Recording Open Artifact Scatters

❑ The location of the scatter (i.e., what enabled you to see it—Is it within an erosion scar? On a vehicle track? In a sparsely vegetated area? Beside a creek?)

❑ The visibility conditions of the scatter (i.e., how much of the ground surface is visible, usually stated as a percentage, and what kind of ground cover)

❑ The visibility conditions away from the scatter (the comparison between this and the conditions of the scatter will help you to determine whether there might be more artifacts present than you can actually see)

❑ The length of the scatter

❑ The width of the scatter

❑ The approximate density of artifacts within the scatter (artifacts per square meter)

❑ The range of artifact "types" within the scatter

❑ The range of artifact sizes within the scatter

❑ The presence of any other indications of human behavior (i.e., charcoal, bone, hearths, contact materials) in the scatter

❑ Any potential for subsurface deposits

❑ Any potential sources of damage to the scatter (e.g., animals, vehicles, people)

RECORDING QUARRIES

A quarry may be anything from a rock outcrop that has been quarried once to a highly prized and carefully managed source that may have been quarried over generations and to which access was tightly controlled. In general, Indigenous people preferred particular kinds of stone when making artifacts. Very fine-grained stone not only makes the sharpest artifacts but also is the easiest to knap successfully. Chert, mudstone, silcrete, quartzite, and chalcedony were all preferred materials for stone artifacts and thus also for stone artifact quarries. A recording form for quarries or quarried stone outcrops is included in appendix A.

RECORDING FINDSPOTS

Findspots are relatively easy to record because they often are a single artifact and rarely more than a few.

- Check carefully to see that there are no more artifacts in the immediate area. Only then should you collect the artifact(s). If there are more artifacts, how many, and what are the relationships between them? Could the artifact(s) be part of a larger nearby site?
- Make note of the conditions that allowed you to find the artifact. Was it on the surface, plainly visible? Was it in a vehicle track or the spoil from an animal burrow?
- Is the location near any particular environmental feature(s) to account for it, such as near a water source or on a high spot?
- Plot the artifact(s) on a map. If easier, you may wish to take GPS readings and note them, placing them on a map later.

Checklist for Recording Stone Artifact Quarries

❏ The material form of the quarry (Is it a rock outcrop? River cobbles?).
❏ The site location (e.g., is it on a hilltop? Beside a creek or river? On a slope?).
❏ The particular features of the quarry (e.g., can you see pits from quarrying activity? Are there flaking or knapping floors there? Are there other imported raw materials at the site? Can you see flake removal scars on boulders?).
❏ If there is surface artifactual material, what is the artifact density?
❏ Are other stone artifacts present? What is the percentage of cortex on them?
❏ If the site is an outcrop, estimate the percentage that is worked.
❏ Any potential sources of damage to the site.
❏ If known, the distance to isolated artifacts or sites in the vicinity.

RECORDING MIDDENS

Recording middens can be problematic because they may be independent of a habitation site or an integral part of it. If they are part of a habitation site, they may be considered a **feature** rather than a standalone site. Some habitation sites literally are middens, with shelters built directly on the midden, with the trash deposit sometimes forming house walls. This is relatively rare but usually happened when the habitation site was in a constricted area, such as inside a fortification.

You should try first to understand the nature of the midden. Is it a midden scatter or a true midden? If a true midden, is it a feature of, and integral to, a habitation site? If a standalone midden, what is its source? How near is it to a habitation site? After all, the trash had to come from someplace. You will need to determine its dimensions, and if you can do any test excavations or see a profile in an erosional feature, determining the midden's depth is especially useful. You cannot always rely on a midden being built on the surface of the ground because people often deposited their trash in natural features such as gullies, old stream channels, or sinkholes. Middens usually have a wide variety of materials in them, so you'll need to get an idea of the range if possible. We have not included a special checklist for middens because it would be very similar to the list for shell middens that follows. Just take the shell midden list and remove the parts that have to do with shells.

RECORDING SHELL MIDDENS

Shell middens present special problems. The first task when recording a shell midden is to establish whether it is indeed a humanly created midden or a natural shell bed. This is not as simple as it sounds, however, because a variety of factors—such as the diversity of the shoreline, the location of the midden in the landscape, and the past land-use history of the area—can affect the form and content of both natural and humanly created middens (Attenbrow 1992; Bonhomme 1999). No single criterion positively identifies an Indigenous midden, but there are some generally accepted criteria that might be helpful in distinguishing a shell midden from other types of shell deposit (Attenbrow 1992; Bonhomme 1999).

When recording a shell midden you need to record its form, dimensions, context, and the numbers and proportions of different shell species that are present, as well as any other artifacts it contains. To understand how the midden relates to its environment you also should take note of whether similar shellfish species are available nearby and what the local estuary, river, rock platform, or beach is like now (Sullivan 1989, 52). Shells are mainly calcium carbonate, and as they decay they create a highly alkaline environment that tends to preserve bone and other organic remains quite well. This means that the excavation of

Checklist for Recording Shell Middens (after Bonhomme 1999; Sullivan 1989)

❑ The location of the midden (beach, dune, lake)
❑ The local conditions (revealed through erosion, or stable environment)
❑ The curvature of the midden (Is it mounded? Is it flat?)
❑ The shape of the midden (Is it elongated? Circular?)
❑ The length of the midden
❑ The width of the midden
❑ Whether it has potentially excavatable deposits
❑ If it has some depth, whether this depth is even or uneven across the midden
❑ The minimum and maximum depth
❑ The estimated volume of the midden
❑ The species of shell(s) to be found in the midden (you should try to record the full range of shells visible on the surface to species level if possible)
❑ The relative proportions of different species (calculated by number and/or weight)
❑ An estimate of the rank and order of abundance of shell species (what are the dominant, rare, and common species?)
❑ The size of different species and their relative proportions
❑ The condition of the shells in the midden (whole, worn, broken, burned)
❑ The nature of any other artifacts in the midden
❑ Any potential sources of damage to the midden

a shell midden can be quite productive in terms of recovering a wide range of organic remains (see "Val Attenbrow's Tips for Excavating Shell Middens" in chapter 5).

RECORDING STONE ARRANGEMENTS

The methods you will use to record stone arrangements will be determined by the manner in which the stones are arranged. Some stone arrangements are linear, and some are circular or oval in shape; others may be piles of stone. Some are very extensive and contain tracks, circles, and other linked sections. When you are recording a stone arrangement you need to remember that the stones may not be in their original positions. Often you won't be able to tell, but sometimes removed stones will have a different pattern of weathering from the other stones in the arrangement, and sometimes the displacement will be really clear, such as when a road has been bulldozed through the middle. In the latter case, you would record each part of the arrangement as a separate feature, but also record in your notes your interpretation that these were once part of the one arrangement.

Checklist for Recording Stone Arrangements

❏ A plan of the site
❏ The type(s) of stones
❏ The size of the stones
❏ The assumed function of the arrangement (fishtrap, ceremonial), if possible
❏ Anything unusual about the arrangement
❏ Any visible artifacts or features
❏ Its proximity to other sites
❏ Any sources of damage to the site

Depending on the amount of ground-cover surface conditions, you easily may be able to tell if any artifacts are associated with the stones. You should not necessarily assume that there are not. Tepee rings, for example, are associated with short-term habitation, so there may be both artifacts and hearths. Usually these are few and near the surface, so at least some test excavations may be needed to determine the nature of the arrangement.

RECORDING ROCK ART

The main challenge with recording rock art is to record the motifs accurately without damaging them. Pictographs (rock paintings), in particular, are often frail, and you will

Checklist for Recording Rock Art

❏ The location of the panel or motifs within the shelter or rock outcrop
❏ A general description of the rock art and the motifs
❏ Detailed drawings of individual panels or motifs
❏ If pictographs, a note of the colors of the motifs (you can identify these by using a Munsell color chart or a Pantone swatch set; see "Drawing Rock Art" in chapter 9)
❏ The time of day that you made the recording (the quality of light hitting the rock surface at different times of the day definitely can affect your ability both to see motifs and to accurately describe their colors)
❏ Photographs of the panels and motifs
❏ Any potential sources of damage to the art (e.g., have wasps or swallows built their nests across the art surface? Is rainfall washing across the rock surface? Have parts of the rock surface flaked or fallen off?)
❏ The condition of each individual motif

Bruno David's Tips to See the Invisible

Pictographs—rock paintings—differ from one place to the next. So too do they vary over time. Yet until recently, rock art researchers around the world have been tethered by two critical factors: (1) the difficulties of dating rock art and (2) the tendency for older art in particular to fade or to otherwise disintegrate. In consequence, until the 1980s few archaeologists systematically incorporated rock art within regional historical studies, and even when they did, much rock art—and particularly the older pigment art—failed to be recognized due to its damaged state.

One solution is nevertheless emerging. During the 1960s, secret spy satellite programs and technologies used in space exploration missions such as the Ranger lunar space craft program (1961–1965) gave birth to digital image enhancement. What is relatively new is the accessibility of this technology to the public on a large scale. The 1990 release of Adobe Photoshop for home computers made the tools for digital image enhancement commercially available, and subsequent versions took the technology to new domestic heights.

Today, image enhancement can be undertaken using commercially available software such as Adobe Photoshop or Paint Shop Pro and hardware that is both cost effective and highly portable. What this means for archaeologists is the possibility of rendering previously invisible rock paintings visible again. The principles work like this:

1 Different colors consist of electromagnetic waves of various lengths.
2 Rock paintings can fade through time through various processes, including the action of water, dust, and the like.
3 The process of fading often involves the development of opaque films—whether silicate or otherwise—over pigment art.
4 These gray films are unsaturated colors—that is, they are a combination of all colors.
5 By asking the computer to change or enhance particular wavelengths or colors on a digital photograph (e.g., by preferentially saturating the distinctive colors of paintings and getting rid of grays), we can highlight pigment colors and thus minimize the effects of fading.

It is best to enhance images by first downloading digital photographs or digital scans of images onto the computer and opening them as uncompressed TIFF rather than JPEG files. Once opened in Photoshop, images can be enhanced through the Image (Adjust) channels.

Apart from revealing previously hidden rock art, digital enhancement has the advantage of being able to produce results immediately, and once the basic hardware and software are at hand (laptop, camera, software), results can be both checked against rock surfaces in the field and shown to community members, including those who may not be able to go to the sites. These potentials are exciting and await to be fully exploited by researchers and communities wishing to document their own ancestral places.

June Ross's Tips for Recording the Color of Rock Art Motifs

Recording the color of art pigments is an important part of recording pictographic rock art. When you draw a motif or a panel of motifs, make sure you note on the pencil drawing the range of ocher colors. Analyzing the color of motifs can help you identify whether the same pigment has been used throughout, suggesting that the art was produced in a single episode, and can also be used to check the spatial distribution of distinctive colors.

- Remember that the consistency of pigment color is often uneven, so "washy" sections will appear lighter than thicker sections. Getting a repeatable reading is sometimes questionable because of this, but it may be necessary.
- Rock art pigment is often poorly mixed, so each motif may need two or more color readings.
- Identifying colors is a difficult task and many people don't have an eye for it, so there can be many different readings for the same motif. For this reason try to limit the number of people recording color so that you can maintain some control over the color recognition process.
- Colors will look different in different lights, so readings may be different at different times of the day. For this reason you should always note the time of day you made your reading and write this on the drawing.
- Recording the color of rock art motifs is usually done through the use of Munsell color charts, although some rock art researchers have used Pantone color swatches. The advantage of Pantone swatches is that the color can be reproduced easily on your computer (although with scanning this has lost its value), and they are easy to use as you can hold the swatches right up to the pigment. Unfortunately they are also expensive to buy, and the colors are often too pure and don't really match the natural earthy tones of rock art pigments very well. Munsell charts, on the other hand, have a much better range and grading of colors, but their format makes them difficult to use because the swatches are small and always surrounded by a distracting white border. On balance, even though not as handy a format as Pantone swatches, Munsell is still the best way to document the color of rock art motifs.

have to use recording methods that do not involve touching the art surface. The most effective way of recording rock art is through drawing the motifs in the field or taking photographs and then drawing from them. When photographing rock art it is especially important to remember to include a metric scale that incorporates a color standard (such as the one supplied by the International Federation of Rock Art Organisations [IFRAO]) as this will help you to judge the authenticity of the color of the paintings. Make sure you note the technique(s) used in producing the art (table 7.1), the location of the rock art panels, and any sources of potential damage.

RECORDING HABITATION SITES

When people choose to live in a place for more than a few days, they tend to locate themselves near important resources such as water and primary food sources. They also consider intangibles such as the view or defensive positioning. They weigh factors such as the need to be close to water with the need to be far enough from it to stay away from possible flooding and insects. Fortunately, basic human needs have never changed, so a certain amount of intuition can be used to locate habitation sites. Good places to live now often were good places to live in the past, although cultural preferences certainly play a part in human locational behavior.

The wide range of habitation sites demands very flexible strategies for recording an excavation, particularly if a site is large. Certainly, the factors that might have gone into the selection of a location need to be considered, so you may need to collect a range of environmental information from a site. Because people from one time and culture tended to choose a particular location, you might expect that people from another time or culture might choose the same location. This means that you will need to determine whether the site has multiple components from uses of the location at different times, which is not always easy. You also will need to determine the nature of shelters on the site, possible activity areas, and any features. Habitation sites tend to have a larger number and wider

Checklist for Recording Habitation Sites

❏ Note pertinent locational information that might be relevant to the selection of the site, including distance to nearest water; key geomorphological features such as a high point, stream terrace, or easily defensible position; and key resources, particularly food, lithic sources, or other items of potential importance.

❏ Locate, if possible, the boundaries of the site and plot them on an appropriate map.

❏ Record the remains of any shelters or features visible on the surface, such as raised platforms, depressions, walls, mounds, and fortification ditches. Note and map them.

❏ Record the range of artifacts on the site and their densities.

❏ Record clusters or relationships of artifacts on the surface that might indicate possible activity areas. You may need to do test excavations to verify them.

❏ Locate any features external to but near the site, such as mounds or middens. Map them in relation to the habitation site. Do not designate them as associated with the habitation site until you can verify it.

❏ Note any evidence that the site may have multiple components or that it may be the product of one occupation at a particular time.

❏ As needed, do block excavations, using 2 m × 2 m units or opening an even larger area, to verify the presence of structural evidence such as post molds, packed earth floors, or **cache pits** dug into the ground for storage or trash.

range of artifacts than do other kinds of sites, so you will need to deal with the variety as you surface-collect or excavate the site, especially in terms of the distribution of artifact types and their relation to other artifact categories and features on the site.

RECORDING ROCKSHELTERS

Rockshelters have been used by Indigenous people as shelter since the earliest habitation of the continent. Rockshelters are a place to rest, to keep out of the sun, to avoid rain, to

Checklist for Recording Rockshelters

❏ The aspect of the shelter (i.e., what direction is it facing?)
❏ The degree of slope leading up to the shelter (measured with a clinometer)

A plan of the rockshelter showing:

❏ The shape of the rear wall of the shelter
❏ The shape of the front of the shelter
❏ The position of the **drip line**(s), or the limit of the dry area under the rock overhang (literally the line along which the rain will drip); this is particularly important to record as it may show you the areas most intensely occupied by people and the area outside the shelter where artifacts may have been disturbed by erosion
❏ The position of the limit of rock overhang (this may or may not, and usually will not, coincide with the drip line)
❏ The location of major features of the site, such as large boulders, major rockfalls, or rock art panels
❏ The location of major rock art motifs
❏ The location of any surface archaeological material

A cross section (side view) of the shelter showing:

❏ The height of the roof
❏ The level of the floor
❏ The extent of the livable area
❏ The location of any major features, rock art motifs, or surface archaeological material
❏ If there is surface archaeological material, the range of artifact types present
❏ The range of raw materials present
❏ The distribution of material across the surface (i.e., are there any obvious concentrations of artifacts that might indicate places for future excavation?)
❏ Whether there is any evidence of animals regularly using the shelter, which could have disturbed the archaeological material and its patterning

sleep, and to provide defense. Some also are prime locations for creating rock art. They are located in most escarpment areas, providing a safe and sheltered place with a view of the surrounding area. Those that are located near water were a favored place for people to live. However, the fact that a rockshelter was inhabited by people in the past does not mean that there will always be archaeological evidence of such use. Surface evidence is often ephemeral. It can blow away or be disturbed by animals or covered by later deposits.

When recording a rockshelter, the first decision you will need to make is where the site's boundaries are. It doesn't really matter at which point you decide that the shelter ends as long as you record the reasons for your decision. You may decide that a group of fallen boulders marks one end of the shelter, or that it comes in sharply at a particular point that works to define the point between inside and outside. Some rockshelters have a slope in the front that contains artifacts because inhabitants threw unwanted materials out the front, downslope and away from the shelter. You may wish to include the slope as part of the shelter. The main thing is to record why you have made your decision, with the aim of making it possible for another researcher to replicate your methods and verify your results.

RECORDING INDIGENOUS SPECIAL PLACES AND TRADITIONAL CULTURAL PROPERTIES

The U.S. National Register of Historic Places recognizes that certain places hold special importance for people even though the place may not have material remains or structures. For Indigenous people these may be places where their traditions say they were created, or they might be places where certain religious rituals are held. They may be places that are just considered to be sacred or held in reverence, but they don't have to be. By definition, they are places that "embody or sustain values, character, or cultural coherence" (King 2003, 1). Non-Indigenous people also have such places, and they also deserve attention. In CHM terms these are **traditional cultural properties (TCPs)** and by more formal definition are associated "with cultural practices or beliefs of a living community that (a) are rooted in that community's history, and (b) are important in maintaining the continuing identity of the community" (National Register of Historic Places 1990, 1).

None of this is straightforward. Because many TCPs have few if any cultural remains, you are unlikely to find them in the field. This means they must be identified by consultation with communities, and that can be difficult (see "Social Significance" in chapter 8). Ethnographic research is important in identifying and assessing the significance of such sites. TCPs do not necessarily have to be sacred places but often are. When they are, "sacred" becomes very difficult, even impossible, to define. In terms of defining properties, you need to record some of the same information you do for any other kind of site, but especially the boundaries of the property. Even this can be a problem. The term *property* is difficult because it implies ownership and often someplace that is relatively small or limited. Can someone "own" a sacred place, and how can you put boundaries on the sacred?

The best advice is to be respectful of a people's beliefs about a place and flexible in your approaches to dealing with them and the information they give. They may not want you to set foot on the site, or they may wish not to tell you information that is normally kept secret from outsiders or even insiders who have not been properly prepared or earned the right to know about a place. Don't press for information. If the site is in danger of destruction, you can explain that identifying the site and its boundaries might offer some protection, but recognize that telling you about a place is their choice. If you are offered information, record and protect it, following any strictures they wish to place on the information.

RECORDING BURIALS, MOUNDS, AND OSSUARIES

Most people, and certainly most Native Americans, are especially concerned about the remains of their dead. Burials can be encountered in many contexts, from burial in the floors of houses to interment in mounds or ossuaries. They may be near habitation areas or at some distance from them in important or sacred places. If burial areas such as groups of mounds are obvious, you follow similar practices for delimiting the boundaries of any sites and mapping the locations of each mound.

- Record the location of the mounds in relation to any topographic features such as high points, ridgelines, or water sources.
- *Do not* remove vegetation from mounds. If you can't map them due to vegetation, use pacing or other methods to estimate size and shape.
- Note the dimensions of each mound and its shape. Most mounds in North America are conical or linear, but there are other forms.
- If a mound has an unusual shape, such as an effigy, do your best to map and photograph the mound.
- In areas of agriculture or high erosion, mounds may be small or barely visible. Do your best to assess size and shape.
- *Do not* do subsurface testing in any mound unless you have explicit permission from proper authorities. To do so may be a violation of law.

What to Do if You Encounter Human Remains

Burials can be located in many different contexts including natural, deliberate, and unintended or "accidental" burial. For this reason it is possible that you might encounter them

Identifying Indigenous Burials

The Skeleton Manual (Thorne and Ross 1986, 32–33) sets out some criteria. Answering yes to any of these questions may mean that the burial is Indigenous.

- Is the grave small, shallow, and/or oval in shape?
- Is the grave outlined by salts from contact with local groundwater (indicating that it may be very old)?
- Has it been dug into hard deposits but without any evidence of metal tools used?
- Is it associated with other Indigenous cultural material (such as stone artifacts, ocher, animal bones, or shell)?
- Does the burial occur within an ancient landscape or is it associated with a known Indigenous burial site?
- Does the grave contain bones from more than one individual?
- Are the bones in a flexed position (i.e., are the legs drawn up to the abdomen or chest, or are the arms folded against or across the chest)?
- Have the bones been made into a relatively small bundle (i.e., are the legs, arms, and torso very close together)?
- Are the bones hard and mineralized, encrusted with carbonate or other salts, or discolored from long contact with the soil?

during fieldwork. If you do encounter human remains during excavation or survey (this is possible if Indigenous burials are actively eroding), it is imperative that work cease immediately until a positive identification of the remains can be made (first, as definitely human—you would be surprised at how many sheep or other animal bones are initially misidentified—and second, as Indigenous). *Under no circumstances should you remove the remains or interfere with the surrounding soil matrix in which they occur.*

In some cases it may be possible to determine whether or not the remains are Indigenous by a careful but nonintrusive examination of the grave and any associated features. Whether Indigenous or not, their treatment is covered by law in almost every instance.

If your answer is still inconclusive, however, you will need the help of a physical anthropologist to examine the bones. Remember that, if the bones are Indigenous, they will be protected by legislation, and if the burial is recent it will immediately become a police matter. *Either way, any unauthorized disturbance of the skeletal remains or the burial will be illegal.* If the remains need further identification you should contact the police and the relevant government authority for Indigenous heritage matters immediately.

If you are charged with removing the remains, remember always to treat remains with the utmost respect. Many people think of archaeologists as graverobbers already, and there have been many unfortunate cases where archaeologists or people working with them have done such things as put sunglasses on a skull or a cigarette in its mouth. Such acts are disgraceful and have serious consequences. Ideally, you should have special knowledge of human osteology to properly understand what you are doing and how to interpret the site. A number of sources (e.g., Bass 2005; White and Folkens 2005) are available to help you with this, but a wise archaeologist will consult with a specialist.

RECORDING EARLY POSTCONTACT SITES

Postcontact sites are best identified through reference to the history of the region and the surrounding material culture or through interviewing Indigenous people (see "Recording Indigenous Histories"). Does the site seem to be meaningfully located in relation to these histories? In North America, especially in eastern areas where contact first occurred, Native Americans usually have been moved away from their homelands. You need to remember that it is very difficult to prove a meaningful association between artifacts in a surface assemblage, because these materials could have been left behind at very different times. So the location of square nails and beads near a stone artifact scatter or hearth does not automatically constitute a postcontact site. You would then need to consider the site in terms of the history of the area. Sites near transportation routes, along rivers, or on good harbors have the highest probability of being postcontact, because they facilitated exploration and trade by Euro-Americans. People have always lived in these areas, however, so pre- and postcontact components may exist in the same place. Postcontact sites also may be found outside of any of these areas.

Contact sites encompass a range of site types (such as habitations, middens, rockshelters, open artifact scatters) but are also likely to incorporate the material culture of non-Indigenous groups. A contact site also can be indicated by the use of material in a context different from that in which it is normally found. Postcontact sites are recorded using the methods suited to that particular site type, but in a sense, you will need to use methods of both precontact and postcontact archaeology, especially the use of documents to support your work. Be aware that the earliest contact is often poorly documented.

RECORDING INDIGENOUS HISTORIES

The methods used to record Indigenous histories are comparable to those used to record any oral histories (see "Recording Oral Histories" in chapter 6). In dealing with Indigenous people or communities, there are several specifics that you should bear in mind:

- Be aware that Indigenous people often think it is rude to ask direct questions. They are therefore likely to be under more stress than non-Indigenous people when a formal interview is being conducted.

- It is important to leave room for Indigenous people to shape the interview process themselves. This can be done by allowing people to go off on tangents, talking about the things that are important to them (but that may not be of immediate importance to you). Often, this will deepen the quality of the interview and is part of establishing trust between the interviewer and the person being interviewed.

- If people avoid answering a question, it is usually because it is not something they wish to answer. Don't harass them, and take constant note of their body language as this will give you a clue as to how comfortable they are feeling during the interview (remembering, of course, that body language may be differently interpreted!).

- Sometimes people may know the answer but will not have a right to speak on that particular topic. In this case, they may direct you to the person who does have a right to speak, by saying, "Ask Joe," or "Mary might know about that." This is not a refusal to help you but Indigenous protocol for dealing with information in a system of restricted knowledge.

UNDERTAKING ETHNOHISTORIC RESEARCH

Ethnohistoric research is an important part of most Indigenous archaeological projects and will form a part of the literature review for any good Indigenous consultancy project. **Ethnography** is the study of living peoples; **ethnohistoric research** uses historical accounts of Indigenous people written by Europeans or Euro-Americans in the early post-contact period to reconstruct what Indigenous culture in this period may have been like. Ethnohistoric sources can provide information on how people were moving through the landscape or using particular areas; what plant and animal resources they relied on (and, from this, where sites might be located); their language, beliefs, diet, ceremonies, dwellings, and hunting techniques; and what objects they made or traded with other groups. Sources of information include explorers' journals, official reports, settlers' diaries, letters or reminiscences, accounts of early anthropologists, and any other early record left by those who came into contact with Indigenous people. You can find this material in any major or state library, even in local historical society collections and libraries, and sometimes still in the control of private individuals (descendants, perhaps).

Archaeologists use ethnohistoric sources to reconstruct in some measure the postcontact cultural environment of Indigenous people. There are obvious problems with this, however, most notably that these sources have the same inherent problems as all written documents (see "Using Historical Documents" in chapter 6). They were written by a particular person for a particular purpose and will tend to include only the information that the observer thought was relevant at the time. The cultural barriers between Europeans and Indigenous people also affected the accuracy of their ethnographic observations—many accounts contain descriptive or other incidental observations of a culture that the Europeans poorly understood and for which they may have had little sympathy. There is also an expectation that the earlier the account, the more closely it will resemble the precontact "truth" of how Indigenous people actually lived, but you must bear in mind that by the time even the earliest accounts were written, European observers already were witnessing a society radically changed by the contact process. Because of the extremely complex social networks linking Indigenous people throughout North America, many groups already had access to European goods through their trading networks long before they first saw a white person. Other problems with the use of ethnohistoric sources are that many observations were made of small groups of people undertaking specific, often highly seasonal tasks and therefore do not reflect the broader range of activities of the larger Indigenous group.

Finally while ethnohistoric accounts are invaluable for the insights they can provide into the immediate postcontact period, they are also tightly restricted in time and space and cannot be applied to geographically separate groups of people or to people inhabiting the same area in even the recent, let alone the distant, precontact past.

REFERENCES AND FURTHER READING

Andrefsky, W., Jr. 1998. *Lithics.* Cambridge: Cambridge University Press.

Attenbrow, V. 1992. Shell bed or shell midden. *Australian Archaeology* 34:3–21.

Bass, W. 2005. *Human osteology: A laboratory and field manual.* Columbia: Missouri Archaeological Society.

Bonhomme, T. 1999. Shell middens on the central coast of New South Wales: A discussion of problems in distinguishing natural shell deposits from cultural shell accumulations. In *Australian coastal archaeology,* ed. J. Hall and I. McNiven, 229–233. Canberra: ANH Publications.

Brink, J. W., and B. Dawe. 2003. Hot rocks as scarce resources: The use, re-use and abandonment of heating stones at Head-Smashed-In Buffalo Jump. *Plains Anthropologist* 48(186): 85–104.

Byrne, D., ed. 1997. *Standards manual for archaeological practice in Aboriginal heritage management.* Sydney: NSW NPWS.

Clegg, J. 1983. Recording prehistoric art. In *Australian field archaeology: A guide to techniques,* ed. G. Connah, 87–108. Canberra: AIAS.

Fullagar, R. 1989. On site functional analysis of stone tools. In *Sites and bytes: Recording Aboriginal places in Australia,* ed. J. Flood, I. Johnson, and S. Sullivan, 39–48. Australian Heritage Commission Special Australian Heritage Publication Series Number 8. Canberra: Australian Government Publishing Service.

Kehoe, A. B. 1998. *The land of prehistory: A critical history of American archaeology.* New York: Routledge.

Keyser, J. D., and M. A. Klassen. 2001. *Plains Indian rock art.* Seattle: University of Washington Press.

King, T. F. 2003. *Places that count: Traditional cultural properties in cultural resource management.* Walnut Creek, CA: AltaMira Press.

Meehan, B. 1982. *Shell bed to shell midden.* Canberra: AIAS.

National Register of Historic Places. 1990. *Bulletin 38: Guidelines for evaluating and documenting traditional cultural properties.* Washington, DC: National Park Service.

Sledzik, P. 2001. Nasty little things: Molds, fungi, and spores. In *Dangerous places: Health, safety, and archaeology,* ed. K. Feder and D. Poirier, 71–78. Westport, CT: Bergin and Garvey.

Sullivan, M. 1989. Recording shell midden sites. In *Sites and bytes: Recording Aboriginal places in Australia,* ed. J. Flood, I. Johnson, and S. Sullivan, 49–53. Australian Heritage Commission Special Australian Heritage Publication Series Number 8. Canberra: Australian Government Publishing Service.

Sullivan, S. 1983. Making a discovery: The finding and reporting of Aboriginal sites. In *Australian field archaeology: A guide to techniques,* ed. G. Connah, 1–9. Canberra: AIAS.

Thorne, A., and A. Ross. 1986. *The skeleton manual.* Sydney: National Parks and Wildlife Service NSW and the NSW Police Aborigine Liaison Unit.

Vaughan, P. 1985. *Use-wear analysis of flaked stone tools.* Tucson: University of Arizona Press.

White, T. D., and P. Folkens. 2005. *The human bone manual.* New York: Academic Press.

Whitley, D., ed. 2001. *Handbook of rock art research.* Walnut Creek, CA: AltaMira Press.

Whittaker, J. C. 1994. *Flintknapping: Making and understanding stone tools.* Austin: University of Texas Press.

Wright, R. 1983. Stone implements. In *Australian field archaeology: A guide to techniques,* ed. G. Connah, 118–125. Canberra: AIAS.

For a range of other useful information, see the website accompanying the text.

CHAPTER EIGHT

MANAGING CULTURAL HERITAGE

What you will learn from this chapter:

What site significance is
How to assess the significance of a site
How to make this process as objective as possible
Strategies for assessing the impact of development
Why good management decisions can only be made after the assessment of significance
How to prepare a bid for a cultural heritage management project

---

Much archaeological fieldwork is carried out within the confines of cultural resource management (CRM) projects, or as it is more generally referred to outside the United States, cultural heritage management (CHM) or heritage resources management. In fact, even in the United States the trend is toward the use of CHM rather than CRM, a usage that makes sense because it provides a broader foundation for study and protection of heritage and avoids the use of the term *resource*, which tends to commodify cultural heritage. (After the introduction to this chapter, please note that the usage shifts mostly to CHM.) CRM/CHM is based on **consultancy**, or what is often called **contract archaeology**, where the archaeologist serves as a paid consultant to a government or private agency whose development work may have an impact on heritage sites that are archaeological, historical, or traditional cultural properties. Cultural heritage management is the branch of archaeology that deals with assessing the effects of development or other potentially harmful human activity on heritage sites and takes steps to either protect sites or to allow their destruction. The latter is no small matter. Although most would like to see all sites protected, all archaeologists accept that not every archaeological site is worth preserving indefinitely. Not only are there insufficient resources for authorities to physically look after every site, but preserving every example of an open artifact scatter is not necessarily going to provide better information than preserving only the best and most informative examples (i.e., preserving a **representative sample**). One of the main tasks of CHM, therefore, is to assess which heritage sites are significant enough to preserve and which are not. This requires an understanding of the process of assessing **significance**, or those aspects of a place that make it of value to society (see "The Categories of Cultural Significance").

To do this, a site must have some capacity to contribute to our understanding or appreciation of the human story (Pearson and Sullivan 1995, 7), but the significance of a site is actually a matter for communities to define. In other words, significance is a quality that is assigned to a place by people—not some inherent quality of the place itself. For this reason, what is considered "significant" can change through time, as history unfolds and communities change. To aid archaeologists and other heritage professionals in making these assessments, many of the U.S. state and federal authorities who administer cultural heritage under the National Historic Preservation Act (notably the Department of Interior, National Park Service) have developed guidelines for assessing cultural significance. Obviously, this is not, and never will be, a truly objective process—cultural heritage management is about how people value a site, something that is often highly emotive and intuitive rather than rational and logical. This does not, however, make cultural significance any less real or any less important, as relating to the tangible remains of the past in some way enriches our lives and deepens our understanding of ourselves.

The process of assessing significance requires a firm understanding of the purposes and limitations of archaeology, the intent of cultural heritage legislation, the range of sites that exist in the United States, the management policies of the relevant state and federal authorities, and the intricacies of appropriate site preservation and management measures. For this reason, the federal government established minimum qualifications that are considered adequate for supervising a CHM project.

These qualifications support the ethical responsibilities of the archaeologist (see "Archaeologists and Ethics" in chapter 1) in that you must be sufficiently well qualified to be able to carry out a job to acceptable professional standards. Poor-quality or ill-informed assessments damage the archaeological resource and the professional standing of the archaeological community, sometimes irretrievably.

Secretary of Interior Professional Qualifications Standards for an Archaeologist (36 CFR Part 61, Appendix A)

1 At least one year of full-time professional experience or equivalent specialized training in archaeological research, administration, or management.
2 At least four months of supervised field analytic experience in general North American archaeology.
3 Demonstrated ability to carry research to completion.
4 A professional in prehistoric archaeology shall have at least one year of full-time professional experience at a supervisory level in the study of archaeological resources of the prehistoric period.
5 A professional in historic archaeology shall have at least one year of full-time professional experience at a supervisory level in the study of archaeological resources of the historic period.

www.cr.nps.gov/local-law/arch_stnds_9.htm (accessed January 2, 2007)

THE BASICS

One-third of any CHM project is simple people skills: liaison, coordination, and negotiation. You may have to consult with tribal members, landowners, historical societies, developers or engineers, construction workers, and architects or town planners, plus members of the general public, all of whom will have different questions and concerns. As a heritage practitioner, you have a primary ethical responsibility for the proper conservation and management of the heritage resource. Nevertheless, you also must be aware of the pressures and constraints that can affect CHM projects and the range of agendas that will often exist in relation to any heritage site. If you are being contracted to undertake heritage work, you must also bear in mind the legal right of the client to have full access to information about the site (see "Archaeologists and Ethics" in chapter 1) and your ethical responsibilities to the administering authority or other groups. The most common constraint on all CHM projects is time: if you are working as a consultant you will not have the leisure of working on a pure-research timetable. In all likelihood you will be working on somebody else's schedule, somebody who may or may not be receptive to archaeology as a valid component of the project in the first place. This means that you will have to be highly focused in how you approach the project and how you carry it out, and also be prepared to be the liaison between the often arcane practices of archaeologists and the realities of construction, engineering, or mining projects. You may have to make rapid assessments of areas or sites, without the leisure time to investigate every square centimeter of ground. Don't be pushed around by developers, but be prepared to be flexible if the situation warrants it.

The most common CHM projects are surveys undertaken as part of a project driven by Section 106 of the National Historic Preservation Act (NHPA), designed to locate heritage sites, record them, and assess their level of significance. Many different bodies require CHM reports for a variety of purposes—private developers, local and township councils, corporate developers, mining companies, government departments, and even in some circumstances, private landowners. While all the basics of fieldwork will be essential in any CHM job, you will also need to develop some extra skills. Most important, you will need a good understanding of the concept of cultural significance and the standards for assessing it. You also will need to know how to make management recommendations for a site or area, because this is the ultimate task of most CHM projects. Remember—your role is to be as objective as possible, but you also are being employed as a heritage professional. Your first duty is to do the best job you can for the heritage values of the place, your second is to try to reconcile the varied goals of the developer or owner and any other interested parties according to those cultural heritage values. This mainly is what CHM is all about—treading the minefield between what should happen in a perfect world and what resolution it is best to achieve in this one. Above all, your recommendations need to be realistic and tailored to suit the individual circumstances of the job—there is no point in recommending the full-scale salvage of an area if you are working for a small client with limited funds.

AN OVERVIEW OF THE CHM PROCESS

The CHM process begins when a private or government entity plans some development. What they plan may be as small as a tennis court or as large as a major interstate highway. Heritage management issues come into play if there is any level of federal involvement, including seemingly minor links such as federal loans or permits. This makes the project a **federal undertaking**. Some states and local governments have similar policies. Section 10 of the NHPA requires that the organization responsible for the development coordinate with the state historic preservation officer (SHPO) or tribal historic preservation officer (THPO) if on certain tribal lands, who assesses whether significant sites may be harmed by the project. If the SHPO or THPO believes that to be true, the officer tells the developer or agency to arrange for identification and inventory of sites in the **area of potential effect (APE)** (i.e., the land area involved in the project and sometimes lands around it that may be affected indirectly). If the APE is large, the officer may recommend survey of a percentage of the area. Most SHPO/THPO offices keep a list of qualified archaeologists or CHM businesses capable of doing the inventory, and the developer hires one of them to do the work. When federal agencies are doing work themselves, they may use their own archaeologists or may request proposals or bids from private CHM businesses. The archaeologists hired or assigned the work begin consultation with all of the stakeholders, from the developer and SHPO to Indigenous people or local communities that might have concerns. Some projects have three phases, and this consultation continues until all phases of work are complete.

Preparing the inventory is usually designated **phase I**. The inventory almost always includes a literature search to see if sites are already known from the APE. This search involves looking at a wide range of records, including site forms in the offices of the SHPO/THPO and the state archaeologist, reports from earlier projects within or near the APE, and any other materials deemed to be relevant. Because relatively few areas are well known archaeologically, the inventory usually includes a **reconnaissance survey** by archaeologists (see chapter 3, "Finding Sites"). The job of the archaeologists is to locate sites that may be eligible for inclusion on the **National Register of Historic Places** (often just called the **National Register**), a list of significant sites maintained by the federal government. Archaeologists conduct their surveys and report their findings to the lead agency and usually to the SHPO/THPO. Their reports provide all the information possible about the site without excavation, except perhaps for some shovel tests or deep testing done to locate the site. The archaeologists recommend whether they believe a site is eligible for the National Register and should receive further testing for significance.

National Register of Historic Places Criteria

In order to be listed on the National Register, sites need to meet key criteria. Do sites "possess integrity of location, design, setting, materials, workmanship, feeling, and association" and also meet one or more of four eligibility criteria? They need to be:

a   sites associated with significant events;
b   sites associated with significant people;
c   sites that embody a type, period, or method of construction; or represent a master's work; or possess high artistic values; or represent a significant, distinguishable entity; or
d   sites "that have yielded, or may be likely to yield, information important in prehistory or history."

Phase II is a detailed evaluation of a site. If the SHPO/THPO agrees with the archaeologist's recommendation that a site may have National Register potential, and the site is not already considered eligible for or not already on the National Register, the SHPO/THPO will recommend an evaluation of the site. This is to see if the site is significant enough to be eligible for inclusion on the National Register. Usually, the developer hires the same CHM company that did the phase I inventory to do the phase II evaluations because they are already familiar with the site. Phase II involves more formal testing of the site to assess its boundaries, the precise nature of the site, stratification, the amount of prior disturbance, and anything the SHPO/THPO or CHM archaeologist believes might provide information to help evaluate the significance of the site. Phase II usually involves a more formal program of subsurface testing, using 1 m × 1 m units placed over the site according to a sampling procedure (see "Sampling" in chapter 3). The archaeologist uses the criteria established in the regulations of the NHPA to recommend whether the site is eligible for the National Register. For precontact archaeological sites, criterion d is the most often used, but for postcontact sites almost any of the other criteria can be used, especially if there is good documentary evidence about the site. Use of multiple criteria tends to strengthen the recommendation. In truth, criterion d has become a bit of a catchall, but it is often all you can use for a precontact site.

The phase II report discusses each site that was evaluated and makes a recommendation about its National Register eligibility. When the report is complete, it goes to the developer or agency first, which then may allow it to be sent to the SHPO/THPO. Almost always, peers heavily review the report to assess its adequacy. These are other archaeologists who have worked in the area, and they may even be competitors in the CHM business. Important decisions about protection of sites will be based on the report. Thus, phase II reports should always be the best work possible.

If the archaeologist recommends that a site is not eligible and the SHPO/THPO and agency agree, the issue of compliance with the law ends for the agency or developer. If the site is recommended as eligible for the National Register, "the process becomes much more formal and deliberate" (Neuman and Sanford 2001, 157). The intent becomes to work around or to avoid the site if it is practical and to recover as much information from it as possible if disturbing the site can't be avoided.

Phase III begins when a site is declared eligible for the National Register. The task of the developer and the SHPO is to figure out how to **mitigate the loss** of sites that are National Register eligible (i.e., how to avoid, minimize damage to, or excavate the site before it is destroyed). The steps are clearly outlined. First comes a determination of **adverse effect** (i.e., that a National Register–eligible site will be harmed by the project). This is followed by a distribution of the results of the phase I and II reports and recommendations to all consulting parties, with an invitation for the public to comment. In consultation, the various parties develop a **memorandum of agreement (MOA)** that spells out the steps that will be taken to mitigate the loss of the site. Finally, archaeologists and the agencies involved mitigate adverse effects to the site by avoidance or excavation. Mitigation does not mean excavation! In fact, avoidance is preferred because it fully protects the site, whereas excavation destroys it (see chapter 5, "Basic Excavation Techniques"). Excavation should be the choice of last resort. The problem is that any redesigning of the project plans to avoid a site is often more expensive than excavation, so **full data recovery** by excavation of the site sometimes becomes the least costly option for the developer. Because excavation is often costly, the project usually is put out for bid in the hope that competition will reduce the

CHM Law and Regulation versus the Real World

Although CHM regulations seem clear and straightforward, the truth is that many developers and project engineers either don't know about the NHPA or disagree with it. Some believe that CHM projects are too costly or stand in the way of progress. Whatever the reason, they often don't build CHM into their planning. One of the greatest tasks of SHPO and THPO offices is to educate these individuals about the laws and processes used, and as people on the frontlines of CHM, archaeologists need to get involved in the education process too. Some developers are so well organized that they build CHM into their planning years ahead of actual construction, thus avoiding having to redesign projects or delay construction. Unfortunately, out of ignorance some don't plan for CHM at all, while others use the philosophy that it is better to build their projects without doing the required surveys and ask forgiveness later, if sites are found or their law breaking is discovered. The penalties can be severe in either case. If a project gets delayed due to a site found during construction, equipment and human "downtime" can be enormously expensive. If a site is damaged, the developer may be asked to make amends. In a case in Iowa, a builder of a cell phone tower ended up spending more that $1,000,000 to relocate the tower and restore a burial mound. They could have avoided the whole problem by paying about $1,000 for a phase I survey!

Another occasion where the real world intrudes is when a developer has failed to plan and desperately needs to stay on a schedule. Sometimes the SHPO/THPO is willing to alter the three-phase process by allowing stages to be combined. Commonly, phase I reconnaissance and phase II evaluation can be combined. Similarly, phase II and III are combined to avoid the time spent in consultation.

In all of this, if you have the opportunity to advise clients, you should urge them to plan well ahead, but if required, let them know about possible shortcuts that the SHPO/THPO may be willing to negotiate. The shortcuts usually save time, however, not costs, and may actually cost a bit more.

overall costs. The archaeologists who did the phase I and II work may not win the contract for phase III work, even though they might know the site better than anyone else. Upon completion of the excavation, a phase III report details the excavation methods, what was found, and any interpretations about the site. This report sometimes includes a public component that informs interested parties about the significance of the site.

THE BUSINESS OF CHM

CHM is a business as much as it is a way to protect heritage sites. The business aspects of CHM often are not a part of training in archaeology but probably should be. If you intend to be involved in CHM you should take training in everything from the basics of accounting to human resources issues. You can't do any of this, however, if you don't know how to prepare a **proposal** or **bid** so that you will be selected to do a phase I, II, or III project. The whole CHM business system is driven by bids and proposals.

When the need for a CHM project arises, the developer or agency may call a CHM company directly, if the project is small, and ask for a bid. A bid is a quotation of the costs for doing the work. For larger and more complex projects the developer or agency may ask for proposals as well as bids. A proposal is essentially a research design that outlines the methods you intend to use to do the work and your justification for them. Your cost estimate (bid) is linked to the things you propose to do by your justification of the costs. Larger projects, especially government-funded ones, get advertised in many ways. If an advertisement is an **RFQ**—a **request for quotations**—all that is required is a bid (although sometimes they require a breakdown of costs). An **RFP**—a **request for proposals**—usually asks for more complete documentation, including a research design. If your company is interested in the project, you request the **scope of work** (**SOW**), which outlines the project in some detail. Proposals tend to be more complicated than bids.

HOW TO PREPARE A PROPOSAL OR BID

Bids and proposals are part of the CHM business; essentially they are job applications, so take them seriously. When preparing a proposal or bid the key is to make sure that you do justice to protection of the resources, properly estimating the real costs of the job so that you don't lose money, and that you remain competitive. Some government departments will issue a detailed project SOW and will expect you to address each selection criterion in your proposal or bid. This is exactly like applying for a job—if you don't address the selection criteria properly, you won't get the job. Other jobs will be less formal, and for these the onus will be on you to find out precisely what the job will entail and to accurately assess what it will cost. The essential first stage in preparing a bid is to get a map of the area and make sure you have a clear idea from the client about the actual scope of the project. Make sure you know how large the area is, what the terrain is like, and what the client intends to do, because this will help you to calculate just how much time and how many people the job will take. If you are bidding for an Indigenous archaeological project, the other essential initial task is to talk to the THPO or other relevant tribal officials. This will establish a good working relationship with them even if you don't get the job and will alert you to any concerns or stipulations they might have.

The second stage of the bid process is to construct a fair budget for the project. As with any application for funding, don't inflate, but don't underestimate either. If in your bid you indicate that you can do the job properly in three days, but then find out in the field that you miscalculated and it will take twice as long, the client is unlikely to be sympathetic. You made a mistake, and you will have to bear the extra costs. If you are genuinely not sure precisely how long the job will take, however, indicate this clearly in the bid, including your reasons for not being able to calculate it precisely. For example, you may be asked to survey an area on tribal lands and then make management recommendations based on what you find. You suspect that you might locate highly significant or sensitive sites and that this might totally change the THPO's views on how intensively the area should be surveyed, thus requiring more consultation time and costs. You cannot predict this with any certainty, so you could indicate in your bid that this possibility is likely and provide an estimate of the additional costs should it happen. If you are really worried about your cost margins, some agencies allow you to include a contingency—often 10%—to cover unforeseen circumstances, such as heavy rain preventing you from accessing sites. Clients may understand that you can't predict every eventuality. In some cases you also may be able to negotiate a budget variation with the client if the work turns out to be far greater than you reasonably expected, although the success of this may come down partly to your negotiation skills. If a client changes the scope of work in the middle of the project due to unforeseen circumstances on the client's side, you may be able to change your contract.

In your bid you also must price yourself and your employees fairly according to levels of expertise. Bear in mind, however, that you may need to balance a professional rate with the needs of the individual situation—a small client with limited funds may not necessarily be able to afford your normal rates. The amount you charge may be governed by classification schemes that your business or university has developed in order to assure fairness of pay among equally qualified employees. Your practice also may vary depending on the conditions under which you are asked to work. For example, you may be able to ask for a greater pay rate if your client is trying to meet a construction deadline or requires you to work in difficult or dangerous conditions. Also remember to calculate any institutional requirements for employee benefits, such as workers' compensation or insurance. Most institutional research or human resources offices have devised percentages of your payroll to cover them. If you are not part of a larger organization, you may still be legally responsible for covering such benefits. The issues of employee costs are complicated, and you need to take this into account when you are working out the composition of your field team. If the project is large, you would be well advised to consult with human resources specialists.

The other key in bidding successfully is to make sure that your budget is sufficient. Make sure, for example, that you remember to include fees for consultation and that you allow for the recommended three days in the office/lab for every one day you spend in the field (see "Finding Funding" in chapter 1). If you are including fees for Indigenous consultants, it is wise to check their consultancy rates before you submit, because it is no good getting the job and then finding out the Indigenous community routinely charges $40/hour instead of the $20 you budgeted for. Remember to include an amount for report production to cover the costs of copying and binding reports, buying film, and developing photographs, as well as the cost of any travel to and from the site. If you intend to get feedback on a draft of your report before submitting the final version, remember to allow extra time for rewriting and extra costs for a second round of copying and binding.

The third stage of the bidding process is to write the bid and sometimes a proposal, usually a requirement on large projects. The bid is more straightforward and usually is a listing of expected costs. Some RFQs ask for a single price as a **fixed cost** (i.e., you are paid the amount you bid no matter the real costs). If you win the bid and the project can be done professionally at a lower cost, the remainder is profit. Mostly this type of bid is done with small- to medium-sized phase I projects. Other projects may be offered as **cost recoverable** (i.e., you are paid what the project actually costs, and sometimes an actual budget line item for profit is allowable). These usually require a bid that is spelled out in

Low-Ball Bidding

One of the main ethical principles for bidding is never to undercut (i.e., to knowingly charge less than your nearest competitor to ensure you get the job), even though it's tempting. It is also unethical to knowingly bid too low a price (sometimes called "low-ball bidding") for a project to ensure that you get the job and then, once it is secured, to turn around and renegotiate the price with the client based on the true value of the work. These practices devalue both your work and that of others. They lead to substandard work and reflect poorly on the professionalism of the archaeological community.

detail, and the items must be justified. Cost-recoverable projects also may allow for contingencies where actual costs exceed your bid due to unforeseen circumstances. Some larger organizations require that you incorporate **indirect costs**, which compensate the organization for such costs as office space and accounting. If you work for a large organization, this usually is a percentage of total employee costs. Check to be certain if this is necessary and whether your client allows for such costs. In all matters, pay careful attention to the RFQ or RFP to see what is expected and allowable.

Proposals required in RFPs usually are much more complicated than bids. A contracting agency, usually with a staff archaeologist, will have a good idea of what the project entails, the types of sites likely to be found, and how they want the three phases to be done. When you respond with a proposal, you need to be certain that you address each element of the RFP. A proposal usually will include a demonstration that you know something

Checklist for Bid and Proposal Documents

❏ Have you remembered to budget for travel time and costs (e.g., cents per mile for your vehicle, the time you will spend in traveling, vehicle maintenance)?

❏ Have you remembered to include a component for postage, telephone costs, purchasing film, developing prints, and any photocopying that may be required, as well as printing and binding your report?

❏ Have you correctly calculated personnel costs and costs for any required benefits or taxes? Human resources or payroll offices of most larger companies or universities can provide rates for these.

❏ If you will be away from home, have you remembered to allow for accommodation and subsistence costs?

❏ Have you checked the fees for any necessary consultants to ensure they are correct?

❏ Have you made any allowance for contingencies, such as rain or difficulty in tracking down landowners or other appropriate people?

❏ Some larger organizations require that you incorporate indirect costs. Check to be certain if this is necessary and whether your client allows for such costs.

❏ If there is a formal proposal for the project, have you addressed all of the requirements?

❏ Even if there is only an informal bid, have you demonstrated how your bid will address the client's needs?

❏ Have you included the latest version of necessary CVs, making sure the focus is on previous relevant experience?

❏ Have you clearly identified any potential problems or limitations that you envisage might affect the progress of the project?

about the area by your doing some relevant background research, though not necessarily a full literature search. You usually will be asked to outline your proposed methods for fieldwork and analysis and an estimate of the total time the job is likely to take, as well as any other essential information that supports your budget. You may be asked to provide current CVs (curricula vitae) or résumés for all key staff members and consultants. You may be required to demonstrate that you have sufficient insurance to cover yourself and anyone working for you. Some clients will stipulate that you have appropriate insurance coverage as an essential part of the bid process and will not hire you as a contractor without it. There are no easy recipes for writing proposals because they are as variable as the nature of the project and the agency requesting the proposal.

CONSULTATION

Many vested interests come into play on CHM projects. Landowners may be worried about the impact of a project on their property. Engineers and contractors want to bring a project in on time and on budget. Community members may be for or against a project for any variety of reasons. Bureaucrats want to be sure that all laws and regulations are followed. As an archaeologist you are trying to make a living and working to protect archaeological sites, but you find yourself in the middle of these often-competing concerns. What should you do?

The answer is to consult. Section 106, at the core of U.S. CHM law, structures **consultation** into CHM as the "central genius of the section 106 process" (King 2004, 86), explicitly providing for broad-based consultation. Whether it is required or not, consultation is just good practice. Too many people or organizations seem to want to keep what they are doing a secret until the last possible moment, and that leads to inevitable disagreements that could be resolved if people just talked to each other early in the process. Why consult? Doing so can provide you with "information you don't have that might influence your decisions." Probably more important, consultation "makes sure that people feel like their concerns have been addressed, so they're more likely to accept the decision when it's made" (King 2004, 87).

There are no reasonable formulas for how to do consultation because situations differ, and believing that there is a recipe for consultation might even be dangerous (Zimmerman 2006, 38). The idea is to talk with as many parties as possible and to keep working with them until all their interests have been expressed and problems have been worked out. Then do it some more.

Remember first that notification or holding public meetings is not consultation. To consult you really need to talk with people. Notice here that the need is to talk *with* people, not

Chris Matthews's Tips for Recognizing Communities and Working with Them

Archaeologists often deal with communities that formed for reasons that archaeology has little to do with directly. Archaeology is useful to many communities because it may be referenced as an authoritative source in land claims, heritage and identity affiliations, historical injustices, and other politically charged issues that shape the contours of social and political life in the present. Working with communities is difficult but rewarding. You'll find the work less difficult by following this advice:

- Understand the specific politics of collaborating communities. Most collaborators have their own agendas, no less than your own as you make a living by doing archaeology.
- Examine tribal affiliation, local proximity, professional interest (who will use the work as well as who does the work), and other sources of identity and affiliation that archaeologists typically use to locate and define collaborators.
- Don't try to verify the statements made by persons who approach you about who they really are. Do you have the right to challenge anyone's self-identification as a community member?
- Try to understand the groups they come from to appreciate the individual positions of the people you have access to. They often consist of those members who reach out to archaeology from within the group, presumably for the benefit of the group, but perhaps also for their own benefit or for the benefit of their particular faction.
- Reflect on how communities and collaborators relate themselves to archaeology. They usually don't directly approach archaeologists with their specific political agendas. They more often attempt on their own to make their interest simultaneously an interest of archaeology.
- Listen to community interests and try to adopt their concerns as the focus of the research. If archaeologists are trained to be useful to the present it is because they see the material basis of social life.
- Make an explicit effort to make your work relevant by knowing first the problems that collaborators identify about the present in the very local situations where your research is enmeshed.
- Realize that it is only an unintended consequence of this process if archaeology eventually elicits feelings that form new communities. This is the most powerful form of community engagement and also the one most prone to error.
- The key is to position the project so that it offers a space where those who have difficulty talking to and relating to each other might find they can speak more freely.
- The lesson here is that archaeologists can show diverse peoples that claims on the past, and on archaeology specifically, are spaces where the present builds opportunities to conceive of novel communities that can remake the future.

to people. Just telling someone or some group that you are beginning a project and what you'll be doing is inadequate. Experienced archaeologists know very well that talking with the "locals" is one of the best ways to get information about where sites might be located, as well as finding out about a wide range of local conditions, including some of the feelings about construction projects for which you may have the archaeological contract. Consultation for Section 106, however, demands more. The agencies involved in CHM projects, including you as an archaeological contractor, should consult with lots of groups and other agencies, but consultation with certain parties is required by regulations (King 2004, 87):

- Indian tribes whose reservation lands may be affected
- Indian tribes and Native Hawaiian organizations who have a particular religious or other cultural attachment to affected lands, on or off reservation
- Local governments with jurisdiction over the lands affected
- Applicants for federal assistance for a project
- Applicants for federal permits, licenses, or other approvals
- Individuals and organizations with a demonstrated interest in the undertaking (which can be just about anyone!)
- State and tribal historic preservation officers

The list is long and includes just about everyone with a potential interest in a project. Without doubt, this raises the complexity of a project, but the benefits of good consultation can be profound.

WORKING WITH COMMUNITIES

If consultation is complex and potentially difficult, working with communities is more so. No single approach can begin to cover the community variations that are possible. Still, there are concerns that seem to be common and of which you should be aware.

Identification of the community and stakeholders in a project can be difficult. What is the group, and what is their relationship to the project? Is the connection legal, cultural, historical, or just a matter of interest? Who has a legitimate concern about the project, and is a particular claim more or less strong than others?

PROPERTY RIGHTS

Certainly legal matters pertain in the identification of stakeholders. In the United States, **land rights** are a paramount concern, as they are in many parts of the world. Individual property owners have a great deal of power when CHM or other actions affect their land. Unless the land has been acquired ahead of your survey or excavation by an agency or organization responsible for the project, you certainly need to have landowner permission to do any work on their property. If they still own the land, they are not obliged to grant permission. Landowners who have been part of the consultation process are much more likely to grant permission than those who have not. Communally owned lands are similar. If the lands are owned by a corporation, a township, a Native American tribe, or a similar group, their permission also is necessary, and they should be made part of the consultation process from the start. If you are refused access to land, you many need to alter your survey or excavation strategy, which may require additional consultation with the SHPO and your client.

Intellectual property includes intangibles such as knowledge that community members have about the landscape in which they live, traditional information about their past, or information about particular practices or sites. Intellectual property issues are complex in archaeology, and we have only started to explore them (Nicholas and Bannister 2004). In CHM, perhaps the most difficult intellectual property concern involves traditional cultural properties. National Register nomination forms for TCPs require specific site locations and detail about why the site is important, both of which may be privileged information. Some communities would rather not divulge this information to anyone, even though they believe a site to be extremely significant to their people, but sensitive consultation may allow for compromises for protection of intellectual property.

ASSESSING SIGNIFICANCE

Making an assessment of significance for a site to the SHPO or THPO may seem straightforward when you read the National Register eligibility criteria (see "National Register of Historic Places Criteria" earlier in this chapter), but there is no simple "recipe" for assessing significance, and in fact, there are differing views of what it means (Tainter and Lucas 1983). The real world can easily intrude on what seems to be a straightforward consideration. As you consult during phase I and II projects, however, you will find that some individuals definitely consider significance to be a political tool, which they hope to use to stop or to alter a construction project. Some may see significance as a threat to their project. Usually these individuals are vocal enough that their agendas are clear, but you constantly need to remind yourself that significance is, and always should be, a well-considered assessment of the complexities of what makes a place of value to society. As a CHM concept, significance attempts to standardize approaches (Neumann and Sanford 2001, 33) and has drawn no small amount of criticism. The problem stems largely from a lack of consistency in the ways in which people define significance and a lack of recognition of the deeply social nature of heritage (Byrne, Brayshaw, and Ireland 2001, 61–72).

If we accept that cultural significance is not an inherent quality of a place, but a social outcome resulting from people's interactions with a place, then the community itself must be the most important source of significance. In trying to quantify how people value places, however, it has become apparent that there is an urgent need to broaden the definition of cultural heritage beyond purely physical traces (the sites and artifacts) to incorporate the intangible traces of people's attachments to place.

In the United States there are at least six theories of significance (King 2003, 14–16) for evaluating sites. **Commemoration and illustration** is pedagogical, seeking to inform the public about a place that commemorates or illustrates an important historical event, process, or theme (i.e., an interpretive construct). A related theory is **uniqueness-representativeness**, which suggests that significant places are one-of-a-kind survivals and representative of a type. **Scholarly value** considers sites to be significant if they can be studied to learn something important. This theory certainly is important for demonstrating significance for most archaeological sites, but it is focused on what scholars need to know, not necessarily what the public is concerned about. **Ambience retention** recognizes that certain places convey a distinct sense of place that most people recognize and value. Ambience retention is usually a key to the nomination of **historic districts** to the National Register. The **kitsch** theory considers significance on the basis of obscure but interesting or amusing places of popular culture. Finally, the **community value** theory says that places that a living community values are significant. The place in some way contributes to a sense of community identity and cultural integrity, or relationships with the biophysical or spiritual environment. This approach is the basis for nominating sites to the National Register as traditional cultural properties.

Whatever the theoretical approach, the central question in assessing cultural heritage significance for any site or place should always be: Who values this heritage and how do they value it? In this model, the archaeological profession is only one sector of the community and, as such, must make a space for other nonarchaeological groups to value places in ways that may be quite different from ours. To do this requires self-reflection about our professional values, and we must recognize that there may be other ideas about what is or is not significant.

In reality, just about any place can be argued to have some level of cultural heritage significance, but not all places are equally worthy of preservation. We can't retain everything, so the assessment process is one of objectively establishing the nature of a place's significance (aesthetic, historical, and so forth), the **level** of that significance (low, moderate, high), and the **degree** of that significance (local, state, regional, national, or global). In all situations, the process of assessing significance must be made as credible as possible be-

No site can be assessed in isolation—the assessment of significance is always going to be a comparative process. Whenever you undertake an assessment you always must try to widen the assessment as much as possible. For an archaeological site, for example, you may need to measure it against other known sites in the local area, across the state, or even in the wider region. Does it contain features that may have been lost from other similar sites? Does it have complementary information that may be missing from other sites? Are there no other known sites like it? (Or conversely, are there many?)

cause others will use your assessment to determine whether they think the site is eligible for the National Register. As a result, in all of your assessments you will need to be explicit about your criteria and precisely what they mean, and to outline any limitations on your assessment that may have influenced your decisions.

Recognizing how intimately people's attitudes, understandings, memories, and desires are connected to the creation of cultural significance makes it no easier to assess. A central component to the process of assessing cultural significance is talking to the community members who interact with or value the site. Gauging the reasons people value a place is the essence of assessing social significance, but it is also a component of the assessment of all other categories of significance as well. "Community" can be defined in any number of ways, of course, and one of your tasks will be to decide who the community is and how they value the place. To do this you will have to take into account how different groups value the same place and the scale at which these groups can be defined (are they local? regional? national?). The community that values such sites as the Cahokia Mounds near St. Louis, for example, could be defined at a national level as the people of the United States or, given its status as a World Heritage Site, people of many nations, while the community that values Boiling Springs in Minnesota might be limited to the Dakota (Sioux) people of the area. You also may have to take into account the existence of varied and potentially conflicting values for the same place.

THE CATEGORIES OF CULTURAL SIGNIFICANCE

Whatever the theoretical approach to cultural significance, you do need to express significance in terms of the National Register criteria. Criteria a and b generally relate to historical significance. Criterion c is associated with ideas about aesthetic significance. Criterion d relates both to historical significance and demonstrated or possible scientific or research significance. All of them are mediated or integrated by considerations of social significance.

None of these categories is mutually exclusive of course: a site that has historic significance also can possess aesthetic significance as part of its locale or scientific/archaeological significance if it also can contribute to archaeological studies. It is also possible for one site to possess significance for both Indigenous and dominant-society people as recognized by several international movements to conserve and restore monuments and sites. Worldwide, many different models can be used to establish how and why places are valuable.

An assessment of significance requires more than merely determining what criteria of cultural significance are appropriate. Each criterion also must be assessed in terms of the degree of its significance. This is essentially an assessment of comparative significance, or of the relationship between the place and other places that are either like or unlike it. Not everything is equally significant, and assessing the degree of significance is the first step in deciding which places are more significant than others (and why). The next step assesses the level of a place's significance in two further ways: against representativeness and rarity. **Representativeness** is an assessment of whether or not a place is a good example of its type, clearly illustrating the attributes of its significance. **Rarity** is an assessment of whether the place represents a rare, endangered, or unusual aspect of our history or cultural environment that has few parallels elsewhere. Thus a place that has historical significance might be representative of the historical development of a region but might not be rare, in that other similar places also might exist in the region. It could, however, be rare locally, if no other similar examples exist in the immediate vicinity. An outstanding place might be both representative and rare on a national scale.

Historical Significance

Historical significance relates to Euro-American structures or archaeological material, although it does not refer to them exclusively (e.g., Indigenous–Euro-American contact sites may possess significance under this category). Such significance commonly is identified in terms of a set of themes that relate to such influences as a historic figure, event, phase, or activity. More specifically a place may have historical significance because it typifies past practices or because it may be the site of an important event.

Aesthetic Significance

This is one of the hardest categories to evaluate, because almost everyone has a personal characterization of what is visually pleasing. In addition, there is a general recognition that aesthetic significance is a Eurocentric concept that may remain quite alien to Indigenous and other non-Western cultures. One should attempt to break away from narrow or conventional—and certainly Eurocentric—definitions of "pretty" or "beautiful" when trying

The Problem of the Viewshed

The **viewshed** relates to the visual impact of a project on a significant site. Although there may be no significant sites within the APE of the project, when a project is especially tall, such as with a cellular telephone tower, it may be visible from the site. Normally this would not affect most archaeological sites, but the viewshed certainly can be an issue for architectural and historic sites, as well as TCPs. The problem is that visual impacts are literally in the eye of the beholder. Does the visual impact of the proposed project offend anyone? Does it matter? What happens when the project comes down in several years? Does that also change the visual impact (King 2002, 70–74)? How far away is far enough?

Many SHPO and THPO offices are starting to be more concerned about viewsheds, some of them suggesting that if a project is visible from a site from a half-mile or some other specified distance, then this will constitute a visual impact. You may be faced with making such an assessment, so it is best to be aware of the standards of the SHPO or THPO. You may be asked to justify your assessments.

to identify and assess aesthetic value and define it very broadly as a response related to cultural attributes linked to the experience of a particular environment. "This response can be to visual or non-visual elements and can embrace emotional responses, sense of place, sound, smell and any other factors having a strong impact on human thoughts, feelings and attitudes" (Paraskevopoulos 1994, 81). This hints at some of the problems inherent in trying to capture aesthetic significance: it is a product of a powerful emotional experience rather than a checklist of attributes.

The qualities that might be considered as part of aesthetic significance have been most clearly set out by James Semple Kerr as the formal or aesthetic qualities of a place that make it visually pleasing (Kerr 1985, 10–11). Kerr argues that aesthetic significance can be assessed in terms of the individual elements present at a place; in terms of the unity of scale, materials, texture, and color that is evident between elements; in terms of the degree of contrasting elements that may or may not be disruptive; or in terms of the entire landscape setting in which each of these elements combines to produce an overall impression (Kerr 1985, 11). Of importance in assessing aesthetic significance is the degree to which a place has a relationship between its parts and its setting, which reinforces the quality of both (Kerr 1985, 11).

Obviously, many archaeological sites will be subsurface and therefore unable to be assessed on aesthetic criteria. You will need to decide on a site-by-site basis whether aesthetic significance is a relevant matter, rather than taking this as a given.

Scientific Significance

This is an assessment of the research potential of a site and the relevance of any data that the site might contain for the pursuit of academic research questions. Bear in mind that the research questions may well be applicable beyond the context of the single site being studied (Schiffer and Gummerman 1977; Pearson 1984).

Significance under this category includes the research potential of the site itself and its representativeness within a wider suite of known sites. Ideally the scientific significance of Indigenous heritage sites would be determined in consultation with an Indigenous community that has or once had a connection to the place, but this is difficult when tribes have been removed from their homelands, as is the case in much of the eastern United States. Most tribes, however, do maintain connections to their homelands, so do not assume that because a tribe was removed that they would have no interest. Tribal histories and legal records usually document the tribes that lived in most areas and where they are now. Many tribes still have a substantial tradition about their homelands and should be consulted. They may have specific research questions your project can address. See Watkins (2000) and Stapp and Burney (2002) for a discussion of many issues related to Native Americans and CHM issues of scientific significance. There is a growing number of models for cultural heritage management and scientific collaboration between archaeologists and Native Americans. Kerber (2006) and Silliman (2008) provide numerous examples.

Scientific significance also is concerned with the potential of a site to address anticipated future trends in academic research interests and should take into consideration the fact that future research capabilities and interests cannot be predicted with any accuracy. Because it is impossible to anticipate all research questions, it is also difficult to identify and conserve suites of sites that may be capable of addressing all future research problems.

There is no nationally set threshold for archaeological significance, partly because the issue of what constitutes an archaeological "research resource" still is highly debated. One guide that may help you to decide whether a site is of archaeological significance rests on its ability to answer three questions (Bickford and Sullivan 1984, 23–24):

- Can it provide information not available from other sources?
- Can it provide information not available on other sites?
- Can it answer pertinent research questions?

In the late 1970s, states were required to develop "state plans" to help address issues of what scholars considered to be significant for research on a state or regional level related to broader trends in American history. States identified "contexts" that were key research questions or themes that needed to be addressed. The dialogue about the questions and themes proved to be interesting and useful, even if the final result sometimes wasn't. Most abandoned this approach, but some maintain the context approach. State historic preservation plans now have evolved more into assessments of threats to historic resources and goals than ways to assess research significance, but if you are unfamiliar with a region, finding a set of those questions about archaeological sites can be instructive (see King 2004, 311–325 for a critique and history of state plans). Most of the questions are still important for research in the area.

Social Significance

The significance of any site, especially for traditional cultural properties (see "Recording Indigenous Special Places and Traditional Cultural Properties" in chapter 7), in terms of its social value lies mainly in its association with a particular recognizable community or parts of a community. Social significance is often defined in terms of the degree of contemporary community esteem that is attached to a place and aims to establish whether, for example, damage to the site or its contents would cause the community a sense of loss, or whether the site contributes to a sense of community identity (Johnston 1994). A site must be both well known and highly valued, have a long history of association, or be valued as a landmark or community signature (i.e., a place people identify with as part of who they are, such as places they show to visitors or places that everyone recognizes as a landmark). Social significance also can be assessed in terms of representativeness and rarity, in light of whether the place represents a seminal or optimal example of a class of items that is valued by a community, or whether it is a scarce example of a particular style, custom, or human activity that is esteemed by a community.

Whenever you assess social significance you will have to make a decision about who constitutes the community. It is not necessarily going to be all the people who live in a particular area, because sectors of this geographic community may be unaware of a place or may value it completely differently from other sectors. If a place is a popular recreation destination, for example, it may be of value to a much wider community than just the people who ordinarily live there. Tourists may come from all over to visit it, making the community who value it much broader. When assessing how socially significant a place may be, ask yourself these questions:

- Is it widely known among community members?
- Is it highly valued by members of the community?
- Has it been known and valued for a long period of time?
- Does it have symbolic value as a local landmark or icon that people identify with?

Answering yes to one or more means the place has social significance. Assessing how large a community values it will give you some guide as to how significant it may be. Figuring out how to express all these factors is another matter!

HOW TO ASSESS CULTURAL HERITAGE SIGNIFICANCE

According to the Australian New South Wales Heritage Office (2001, 6–7), there are eight essential steps in the significance assessment process, and they work well in most cultural heritage cases anywhere (figure 8.1):

- Summarize what you know about the site, place, and artifacts.
- Describe its previous and current uses, associations with individuals or groups, and its meaning for those people.
- Assess significance using valid heritage assessment criteria.
- Check whether you can make a sound analysis of heritage significance based on this.
- If you can, determine and recommend the level of significance.
- If you can't, find out whether there are other sources of information that might be helpful.
- Prepare a succinct statement of heritage significance.
- Get feedback from all interested parties.
- Write up your information.

WHAT COMES NEXT?

Sites that you recommend as eligible for the National Register may not be nominated to the Register. If the loss of the site has been mitigated by excavation, then it may have been destroyed completely by both the excavation and development project, so there is no need to nominate a nonexistent site. If significant parts of the site remain and retain enough integrity to remain eligible, or if mitigation was accomplished by avoidance of the site, your contract may require that you fill out **National Register nomination forms** and shepherd them through the state or tribal levels of the National Register system. Forms are very similar to most state archaeological site recording forms, so the information requested should not be unfamiliar. The narrative statement regarding the site's significance must be clearly written and as jargon-free as possible because nonspecialists will read the nomination. Your responsibilities do not necessarily end there. You may be asked to draft a set of management recommendations that indicate in detail how the place should be treated in the future, and you cannot make management recommendations without a sound statement of significance.

FIGURE 8.1: These steps in the significance assessment process would work well for assessing significance in most countries (after NSW Heritage Office 2001, 6–7).

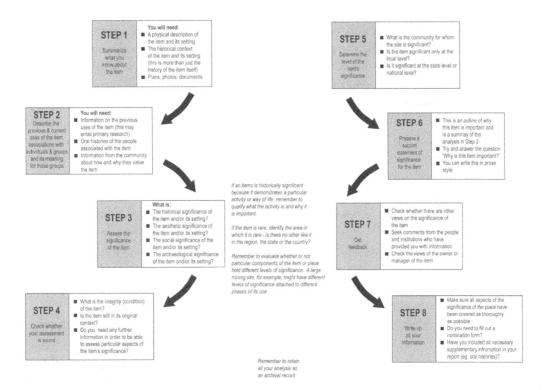

MANAGING CULTURAL HERITAGE SITES

More and more in North America, archaeologists are involved in consultation over the actual management of heritage sites. They may be employed by a federal, state, or provincial agency, and municipalities also sometimes hire heritage specialists. Management is about controlling the type and degree of interference at a site so that the cultural heritage values of the place, their levels of significance, and any essential physical changes to the sites can be properly balanced. Management strategies may be directed toward preventing any interference with the fabric of the site; they may require interference to be carefully conducted; or they may outline the way in which the site can be used by an organization, agency, or the public for education, interpretation, heritage tourism, and conservation. Sometimes as part of a large CHM project, agencies ask for recommendations as part of your final contract report, and recommending management strategies should be taken seriously. Most involve consultation with a wide range of stakeholders.

BEFORE YOU SUBMIT YOUR REPORT . . .

All of the previously mentioned issues may be a part of a report you prepare on any phase of the CHM process. Phase I may require the briefest report, and if you have negative results, you may not need to do anything more than file a letter stating the nature of your survey, your field methods, and that you found no sites. Most states, even for negative results, require a particular **format for phase I–III report contents and structure** so that they can rapidly assess the quality of your work and compliance of the developer with heritage preservation law and regulations (the process is sometimes called **review and compliance**). You would be advised to find these report guidelines before you set foot in the field, because sometimes they also contain minimal guidelines for such matters as subsurface testing by shovel tests or some kind of deep testing. These can affect your proposal and bid preparation. Be certain that you have met all these guidelines and report formats. Similarly, there may be minimal requirements for phase II evaluations. Phase III reports are more like standard archaeological reports in that they discuss excavation methods, artifacts and features discovered, and your interpretations, but they also usually require a full set of documents related to consultation and the entire mitigation process. They may also require National Register nomination forms and, in some cases, management recommendations if the site hasn't been destroyed.

Where possible, get feedback from groups of people with a vested interest in the site. This may involve submitting a draft report to the client and to any other interested parties and waiting for responses before you submit the final version. In many cases, this is required in your contract, especially one with government agencies, but in some cases it is forbidden until the agency or the organization gives permission. Getting feedback gives all stakeholders, including professional colleagues, an opportunity to comment. This is particularly important if you are working with Indigenous communities, because they are likely to have definite and often quite specific ideas about what they think are adequate interpretations or recommended management strategies. Before you submit your report, take your recommendations back to the community, and carefully go through them together to make sure that everyone understands what is at stake and has an opportunity to comment on whether they think the recommendations are suitable or unsuitable.

Finally, remember that you are submitting your report not just to a client but also to the government authority that administers cultural heritage in that state, to archaeological peers who may be CHM competitors, and often to members of the public. They will assess the report in differing ways, so it behooves you to follow current best-practice guidelines (See chapter 10, "Getting Your Results Out There: Writing, Publication, and Interpretation"). All of them may ask you for clarification on certain aspects of your work, to rewrite sections of your report, or even to do more research or fieldwork before they accept it. You must also satisfy your clients, of course, because they are the ones paying for you to do an adequate job in the first place. Clients are unlikely to be sympathetic if they have to pay more money because you did a substandard assessment to begin with that later requires substantial reworking before the state government authority will accept it.

REFERENCES AND FURTHER READING

Bickford, A., and S. Sullivan. 1984. Assessing the research significance of historic sites. In *Site surveys and significance assessment in Australian archaeology*, ed. S. Sullivan and S. Bowdler, 19–26. Canberra: Australian National University, Department of Prehistory, RSPacS.

Byrne, D., H. Brayshaw, and T. Ireland. 2001. *Social significance: A discussion paper.* Sydney: NSW NPWS.

Hardesty, D., and B. Little. 2000. *Assessing site significance: A guide for archaeologists and historians.* Walnut Creek, CA: AltaMira Press.

Johnston, C. 1994. *What is social value? A discussion paper.* Canberra: Australian Government Publishing Service.

Kerber, J. E., ed. 2006. *Cross-cultural collaboration: Native peoples and archaeology in the northeastern United States.* Lincoln: University of Nebraska Press.

Kerr, J. S. 1985. *The conservation plan: A guide to the preparation of conservation plans for places of European cultural significance.* New South Wales: National Trust of Australia.

King, T. 2002. *Thinking about cultural resource management: Essays from the edge.* Walnut Creek, CA: AltaMira Press.

King, T. 2003. *Places that count: Traditional cultural properties in cultural resources management.* Walnut Creek, CA: AltaMira Press.

King, T. 2004. *Cultural resource laws and practice.* Walnut Creek, CA: AltaMira Press.

Neuman, T., and R. Sanford. 2001. *Practicing archaeology: A training manual for cultural resources archaeology.* Walnut Creek, CA: AltaMira Press.

Nicholas, G. P., and K. P. Bannister. 2004. Copyrighting the past? Emerging intellectual property rights issues in archaeology. *Current Anthropology* 45(3): 327–350.

NSW Heritage Office. 2001. *Assessing heritage significance.* Sydney: NSW Heritage Office.

Paraskevopoulos, J. 1994. Deliberations of the working groups—summary. In *More than meets the eye: Identifying and assessing aesthetic value*, ed. J. Ramsey and J. Paraskevopoulos. Canberra: Australian Heritage Commission.

Pearson, M. 1984. Assessing the significance of historical archaeological resources. In *Site surveys and significance assessment in Australian archaeology*, ed. S. Sullivan and S. Bowdler, 27–33. Canberra: Australian National University, Department of Prehistory, RSPacS.

Pearson, M., and S. Sullivan. 1995. *Looking after heritage places: The basics of heritage planning for managers, landowners and administrators.* Melbourne: Melbourne University Press.

Ramsey, J., and J. Paraskevopoulos. 1994. *More than meets the eye: Identifying and assessing aesthetic value.* Canberra: Australian Heritage Commission.

Schiffer, M., and G. Gummerman. 1977. *Conservation archaeology*. New York: Academic Press.

Silliman, S., ed. 2008. *Collaborating at the Trowel's Edge: Teaching and Learning in Indigenous Archaeology*. Tucson: University of Arizona Press.

Smith, L. 2004. *Archaeological theory and the politics of culture heritage*. London: Routledge.

Stapp, D. C., and M. S. Burney. 2002. *Tribal cultural resource management: The full circle to stewardship*. Walnut Creek, CA: AltaMira Press.

Tainter, J. A., and G. J. Lucas. 1983. Epistemology of the significance concept. *American Antiquity* 48(4): 707–719.

Watkins, J. 2000. *Indigenous archaeology: American Indian values and scientific practice*. Walnut Creek, CA: AltaMira Press.

Zimmerman, L. J. 2006. Consulting stakeholders. In *Archaeology in practice: A student guide to archaeological analysis*, ed. J. Balme and A. Paterson, 38–58. Malden, MA: Blackwell.

For a range of other useful information, see the website accompanying the text.

CHAPTER NINE
PHOTOGRAPHY AND ILLUSTRATION

What you will learn from this chapter:

How a camera works
The relative benefits of digital and SLR cameras
The advantages of maintaining a good photographic record
Techniques for photographing sites
Techniques for photographing artifacts
What makes a good illustration
Conventions for drawing different kinds of artifacts
How to produce high-quality photographs and drawings for publication
Procedures for archiving your photographs and illustrations

Archaeologists have an ethical responsibility to produce high-quality and accurate recordings of their work. This is done not only through written reports but also through photographs and illustrations. All of these materials eventually become part of your fieldwork archive and will be an invaluable aid to anyone involved in subsequent analysis or reanalysis of your work. Archaeologists use photographs and illustrations for a variety of purposes: to record a site or an artifact, to document the process of excavation or survey, to record field conditions, to illustrate the technical data provided in a report, to accompany National Register or other nominations of sites, or to interpret a site to the public. The best way to learn how to take good photographs or draw good illustrations is through

The Basic Photography Toolkit

A square of black, nonreflective cotton material (velvet is ideal)
A 10 cm IFRAO* color scale for photographing small objects
A 1 or 2 m scale for photographing large objects
A three-in-one collapsible gold and silver reflector and diffuser
Information board with chalk or plastic letters
Blu Tack
Lens tissue
Lens cleaner
Q-tips or other cotton swabs
A small packet of tissues
A squeeze bulb, or blower brush
Two pieces of chamois for cleaning the outside surfaces of the camera
A sable- or camel-hair brush for cleaning the camera lens
Small jeweler's screwdriver
Spare camera batteries

*International Federation of Rock Art Organisations (www.cesmap.it/ifrao/scale.html)

practice. Both activities will hone some of the basic skills of an archaeologist: detailed observation and accurate recording.

THE BASICS

A photograph is a visual recording of a moment in time. Photography is perhaps one of the most important ways in which archaeologists record all aspects of their fieldwork on a daily basis. Because they are usually seen as objective, photographs have always played an important role in the scientific documentation of sites and excavations, as well as constituting important historical documents in their own right. This visual record also can be used to fill in some of the gaps that every archaeologist occasionally finds in the field notes or to revisit troublesome problems. In the case of contested finds, a detailed photographic record may become the ultimate verification of your field technique.

Many publications detail the essence of good photography, but a "good" archaeological photograph is not the same as a "good" artistic photograph. Because archaeological

The Basic Illustration Toolkit

Technical pencil or lead pencils, preferably HB or the hardest of the B series

Clean erasers (soft eraser for pencil drawings, fiberglass or special ink eraser for final ink drawings on tracing paper)

Pencil sharpener (metal ones are best, but in a pinch fine sandpaper will do just as well)

Scale ruler

Graph paper

Masking tape

Invisible or "magic" tape

Calipers or dividers

T square or set square (make sure this is flat and right angled)

Protractor (a full circle or square Douglas protractor is easiest to use)

Permatrace (translucent drawing film) or good-quality tracing paper

Drawing board (you can make one easily from plywood covered with laminated graph paper)

Blu Tack

Scissors

Clothespins (spring type)

String

Nails

Carpenter's line level

Optional:

Portable camp stool, to sit on while you are drawing

Planning frame (this is a square wood or metal frame with an internal metric gridwork of string; it is most useful for drawing rock art panels and detailed horizontal surfaces such as excavation squares)

For final inked illustrations, you will also need a range of technical drawing pens, preferably of at least three point sizes (0.25, 0.35, and 0.5), good-quality ink, a sharp scalpel or X-ACTO knife with a rounded or pointed blade, and replacement blades.

photography has a particular and quite narrow aim (to document a site or artifact in the necessary technical detail), it is much more analytical and precise than taking snapshots. For this reason, while you will still need to follow some basic rules of composition and lighting, archaeological photography has its own standards. While there is always room for artistic or personal shots on a dig, the three basic elements to all archaeological field photography are:

- Learn enough basic technical skills to ensure you can take photographs that show sufficient technical detail (see "Taking Good Shots").
- Always include a scale, because there is no point in photographing a site or artifact without also indicating how big or small it is, and a north arrow for orientation (if that may later be useful information) (see "Scales, North Arrows, and Information Boards"). Pointed trowels often are used if no formal arrow is available.
- Always record the details of every photograph on a written recording form. Because all photographs ultimately become part of the permanent site archive, written descriptions of each photograph are always noted on recording forms, so that no detail of any photograph is lost (see "Keeping Photographic Records").

In general, archaeological photographs should be descriptive and realistic, rather than interpretive. Think about the purpose of the photograph—what are you trying to show? What point of the report or article is this photograph intended to illustrate? Are there specific features or elements that you want to emphasize? Always imagine that someone else will be analyzing your results or reanalyzing your material: will they be able to grasp what you are doing and understand the point of the photograph? Don't just snap photographs; always look critically at what you're recording and assess whether this particular photograph will help you to show it.

HOW A CAMERA WORKS

A camera works by capturing the light reflected from an object on film or some other sensor according to the light intensities that come through its lens. A camera has a lens to focus the light; an aperture, which allows a fixed amount of light to pass through the lens; and a shutter, which opens and closes to allow the light in for a specific period of time. All of these mechanisms are designed to control the amount of light reaching the film or sensor so that the final picture will be neither underexposed (as a result of too little light) nor overexposed (as a result of too much light).

The **aperture** is literally the "iris" of the camera's eye: it is the adjustable opening through which light passes in the lens. It is controlled by the aperture ring on the lens barrel and can be opened or closed to allow in more or less light, depending on the situation. The aperture controls the **depth of field** of a photograph, or the area that will be in focus (see "Getting Things in Focus").

FIGURE 9.1: The relationship between the aperture and the amount of light passing through the lens. Apertures with smaller f-stops let in more light.

F/16   F/5.6   F/2.8

F-stops on film cameras are the numbers on the aperture ring that describe the size of the aperture. The important thing to remember is that as the f-stop number increases, the area of the aperture decreases, so that moving one f-stop will either double or halve the amount of light allowed through the lens. Basically, the bigger the f-stop number, the less light will be allowed to reach the film through the iris of the camera (figure 9.1).

Shutter speed is the amount of time that the shutter remains open to allow light into the camera. The speed of the shutter is measured in fractions of a second: 1/2, 1/4, 1/8, 1/15, 1/30, 1/60, 1/125, 1/250, 1/500, 1/1,000, and so on. Shutter speed is closely related to aperture, and one of the main rules of film photography is to make sure that you have the right balance between them. They have an inverse relationship, which means that whatever you do to one, you will have to do the opposite to the other. In other words, if you are increasing the size of the aperture (i.e., moving down through the f-stop numbers), you will need to decrease the shutter speed to compensate for the greater amount of light being allowed through the iris. Conversely, if you are making the aperture smaller (moving up through the f-stop numbers), you will need to increase the shutter speed to allow the smaller amount of light being let in by the iris to expose the film for a longer period of time (figure 9.2).

In archaeological photography, particularly for small artifact photography, you should always choose the aperture before you choose the shutter speed, because the aperture controls the depth of field.

FIGURE 9.2: An exposure calculator to help you get used to the inverse relationship between aperture and shutter speed

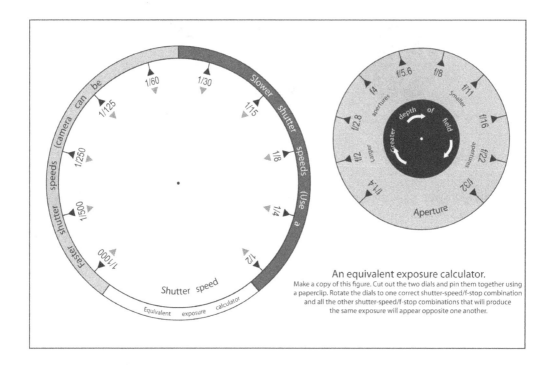

An equivalent exposure calculator.
Make a copy of this figure. Cut out the two dials and pin them together using a paperclip. Rotate the dials to one correct shutter-speed/f-stop combination and all the other shutter-speed/f-stop combinations that will produce the same exposure will appear opposite one another.

Exposure is the total amount of light that is allowed to reach the film. You can calculate exposure by multiplying the aperture by the shutter speed.

Lenses alter a camera's field of vision. The main ones used in archaeology are telephoto and wide angle. A telephoto lens (usually from 85 mm to 200 mm) brings the distance close, magnifying a subject. A wide-angle lens has a focal length below 35 mm and is ideal for taking landscape shots.

Filters are used to help control contrast and create special effects. Polarizing filters control the effects of reflection, soft-focus filters soften hard edges, and UV filters reduce the blue cast that occurs in photographs taken in the shade or on overcast days. In archaeology, filters also can be useful for bringing out details on artifacts.

Film speed refers to the film's sensitivity to light and is expressed in terms of an ISO number. A slow film will have an ISO of 25 or 40, a fast film of 200 or above. Standard film speed is ISO100. Basically, the faster the film the less time it needs to be exposed to light to produce a suitable image. There is a trade-off to consider here. Fast film allows you to take a good image in poor light but will also appear much grainier than a slow film.

Because they are finer grained, slower films are better if you want to make big enlargements. An equivalent in digital cameras is related to the resolution at which the sensor detects and captures light intensities. Generally the higher the megapixel rating of the camera, the finer the "grain" and the better quality you will get on big enlargements.

Grains are the tiny light-sensitive particles of silver that make up the negative and are much smaller and finer in slower films, giving them higher definition (Hester, Shafer, and Feder 1997, 163). If you are using a manual camera, make sure you have it set to the appropriate film speed.

TAKING GOOD SHOTS

The direction and intensity of lighting can make all the difference between a great and a poor photograph. Very directional light, such as through a window, can maximize textures, cast strong shadows, and reduce the midtones. It also can create shadows, however, and obscure the outlines of objects. Very bright or harsh light can create deep shadows and intense reflection, washing out details and making some parts of the photograph overexposed (very bright) and others underexposed (very dark). Very dim light will be too dark and will not reveal enough to make the outlines of any object clear. Because of the softer lighting, the best times for taking field photographs are early in the day (preferably just before sunrise) or later in the afternoon at evening or twilight. Obviously you will not always be able to control the lighting conditions or wait until the perfect time to take each photograph. In these cases you will have to make the best of the circumstances you find yourself in, but if you have a basic working knowledge of what is important for taking a good photograph, you should know enough to be able to avoid the worst.

Essentially the main principle in taking a good photograph is to even out the highs and lows so that all the detail of the bright and dim areas can be captured. All good cameras will allow you to regulate the amount of light coming through the lens via combinations of shutter speed and aperture to achieve the correct exposure for the speed of the film. If your camera is set to automatic, these decisions will be made for you, although this does not mean that your photos will always be perfect. Part of the problem with light meters in cameras is that they tend to average the amount of light using the middle 30–50% of the scene. This means that the light reading that the camera will use to determine the aperture and shutter speed actually may not be reflecting off the subject, and you may run the risk of under- or overexposing your shot. This particularly can be a problem if you are

Gray cards can be purchased from any photography dealer, although if you find yourself caught without one you can improvise. A reading taken from a nonreflective brown paper bag, a burlap bag, or even from the palm of your hand will come within about one f-stop of a reading taken from a gray card (Howell and Blanc 1995, 24–25). A reading taken from a piece of plain white paper will come within about two. To compensate, take the reading from the bag or the palm of your hand, and then overexpose the reading by one f-stop (i.e., drop the aperture one f-stop down from that suggested by the reading). If the reading from the palm of your hand suggested a shutter speed of 125 at f8, for example, then the corrected reading would be 125 at f5.6. If you are taking a reading from a piece of white paper you will need to overexpose it by two f-stops, so drop the aperture ring down two f-stops.

trying to photograph artifacts on a black background, because it is very easy to include too much of the background in the meter reading (Howell and Blanc 1995, 24). Photographers often use a gray card (a piece of poster board with a neutral gray tone) to counter this problem and to determine the correct exposure for photographs. An exposure reading taken from a gray card provides a mean reading between extremes that will allow you to capture the detail in both the highlights and the lowlights.

You also can try physical solutions to problems of too much light or shadow. One way to remove shadows is to use a reflector to brighten the darker areas (figure 9.3). If you don't have a commercial reflector, you can use almost any bright object that comes to hand, even something as simple as a large sheet of white card, a space blanket, or aluminum foil taped to a flat surface. The reflector should be placed on the shadowed side and moved just close enough to lighten the shadow, so that you are able to record detail in those areas. If you are also using artificial light, this should be shone directly at the reflector, which can then be positioned so that it reflects the light onto the precise spot you want illuminated.

One way to even out the light is to use a diffuser to spread the light and minimize both shadows and highlights. One of the best commercial diffusers available is a combination gold reflector, silver reflector, and diffuser in one collapsible package. The gold and silver surfaces diffuse different wavelengths of light and so give quite different results. If you are photographing artifacts outdoors, you may have to diffuse the light, because direct sun often is too harsh to give a satisfactory result. Photographs taken without diffusion in direct sunlight will have high contrasts, with the light areas very light and the dark areas very dark, and are unlikely to show details well. This may not be necessary if the day is overcast or if the light is shadowed or hazy because cloud cover is ac-

FIGURE 9.3: Reflecting light to eliminate shadows (photograph courtesy Aidan Ash)

tually one of the best light diffusers you can have. If you can't wait for an overcast day, however, and don't have a commercial diffuser at hand, try improvising with a large piece of paper, a white cotton shirt or sheet, or the lid of a white plastic container if you are photographing small objects. Experiment with a diffuser to work out the best effect before you take the photograph.

Getting Things in Focus

The aperture in a camera controls two things: the exposure (i.e., the amount of light reaching the film) and the depth of field, or the area of the photograph that is in focus. Controlling depth of field is an important way of concentrating attention on particular features in your picture and is also essential for maintaining sharp focus (figure 9.4). A shallow depth of field can help soften unwanted or distracting detail, while a greater depth of field will bring into focus objects that are in front of and behind the main image. The overall depth of field is influenced by three factors: the focal length of the lens (how long or short the lens is), the distance the photographer is from the subject, and the size of the

A simple rule to remember is that the smaller the aperture (the larger the f-stop number), the more narrowly the light coming through the lens will be focused and therefore the greater the depth of field.

aperture. For a large depth of field, select a small aperture (a large f-stop number). For a small depth of field, select a large aperture (a small f-stop number).

When you're photographing artifacts, getting them into sharp focus by maintaining the maximum depth of field is one of the most difficult things to do. A general rule to follow is the **one-third rule**, which suggests that you focus on a point that is one third of the way into your composition (figure 9.5). The depth of field in a photograph extends from approximately one-third in front of the point of focus to two-thirds behind. If you focus on the background, this will waste the one-third that is behind the point of focus and give an image that is blurred for one-third in the front. Remember that you can't see this zone of sharpness through your camera viewfinder, so you'll find out which parts of the object are out of focus only when you get your finished prints back. If you're photographing a ceramic vessel, for instance, and focused only on the very front of the vessel, you might find that the sides and rear edges are blurred. Using the one-third rule, however, you would focus approximately one-third of the way back from the front edge, bringing both the foreground and the background into sharpness. Some good SLRs may have a depth of field button that will let you see before you shoot.

FIGURE 9.4: The effects of varying depths of field on the sharpness of a photograph

F4.5 (50 mm lens)   F11 (50 mm lens)   F22 (50 mm lens)

FIGURE 9.5: The one-third rule

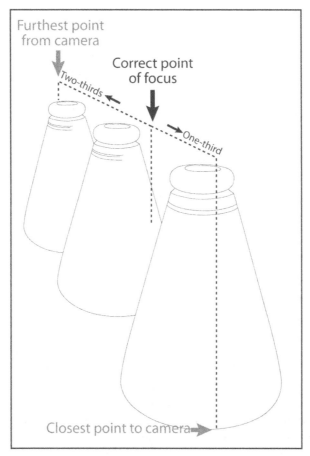

Furthest point from camera

Two-thirds

Correct point of focus

One-third

Closest point to camera

F22 (50mm lens)

HOLDING THE CAMERA

The quality of your image will be enhanced by how well you hold the camera. The stiller it is, the sharper the resulting image will be. How steady the camera needs to be to take a good photograph is directly related to the shutter speed. In other words, if the shutter needs to be held open for a longer period of time to let in more light, then the camera needs to be held steady for a longer period of time. Very few people can hold a camera steady at a shutter speed of 1/60 or lower, so if your exposure time will be long you'll need to use a tripod (see "When to Use a Tripod").

Tips for Taking Good Archaeological Photographs

- Always keep the plane of the film (i.e., the back of the camera) in the same plane as the subject to avoid distortion.
- Always take light meter readings from your subject and not the background or foreground. If you can't get close enough, take a reading on something that's a similar color or is in similar light.
- Try to diffuse the light wherever possible, or use reflection to reduce contrast in dark shadows.
- Always include a scale and some device to help you orient the photograph.
- Always record the details of each photograph in a log or on photographic recording forms.
- Shoot the first frame of each roll of film on an information board noting the site, date, and location in case your logbook or recording forms are lost. Also be sure to label the exterior of each roll of film.
- Make sure there is no extraneous material intruding on your shot (you'd be surprised at how distracting a yellow bucket or a red folder off to one side can be).
- Check regularly to make sure your camera is set to the correct film speed and hasn't been moved inadvertently.
- Remember that film is cheap in comparison to the cost of returning to a location. Always take at least twice as much film as you expect to use. It is also a good idea to take more shots than you think you will need, especially if you are planning to include the images in a report or publication.
- You can never plan for the weather. Take film in a variety of speed ratings so that you'll be prepared for a range of lighting conditions.
- If you are in doubt that your choice of aperture and shutter speed will actually give you the correct exposure, try bracketing your photographs. This is the photographic equivalent of an insurance policy. Take one shot at the exposure that you think is correct, and then take additional shots on either side (sometimes called "bracketing") of this to give more and less exposure. If you took one photograph at 1/125 of a second at f-stop 8, for example, then you would also take one shot at 1/125 at f/5.6 and one at 1/125 at f/11.
- Keep it simple. Whereas a painter starts with a blank canvas and builds on it, a photographer starts with a multitude of images and edits them down. For effective composition, especially when photographing small objects, take elements away until images are reduced to their simplest components. One of the most common errors is trying include too much.

When taking a handheld photo:

- If standing, make sure you are relaxed and comfortable. If you place your feet slightly apart and tuck in your elbows, this will help distribute your body weight more evenly and provide a secure platform for supporting the camera.
- Try bracing your body on a solid object, such as against a tree, a table, or the side of a building.
- If squatting, steady the camera by supporting your elbow on your knee.
- If kneeling, distribute your weight evenly.
- If lying down, use your camera bag or case to support the camera.
- Try holding your breath when you press the shutter release button.
- Press the shutter release button softly to avoid sudden movement.

WHEN TO USE A TRIPOD

A tripod (figure 9.6) anchors the camera in a way that is impossible for the human hand. Remember to use a cable release or remote control to take tripod pictures so that

FIGURE 9.6: The advantages of using a tripod to photograph archaeological sites

Tripod Tips

- If you need to steady the tripod, tie a bottle of water, bag of sand, or heavy tool to it to balance the weight of the camera.
- In gusty weather, try putting a weight (such as your camera bag) on the tripod to stop it from moving.
- If you don't have a tripod with you, a small beanbag or similar object placed on a fencepost can be used to cradle the camera.

you do not have to touch (and thus jar) the camera with your hand. If you don't have a cable release or remote, or if you lose it, you can also use the self-timer built into the camera to avoid unnecessary camera movement. You will need to use a tripod if you are taking photographs:

- With long exposures at night
- In close-ups, where any camera movement will have a serious impact upon the quality of the image
- In rough terrain, where it is hard to maintain a steady stance
- With a very small aperture (a high f-stop) to allow for maximum depth of field
- With a telephoto lens when shooting objects at a long distance from you

CHOOSING THE RIGHT CAMERA: FILM VERSUS DIGITAL

Until recently most archaeological photography was done with 35 mm SLR (single lens reflex) cameras, but with digital cameras becoming more common, their quality vastly improved, and their price dropping sharply, they are rapidly becoming the standard for field photography. Most standard manual/automatic film cameras are 35 mm SLR and usually come with a range of lenses. They use mirrors and prisms to focus the light coming through the lens onto the film. Digital cameras, by contrast, do away with film altogether and instead use a light sensor (CCD, or charge-coupled device) to capture an image. Many of the principles of photography discussed for an SLR also apply to digital photography.

The quality of the lens (point-and-shoot cameras tend to use plastic) and the number of pixels the camera can create determine the resolution of digital images: basically, the better the lens and the more pixels, the higher the quality of the image will be. Point-and-shoot digital cameras are extremely affordable, and quality has gotten extremely good.

They work especially well if you are planning to use the images on an Internet site or on your computer. A relatively inexpensive 4-megapixel camera will now produce images that rival film cameras at 8" × 10" print size, but the equivalent image quality of a 35 mm transparency from an SLR camera is an 8-megapixel digital camera. Many digital cameras are now SLR with a range of lenses available. Most of these are relatively expensive, but costs are coming down rapidly.

Digital cameras do offer distinct advantages over film cameras in that you can look at your images almost immediately and retake the photo if the quality is poor or doesn't contain the information you need. You can take many more images with even the smallest storage device than you can on the largest roll of film (100-plus at medium resolution versus 36 on film). Having film processed takes substantially longer, and if you didn't get what you wanted in the photo, your opportunity to retake the shot probably will be gone. Because the images are digital, they also can be manipulated by graphics programs on your computer. This often allows you to salvage a poor-quality photograph easily, something vastly more complex with film.

The disadvantage of digital is that high-quality images require large-capacity storage devices, such as compact flash cards or microdrives, which adds to your up-front costs. Simple record shots can be made at relatively small file sizes, but any photograph you think you may want for future publication should be taken at the maximum file size your camera allows. Most cameras use JPEG format for images, which is fine for web or small prints, but for the best possible quality, making larger prints, and publication, buy a camera that will allow the raw image format. Raw file sizes are very large, requiring large storage devices, but such devices have also come down in price while increasing in capacity to hold images. As with film, be sure you have enough storage for all your photographs. You can easily download your images to a computer at the end of the day and empty the storage device. However, be warned: be sure that you make a backup of the images on a CD-ROM or DVD-ROM before you remove the images from your storage device. Do not manipulate the original images; keep them as they were downloaded from the camera. Work only with copies of your images. Because the images are digital, the copies are always the same quality as the original unless you have altered the original.

Many organizations now are moving toward complete use of digital images, but questions remain regarding quality and archival storage of images. For example, technology is changing so quickly that images stored using one technology will inevitably need to be transferred to a more current technology. If they aren't, they may become inaccessible in the future. There is also concern about prints done on inkjet printers (the most common approach). Some archival experts feel that prints will last as many as 150 years depending on ink, paper, and storage quality. But these concerns may fade (every pun intended) as the technology improves.

Whether digital or film, you still need to learn the basics of photography. You also should consider the advantages and disadvantages of each medium. The reality is that archaeology will follow the technology and the market, which means that digital cameras largely will replace film cameras. By the time the next edition of this text appears, the emphasis is likely to be on digital instead of film photography.

MAINTAINING YOUR EQUIPMENT

Try to establish a daily and weekly routine for checking photographic equipment. Inspect your cameras, lenses, and tripods on a daily basis and wipe them clean. Inspect them closely once a week, and clean all their outside surfaces with a clean, soft rag or piece of chamois. Pay special attention to the interior of the camera case if you have access to it. Blow dust from the interior of a camera body and case using a squeeze bulb, or blower brush, or a can of filtered compressed air. Commercial lens tissues are good for lint-free dry cleaning of lenses and cameras. Special tissues and lens cleaner should be used for wet cleaning, with cotton swabs for cleaning in spots that are difficult to access. Do not use paper towels or similar paper products, which will easily scratch plastic lenses. When cleaning the lens or filter, remove as much dust as possible with a soft brush and blower, then use lens cleaning fluid and tissues. *Never* apply lens cleaner directly to the lens, as it may leak through the casing. Instead, apply it to the lens tissue. Rub the dampened lens tissue in a spiral motion outward from the center of the lens.

Some basic precautions:

- Make certain that the equipment is operational a week or so before you leave, so that you will have time to fix any faults.
- Store all items in dustproof containers.
- While in the field, inspect and clean cameras and other equipment regularly.

CHOOSING THE RIGHT FILM

Black-and-white or color prints are the usual choice for archaeological reports. Color transparencies (slides) are also common as archival documents because they are more stable than prints. Black-and-white transparency film is rarely used in archaeology. The most stable color print or slide film is Kodachrome, which is also relatively cheap and has good color balance. Your choice of film will also be determined by what you're photographing and what you're trying to show. Color slide film can record only a relatively narrow range of light, color print film a slightly greater range, and black-and-white print film a greater range again (Howell and Blanc 1995, 20). This means that if you're trying to photograph artifacts outdoors, where high contrast between light and dark areas might be a problem, black-and-white film will be able to capture more detail in both the very dark and very light areas. Color slide film, on the other hand, will probably increase the contrast and make your artifacts highly shadowed. If in doubt, use color print film—ISO100 outdoors and ISO400 or 800 indoors.

Be aware that changing technology may affect the availability of certain films. Slides, for example, may see less use in archaeology because slide projectors no longer are being produced and repair parts will become limited within a few years (and because of this many archaeologists are scanning and storing their slides digitally).

Caring for Film

- Always check the expiration date on the outside of the film carton. When you purchase film make certain that it is not near the expiration date.
- In the field, store film in a cooler, or wrapped in a wet towel, to keep it cool. Remember to keep the film in an airtight container so it doesn't become damp, and remove it an hour or so before you plan to use it so it is at room temperature when you load it into the camera.
- Load and remove film in the shade, or at least shield it from direct sunlight with your body.
- Never leave a loaded camera in the glove compartment or trunk of your car. The high air temperature in confined spaces such as these can damage the film's speed and color. High temperature can also affect digital storage media.
- If the air is very humid do not return exposed film to the canister. Keep it in an airtight bag with a few packets of silica gel to absorb any moisture.
- Have exposed film processed as soon as possible so that if there have been major mistakes or problems you can fix them immediately.
- Keep digital media away from strong magnetic fields, but they don't affect CD- or DVD-ROMs.

SCALES, NORTH ARROWS, AND INFORMATION BOARDS

All archaeological photographs for technical purposes should include a scale, whatever the subject being photographed. The purpose of a scale is to provide something of known dimensions against which the size of the object can be judged (Dorrell 1994, 51), so a clear and readable scale is essential. Ideally you should have a variety of scales to suit any circumstance, but each one *must* have the unit of measurement clearly marked on it (e.g., millimeters, centimeters, or meters) and, if possible, at least one, if not more, major length divisions (e.g., 10 cm, 15 cm, 50 cm, 1 m). The standard scale for site photography is a 2 m range pole, marked in 50 cm sections in alternating red and white. If you do not have this you can make your own scale from a length of lumber by painting the divisions in either red and white or black and white. The standard scale for object photography is 10 cm, marked in 1 cm sections in alternating black and white, though a range of smaller scales can be used for some laboratory shots. The International Federation of Rock Art Organisations produces a free 10 cm color scale for use in artifact recording. The advantage of this scale is that it also includes a color reference strip that can be used to assess the degree of color distortion resulting from lighting conditions or the development process.

The most important principle when using a scale is that it should not overwhelm, or detract attention from, the object. *Never* place a scale on top of an artifact, even if you feel that it does not obscure essential information. The scale should be placed to the right or left of the object or centered across the bottom or top of the picture. Because distortion is an inherent part of the photographic process, make sure you align the scale parallel to either the horizontal or vertical frame of the photo. This means making sure that the scale is not leaning at an angle or twisted so that it faces away from the camera. If you happen to be caught in a situation without a scale, then it is still essential to include some object in the photograph for the same purpose. A person (of average height) is acceptable for larger features or site photography; for small items or areas, use a relatively common and recognizable object such as a lens cap, coin, or pencil, but remember *always* to include a note of the length of the object in your field notes and figure captions.

In site photography, but especially in an excavation unit, a north arrow is often useful to help you orient the photograph. Sometimes north arrows are included on the scale. Even a crude north arrow helps. Trowels can be used to fill in when no north arrow is available. Even though your excavation grid may be oriented to the cardinal directions, you will often find that you cannot orient a photograph of an excavation unit. You can also write in your photo log which direction the camera lens was pointing when the photo was taken.

An information board is also useful because it can be used to provide a basic record of the photographic event, which can be checked against other records. A small child's blackboard not only is effective as an information board but also is cheap and can be reused quickly and easily. Letter boards with vinyl or metal letters are also inexpensive and easy to use. They also give a consistent appearance to the information board and may be more legible than hand-drawn lettering. Information boards should be marked with the location, date, and roll number. If photographing an excavation, you also should include information on the unit, square, context, or trench. Such photographs are not always attractive, so if your aim is to produce images for publication in articles or reports, it can be a good idea to take two photographs: one with and one without the information board.

PHOTOGRAPHING STANDING STRUCTURES

The conventional approach to architectural photography requires a measure of technical skill and a camera or lens that can be adjusted to correct for converging vertical lines. At their best, these pictures convey the proportions, textures, and colors of a building. When you are photographing the outside of a building, try to visit it at different times during the day so that you can view it in different lights. Then choose the lighting angle that best shows the shape and texture of the materials. When photographing the inside of a building use available light wherever possible, but if this is insufficient, try bouncing the beam of a flashlight from a ceiling or wall or using a reflector.

To record perspective accurately it is necessary to keep the back of the camera parallel with the subject. When you photograph a building from ground level, however, it is usually necessary to tilt the camera back a little so that you can include the top of the building in the frame. This means that the bottom of the building will seem larger than the top, and the sides will appear to converge. The easiest way to deal with this is to stand well back or use a telephoto lens so that you will not have to tilt the camera. Some digital cameras have perspective correction built into them that will prevent this problem.

When photographing a standing structure:

- Always take orienting shots that show the building in its context, including the surrounding landscape and other buildings.
- Take external shots of the facade with a normal or telephoto lens, and then individual shots of the details on the facade.
- If you are taking many shots of the exterior or interior of a building, it is wise to note the direction and location of each shot on a photographic plan. Draw a sketch map of the building or site, and indicate the physical location of each shot tied to the exposure number and the approximate direction you were facing for each shot with an arrow.

PHOTOGRAPHING EXCAVATIONS

It is particularly important that you produce an accurate photographic recording of archaeological excavations. When photographing excavations it is worthwhile taking two types of photographs: accurate recordings of the results of excavation and photographs that record the work in progress. In terms of recording the past, the important point is to make a complete record of the site before, during, and after excavation. In more general terms, you need to think of the many purposes to which archaeological photographs can be put.

You should take each of the following:

- An establishing shot, taken with a wide-angle lens, that shows how the area to be excavated fits into its surroundings. Digital cameras make it especially easy to take panoramic shots by "stitching together" a series of overlapping images. These should always be taken from a tripod. You can take a 360° panorama from a central point on the site (these are easy but distort the image) or overlapping shots along a straight line (these don't distort but need to be carefully set up).
- A "before" series of shots that records the excavation area before it is disturbed.
- Overall shots of people in action. This can give a vivid impression of the excavation process.
- Full-face portraits of people in action. Try to get candid shots of people performing routine activities, such as troweling and screening. The best technique here is to take lots of photographs. While people will be stiff at the beginning, after a while they will become less aware of you, and you will be able to get increasingly natural shots. Don't direct people too much. Let them be themselves, and try to capture this.
- Shots of sponsors or visitors to the site, which may be used subsequently for publicity purposes.
- Close-ups of special finds, which should be photographed *in situ*. Bear in mind depth of field, and make certain that the entire object is in focus.
- Close-ups of individual features as they are exposed.
- Individual photographs of the spatial association between artifacts.
- Individual photographs of the step-by-step excavation of a significant discovery.
- Individual photographs of each context or unit once it has been excavated, recording the particular surface characteristics of each unit. These should include both vertical and horizontal faces (i.e., separate shots of the walls and floor of the trench). They should be taken after the walls have been straightened and the surface tidied and brushed clean (see "Recording Sections" in chapter 5).
- Some archaeologists recommend taking such photographs of each excavation unit as you complete the excavation of each level in the unit. Sometimes called "record shots," these photos can help to reconstruct the unit should there be questions about the excavations later.

When taking shots of successive levels in an excavation unit or trench, make sure that all shots are oriented in the same direction. In other words, if the first photograph of the excavation unit is taken facing north (the standard), then all subsequent shots documenting the excavation of that square should also be taken facing north, so that the complete series of photos can be easily compared. Here is where using a north arrow really helps. Obviously, if you are also taking individual shots of particular features within the unit, these can be taken from any angle, but again, a north arrow really helps. To avoid problems of distortion when photographing whole excavation units, you should try to keep the plane of the film (i.e., the back of the camera) parallel to the ground surface. This may mean elevating the photographer above the site so that the photograph can be taken looking down (see "Taking Aerial Photographs").

- An "after" series of shots, which records the excavation area once work is complete but before the site is backfilled.
- A series of shots of the area after the site has been backfilled.

Trouble Shooting?

- If you have problems with shadows in deep trenches, try using a reflector or diffuser (or both) to make the light more even.
- If the stratification is unclear, you can lightly spray the walls with water. This will darken the earth and can highlight differences in soil color. In fact, at some sites differential drying is the best way to record important stratigraphic boundaries. If you do use spraying to enhance stratigraphic resolution, however, this should be recorded in your notes and on the photographic recording form.
- Take close-ups of any areas that are difficult to interpret, such as postholes, because you may want to revisit these problems later or rethink your previous assessments.

TAKING AERIAL PHOTOGRAPHS

The purpose of aerial photography is to obtain a bird's-eye view of an archaeological site. This can give you quite a different view from that which you would normally take. For example, if you are on the ground you may be able to see a large number of mounds, but it is only from above that it is possible to see the relationships between them. Aerial photography can be undertaken in two ways. Either the archaeologist has to find a way to get above the site or has to find a way to elevate the camera. The elevation of the archaeologist can be achieved through the use of a light plane or a hot air balloon (figure 9.7). In some instances, low elevations may be all you need, and it may be enough to climb a ladder, a tower, a tree, or a rock outcrop. A "cherry picker" is another possible solution, although they can be quite expensive and are not always easily maneuverable on site. A higher viewpoint will enhance your ability to interpret the site in terms of its surrounding environment, as well as to make sense of the relationship between different parts of the site. In terms of site photography, elevating the photographer or the camera can be a solution to problems of distortion inherent in photographing large areas from ground level. Alternatively, the camera can be elevated independently through a variety of means, such as balloons and bipods.

FIGURE 9.7: Tethered hot air balloons can provide a useful platform for taking aerial site photographs, such as these taken over an earthlodge excavation in eastern South Dakota in 1976.

Fred Cooper's Simple Bipod

FIGURE 9.8: An inexpensive bipod in detail and action

Whittlesey bipod camera supports have been used since the 1960s to elevate cameras at archaeological sites. Commercially prepared bipods are available but costly. You can make a simple and inexpensive bipod for under $100 with equipment from hardware and camera stores. Get two telescoping fiberglass or plastic extensions for window and house washing. These extend about 20 feet. On the  narrow end of each, carefully drill a hole through which a small-diameter 6- or 8-inch bolt will pass. Take a camera monopod or the core of a tripod and drill a similar hole through which the bolt will pass. Put bushings of the appropriate length on either side of the monopod/tripod head so it will swing freely but not move from side to side. Bolt this assembly between the two telescoping poles so that it swings freely. Mount the camera on the monopod/tripod head. Extend the legs to the length you need. Attach a small rope at least twice as long as the height of the bipod to allow you to raise the bipod. Swinging freely, the back of the camera will be in the same plane as the ground. Brace the legs over the objects or excavation, and pull the bipod and camera assembly up. A digital camera with an infrared or other remote works best because you can activate the shutter easily (except in bright sunlight, which defeats the infrared) and check photo quality immediately. Film cameras with a long shutter release also can be used. With practice, you can become proficient quickly.

PHOTOGRAPHING ROCK ART

Unlike cave paintings in Europe, rock art in many places is usually found in rockshelters, or outdoors on more-or-less vertical cliff faces and on boulders. Normally, there is sufficient light to take good photographs. Digital images can sometimes be more useful than film because colors and contrast easily can be changed on the computer to allow better visualization of the art. When photographing rock art, take each of the following:

- Orienting shots, showing the immediate environmental context
- A close-up of each motif, which can be used as the basis for tracing
- Wide-angle or panorama images, which show the motifs in relation to each other
- Close-ups of details, such as superimposition or areas of damage, which can be used in site interpretation

Remember to keep the back of the camera (i.e., the plane of the film) in the same plane as the rock surface as much as possible to avoid distortion.

As opposed to rock paintings, petroglyphs are often located at open sites and can be difficult to photograph. The best time to photograph a particular petroglyph site will depend on that site's orientation and location in the landscape, but as a general rule it is best to take photos in the early morning or late afternoon, when the sun is at an oblique angle and will reveal more clearly the pecked and engraved lines.

It is especially important to visit rock art sites at different times of the day to work out which is the best light for photography. Experiment with filters and diffusers to see if they help bring out different features in the art. If the rock art is in an area of little sun, it may have to be photographed using artificial light. In this case, it is important to make certain that the light spreads evenly across the surface so that you can record the greatest detail. Sometimes, it can be helpful to photograph petroglyphs at night using an artificial light source held very close to the surface of the rock so that the light shines *across* the art surface rather than straight at it. You also can try holding a handheld mirror close to the rock surface in daylight to redirect sunlight to the same effect. If you are trying this during the day it is much more effective to shade the area you are trying to illuminate, so that the light cast from the mirror is not washed out by the brighter sunlight (Clegg 1983, 99). Using oblique light in this way highlights the relief on the surface and can be very helpful in providing detail for tracings. This technique can also be useful for recording other hard-to-interpret relief surfaces such as weathered gravestones.

For petroglyphs, another photographic approach is to use a laser scanner, which can take as many as 25,000 data points a second with remarkable accuracy (0.05 mm or better). This allows a level of recording that regular photography cannot match, as well as ma-

Never use chalk, paint, or any chemical to outline or emphasize rock art motifs because this can cause permanent damage to the art surface. For the same reason, never remove graffiti, lichen, or moss from the art surface so that you may see it better. Removing any such coverings is likely to cause unforeseen damage, and you must have permission from the relevant authorities before you can "clean up" any archaeological site. If you cannot manage to bring out the best in the rock art through the use of filters, oblique light, or other lighting conditions, then you will have to rely on tracing or drawing the rock art panels to show their detail (see "Drawing Rock Art").

nipulation of the images into 3-D or false colors (Barnett et al. 2004). With a laser scan, you often can see elements that the naked eye and photography don't. The equipment is relatively expensive and takes special training to use, however, but costs rapidly have come down and the technology has been simplified.

PHOTOGRAPHING ARTIFACTS

Because artifact photography is designed to reveal technical details, it is very important that you can see all parts of the artifact clearly. Lighting is crucial in close-up photography of artifacts. If you are photographing something small like a coin or a stone tool, mount it so that it is a centimeter or two above the background. This will allow you to focus on the object while throwing the background out of focus. Plasticine or Blu Tack are not ideal, as they may mark the material, but will work.

When photographing artifacts make sure that the background contrasts with the color of the artifact so that the entire margin of the artifact is clear. Dark artifacts against a dark background, for example, don't work well. A plain colored background is best: either black or some other relatively neutral color. Try to avoid casting shadows, which can obscure the margins of the artifact, and try to ensure good, even light. Take the time to get it right, because you may never find that object again!

KEEPING PHOTOGRAPHIC RECORDS

Given the enormous cost of getting into the field, it is absolutely essential that you make certain the information relating to your photographs is not lost. Some form of record

Tips for Good Artifact Photography

- The most important factor in taking a good artifact photograph is to ensure that you use the entire negative to frame the artifact. There is nothing worse than looking at a vast expanse of background with a tiny artifact in the center. While you can crop photos later, if you are not focusing sufficiently closely on the artifact, your photograph will lack the detail necessary for a good archaeological photograph. If you are going to be taking lots of photographs of small artifacts (e.g., stone artifacts), this may mean investing in a macro lens to get the necessary close-ups.
- Glass artifacts are some of the most difficult artifacts to photograph well. When photographing glass, try holding the artifact up to the light in order to reveal details.
- If you're photographing several artifacts in the one shot (e.g., an assemblage of bone buttons or stone artifacts), arranging the artifacts in rows and grouping together artifacts of similar size usually works best.
- Choose the appropriate background for your photographs. This doesn't always have to be artificial (e.g., a background of pale sand can work as well as a piece of cloth or paper), but make sure that the color of the background doesn't make it difficult to see the artifacts clearly.
- Use a scale with designations appropriate for the size of the artifacts (i.e., usually with centimeter markings).
- If you must photograph artifacts underwater, remember that the deeper you dive, the less light there will be to take good photographs. You will also lose different wavelengths of light at different depths, which will give a color cast to your photographs.
- Also remember that objects underwater will actually be one-third farther away than they appear.

keeping in the field is essential if the images are to remain meaningful for archaeological purposes. Precise information on when, where, and why a photograph was taken can be permanently lost if photographs are not securely correlated to good records.

- At the beginning, number each roll of each type of film in sequence (color slide film 1-X, black and white 1-X, and so on). When you take the first shot on each roll, make certain that it includes either an information board or a piece of paper with the roll number, date, and location. This means that at least one frame within each roll will have basic identifying information. This can be especially important if the photographic recording sheets are ever lost, not filled in, misplaced, or filed separately from the images.

- Basic information, such as date, time, location, subject, frame number, and roll number, should always be included on a photographic recording form (appendix A), which should also include specific remarks. It is also a good idea to carry a small notebook and jot down basic information, or record this in your field diary.
- *Never* succumb to the temptation to write up your photographic records later. Record the information after each photograph is taken, and update remarks and general information throughout the day. While it can be tempting to wait until evening, by then the nuances will be lost, and if you put it off until morning or for a few days, you can easily omit important details.
- If several sites are involved, you should record the photography on a site-by-site basis, especially making certain to enter information on the first frame used on a new site on the recording form. With the large capacity of some digital media, be especially careful to provide markers distinguishing between sites. If you have multiple digital storage devices, recording the photos from only one site on a single device may be the best practice.
- Another way of protecting information is to take photographs using a Polaroid camera. When setting up to take a series of photographs, take a couple of Polaroid images first and mount them directly into your field notebook. Record the roll and frame numbers alongside the appropriate Polaroid print. If other records get lost or misplaced, you can locate where the main prints were taken by comparing them to the Polaroid scenes in your field notebook. Note that Polaroid prints are unstable and will become darker with time. For this reason they are not suitable for archival purposes. If you have a digital camera and a way to print photos in your field camp, you can use them instead of Polaroids.

THE BASICS OF FIELD ILLUSTRATION

Just as a "good" archaeological photograph has a particular role to fulfill, so too does a "good" archaeological illustration, but it is not the same as an artistic representation of an object. The general aim of all archaeological illustration is to produce an objective drawing that can be used for the purposes of comparison (Drewett 1999, 177). For this reason, all archaeological drawings must be carefully measured and are designed to reveal technical information of use to archaeological analysis. Good-quality illustrations are an important part of archaeological recordings. Journal articles and archaeological reports will include a range of illustrations, such as maps, site plans, section drawings, illustrations of artifacts, and, in some cases, imaginative reconstructions of past lifeways. The quality of illustrations can make an enormous difference to the final publication. Good illustration demands training and skill, so if you do not draw particularly well yourself, pay someone skilled to produce good illustrations for you. However, work closely with them so that they understand the features you wish to emphasize.

The essential equipment for any good field illustration is graph paper, a sharp pencil, a scale ruler, and a good eraser (see also figure 9.9). You can either draw your illustrations directly onto graph paper or draw them onto translucent drawing film (such as Perma-trace) or tracing paper held down with sticky tape over graph paper. You can buy drawing film from any art supply shop.

FIGURE 9.9: Many archaeologists use a drawing board when in the field made from a light sheet of Masonite or plywood holding a fixed sheet of laminated graph paper. You can then easily tape drawing film or tracing paper directly over the laminated graph paper.

The archaeological illustration process has two parts: the initial in-the-field pencil drawing of the plan, section (see chapter 4, "Site Survey and Mapping"), or artifact and the final inked version for publication. The final inked part of the process is not so much part of the fieldwork, but something that is done later in the lab. It is essential for publication, however, so has been included here as part of the general process (see also chapter 10, "Getting Your Results Out There: Writing, Publication, and Interpretation"). Many computer programs also can be used to produce high-quality professional illustrations from your initial pencil drawings.

An inked drawing is essentially a tracing of your penciled original. Use high-quality translucent drawing film or high-quality tracing paper (make sure you avoid cheap and nasty "lunch-wrap"-style tracing paper). When inking drawings you should use high-quality technical pens (such as Rotring Isograph or Castell Rapidograph pens, which come in a range of point sizes) filled with good-quality ink. Don't try to draw inked illustrations directly onto paper, because the fibers in the paper will cause the ink to bleed and make the illustration messy. Because you cannot simply rub mistakes out when you are using ink, you need to exercise care. Remember that, because you are making a copy of the original pencil master drawing, you can make as many copies as you like and keep practicing until you get it right. On good-quality drawing film you will have to use a scalpel or similar knife to scrape off any mistakes. The blade must be very sharp, and you cannot do it too often as eventually it will permanently damage the surface of the drawing film. When removing mistakes by scalpel, hold the blade perpendicular to the surface and remove the ink with a firm, smooth sweep, using as few passes as possible. Be careful not to let the point of the scalpel gouge the surface or to let the blade start and stop jerkily, as this will create cavities in the drawing film, which will make the ink bleed or pool and mess up your drawing.

DRAWING HORIZONTAL SURFACES (PLANS)

The drawn record of any piece of archaeological fieldwork will consist mainly of measured drawings of surfaces, either horizontal (plans) or vertical (sections) (Drewett 1999, 130). Site plans are one of the most common types of archaeological illustration. Because it is usually impractical to photograph a site from the air, a plan is often the only way to document and convey spatial information about a site quickly and easily. Plan drawing uses the measurements taken from a survey (see chapter 4, "Site Survey and Mapping") and converts these to a suitable scale to fit onto a sheet of graph or drawing paper.

Because sites are rarely if ever drawn at a scale of 1:1, the first and most important thing to consider when drawing a plan is the appropriate scale (table 9.1; see also table

TABLE 9.1: The relationship between scale and the level of detail that you can reasonably expect to include on a site plan. For any objects smaller than specified, you could indicate their location with a dot but would not be able to include any details of their shape or form.

Scale	Means	Main uses	Level of detail
1:1	Life size	Only for small artifacts or examples of decoration on artifacts	Excellent, can include everything
1:10	10 cm on the ground = 1 cm on the plan	Sections and elevations; skeletons; and small, complex deposits	Expect to draw every object above 1 cm in length (which will be 1 mm on the plan)
1:20	20 cm on the ground = 1 cm on the plan	Feature plans	Expect to draw every object above 2 cm in length (1 mm on the plan)
1:50	50 cm on the ground = 1 cm on the plan	Site plans; large, simple sections; and elevations	Expect to draw every object above 5 cm in length (1 mm on the plan)
1:100	1 m on the ground = 1 cm on the plan	Simple site plans only; sketch plans	Expect to draw every object above 10 cm in length (1 mm on the plan)
1:250	2.5 m on the ground = 1 cm on the plan	Larger sites or sketch plans of sites	Expect to draw every object above 25 cm in length (1 mm on the plan)
1:500	5 m on the ground = 1 cm on the plan	Large, complex sites	Expect to draw every object above 50 cm in length (1 mm on the plan)

2.1). Obviously the drawing can't be so large that it won't fit onto the paper, but by the same token, there is no point drawing it so small that you can't see any of the details.

How to Draw a Plan in the Field

- Decide on the most appropriate scale *before you begin.* There is nothing more frustrating than getting halfway through a plan before you find out that part of the site literally will not fit. To work out the scale, find out the longest measurement that you will be required to plot, and work out a scale that will fit this onto the drawing. Obviously if you can fit the longest measurement, then everything else will fit too.
- Work out roughly where this measurement will be located on your drawing to ensure that you can fit the other elements of the site around it (i.e., if the longest measurement is running through the middle of the site, there is no point placing this on one edge of the drawing).
- Mark the baseline or the edges of the planning frame *lightly* onto the drawing, and indicate the measurement gradations.
- Work out where north is with a compass, and convert this to a north arrow on your plan using a protractor. To do this, first take a compass bearing along your baseline (see "Using a Compass" in chapter 2). Then orient your protractor over the drawn version of the baseline from the same point so that it faces the same direction. If you took a compass reading of 90° from the southern end of the baseline, for example, you would position the center of your protractor over the southern point of the drawn baseline so that the 90° mark lined up with the baseline. From this you would mark the direction of north (0°) at the edge of the protractor and then draw a short, solid line capped with an arrow to represent north. While it is the convention for all plans and maps to be oriented with north to the top of the page, because you will have established your baseline according to where it is most useful to record archaeological information, you probably will not have the luxury of being able to automatically place north at the top of your field plan. In this case, don't worry. When you eventually come to draw the final inked version of your plan, you can redraw it in a new orientation so that north will face the top of the page.
- Use the same method to convert any directional bearings from a compass that you make during the course of the plan to directions in degrees on your plan.
- Draw in the larger, dominant features first. This will help you to position the smaller features around them and may save you time if you are running short at the end. If all else fails, as long as you have the dominant site features accurately plotted, then you can always draw in the lesser features by eye.

- Clearly label the drawing with the site name, trench or square designation (if you are drawing a plan of an excavation), your name, the names of any people who have measured for you, and the date.
- Always draw the scale of the plan as a linear (bar) scale, rather than just noting down the scale ratio (1:10, 1:100, and so on), and make sure that you note what units of measurement the scale refers to. If the scale is in centimeters, mark it with a "cm," if in meters mark it with an "m," and so on. There is absolutely no point in drawing a beautiful, accurate scale if nobody knows what units it represents.
- If you are drawing a very large or extensive site it may not be possible to fit the entire area onto a single plan and still preserve the detail. In this case you may need to break the site down into discrete parts that can be drawn separately, but you will also need to draw an overall plan of the site showing each part in relation to the other. If your plan is running across two or more sheets of paper, make sure that you note how they fit together and that you write this on *both* sheets. One way to do this is to make sure that the adjoining parts contain the matching halves of a single symbol (such as a circle, square, or solid line) so that you can literally put the two halves back together again. Another way is to number the sheets and mark the adjoining edges "Plan 1 adjoins Plan 2" and so on. If you adopt this latter method, make sure that someone else will know precisely *where* they join: there is no point noting which plan joins which if there is no other indication of which edges actually join.
- When you come to draw the final inked version of the plan, always remember to include the scale and your north arrow marked with the letter *N*.

There are various conventions for drawing slopes. A plan makes the distance between any two points appear horizontal, as if both were at the same level. In reality, of course, your site may include various kinds of slopes, which needs to be indicated on your plan. This will help you to convey an idea of the contours of the ground and will be essential if the site you are recording consists of hummocky relief (i.e., mounds and hollows), or if there are distinct changes of slope that are an essential part of the arrangement of the site (such as mine-processing plants, which were commonly built along the slope of a hill to take advantage of gravity to move materials between different stages of the process). You indicate slope by using **hachures**, or short lines that indicate the top of the slope with an arrow and the length of the slope with a line (figure 9.10).

DRAWING VERTICAL SURFACES (SECTIONS)

A section is the drawing of a vertical, rather than a horizontal, surface but employs all of the same basic techniques. You can apply these techniques to any vertical surface, whether the side of an excavated unit or the wall of a standing structure.

FIGURE 9.10: Conventions for illustrating slope

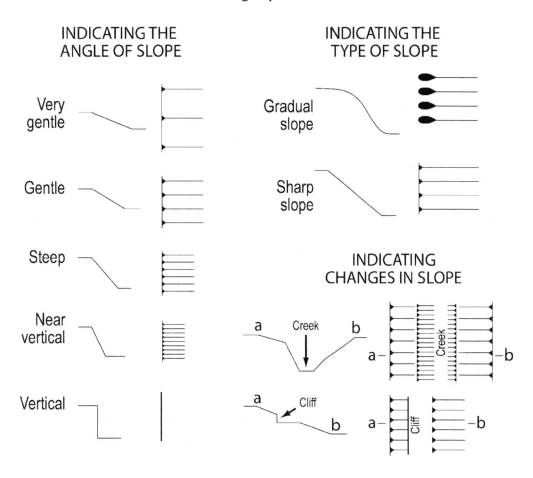

When drawing vertical surfaces:

- Set up a horizontal baseline (datum) across a suitable part of the section—either at the top if it is a small section or halfway down if it is a large section. To do this, first set out the datum using a piece of string secured firmly to two nails. These can be inserted into the corners of the section if you are drawing a unit profile, or into cracks in the masonry if you are drawing a wall. Use a line level to make sure that the string is horizontal. Once you have established this, fix a tape measure to the string baseline with clothespins.
- Draw the datum line *lightly* onto your graph paper or drafting film as a horizontal line parallel to the top of the drafting sheet, and mark the gradations of the tape measure

If you are excavating a large and complex site, you can secure an aluminum tag clearly showing the unit number to the trench section as the surface of each new unit is identified. This will help you later when drawing up the sections.

onto it. Remember to place this appropriately on your page (i.e., at the top if your baseline is at the top, in the middle if your baseline is in the middle, and so forth).

- Begin by drawing the gross elements, such as the limits of the section or wall, the level of the topsoil, and the base of the trench, by taking offset measurements above and below the datum line.
- Once you have established the boundaries of the drawing, begin on the details, such as the layer boundaries and features. If you are drawing an excavation unit, you may have to go back and forth between your drawing and the unit notes and recording forms to make sure that you have all the layers.
- Remember that it is okay to draw in some smaller features by eye or to fill in some details by eye, and as you gain experience this will become much easier to do.
- If you are drawing a unit profile, make sure that you label each excavated context that appears in the section with its correct context number (usually represented according to the Harris matrix system by the number inside a square; see "Interpreting Stratigraphy" in chapter 5).
- If the four sections of a unit are to be drawn on the one sheet, then draw them in the order of N, S, E, W.
- Clearly label your drawing with the site name, unit number and profile description if appropriate, date, scale, your name, and the name of anyone who has taken measurements for you.

While there are standard systems of symbols to use in drawing sections and plans (figure 9.11), it is difficult to achieve a uniform system because sites and their contents vary so widely. See Adkins and Adkins (1989, 74) for some suggestions.

DRAWING ARTIFACTS

Measured drawings of individual artifacts are time consuming and usually only done for publication. The drawing of any artifact is not simply a mechanical process but requires some interpretation and selection (Drewett 1999, 177). First, carefully examine the object and decide which aspects are most important to convey. The size and shape of the object

FIGURE 9.11: Some conventions for section or profile drawings

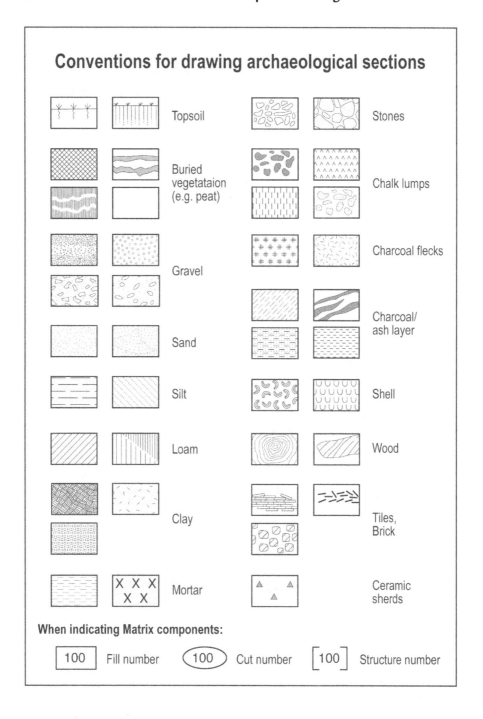

always will be important, but what about its material? Evidence for how it was made? Different surface finishes or areas of damage? What will need emphasizing in the final drawing? It is also important to consider how you will convey the three-dimensional nature of the object on a two-dimensional surface: which side or aspect is the most important to draw? This will determine what will be regarded as the "front" or the "back" of the object and therefore what is also drawn as the side, top, or basal view. All good artifact drawings will not only be technically correct and convey the relevant technical information but also be pleasing to the eye.

The basic process to be followed is similar for all kinds of artifacts. Unlike plans, it is far easier to draw an object at a scale of 1:1 (i.e., actual size) rather than to try to reduce or enlarge it. If an object is particularly large or small, however, the drawing may need to be reduced or enlarged as appropriate, for ease of working. There are four main stages in drawing most artifacts:

- Drawing the outline
- Drawing the details
- Drawing a side view
- Drawing a cross section

Some more complex artifacts may require more views than this (such as a top, base, or back view for instance)—use your own judgment as to which will convey the most useful information, or look at published drawings of similar artifacts as a guide.

If you are drawing more than one artifact, you will also have to give some thought to the placement of artifacts together on a page:

- Set your drawings in horizontal rows to the extent allowed by their shape and size.
- Don't be tempted to rotate the artifacts to fit them in. Always keep them in their correct conventional positions.
- Put the smallest, lightest-looking artifacts at the top of the layout and the darkest, heaviest ones at the bottom (Addington 1986, 68).
- Try to keep all the specimens of one artifact type together in a series. Do not randomly mix your drawings in complete disregard of their classifications (Addington 1986, 69).
- If you are numbering each artifact, put the numbers in the same relative position by each artifact and make sure that the numbers or letters are arranged in a logical order (i.e., running from left to right and top to bottom).
- Make the numbering or lettering as unobtrusive as possible.
- Consider placing a border around the drawings to visually draw them together.

Drawing the Outline

To draw whole objects, place the object flat on a piece of graph paper (it can be held in place with Blu Tack or small wooden blocks if necessary). If you are drawing a small artifact, you may be able to trace directly around it using a sharp, long-pointed lead pencil. If you can't trace directly around it, use the pencil to project points around the edge of the artifact that can be joined to give the outline (figure 9.12). If you are drawing a large

FIGURE 9.12: Measuring the outline and details of an artifact for illustration (after Griffiths, Jenner, and Wilson 1990, 96; Mumford 1983, 161)

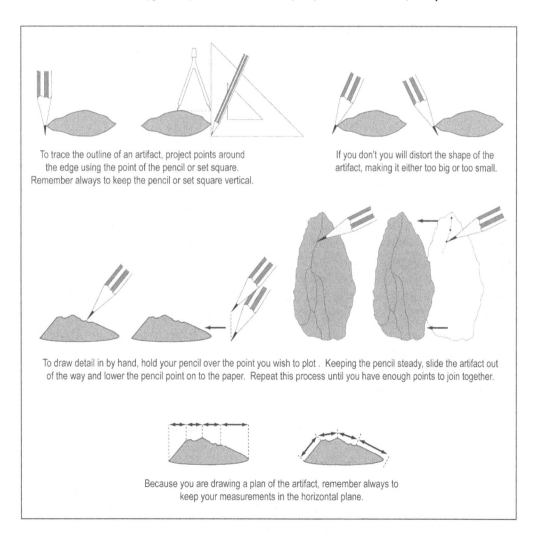

To trace the outline of an artifact, project points around the edge using the point of the pencil or set square. Remember always to keep the pencil or set square vertical.

If you don't you will distort the shape of the artifact, making it either too big or too small.

To draw detail in by hand, hold your pencil over the point you wish to plot . Keeping the pencil steady, slide the artifact out of the way and lower the pencil point on to the paper. Repeat this process until you have enough points to join together.

Because you are drawing a plan of the artifact, remember always to keep your measurements in the horizontal plane.

artifact, use a set square to project points in the same fashion around the edge of the object onto the paper. If the object is regular in shape you probably can get away with relatively few points, but if it is irregular you will need to draw as many as are necessary (generally, wherever there is a major change in angle/shape) to indicate its precise outline. Remember to keep the pencil or set square vertical while you are doing this, otherwise you will distort the shape of the object. Even if you do this, there will be a slight enlargement of the object due to the width of the casing of the pencil.

Now place the artifact to one side of the outline and compare them critically by eye. You will no doubt see several anomalies in the outline that have dropped out or become "softened" through the tracing process (indentations will be smaller than they ought to be and bumps bigger). Correct the outline to define the details of the edge more sharply. If necessary check your measurements with calipers to ensure that your outline is accurate. Remember that you are drawing a plan of the artifact; therefore make sure that all of your measurements are kept in a horizontal plane (figure 9.12). If you are drawing a stone artifact, make the lines of the outline angular rather than rounded, because this will emphasize details rather than obscure them (Mumford 1983).

Drawing the Details

Once you have a measured outline you can begin on the detail. You can plot in details of the surface of an artifact by hand (figure 9.12) or by measuring the artifact with calipers. If you are doing it by hand, place the artifact over its drawn outline and hold your pencil over the point you wish to plot. Keeping the pencil steady, slide the artifact away, then lower the pencil point onto the paper immediately below. You can repeat this process until you have enough points on the paper to draw the feature in fully.

This will give you a complete "skeleton" of the artifact: its edge and all its features in outline. Sometimes this is all that you will need to show the artifact clearly and indicate its main features. If you think your artifact requires more interpretation, you can do this by adding shading to make it three dimensional (figure 9.13). Shading can be added as stippling (small dots that increase in frequency in darker, more shaded areas) or crosshatching (diagonal lines that increase in frequency in darker, more shaded areas). If you are at all hesitant about adding shading then don't attempt it—it takes as much effort to do it badly as to do it well, and it is not always vital to the understanding of the object (Mumford 1983, 166) (for more tips on shading see "Golden Rules for Drawing").

Drawing a Side View and Cross Section

A side view is drawn by rotating the object through 90° from the surface or "front" view. Always place a side view parallel and to one side of the front view—it doesn't really matter which, although the convention is to place it to the right.

FIGURE 9.13: Shading is not always essential to an understanding of an artifact but can be used to add three-dimensional form

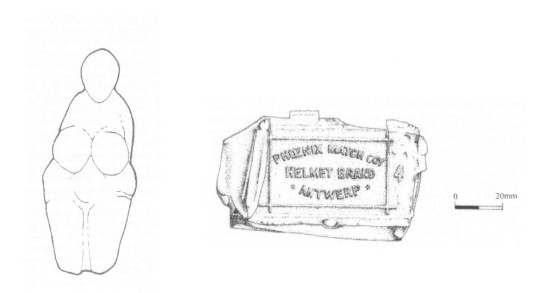

Many object drawings also require a cross section to show the thickness or shape of the artifact. This is not a substitute for a side view. For ceramic vessels a cross section will be a half profile divided down the long axis of the pot; for stone artifacts it will be a cross section through the middle or the most informative section of the artifact. When measuring the thickness of an artifact for a cross section, make sure to measure it at as many points as are necessary to convey the object's precise form (because its thickness may not always be constant).

Whenever you draw a cross section, make sure you indicate the line of the section (i.e., the place on the object that the section passes through) with a short line on either side of the object in the appropriate spot. Make sure the cross section is always placed parallel to the axis of these lines and to one side of the front (surface) view. In Britain and Australia the convention is to place this on the left-hand side, in the United States to place it on the right. Either way, the cross section should be either colored in solid black (if it's a cross section of a pottery vessel) or cross-hatched (if it's a stone artifact).

Reduction

Very few finished drawings of artifacts will be reproduced at life size. Drawings are reduced for many reasons, most of them economic (some artifacts are simply too large to fit

The positive side of the reduction process is that it can actually make your drawing look better because it reduces any flaws. If you want to get an idea of how reduction will affect your drawing, try reducing it on the photocopier to see how it will look.

on a page, and many will often need to be included on the same page). This means that the scale and level of detail you choose for drawing an artifact is very important. Bear in mind that reduction will affect every aspect of your drawing: every line will be reduced in thickness; the white space will be reduced in area; any shading, stippling, or cross-hatching you have used will be closer together. This will be particularly important if your drawing is going to be reduced to one-third or one-quarter of its size for publication: if you think of how your drawing will look even when reduced to only half its size, how much of the decoration or fine detail will still be visible? When it comes to making decisions as an illustrator, one of the most important things to think about is the final scale of the published drawing: large artifacts are usually drawn at a scale of 1:1 but then reduced to 1:4 or 1:3 in the final publication; while small artifacts are usually drawn at a scale of 2:1 so that they can be reduced to life size in the final publication.

When preparing an illustration for publication:

- Draw lines that will be thick enough to reduce without disappearing. The thinnest line that can be printed confidently is 0.1 mm; any less than this and the line will break up (Griffiths, Jenner, and Wilson 1990, 8). Your lines will therefore have to be proportionally thicker than this. For those that will be reduced to one-quarter their size, the safest thin line would need to be 0.4 mm thick, for example; for drawings that will be reduced to half their size, the safest thin line would need to be 0.2 mm thick, and so on.
- When shading or cross-hatching, make sure the lines are not so close together that they will appear black in the published drawing.
- If you are using different shades of gray for infill, make sure that reducing the drawing will not make them all look the same. In general, go for readily distinguishable and separable shadings (e.g., white, 50% black, or 100% black) and not minute variations in between.
- Think about the size of your lettering or numbering, including the size of your scale, and how this will look when reduced. For scales it is best to stick to simple and easily legible black-and-white bar scales with lettering that is still large enough to remain legible after the reduction process.
- Bear in mind that the white space is just as important as the black lines when it comes to the reduction process.

Golden Rules for Drawing

- Keep your pencil sharp.
- Try not to use a hard-lead pencil (H series), as this will leave an indelible mark on the paper or drawing film, which will remain even if you rub the pencil itself out. HB or B series pencils are softer and can be rubbed out completely.
- Never give only a written description of a scale (e.g., "Drawn at 1:1"), as the size at which an illustration will be published is unlikely to be the same as the original (Mumford 1983, 168). Always include a simple bar or line scale.
- Always include your name as the illustrator and the names of any others who have taken measurements for you, as well as the date and the name of the site or other title.
- If you are drawing a plan, always include a north arrow.
- Use conventional symbols wherever possible.
- Use a heavy grade of tracing paper, because lighter grades crinkle too easily and absorb moisture from your hands.
- If you decide to use drawing paper, choose one that has a smooth surface, because a textured surface will break up the lines of ink, making copying difficult.
- Never use felt-tip pens, magic markers, fountain pens, or ball points to make final illustrations.

For artifacts:

- Always draw an artifact as if the light is coming from the top left-hand corner. This means that shading will be to the right and on the lower right-hand sections of the artifact. If you are unable to arrange lighting from the left-hand corner, use your imagination to guide your shading.
- The main component is the front or surface view (remembering that "front" will be arbitrary in some cases).
- Always use a consistent orientation, and make sure the vertical axis of the object is always kept parallel to the vertical axis of the page.
- Other standard components for most artifact drawings are a side view and a cross section. Some very complex artifacts may require a view of the top and bottom of the artifact as well.
- Draw views of the top or the bottom of the artifact above or below the object, respectively.
- Side or back views should be drawn to the right of the front view.

(continues)

Golden Rules for Drawing (*continued*)

For stippling:

- When stippling, hold your pen upright to produce a discrete dot rather than a small comet. If the drawing is used in a publication it will be reduced, and stippling can easily become a black blob. Start with an overall light covering, and work from lighter (less dense) to darker (more dense) areas.
- Remember that the dots should be randomly placed and not ordered in rows or lines (this is harder to do than you might think). They should be evenly spaced, and their density should increase gradually (Mumford 1983, 167).
- If the surface of the artifact is smooth and uniform, keep the dotting fine and uniform, with only gradual changes in tone.
- If the surface is rough and coarse, stipple with more vigor in some areas according to the character of the surface features (Addington 1986, 18–19).
- When stippling, remember that variation in the amount of white space between dots can give an impression of an undulating surface.
- Add the dots for the more heavily shaded areas last. Try to fade these areas gently into each other, unless you are trying to indicate a change of plane. Bear in mind that the densest parts should be on the right-hand side, if the light is coming from the upper left-hand corner.

For cross-hatching:

- Cross-hatching should be at the same spacing as the line shading and generally should be at right angles to the lighter tones.
- On curved surfaces, hatching should follow the curves, either around the edges or radiating down curved surfaces.
- If you need a particularly dark shadow, add a third level of diagonal hatching across the cross-hatching (Griffiths, Jenner, and Wilson 1990, 31). Avoid the temptation to add a fourth level of hatching because it will appear solid black.
- It is always easier to add extra lines, cross-hatching, dots, or stippling than to take them away from too crowded a drawing. If you are unsure, it is better to do less rather than more.

DRAWING STONE ARTIFACTS

Stone artifacts are probably one of the most difficult things to draw because they come in a wide variety of raw materials and sometimes show extremely detailed evidence of working. One of the main conventions to follow is to use different drawing techniques to represent the different kinds of raw materials: stippling for coarse-grained material such as sandstone, commonly used in grinding implements, and hatching for smooth, fine-grained materials such as obsidian, chert, or flint.

To draw a stone artifact you follow the same basic sequence as for any other artifact: outline, details, side view, and cross section. There are some specific conventions to follow (table 9.2), however:

- When drawing the outline, remember that pencil lead will leave a residue on the artifact. If you are intending to analyze residues, use only a set square to project the outline, and don't trace around the artifact with the pencil.
- Draw the outline of the artifact first, followed by internal features such as scars and ridges.
- Draw the positive features of the ventral surface, such as ring cracks, eraillure scars, and undulations.
- The position of the flake scars can be measured with dividers or calipers. Remember that you are drawing a plan of the artifact, so all measurements need to be taken from a horizontal plane (see figure 9.12).
- Do not leave flake scars or retouched edges incomplete. If you cannot decide where each starts and ends, either dot it in or do not show it at all.
- If the outlines of the flake scars and other details have been drawn precisely, then the direction of flaking will be self-evident (Mumford 1983, 165). You *can* draw curved

TABLE 9.2: Conventions for drawing stone artifacts

Feature	Convention
Cortex	Stippling
Polished or ground artifacts	Stippling
Flaked stone artifacts	Lines
Use polish	Stippling
Gum	Black or stippling
Cross sections	Blank or filled with cross-hatching
Part of the artifact broken or missing	Short dashed lines indicating how the missing piece must have continued the outline

Alice Gorman's Tips for Stone Artifact Illustration

For the pencil drawing:

- Although it is not generally recommended, it is possible to make a pencil drawing from a photocopy of the artifact. This is particularly useful when you have limited access to the artifact, such as when you are working in a museum, or when you are dealing with use-wear and residue analysis, as it greatly reduces the amount of handling of the artifact. Photocopy both the ventral and dorsal surfaces, and label these clearly. Then copy the outline onto tracing paper, referring constantly to the artifact and checking the measurements.
- If you want to enlarge a drawing, this is easily done with a photocopier.
- Remember a bar scale is essential if you, or the printer, is going to enlarge or reduce the drawing. This will remove all doubt about an artifact's size, but only if you label it (e.g., in cm or mm).
- Begin with the outline and finish with the fine details.
- Keep the pencil drawing as a master copy. If the ink version does not work out, you can easily begin again.

For the ink drawing:

- Wash your hands before you begin to prevent grease from your fingers being transferred to the drawing film. If you are attempting the final inked version of a drawing this will be essential, because the grease from your fingers will prevent the ink from taking.
- Keep a clean sheet of paper handy on which to rest your hand as you are working to cut down on dirt, grease, or smudging.
- If you are right-handed, work down and toward your right so that the movement of your hand does not smudge the ink.
- Keep your wrist straight. Draw lines by moving your whole arm rather than your wrist. It is very hard to keep your hand perfectly steady just using wrist movement.
- Hold the pen as upright as possible. This ensures a more even line.
- Don't exert too much downward pressure on the pen, as you can easily break or bend the nib.
- Always use at least two pen widths: a thicker line (such as 0.35 or 0.5) for the outline, and a thinner line (such as 0.25 or 0.35) for internal lines and detail. This is part of conveying the three-dimensional feel of the artifact; if you draw it with all lines of the same thickness it will look flat and uninteresting.

- Make sure all the lines meet exactly. Even the tiniest bit of overhang can make a drawing look untidy, as can lines that do not quite meet. If necessary, when you are drawing the final inked version, remove any overhanging bits with a scalpel, and thin down any lines that are too thick.
- When removing ink with the scalpel, scrape only in one direction as this will cause less damage to the drawing film. If you have to draw over the area you have just removed, the ink may run if you have damaged the surface. However, a light burnishing can help restore it partially.
- When stippling (i.e., to represent cortex), be aware that your drawing may be reduced, which can make the stipples look like untidy blobs.

Good drawing skills require practice. Don't be too disappointed with your first attempts. It is worth putting in the time, however, as drawing is an employable skill, and it fine-tunes your observation skills for artifact analysis.

lines within each flake scar to indicate the direction from which flakes were struck, for both positive and negative scars, if you wish, but this is not generally recommended unless you are sure you can do it well. If you are not confident that you can, then leave it out.

- Indicate the point of force application with a small arrow outside the drawing.
- Cross sections are used to show the form and thickness of an artifact. When drawn, they should be parallel to the axis on which they were taken. Draw two identifying marks outside the artifact plan to show the line of this axis.
- If drawing cross sections of several flakes, make sure all cross-hatching lies in the same direction.
- If you are in any doubt about how much detail to include, understate, don't overstate. An artifact is much easier to interpret if it is simply and clearly drawn.

DRAWING CERAMICS

Just as there are conventions for drawing stone artifacts, there are also conventions for drawing ceramic vessels. The point of most ceramic drawings is to give an impression of the overall shape and size of the vessel, even if only fragments are available for drawing. If you are drawing a whole pot, the convention is to draw it as though it were standing upright but had been cut in two, with one half of the drawing showing the external surface of the vessel, and the other half depicting the section and interior. The two halves of the vessel are demarcated by a solid vertical line. Similar to the process followed when drawing stone artifacts, to capture the shape of a ceramic vessel, lay it down upon the drawing paper and use a set square to project points around the vessel down onto the paper, and join these dots. When drawing the section, don't assume that the thickness will be even. Use calipers to measure the thickness of the wall of the vessel at various points.

If you are drawing ceramic fragments, the focus is usually on rim or base sherds, rather than body fragments, unless the body fragments have particularly interesting or diagnostic decoration. If you are drawing fragments of a larger artifact they generally should be drawn in their correct relationship to the whole object. In other words, if you are drawing a pot, then rim fragments should be drawn in their correct location at the rim, base sherds at the base, and so on. If you do find yourself drawing body sherds, then you will have to make your best guess as to where they fit in relation to the original curvature of the complete vessel.

To estimate the original curvature of a vessel from a rim or base sherd only, use a rim chart such as the one provided in appendix B. Hold the sherd upright with its rim or base flat on the chart so that all parts of the rim or base are touching the surface at the same time. Line up one end of the sherd with the 0% line on the rim chart, and slide it slowly along the line until you find the concentric ring that best fits the curvature of the sherd. This is your estimate of the original diameter of the vessel. The radiating line closest to the end of the sherd will give you an estimate of the proportion of the vessel's rim or base that the sherd represents.

DRAWING ROCK ART

Drawing is a particularly important way of recording rock art. Sketching a rock art panel in the field makes you first focus closely on the motifs, working out what is really there and which motifs overlap. Many rock art panels contain an apparently bewildering variety of motifs drawn around, on top of, or through each other and are often confused further by natural striations or planes in the rock itself. A photograph of this alone would be unlikely to help you sort out what was and wasn't art and may result in your confusing or not recognizing a certain proportion of the motifs. The analysis involved in drawing each part of the panel by hand, which often seems impossible to begin with, will actually force you to sort out each motif and give you an understanding of how the whole panel works together. The time spent drawing motifs at a rock art site means that you have a greater opportunity to get a "feel" for the site, so that you don't just dash in, take a photo or two, and dash out. This time spent at the site will give you a better understanding of how the art operated in its local environment.

Drawing is essential for establishing patterns of **superimposition** (where one motif covers another), which is the major nondestructive way of dating rock art. Sometimes, however, what appears to be overlap is actually the result of microerosion in that part of the rockshelter, so you need to look for a pattern of overlap to establish regular superimposition. These patterns can then be interpreted in terms of sequences of painting events. However, you have to be very careful when undertaking these analyses because differences in superimposition could be the result of time differences of one minute, one year, one thousand years, or ten thousand years. As a result, to make some decisions about which motifs are older and which are younger, you also will need to take into account the differential weathering of motifs when you are developing a superimposition sequence.

One effective way of recording rock engravings is through tracing. This can be done with heavy plastic and a range of colors using permanent-ink pens (figure 9.14). It is best to use permanent markers, in case it starts to rain when you are working and so that the

FIGURE 9.14: Tracing the outlines of petroglyph sites onto plastic sheets

Inés Domingo-Sanz's Tips for Digitally Drawing Rock Art

In recent years several research teams (e.g., Domingo and López-Montalvo 2002) have developed methods for applying new digital imaging technologies to rock art recording. This new system is more objective than previous methods and is less destructive because it doesn't involve direct contact with the paintings. The method is accurate but slow, as it involves a meticulous process of deciphering and continuously checking the tracings against the original images.

In the field:

- **Identify motifs.** Check whether previous documentation on the site exists. If it does, check previous recordings to identify motifs and assess the damage suffered since the site was last documented. If there is no previous documentation, draw a sketch of the motifs and their location in relation to each other, as part of the recording process.
- **Draw a site plan.** It is important to draw a plan of the site, recording dimensions and the main structural features. The more detail the better.
- **Take photographs.** To trace a motif using digitized images requires high-resolution photographs. Use conventional photography (6 mm $\times$ 7 mm negatives) with large-format cameras or high-resolution digital cameras. The process also can be undertaken using any 35 mm SLR or digital point-and-shoot camera, though the quality of the image will not be quite as good. For tracing rock art, three kinds of photographs are necessary:

  —Close-ups of each motif. These will form the basis of the tracings.
  —Close-ups of details of motifs, such as areas of superimposition, which you can refer to later for clarification.
  —Wide-angle pictures, which show the motifs in relation to each other.

- **Record measurements of each motif and the distances between them.** Inevitably, your photographs will generate some distortion. To counteract this, measure the shape of each motif as well as the distances between motifs.
- **Identify the color range of each motif** using a Munsell color chart.

In the lab:

- **Scan the negatives (if using film).** These must be scanned at a high resolution because you will be working with fine details. A dpi of 2400 is best, although you can use other combinations of size and resolution to give the same result (e.g., scanning the negative at 800 dpi but at 300% size so the result is the same).

- **Trace the motifs** using Adobe Photoshop or a similar program, as follows:

  —Open the scanned photo you want to trace (figure 9.15a).

  —Select a portion of the image using the lasso tool (figure 9.15b).

  —Copy and paste this area into a new layer (figure 9.15c). It is best to work separately with each portion of the motif, as different sections may have different color values.

  —Click on one of the two available color selection tools (the "magic wand tool" or "color range") to select surfaces of similar chromatic range. The width of the range depends on the tolerance values given to the selection (using the fuzziness tool). Modify fuzziness values to small units in the dialogue box, because this will allow you to select more homogeneous colors than if you work with high fuzziness values (figure 9.15d).

  —**Copy and paste the selection into a new layer** and save it (figure 9.15e).

  —Return to the scanned image and **select a new area to trace**.

  —**Repeat these steps until you've traced the whole figure.** Each time you save a new selection, make sure you save it at the same resolution as the old.

  —Sometimes Adobe Photoshop will include pixels from shadows, cracks in the wall, or the adjoining rock surface as part of the selection because these can have similar chromatic ranges to the motifs. You will have to erase these manually by comparing the tracings against the original images (figure 9.15f).

  —Each selection will generate a new layer, and you'll need to fit them together to see the tracing of the entire panel (figure 9.15g). When doing this, check that all of your tracings are scaled to their original size, saved at the same resolution, and oriented correctly.

- Once you've finished the tracing process, **scale the figure to its real size** (which you know from your original measurements).

- **Check the accuracy of the tracings.** Once the tracings are complete you will need to return to the field to compare them with the original motifs. Keep checking until all the measurements on the tracings agree with the measurements on the motifs.

- **Assemble the whole panel.** You can assemble the completed, traced panel in Adobe Illustrator. Make sure all tracings are scaled to their original size, have been saved at the same resolution, and are oriented correctly.

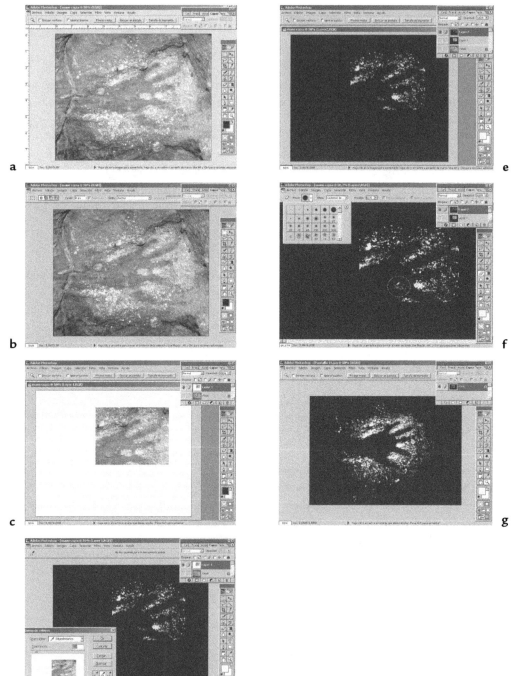

FIGURE 9.15: Using digital technology
to record rock art

colors do not rub off over time. You can use different colored pens to code different types of information. For example, you might draw the main motifs in brown but indicate areas of overlap with blue or red. Or you might use a different color to dot in an area where a motif has become "fuzzy," or to indicate areas where you can't quite determine if the markings are made by people or nature. As with all archaeology, it is important that you record as much information as you can because patterns may emerge later in your analysis that you were not aware of in the field. Another effective way to draw rock art is with a planning frame: a light, portable wooden frame with a metric grid marked out in string that simply rests against the rock surface and visually divides the area into small squares for ease of drawing. If you use this frame, make sure it doesn't touch the art surface.

STORING PHOTOGRAPHS AND ILLUSTRATIONS

Once you have completed a project you have an ethical responsibility to store the complete archive of your fieldwork properly (see "Archaeologists and Their Profession" in chapter 1). Photographs and illustrations need special handling:

- Film negatives should be archived in a dark, cool place, such as a filing cabinet.
- Always store negatives in acid-free negative strip holders, not Mylar, polyester, or polyethylene plastic.
- Never store prints in commercial "sticky-backed" photograph albums. The adhesives will disintegrate over time, but probably not before they have damaged your photos. Ideally you should store your photographs in Mylar envelopes or stacked, but separated, with acid-free tissue paper.
- When you get your film back from the processor, put your rolls in chronological order, and compare the frame numbers on the negatives with the numbers recorded in the log or on the recording sheets. Adjust the numbers in the log or recording sheets if necessary to make sure everything matches up.
- Make sure that you label *every* image individually, otherwise they lose their value as an archival recording. Imagine if your photographs became separated both from each other and from the photographic recording forms—would anyone else ever be able to identify whose photographs they were or what they were of? A *minimum* of information to include is the roll number, the negative number, the place, the date, and the subject.
- CCD images from digital cameras can be stored by direct connection to your computer's hard drive or through removable PC cards that are slotted into the camera and then into the computer. Be careful to keep media away from strong magnetic fields.

- CD-ROMs and DVD-ROMs can be used to archive both digital and scans of hard-copy film images.
- Remember that archiving images on CD-ROMs or DVD-ROMs is not foolproof. They are not affected by magnetic fields but can be affected by fungus, scratches, or even using the wrong kind of marker to label the media.
- For archiving digital images, and given the very low price of digital storage, keep at least one copy of each original photo taken at your camera's highest resolution. This will maintain each image with maximum resolution and information regarding color and other image attributes. File sizes are large, but if you have compressed the image into small file sizes using JPEG, you will lose potentially important information. Remember, a TIFF file, which most digital cameras allow, can be about 17 megabytes. You can store 30 TIFF files on a CD-ROM; a single-layer DVD can store about 300.
- For digital images, cataloging software will catalog your images much more efficiently than memory. Cataloging applications work by making a record like a card index. You can add key words, such as date or location, which makes for easy searching of the catalog.
- Standard 8.5- × 11-inch drawings can be stored in three-ring binders.
- Larger drawings can be kept in a planning folder. If the drawing is going into a planning folder, attach a small tag of masking tape on the top right-hand corner, and write the plan number on it so you can find it again easily (Hawker 2001, 39).

REFERENCES AND FURTHER READING

Addington, L. 1986. *Lithic illustration.* Chicago: University of Chicago Press.

Adkins, L., and R. Adkins. 1989. *Archaeological illustration.* Cambridge: Cambridge University Press.

Barnett, T., A. Chalmers, M. Díaz-Andreu, G. Ellis, R. Gillibrand, P. Longhurst, K. Sharpe, and I. Trinks. 2004. Breaking through rock art recording: Three-dimensional laser scanning of prehistoric rock art. *VAST2004* (December): 70–71.

Clegg, J. 1983. Recording prehistoric art. In *Australian field archaeology: A guide to techniques,* ed. G. Connah, 87–108. Canberra: AIAS.

Daly, T. 2000. *Digital photography handbook: A user's guide to creating digital images.* Cincinnati: Writer's Digest.

Domingo, I., and E. López-Montalvo. 2002. Metodología. El proceso de obtención de calcos o reproducciones. In *La Cova dels Cavalls en el Barranc de la Valltorta,* ed. R. Martínez and V. Villaverde, 75–81. Monografías del Instituto de arte Rupestre, 1. València: Generalitat Valenciana.

Dorrell, P. G. 1994. *Photography in archaeology and conservation.* 2nd ed. Cambridge: Cambridge University Press.

Drewett, P. 1999. *Field archaeology: An introduction.* London: UCL Press.

Griffiths, N., A. Jenner, and C. Wilson. 1990. *Drawing archaeological finds: A handbook.* Occasional Paper No 13 of the Institute of Archaeology. London: University College.

Hawker, J. M. 2001. *A manual of archaeological field drawing.* Hertford: RESCUE—The British Archaeological Trust.

Hester, T. R., H. J. Shafer, and K. L. Feder. 1997. *Field methods in archaeology.* 7th ed. Mountain View, CA: Mayfield.

Howell, C., and W. Blanc. 1995. *A practical guide to archaeological photography.* Archaeological Research Tools 6, Institute of Archaeology. Los Angeles: University of California.

Mumford, W. 1983. Stone artifacts: An illustrator's primer. In *Australian field archaeology: A guide to techniques*, ed. G. Connah, 160–168. Canberra: AIAS.

For a range of other useful information, see the website accompanying the text.

CHAPTER TEN

GETTING YOUR RESULTS OUT THERE: WRITING, PUBLICATION, AND INTERPRETATION

What you will learn from this chapter:

Tips for getting started on writing
The basics of good archaeological writing
How to write for different audiences
The essential components of a good archaeological report
What makes for good interpretation
How to plan and design interpretive materials effectively
How to produce a professional product

Publication of the results of archaeological fieldwork is a critical ethical responsibility. Once your fieldwork is completed you must make your work available to those people who have an interest in it. You should publish as quickly as practicable and in as many forms as reasonably feasible, to inform as wide an audience as possible. Although writing up your results is an obligation, you also have the pleasure of sharing your knowledge and experiences and voicing your opinion. The major venues for publishing your results are:

- Technical reports
- CHM contract reports
- Community reports
- Articles for academic journals and chapters for edited volumes
- Books and monographs
- Websites
- Press releases
- Interpretive material

WRITING WELL

As with all archaeological skills, writing is a skill that can be acquired and honed only through study and practice. The more you study writing, the better you understand its intricacies and techniques, and the more you write, the easier it becomes. That people can either write or not write is a myth. Everyone can learn to do it well if willing to put in the time and effort.

You can employ many strategies to enhance the quality of your writing. Because the purpose of writing is communication, the best are those that make your writing accessible to as many people as possible, without losing the nuances of your arguments. Although you will have to adjust your writing style to suit your particular audience, making your writing user-friendly is a great start to communicating your ideas, whatever your audience. Above all, this means presenting your work in a professional manner (see "Producing a Professional Product").

GETTING STARTED

> It's simple. First I get all the words out, then I push them around a little.
>
> —Evelyn Waugh

> Writing is easy. All you do is stare at a blank sheet of paper until drops of blood form on your forehead.
>
> —Gene Fowler

Most of us are more like Fowler than like Waugh: the hardest part of writing anything is getting started. Writing is scary. It is scary for people who are writing for the first time, and it can be scary for people who are writing for the hundredth time. Because being faced

Ask Oxford's Tips for Keeping Your Writing User-Friendly

- Over the whole document, make 15 to 20 words the average sentence length.
- Use words your readers are likely to understand.
- Use only as many words as you really need.
- Use active voice unless there's a good reason for using the passive.
- Use the clearest, crispest, liveliest verb to express your thoughts.
- Use vertical lists to break up complicated text.
- Put your points positively when you can.
- Reduce cross-references to the minimum.
- Try to avoid discriminatory language.
- Make accurate punctuation the heart of your writing.
- Plan before you write.
- Organize your material in a way that helps readers to grasp the important information early and to navigate through the document easily.
- Consider different ways of setting out your information.
- Use clear layouts to present your words in an easily accessible way.

www.askoxford.com/betterwriting/plainenglish (accessed March 12, 2007)

with a blank sheet of paper (or computer screen) is daunting, one good strategy is to fill that paper as quickly as you can. This can be done through a process known as freewriting, in which you sketch out your ideas without editing them or judging them against the standard of what you want to produce. The point is to get rid of the scary, unfilled page. Once you have something written, you can edit it later to make it into the document you want it to be.

David Schmitt's Tips for Getting Started

- Don't wait for inspiration, just DO IT NOW.
- Write the easiest parts first.
- Begin each writing session by revising what you wrote last time.
- Set clear writing goals on your schedule.
- Avoid "one best way" thinking and realize that there is never a perfect way.
- Don't get down on yourself if you are stuck.
- Develop a positive attitude toward your work and your potential success as a writer.

From Schmitt 1992, 239

THE STAGES OF WRITING

Research

You already should have conducted a thorough search of the archaeological literature, the web, and appropriate databases as part of writing your research design and researching the history of your project or archaeological site. The point here is to start to shape this mass of information into a cohesive and focused report. Start by identifying comparable reports or papers, because their structure and content may be useful models for your own work. You may find that major and minor headings, the range of information in each section, the sequence of points, or effectiveness of tables and diagrams will provide you with a useful template for your own writing. You will find that there are similarities and differences between publications; some ways of presenting information will appeal to you, and others will not. In addition, various categories of archaeological writing will have different requirements. For instance, the aim of a community report is quite different from a research paper, and this is reflected in the format, style, and language of each. It is important to select appropriate models that you can then use to develop the approach, structure, and style of your own writing.

Much of your research will be directed toward a **literature review**, the main purposes of which are to:

- Make certain that somebody else has not already done this project.
- Establish the significance of your project through identifying important gaps in existing research.
- Identify methods used by others to deal with comparable issues, as well as any potential problems with your research methods.
- Find out how your project fits with other people's work.
- Prove that you are familiar with and can critique current research in the subject area.

A typical archaeological literature review is a synthesis of the known archaeology of the region, including major sites previously found within or near to the study area. The review also will identify the main archaeological issues and questions being addressed by your study and assess the results of earlier studies in terms of what you propose to do. The literature review should include three main features:

- A geographical review in which you show not only that you are familiar with previous research conducted in the study area but also how your own research builds on this.

- A thematic review, which identifies important gaps in previous research and shows how your research has built on this. This emphasizes the importance of your project.
- Case studies, which highlight the importance of your questions.

First Draft

The first thing to do when putting together an initial draft is to write an outline, with chapter titles, headings, and subheadings. Spending a day or more on this is a good investment in time. An outline may be a guide only and probably will need revision as your ideas develop and you get a better handle on the topic. However, it is an excellent way of thinking through your project and will help you identify the various elements that need to be included in your writing. This is the time for making sure that your argument is structured logically, because an outline is much easier to shape than passages of text.

When writing a first draft, concentrate on writing whatever comes into your head related to each element of your outline, and save the critical appraisal till later. The important thing is to write down as many ideas as you can. Remember, writing an idea down does not commit you to it. If it is a horrible idea, you'll edit it out. Writing it down will give you the material to make links between ideas later. A different but conceptually related approach is mind-mapping, or branching. This is a visual method, based on writing down as many ideas as you can as they radiate outward from the central or core idea (figure 10.1). Don't be afraid to include even silly or absurd ideas in this process, and remember that it is important not to impose a pattern. Allow the pattern to emerge from the material itself.

Revision

> Perfection is achieved, not when there is nothing left to add, but when there is nothing left to take away.
>
> —Antoine de St. Exupery

You are not likely to produce a perfect document in one draft. You may write three or more drafts before you are happy with the logical progression and your expression. Revision is an essential part of good writing. This is the stage where you refine your ideas and focus your writing so that every part of it is relevant to the original question or aim. Normally, whatever you write needs redrafting at least twice, but sometimes many more times. This is the time when you make sure your argument is cohesive and well organized, find details and examples to support your argument, revise those sections that are not up to

FIGURE 10.1: Getting your information out there

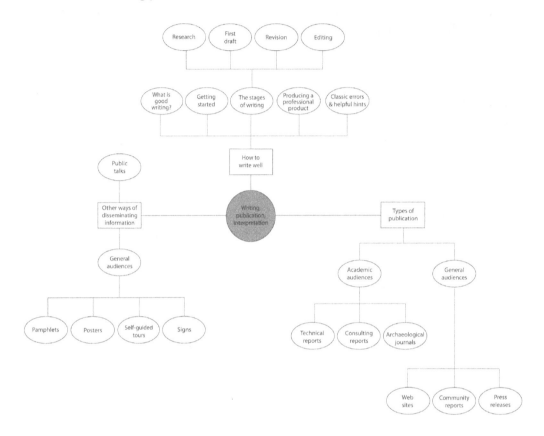

scratch, and refine your expression. An important part of revision is deletion. Remember that if you can write one set of words, you can write another. Do not treat your words as precious. In fact, deleting words (even whole sections) can be quite cathartic, as you work toward the lean, clean work that you wish to produce.

When using a computer, one way of finding the emotional courage to cut words drastically is to save the new draft with a new name, so you can go back to the old words if you need to. Another way is to open a new document, revise your outline, and cut and paste into the new outline.

Editing

The quality of your work will be established in the editing phase. Sloppy editing conveys the impression that your work has been rushed, while painstaking editing conveys the im-

Robyn Najar's Tips for Rewriting

- Don't be afraid to cut and paste. If you are not working on a computer, then a pair of scissors and sticky tape will work fine.
- Read your draft version aloud. This is an effective way to detect grammatical errors and unclear thinking.
- Tidy up your writing by eliminating or tightening your words.
- Avoid lengthy quotations, as these may convey the message that you don't know enough about the topic to write about it yourself. On the other hand, brief quotations can add force to your writing.
- Allow time for your paper to get cold. This allows you to return to it with a fresh and more objective perspective.
- Keep it simple. Do your best to avoid jargon, big words, and long sentences.
- Double-check the paper for accuracy. Be sure you have documented your sources correctly.

pression that your work has been conducted in a meticulous manner. Work that is full of spelling, stylistic, or grammatical errors makes you look bad whether you are a student writer or a university professor.

If possible, have other people read through your work at this stage. Although it can be hard to accept criticism, getting it from your friends, family, or close colleagues is easier than getting it from strangers. Their comments will help you improve your writing skills as well as the final product. People who are not archaeologists can be especially helpful here, because they will be able to tell you if your writing is clear and understandable.

An essential part of editing is proofreading. This should be done at least three times. First, see if the text flows and the ideas link coherently. Second, look solely for errors in grammar, punctuation, spelling, and word usage. Third, check that you have formatted your work consistently. Inconsistent styles for headings, font styles, and layout can indicate to the reader that you don't care about the quality of your work. Those "silly little formatting issues" make all the difference between an amateur and a professional product.

TECHNICAL REPORTS

The basic nature of technical reports is that they are based on evidence. All such reports are aimed at readers with a special interest in the subject. Technical reports present

Klauser's Five Rs for Writing Using Both Sides of the Brain

Klauser (1987) believes that most forms of writing follow a pattern that alternates between using the left- and right-hand sides of the brain. Following these five steps religiously will increase your "fluency and persuasion" dramatically:

- *Ruminate.* This first stage involves leftbrained activities, such as planning, thinking about the main issues and exploring a range of possibilities for presenting the data.
- *Rapidwrite.* This stage uses right brain techniques, such as rapidwriting and branching. Rapidwriting (or freewriting) is similar to brainstorming, in that the aim is to access your creative thinking without the censoring that can cripple so many writers. This is similar to the process of mind-mapping.
- *Retreat.* This is a period of about a week during which you put the work aside and think about something else. This will allow you to go back to your writing with fresh eyes. This period of rest is "non-negotiable."
- *Revise.* When you return to your work, you will find it much easier to understand what works and what doesn't. Try penciling notes alongside the sections that are weak or unclear. Read the work with the following questions in mind: Does this contain all the data I need? Is there anything missing? Does the argument flow smoothly? Don't make major corrections at this stage, just look for the overall flow (however, jot down your ideas as they occur).
- *Repeat.* Now go through the cycle again.

From McLaren 2001, 139–140

original data and, most important, present these data in such a way that the information can be checked and verified.

The basic format of a report is like the shape of an hourglass (figure 10.2): it leads the readers from a wider, general view (such as placement of the research problem within its theoretical context), to the particular (the background of the region, methods, and results), back to the general (placing the results of your research into a broader regional, international, or theoretical context). The logical progression of your argument is established through this format, making it easy for the reader to follow your actions and understand your reasoning. A technical report has four main sections:

- Aims and significance
- Methods
- Results
- Discussion

FIGURE 10.2: The shape of a technical report

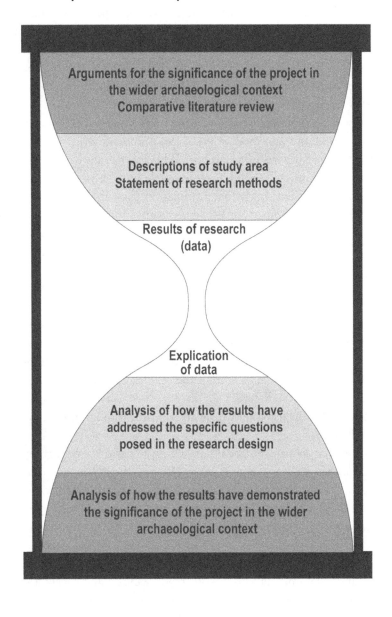

The *aims* section tells the readers what was done and why, what the report will cover, and how the research articulates with other projects or fits into current theoretical debate. When writing this section you need to think about the gap in knowledge that is going to be filled by your research. Definitions and assumptions can be outlined in this section, although they also can be placed in a glossary. In archaeological reports, the aims section normally includes your literature review, highlighting the significance of your project in terms of previous research.

The *methods* section describes how and where the project was undertaken and how the data were collected and analyzed. A clear and precise description of your methods is one of the most essential parts of any report. This is what allows others—either other researchers who may want to expand or reanalyze your data or, more important, reviewers within the government body that administers the cultural heritage legislation—to decide whether your methods were adequate to answer your research questions, and whether they need to gather any further information before they can make a decision. In theory, this section should provide enough detail so that readers could replicate your research if they wished.

The *results* section outlines what was found. This is a statement of findings or observations, presented with very directed discussion. You need to present your results in a logical progression. Graphs and tables are an excellent way of communicating your results, because they present your findings in an easily understood visual format and in part allow the readers to make their own interpretations. If you use percentage graphs, make sure that you always include the raw data so that the readers can assess whether the numbers you present are likely to be statistically significant. Normally, numbers less than 10 are considered to be insufficient to be statistically significant (though they may still represent a genuine phenomenon).

Interpretation of the significance of the results to the wider world is presented in the *discussion* section of the report. Tie your interpretations closely to the aims or questions that were posed at the beginning of your study. This is your opportunity to answer those questions. If the results are inconclusive, then say so, and provide some possible explanations as to why. Any recommendations for future research also should be included in your discussion.

Technical reports require an *abstract* at the beginning that allows the readers to determine the results and recommendations of your report quickly and succinctly. The abstract should contain a brief overview of the major sections (aims and significance, methods, results, discussion, recommendations) but should be as short as possible. Ideally, an abstract should be one page or less. One tip for putting an abstract together is to take the first and last paragraph of each of the major chapters and reduce them to one paragraph. When you have one paragraph per chapter, you only need to polish the text so that it flows from one paragraph to the next.

CHM REPORTS

These follow the same basic structure as technical reports but require some specific features. Be certain that you follow the report-writing standards that many state, provincial, or federal agencies require. Be sure to ask if there are such standards and where to find them. The most important thing when writing a CHM report is to make your data and results comparable with that of others. This means that you need to be absolutely clear about all of the methods you followed, the limitations you faced, the definitions you used, and the data you collected and analyzed. Precise descriptions of the extent of survey areas and the amount of coverage the survey achieved are essential (and, indeed, are mandatory in most states) and wherever possible should be supplemented with clear diagrams showing the size and location of your transects, survey areas, or sampling zones. For more information on determining effective survey coverage, see "Sampling" in chapter 3.

Instead of an abstract, some agencies require that a CHM report include a brief executive summary at the very beginning that encapsulates all of your findings and recommendations. This is a device for site managers who do not wish to wade through your entire report to assess your findings. The executive summary also allows you to be absolutely clear to your clients about what their responsibilities are and what the proper management of the site requires. At minimum, copies of reports need to be sent to the SHPO/THPO in the state, any permitting or licensing agency (the state archaeologist or state historical society), and the organization that hired your services. The report may be considered as proprietary by the contracting agency, so before you give it to *anyone*, including the SHPO/THPO, check with your clients first so that you don't violate your contract. They may have good reason for withholding the report. They paid for the work, so the report is theirs. To get clearances for their project they eventually will have to send it to the appropriate cultural heritage agencies.

With permission, you may wish to send copies to local public libraries as well as government departments, but be aware that precise site locations usually are considered to be sensitive or privileged information. You may need to mask precise locations to protect sites from looting. If you are working on or near tribal lands, you also should give copies to Indigenous community groups if allowed by the contracting agency. Any reports that will be read by the public are best accompanied by plain English (or community) reports, which some federal projects require. A checklist for what to include in a CHM report is included in appendix F.

HOW ACCOUNTABLE IS YOUR REPORT?

Finally, before you submit your report, check how closely it conforms to these best-practice expectations:

❏ Have you used standard measures and terminology to describe sites and artifacts?
❏ Have you defined all your terms and categories, either in the body of the report or in a glossary?
❏ Have you been explicit about how you chose to define a site and the way that you decided on the site's boundaries?
❏ Have you outlined the logic of your sampling strategy?
❏ Have you shown clearly on a map where your sampling unit/transect/excavation squares were located?
❏ Have you shown clearly on a map the location of all of your sites (unless requested to keep details of sites secret)?
❏ Have you been explicit about your methods during all phases of the project?
❏ If you have used a new method, have you been explicit about how you went about it and what its limitations were?
❏ Have you been explicit about the limitations you encountered during all phases of the project?
❏ Have you evaluated the effectiveness of your survey coverage?
❏ Have you evaluated the usefulness of your historical or ethnographic sources?
❏ Have you provided locational references for all of your sites (unless requested to keep details of sites secret)?
❏ Have you made your data accessible to reinterpretation (i.e., included all supporting material relevant to your data analysis as an appendix, such as your tables of raw data, your database, and/or your recording forms)?
❏ Have you included details of all consultation undertaken with any parties or individuals as part of the project?
❏ If you obtained a permit or license to survey or excavate, have you included details (such as the permit number) about it in the report?

COMMUNITY REPORTS

Community reports are shorter, more accessible versions of technical or CHM reports. Their purpose is to make archaeological information accessible to members of the public. Such reports are written in plain English. Use clear language at a level that is suited to the

Jack Radley's Tips for Writing for a General Public

- Whenever you are not pleased with something you can always do better. How? You have learned many of the facts of the profession you have chosen, but this does not mean you automatically have the word-power to write down your own ideas well enough for other professionals, let alone the world in general. You might imagine your proposed work to be a tapestry upon which you can stitch facts. However, factual evidence alone can be boring to a nonspecialist reader, so you must find suitable words to embroider between your facts.
- Remember the taboos. Don't use clichés. Tautology—the contextual repetition of the same phrase, idea, or statement in different words—is a wickedness that can creep up on you, often in the same sentence or paragraph. Even the simplicity of "a quick riposte" is a tautology, as a riposte is a quick retort.
- Perhaps the greatest traitor of all is jargon, because it fools the author with its "educational approach." The use of jargon is irresponsible. It wastes the value of words by being used to perplex and confuse the reader rather than to communicate information.
- Never forget your readers and the fact that clear communication is the real purpose of all writing.

average person, and structure the layout of your report so that people easily can find the information they want.

Writing in plain English is not as easy as it sounds. It takes effort and practice to write simply without being patronizing. Plain English does not mean always using words simplistically, especially when there are other words that are more accurate, or structuring your report in an unsophisticated manner. It means writing simply, clearly, and effectively. One trick is to steer clear of jargon, which is often just a way of showing that you are part of an in-group (and which can automatically make the reader feel part of an out-group). Another trick is to avoid using long words or sentences. If you can say something simply, then do so. As with other types of writing, the best strategy is to look at some examples, decide on the ones that you think work well, analyze how they are constructed, and model your own work on them.

SPECIALIST PUBLICATIONS

When writing for specialist publications remember that you are writing for specialist readers. When writing in this sphere you can assume an intelligent and informed interest on

Tips for Writing for Archaeological Journals

- Submit articles strictly in the format of the particular journal. You usually can find style guides or author submission guidelines somewhere in the journal (often inside the back cover) or on the journal's website.
- Use specialist or technical terms to give clear descriptions, but be careful not to allow this to degenerate into inappropriate use of jargon.
- If using specialist terms, remember to define them the first time you use them, even if your audience may know them. For example, TL dating should be defined at thermoluminescence dating the first time you refer to it. Other clarification can be given in footnotes, but only if this is essential to a thorough understanding of the main point.
- Journal articles need to be precise. They should contain exact details, which are presented in a way that makes it possible for this information to be checked.
- Use headings and illustrations to clarify your points, but remember that each figure should be presented so that it can be understood by itself, without reference to the text.
- Clean copy is important. Make sure that the professionalism of your work is not marred by typographical or grammatical errors or by poor presentation.
- If you submit to a peer-reviewed journal, such as *American Antiquity* or *Archaeologies: The Journal of the World Archaeological Congress*, your paper will be assessed by one or more referees. If asked to revise and resubmit your paper, do so. Use the referees' comments to identify any holes and to improve the quality of your paper, but remember that you can argue against the comments in a reply to the editor if you feel they are unwarranted. You will have a much better chance of acceptance the second time around.

their part, and they probably know the jargon. You don't need to spoon-feed them or engage their interest with a showy writing style. In fact, you should use restrained language for specialist publications because this conveys the impression (correctly or not) that your research has been conducted in an objective manner. Nevertheless, don't let yourself be fooled by objective, scientific language: it does not necessarily mean objective, scientific research, just as subjective language does not necessarily mean that the research has been conducted in a nonscientific manner.

WEBSITES

Writing for the web is different from writing for paper publications. We read screens differently from the way we read paper, and we must write differently for them as well. The

Tips for Writing Your Dissertation (and Beyond) from Sonya Atalay and Amy Lonetree

In preparation for writing, we both attended a dissertation-writing workshop at the University of California, Berkeley, led by Dr. Dorothy Duff Brown. We found Dr. Duff Brown's advice both inspiring and helpful, and in the course of dissertation writing we modified her advice to fit our needs. Here's the strategy that worked for us (based on Dr. Duff Brown's workshops):

- Begin by envisioning the completed product. It helps to create a mock-up of your dissertation with 200–300 blank pages in a binder, including cover page and title, following your university's guidelines. As you write, replace blank pages with your work at the end of each day.
- Print out everything you have already written concerning your research—any drafts, field statements, grant proposals, sections of other papers that seem appropriate. Remove the corresponding number of blank pages from the binder and replace them with your work, even if major editing is needed.
- Develop a daily writing strategy. Research indicates that people work best in 45-minute blocks, so retrain yourself to work in 45-minute shifts.
- Take 15- to 20-minute breaks between shifts to restore your energy and creativity.
- If you can't seem to write during a shift, then don't, but try to outline your thoughts and continue engaging with your topic in some way. Make yourself do something related, even if just freethinking about the ideas you are trying to convey.
- Do four or five shifts each day, but NO MORE! You need restoration time (for e-mail, eating, recreation, personal relationships)—limiting your daily shifts will help your writing as it renews your energy and creativity.
- If you must do further research, save it for later 45-minute shifts and do your writing in the first shifts of the day.
- Give yourself one day a week to get away from it and relax: NO WORK!
- Abandon perfectionism:

  1 Stop obsessing over reading every source—it's a major excuse for procrastination.
  2 Don't worry that your prose isn't perfect—it's easier to revise something that is already written.
  3 Keep writing even if you have a gap in your research. Note the gap in the text and save the research for later.

- Find a writing partner to work with. This person doesn't need to be in archaeology. The idea is to make yourself accountable to your partner. Peer pressure works well for keeping your writing on track.

(continues)

Tips for Writing Your Dissertation (and Beyond) from Sonya Atalay and Amy Lonetree (*continued*)

Writing Beyond the Dissertation

Finding uninterrupted blocks of time to write is tough, but after we got our dissertations done, we each developed strategies for daily writing shifts. Sonya gets the day started with a writing shift while drinking her morning tea, then uses the restorative break to check email and to read daily news online. Amy does her best writing in the morning before the teaching demands get too heavy. Even one morning shift will provide you with noticeable results.

Don't allow yourself to be paralyzed by the seeming lack of time to write. Here it may help to think in page numbers. Writing about one page every workday yields about 25 pages at the end of the month (i.e., a chapter)! Only one shift a day for eight months gives you a 200-page draft!

Realize that most writing is done slowly. Some days are very productive, others sheer writing agony. Count the time you've just spent reading these "tips" as your first shift of the day. Now do what we're both about to do: take a restorative break, set your timer, and begin writing another chapter.

most important things to do are to structure the site for the audience you plan to attract and use an appropriate tone. Is the site instructional? Promotional? Personal? Each of these will require a different tone. When writing for the web, write concisely to help your reader get to the point. "Waffle" in a website is a particularly heinous crime and, because the web is self-driven, as soon as you start to bore people they will leave (either the section or the site). Clear headings and navigation tools help readers find their way around the site, and the multidimensional capacity of hot links (which link through to another page or site) can be used to deepen your arguments or direct people to other useful sites. Our best advice here is to find a site you like and can read easily, and use this as a model for the construction of your own.

PRESS RELEASES

A press release is the basic communication tool for those wanting journalists to publish their story. The writing style of journalists, developed through fierce competition for readers, is a good model to follow. Take the current front-page story in your local newspaper.

Tips for Good Web Writing

- Figure out who the audience will be and the purpose of your site.
- Choose the appropriate style and tone.
- Put the main points at the top of the web page.
- Write short paragraphs.
- Write short, simple sentences. Use one idea for each sentence.
- Use the present tense because this makes your writing active rather than passive.
- Be friendly. Use "I," "we," and "you" instead of "the archaeologists," "the researcher," and so on.
- Use hot links to deepen your argument.
- Don't clutter your site with too much color or too many gimmicks.
- Make sure that the size, font, and color of the text can be read easily against the color and contents of the background. A common mistake that many people make is to have a highly cluttered, "busy" background against which the text can't be read, or to use a text color that does not read or print easily. Dark-colored texts against light-colored backgrounds will always print more easily than the reverse.
- Maintain any hot links to be sure the site is up to date.
- Include a date of last update and contact information for people to reach you with questions or concerns; in other words, take responsibility for what you put on the web.

Go through it and mark where it answers the questions *who, what, when, where,* and *why*. Use this as a model for formatting your own press release. All press releases follow a basic format. They are normally a single page with the words "For Immediate Release" at the top, just under your letterhead. Follow this with an eye-catching headline. They are dated and have a contact name and number at the bottom (or top) of the page. As with most other kinds of writing, there are differences of opinion about the order of material, but be certain you have the basics.

The basic rule for writing a good press release is to ensure that it engages the interest of the reader immediately. You need to find a "**hook**" to grab the reader's attention in the first sentence or two. Journalists usually only have time to scan press releases when they are making an initial assessment of them, so keep your words interesting, your sentences short, and your message clear:

- Present your information in short, punchy sentences using vivid language, and include only a minimal number of ideas in each sentence.
- Use active rather than passive voice and concrete details rather than generalizations.

- Present your ideas in the order of their importance, with the most interesting or significant information first (i.e., the hook).
- Use direct quotations from principals involved in the project to give the release life and a personal angle.
- Allow plenty of white space to avoid a cluttered look.
- Keep the press release to no more than a page if at all possible.

When you have written your press release, put it aside and read it again a day or two later, preferably aloud. Get a friend to read it as well, because this will help you to see if you are communicating your ideas simply and clearly. If your friend stumbles when reading it, it needs rewriting, which probably means editing to make it shorter, sharper, and crisper. Don't forget to keep a file of any media coverage generated by your release. This information can be useful in showing public outreach for your project, as support for funding applications and as a model for future press releases. A sample press release is included in appendix C.

---

10 Essential Tips to Ensure Your Press Release Makes the News from Press-Release-Writing.com

1 Make sure the information is newsworthy.
2 Tell the audience that the information is intended for them and why they should continue to read it.
3 Start with a brief description of the news, then distinguish who announced it, and not the other way around.
4 Ask yourself, "How are people going to relate to this and will they be able to connect?"
5 Make sure the first 10 words of your release are effective, as they are the most important.
6 Avoid excessive use of adjectives and fancy language.
7 Deal with the facts.
8 Provide as much contact information as possible: Individual to contact, address, phone, fax, email, website address.
9 Make sure you wait until you have something with enough substance to issue a release.
10 Make it as easy as possible for media representatives to do their jobs.

www.press-release-writing.com/10_essential_tips.htm (accessed March 27, 2007)

PRODUCING A PROFESSIONAL PRODUCT

Quality of presentation, while important, is no substitute for content, but a well-designed document is easy to read and reduces the chance that you will be misunderstood or misinterpreted. Think carefully about how you present your work. Producing a professional product is largely a matter of adhering to the conventions for the type of writing you are undertaking and taking care that your work is as free of errors as possible and formatted in a consistent manner. Because the object of writing is to communicate ideas, present your work in such a way that it can be read and understood easily. Don't forget that the quality of your work reflects directly upon you: if it looks sloppy, people will assume (rightly or wrongly) that you are sloppy and may be less inclined to believe you or hire you. Professionalism is a matter of pride in what you do. Here are some tips:

- Make certain your grammar, spelling, punctuation, and word usage are correct. Poor expression makes writing seem unprofessional.
- Make sure the formatting is consistent.
- Choose a clear font.
- Use headings carefully as signposts to your argument, and format them consistently.
- Use maps, illustrations, graphs, and diagrams to present your information clearly.
- Always have the final publication proofread by somebody else.
- Make certain you submit the project on time.

Modern technology makes it possible to choose between a wide range of fonts and layout styles and to produce professional-quality reports from your own desktop. While there are many different fonts, they do not all function in the same way. Fonts can be divided into three broad categories: script, display, and text as discussed on AskOxford.com (www.askoxford.com/betterwriting/osa/reports/#presenting [accessed January 4, 2007]):

Brush Script is a *script* font that simulates handwriting and gives text a light, easy feel.

COPPERPLATE LIGHT is a *display* font, which is effective at getting people's attention. Display fonts are used in advertising and posters but are difficult to read for an extended period.

Text fonts can be divided into two types: serif fonts, such as Times and Times New Roman, and sans serif fonts, such as **Arial** and Optima. Serif fonts are a little more formal than fonts without serifs, while sans serif fonts are slightly easier to read.

Tips for Successful Publication

- Get into the publishing habit. Start with book reviews or conference papers.
- Divide a project into several publishable sections (e.g., history, theory, minor data, the big picture).
- Publish in a range of media (e.g., academic and general publications, film/video, exhibitions) to give your ideas maximum exposure.
- Offer opinion pieces to local or national newspapers and magazines.
- Try to arrange publication *before* rather than after you have done the writing. Submit a synopsis for a journal paper or a prospectus for a book.
- Don't publish the same thing twice. The exception might be when the audiences are very different. The ideas can be identical, but the style should be appropriate to the audience.
- Be prepared for critical analysis of your work. Learn how to take criticism and use it to your benefit on future writing.
- Submit to one journal at a time. Where you choose to submit your work depends on the audience, but for professional publications, seek the journal most appropriate to the nature of the material and start there.

The font you choose will depend upon the nature of your publication and its planned audience. For example, it would be considered distinctly odd to submit an article to an academic journal using a script font. Formal submissions, such as journal articles and technical reports, always should be in a text font. A community report, however, could well be suited to the relative informality of a script font, and you may choose to experiment with something quite different for interpretive materials. Press releases and websites are best written in a very clear text font.

PUBLIC PRESENTATIONS

One of the most effective ways of sharing information about your project is by giving a public presentation. The kinds of presentations that archaeologists regularly give range from conference presentations and talks at local schools to public lectures and interpretive tours.

USING POWERPOINT

Even if you've never used it before, PowerPoint lets you produce an impressive and professional-looking presentation the first time around. The best feature of PowerPoint is that

Tips for Successful Public Speaking

- Know and target your audience! What might they be expecting? Knowing the backgrounds of the people who will be your audience allows you to shape your speech to their ages, interests, and levels of knowledge.
- Speak only on topics that you know well and have prepared fully.
- The best ways to be sure of giving a good presentation are to be well prepared, have a written text to refer to if you lose focus, and rehearse your presentation.
- The best way to deal with nerves is to be well prepared, practice your speech, and have some visual material to support you.
- Never give a public talk where you merely read a written text aloud. For formal occasions, prepare a full script, because this ensures your speech develops logically and without serious omissions. When writing the text, write it in a conversational manner, rather than an essay form. Remember, your aim is oral communication, not written. Edit the script into a good outline, which you can write on palm-sized cards, and speak from this outline, not the full script.
- Keep your message simple. A speech cannot take the density of information and nuance that can be included in an essay. Listeners have to grasp the ideas immediately and, unlike readers, do not have time to review the text if there is something they do not understand immediately.
- If you know individual people in the audience, referring to them occasionally can make your talk more friendly and relevant.
- Use audiovisual materials to clarify important points (say, through graphs or maps) and to add interest to your presentation. Just be certain they are relevant and capable of being read by an audience.
- Check the room and any audiovisual equipment before you have to speak. Make sure the equipment works and that you know how to use it.
- Answer questions effectively. Try to repeat or paraphrase the question in the first part of your answer; other audience members may not have heard the question. If someone asks a two-part question, don't try to remember both parts. Concentrate on the second part, and after you have answered that, ask for clarification of the first part.

it allows you to integrate images (including moving images), text, and sound into one presentation. As with all things, however, there are a number of guidelines that you should follow when using it:

- The judicious use of moving parts (such as moving arrows or sequentially appearing text and images) will not only emphasize your key points but also catch the audience's attention. However, having too many moving parts is confusing (not to mention annoying) and should be avoided. The same is true for sound effects that have the potential to be very distracting. Think *emphasis* rather than *everywhere*.

- As with any presentation, go through it beforehand (preferably more than once) until you're happy with the timing and are sure that you have the slides in exactly the right order. A nonspecialist audience is ideal at this stage (your friends, neighbors, parents), because they can give you feedback on anything they find confusing or tell you if you're rushing things. The more you practice, the better you'll feel and the more relaxed you'll be when you actually present.
- Don't just read your slides to the audience (they can do that for themselves). Make the images and text complement your words, so that people are looking, listening, and reading simultaneously (and therefore staying awake).
- Don't include enormous amounts of text as part of a PowerPoint slide. People only want to read the key points, not the detailed explanation of each point (that's for you to expand upon).
- Make sure the font size is large enough to be read easily by someone sitting in the back row. A minimum of 20- to 24-point font is advisable.
- Because PowerPoint can incorporate colored and textured backgrounds as well as text, make sure that the combination works. As with websites (see "Tips for Good Web Writing") the size, font, and color of the text must be able to be read easily against the colors and contents of the background.
- If you are presenting in a new environment, or using someone else's technology, *always* have an old-fashioned backup on hand in the form of overheads or slides in case the technology fails. We can't emphasize this enough—the alternative will be completely improvising your presentation in front of the audience with no visual support (which is not impossible for a skilled and practiced speaker—just a lot more challenging).
- For more information, including step-by-step guides and tutorials to the many features of PowerPoint, try the tutorial supplied with the program or visit Microsoft's website: www.microsoft.com/office/powerpoint/using/default.asp (accessed March 27, 2007).

INTERPRETING ARCHAEOLOGY TO THE PUBLIC

Interpretation is different from information—the latter is facts; the former is intended to provoke ideas, create new associations, or even jolt people into new understandings (Carter 1997, 6). The essence of good interpretation is that it reveals new insights into what makes a place or object special (Carter 1997, 6). Depending on the nature of your research you might choose to produce a poster, a pamphlet, a self-guided tour guide, an interpretive sign, or the text for a more formal guided tour. Regardless of which type of interpretation you choose, you will need to think through what you want to do and how you are going to do it, particularly in terms of how the interpretive story can be linked to physical artifacts or places.

The goal of any successful interpretation is to make the information you have support an interesting story or idea. Plan carefully rather than just throwing a whole lot of information together and seeing what comes out. Start by focusing on what you want to achieve (Carter 1997, 4):

- What do you want people to *know* as a result of your interpretation?
- What do you want people to *feel* as a result of your interpretation?
- What do you want people to *do* as a result of your interpretation?

The core of interpretation is to capture the essence of a place or idea, not to tell people everything there is to know. If you try to present every interesting aspect of a place, people will be overwhelmed or bored, or both. At some point you will have to make a choice about what to interpret and what to leave out, which will undoubtedly involve drastic editing. The best way to do this is to use some form of interpretation project planner (figure 10.3) to give your ideas structure and to force you to consider (Carter 1997, 9):

- Why you want to communicate with visitors
- Who your audience will be
- What your site or object has to offer
- What you want to say
- How best you can say or show it

Only by working systematically through these questions will you be able to tread a concise path through the mass of material you have collected. This is a central part of making sure that your story will be coherent and that the form and content of your interpretation will be focused in a way that actually will achieve your objectives. If you don't want to use a formal planner, try to write a storyline, breaking your narrative into its component ideas, each of which can serve as the basis for a paragraph. A sample interpretive planner is included in appendix D.

Once you have a plan, you need to write the text and design the layout for your interpretation. Writing good interpretive text requires a totally different approach from writing a CHM report or academic paper. You are not only trying to make information available to a much wider audience than your professional peers but, more important, trying to make it *meaningful* for them as well. This is more easily said than done, and in the end you will never be able to cater to everyone. You will have to decide who your priority is

FIGURE 10.3: The interpretive process (after Carter 1997, 10)

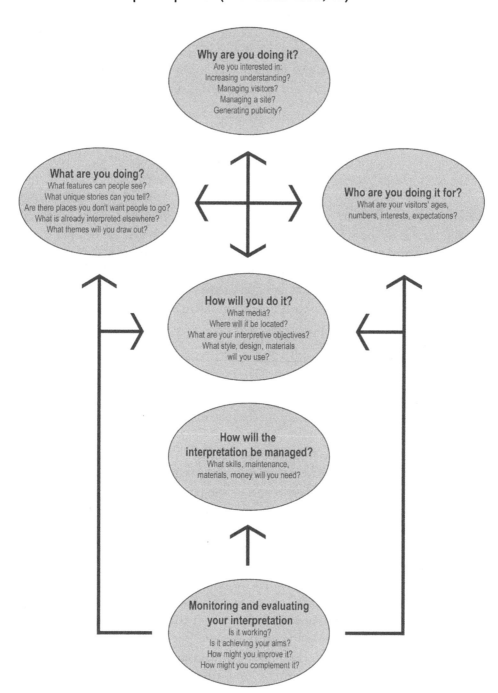

Liz Kryder-Reid's Tips for Giving Tours of Archaeological Sites

With thanks to Phil Arnault, director of the Baltimore Theatre Project, who coached many a student in the Archaeology in Annapolis field school on the art of archaeological tour giving.

- Have a script developed (at least in your head) that makes a compelling story. Start with a "hook" such as a question ("Why on earth would we dig here?" "Anyone know what this is?") or a first-person account ("The first time I saw this site . . . ," "I never would have thought this site would tell us what it did. . . ."), and build the narrative from there.

- Block your tour the way any piece of theatre performance is blocked—where you will stand and where the visitors will stand so that they are looking at what you want them to. How will you move from one spot to another? How can you create seamless crowd control that ensures people can hear you and follow what you are directing them to look at? What props will you use (images, artifacts, maps, photographs), and are they at an appropriate scale for the size of group? Can they be passed around without distracting people from the rest of your talk?

- Is there any element of your tour that a volunteer from the group can participate in? Nothing engages a crowd like feeling a part of the endeavor, even vicariously. Can they try shaking a screen? Tongue-test a ceramic for its porosity? Try to find a date on an artifact? Compare two lithics for use wear?

- If you are expecting a visit from the press, work out your main message and get everyone on the crew on board with the storyline. It will not only help to make sure you get the key points out but also can prevent some embarrassing "off-message" comments or asides being printed. As humorous as comments may seem in the field, they can read quite differently in a front-page story.

- Similarly, if there is sensitive information about the site that is not appropriate to share with the public (sacred objects, burials, interpretations that are problematic for collaborating partners, security concerns about areas vulnerable to looting), be sure that everyone on the site is informed about the issues and given a chance to discuss the reasons for editing some of the interpretation.

- A helpful technique for crowd control is to hold your arms out in front of you at about an 80° angle. If you can't see everyone in the group between your arms, ask them to move a little closer to each other so they can have the best vantage point and hear you clearly.

- If you are turning to point out something in a unit, pause in your talking while you point, and then resume talking after you turn back to face the audience.

(continues)

Liz Kryder-Reid's Tips for Giving Tours of Archaeological Sites (*continued*)

- If there is a loud disruption such as a plane passing overhead, just pause (with a smile) and let it go over, rather than trying to talk over it.
- If something is happening that the visitors can see, acknowledge what is going on, and then either get back to your planned narrative or incorporate it into the script. If the tripod screen has tipped over or someone is standing up in a nearby unit with an exciting new find, no visitor will be able to absorb anything you say.
- No matter how bright the day, remove your sunglasses while you are talking to people. Your eyes are some of your most powerful communication channels.
- Even if it is just a simple sheet of paper, have a "takeaway" that summarizes your main messages, acknowledges your sponsors, and gives people leads to get further information.

and interpret for them. Consider four key dimensions when actually writing and designing your interpretive materials (Carter 1997, 40–41):

- Make it grab attention (color, font size, catchy or provocative titles, activities, things to handle). Audio or tactile labels, pictures, and "hands-on" components can actually double visitors' attention spans.
- Make it enjoyable (make it meaningful, make it personal—link it to people's own lives if you can. Emotion is a powerful trigger that makes people pay attention and remember).
- Make it relevant. Try to give greater dimension to your interpretation by telling the story from different perspectives or through the eyes of different people. Wherever possible, use stories and quotations to refer to real people and their lives, and use dynamic photographs of people or activities rather than static shots of buildings or scenery. The key to any good archaeological interpretation is to forge a connection between people then and people now.
- Make sure it has a structure. Use everyday language—not everyday archaeological language!—so that everyone will understand. If you are going to use specialist terms, you will have to explain them. The idea is to create closeness between the readers and the material, not to distance them by making the text difficult to read or understand.

Try to keep your writing style personal and "chatty" rather than formal and academic. In particular, try writing for an individual, not for the "general public" or another archaeologist (Binks, Dyke, and Dagnall 1988, 113). If you're worried about the tone of your text, give it to someone else to read, and listen to their comments. A good starting point is to look critically at other leaflets, posters, or signs and decide what you think works and what doesn't.

There are also various practical issues to consider when designing interpretive materials. In terms of legibility, some fonts work better than others, and short, well-spaced paragraphs are much easier to read. Unless your text will be internally illuminated (e.g., from a light box), white or pale-colored backgrounds with contrasting text work best. Give careful consideration to what illustrative material you include, and don't just duplicate in images what people can already see around them. Make your illustrations or photos complement the text and tell their own story (e.g., try using them to show what people can't see or what things may have looked like at another time) (Carter 1997, 43–44).

Tips for Making Your Text Work

- People will seldom read more than 150–200 words at a time. Don't be tempted to write long paragraphs; stick to short, sharp ones.
- Keep your sentences short—around 20 words each.
- Keep your titles short and sharp—a maximum of around 5 words for each heading.
- Keep your lines well spaced so that the text does not look dense and crowded.
- Remember, the greater the distance between viewer and text, the larger the font size and the greater the spacing between words, lines, and paragraphs will have to be.
- Break the text into plenty of paragraphs, and keep them well spaced so that people can distinguish visually manageable parcels of information. Try to make each paragraph represent a particular idea or related set of points.
- Vary the font size you use throughout—such as a large font for titles, a lead-in sentence that is smaller than the title but still larger than the main text size, and then main or body text that is smaller again.
- The size of headlines and titles needs to be at least 30 point. For subheadings use at least 16–18 point and 12–14 for general text.
- Only some fonts, such as Helvetica and Times, are easy to read in long runs (Binks, Dyke, and Dagnall 1988, 115). Restrict the use of more exotic fonts to titles or subheadings.
- For overall consistency try not to use more than two fonts.
- Make sure there are no spelling mistakes or typos—nothing looks worse!

Tips for Making Your Layout Work

- Keep text to a minimum, and break up large columns of text with illustrations.
- Many graphic designers use a preset grid in which the text and illustrations balance each other, so that the spacing between blocks of text and between images and text remains consistent (see figure 10.4).
- Remember that you don't have to fill up all the space. Blank or "white" space can be used to emphasize different elements, particularly images.
- Wherever possible convert written information to a graphic or visual form.
- Use large images that can attract attention from a distance.
- Use headings to attract attention or to emphasize main points.
- Include important or one-off information separately from the main text (in a box, like the tips in this book). Don't bury it in a welter of other words.
- Make all aspects of the project work together—the choice of color, font, style, design, and materials can all tell a story apart from just the words.

PRESENTING YOUR RESEARCH AS A POSTER

One way of sharing information about your project is by presenting a poster, which can be presented at a meeting or used as a display at a school or community office.

Tips for Preparing a Poster

- Remember that posters are initially seen from afar and need to be designed so that people want to go closer to view them. The poster title and the images are what will draw the viewer, not blocks of text (see "Tips for Making Your Layout Work").
- Keep your text to a minimum. The major mistake that many people make is to try to fit their entire project onto their poster. Remember that people will not read blocks of more than 200 words at a time (see "Tips for Making Your Text Work").
- Think of a poster as telling the story in images. For the poster to be effective, you almost need the images to stand alone. Think of the adage "a picture is worth a thousand words" and choose only images that will convey the story you want to tell.
- Use no more than two or three sentences, in no less than a font size of 20, to explain each image.
- Use images to convey several forms of information at once. For example, an image of an archaeologist conducting fieldwork with an Indigenous elder can convey information about local environment and collaborative relationships, as well as the way in which the actual task has been undertaken.

Lyn Leader-Elliott's Tips for Presenting the Perfect Poster

Interpretive posters need a strong storyline and the best images you can find to attract attention and tell the story.

Your first step is to answer these questions:

- What idea should the poster convey?
- What story will it tell?
- Who is it aimed at?
- What is the best way to convey the idea and tell the story to your chosen audience?
- Where will the poster be displayed? This will affect your design, choice of materials, and colors.

Images

Photographs, maps, cartoons, graphs, and charts all have their place, depending on the ideas you are working with.
Use clean, uncluttered design—don't try to put too much in.
Use empty space to separate different ideas.
Keep related ideas, images, and text together so that the poster is easy to read.

Text

Choose a heading (title) that immediately conveys the big idea or theme of your story.
Focus on the main messages you want to convey—strip out the detail until you have the essence.
Most people won't read blocks of text on a poster.
The amount of text will depend on the purpose of your poster and its audience. You may choose to use only a title and captions for your images, or you may want to include more text.
Use simple language and sentence structures. Make every word count—you have very few to work with.
Choose fonts and font sizes that are easy to read. Avoid *italics*, UPPER CASE, and fussiness.
And always make the images and text work together.

FIGURE 10.4: Using a grid to lay out your interpretive text ensures that your text and images complement each other, are arranged in a logical order, and are easy to read. The grid is a guide only—your columns don't have to be equal widths, and you can cross over columns to fit in illustrations, titles, or quotations.

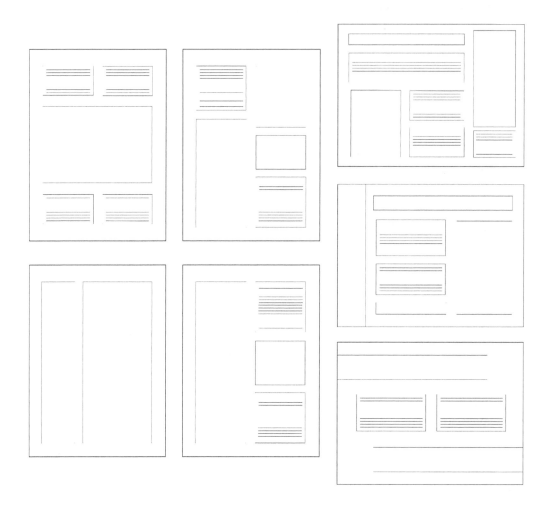

CLASSIC ERRORS AND HELPFUL HINTS

Discriminatory Language

An important part of good writing is choosing language that doesn't offend the audience. Some choose to label this "political correctness," making an attempt to link it to "identity politics," and they almost use the phrase as if it were negative or somehow weak and silly. Certainly seeking to avoid offense can be carried too far, but mostly it is about respect for others. Why use terms or labels that you know will hurt or anger someone? Language is a powerful tool, and it is important to use it in ways that empower people rather than stereotype or trivialize them. Government departments, universities, and many private businesses have policies requiring the use of nondiscriminatory language. One definition (AGPS 2002, 112) of discriminatory language is:

> Language use is discriminatory when it makes people invisible; when it excludes them, or highlights only one characteristic to the exclusion of other often more relevant ones; when it stereotypes people; treats people asymmetrically; and denigrates or insults people.

The most common form of discriminatory language is gender bias, which either overlooks or trivializes the roles of women or assumes that something can be done by, or applies to, only one gender, when it is really applicable to both. Often, this style of writing is done inadvertently, but it should be avoided. It is poor English usage and makes your work appear dated and unprofessional. It also detracts attention from the very worthwhile ideas that are being put forward. There are a number of ways of dealing with gender bias in language. For example, from an original that reads:

> This requires not that the writer make all his sentences short, or that he avoid all detail and treat his subjects only in outline, but that every word tell. (Strunk, in Strunk and White 1979, xiv)

you could try to:

Make it a direct address:

> This does not require you to make all sentences short, or avoid all detail and treat subjects only in outline, but to make every word tell.

Make it passive:

> This does not require that all sentences be short, or that all detail be avoided and subjects be treated only in outline, but that every word tell.

Turn it into a plural:

> This requires not that writers make all their sentences short, or avoid all detail and treat subjects only in outline, but that every word tell.

Other ways of dealing with this are to use "his or her" instead of "his" or to alternate between "his" and "her" as generic pronouns. These two methods are a little clumsy, so we do not recommend them. Neither do we recommend using "her" as a generic pronoun, as this simply replaces one form of discrimination with another.

The other form of discrimination regularly found in archaeological publications is ethnocentric bias. The unthinking use of ethnocentric, even racist, language has been a part of earlier stages in the history of archaeology. Using value-laden terms to describe Indigenous people is one example of this. A short perusal of the early archaeological literature will find descriptions of Indigenous peoples as "savages," "primitive," "backward," or "children of nature." Even choices of words such as *ruin, abandoned,* or *disappeared* may have connotations that offend Indigenous sensibilities (Collwell-Chanthaphonh and Ferguson 2006). As some say, "Our culture isn't in ruins and didn't disappear. It just changed like everyone else's does." All of these terms reinforce erroneous stereotypes and deny the complexity, diversity, and continuity of Indigenous cultures. It is particularly important that archaeologists deal with such biases. We write the pasts of other peoples and have a responsibility to do so without discriminatory bias.

Placing Illustrations Apart from the Text

Some archaeologists choose to separate their illustrations in an appendix at the end of their report rather than integrate them within the text proper. We do not recommend this because it can make the report difficult to follow, forcing the reader to move back and forth between text and illustrations. As a general rule of thumb, illustrations should be included in the body of the report, preferably as close as possible to the in-text reference. Word processors and digital images make doing this very easy. Any additional material that you think would be of interest to people researching a similar topic, but that is not essential to the main argument (such as your raw data), should be included as an appendix.

Listing Figures in a Confusing Manner

When you are listing figures, don't bother separating plates from other figures—this is an old-fashioned method and will increase your workload. Treating all photographs, illustrations, and maps as "figures," numbered consecutively within each chapter (figure 1.1, 1.2,

2.1, 2.2, and so on), is far simpler. Do separate tables from figures, however, because they contain totally different types of information. A checklist for tables and figures is contained in appendix E.

Presenting Numbers in a Confusing Manner

Presenting your data numerically is an important part of archaeological writing but is often done in a confusing or inconsistent manner. Whatever the suggested style, the key is consistency in usage within a document. Many style manuals make essentially the same recommendations (e.g., AGPS 2002; University of Chicago Press 2003). The accepted convention is to spell out the numbers from one to ten, then to use numerals for all figures above ten (11, 12, 25, and so on) unless your number is at the beginning of a sentence, in which case it is spelled out. Follow the same rules for ordinals: first, second, third . . . then 11th, 12th, and so on. Use figures if you are dealing with measurements (1 km, 2 percent), ranges of numbers (2–4 months), or fractions and decimals (4½, 4.5 months). When using fractions, write them out (two-thirds, three-quarters), write out percentages (percent, not %), express ranges of numbers as 10,000–12,000 (not 10–12,000), and present periods as 1914 to 1920 or during 1914–20. When indicating dates or ranges of years there should be no apostrophe, as in 1960s instead of 1960's.

Failing to Acknowledge Sources Adequately

In all writing it is important that you adequately acknowledge all sources. Any ideas that are not your own must be referenced, even if you are not using direct quotes. Otherwise, you can be accused of plagiarism, which is stealing other people's ideas and pretending they are your own. One way to avoid this is to always include page numbers in references for ideas or direct quotes. When referring to an Internet source, your in-text reference should provide either the author or site name and a date (either the date of publication, the date of revision, or the date you accessed the site). Your reference list should include a document title or description, a date, and a uniform resource locator (URL). Whenever possible, identify the author of the document, and direct readers as closely as possible to the information being cited. If you can, reference specific documents rather than home or menu pages (www.apastyle.org/elecmedia.html [accessed March 27, 2007]).

How frequently you cite your sources and where you put the references cited depends on your audience. Technical writing for reports or journals requires a greater number of in-text citations, but for community reports these break the flow of the text. Most community members will not care for a string of citations and from whom you got ideas. They are more concerned with ideas. Putting a list of sources at the end of the report may be

Tips for Referencing

When you are conducting your research you will need to read widely. It is very easy to forget where a quotation or piece of information came from, even though that seemed impossible at the time you were reading it. As a minimum you need to record the following information for each quotation or piece of information you record:

- The title of the work
- The author's full name, if this information is available
- The title of the journal (plus volume and number) or book from which the work was taken
- The publisher
- The date of publication
- The place of publication
- The page range of journal articles or edited chapters

If you take the time to do this as you go along—and do it for everything you read—you will save time later.

adequate, and then only key sources in case someone wants more information. Interpretive documents may need no cited sources at all, or at most a few key sources accessible to nonprofessionals.

Distinguishing between a Reference List and a Bibliography

A reference or bibliography section must be included with all reports and published papers. Many people confuse a reference section and a bibliography. They are different. A reference list records only the references used in the text, while a bibliography includes these references as well as other publications that may be of interest to the reader but that are not referred to directly in the text. Sometimes, as in this book, this is called "references and further reading." A bibliography can also be a list of recommended reading.

REFERENCES AND FURTHER READING

Australian Government Publishing Service. 2002. *Style manual for authors, editors and printers.* 5th ed. Canberra: AGPS.

Binks, G., J. Dyke, and P. Dagnall. 1988. *Visitors welcome: A manual on the presentation and interpretation of archaeological excavations.* London: English Heritage.

Carter, J. 1997. *An interpretive planning handbook.* Inverness, UK: Tourism and Environment Initiative.

Colwell-Chanthaphonh, C., and T. J. Ferguson. 2006. Rethinking abandonment in archaeological contexts. *SAA Archaeological Record* 6(1): 37–41.

Dwyer, J. 1993. *The business communication handbook.* Melbourne: Prentice Hall.

Eagleson, R. D. 1990. *Writing in plain English.* Canberra: Australian Government Publishing Service.

Fagan, B. 2006. *Writing archaeology: Telling stories about the past.* Walnut Creek, CA: Left Coast Press.

Klauser, H. 1987. *Writing on both sides of the brain.* San Francisco: Harper and Row.

McLaren, S. 2001. *Easy writer: A student's guide to writing essays and reports.* Glebe, NSW: Pascal Press. *One Step Ahead* series by Oxford University Press.

Schmitt, D. 1992. *The winning edge: Maximising success in college.* New York: HarperCollins.

Strunk, W., and E. B. White. 1979. *The elements of style.* 3rd ed. New York: Macmillan.

University of Chicago Press. 2003. *The Chicago manual of style.* 15th ed. Chicago: University of Chicago Press.

Zimmerman, L. J. 2003. *Presenting the past.* Vol. 7 of *The archaeologist's toolkit.* Walnut Creek, CA: AltaMira Press.

For a range of other useful information, see the website accompanying the text.

APPENDIX A
SAMPLE RECORDING FORMS

SURVEY: ENVIRONMENTAL BACKGROUND INFORMATION

ENVIRONMENTAL BACKGROUND RECORDING FORM
Page 1

SITE/LOCATION: _____

RECORDER/S: _____ DATE: _____

RECORDING FOR: ☐ Site location (single exposure)   ☐ General survey information only (multiple exposures)

WEATHER:
☐ Clear
☐ Cloudy
☐ Raining

LIGHT CONDITIONS:
☐ Good
☐ Poor

ATTACHMENTS/OTHER FORMS:
☐ Open Site   ☐ Historic
☐ Rock art   ☐ Sketch map
☐ Other _____

PERCENTAGE OF GROUND SURFACE VISIBLE: ☐ %
☐ Average across survey area
☐ Average within exposure

SEDIMENT/SOIL: ☐ Clay   ☐ Silt   ☐ Sand   ☐ Other: ....

DISTURBANCE: ☐ Stock   ☐ Insects   ☐ Erosion
☐ Vegetation   ☐ Other animals   ☐ Development   ☐ Other: ....

GEOMORPHOLOGICAL REGIME:
☐ Aggrading
☐ Eroding
☐ Stable
☐ Unknown

EXPOSURE(S):
☐ None   ☐ Erosion patch   ☐ Dam bank   ☐ Patchy ground cover
☐ Unformed track ☐ Fence line   ☐ Backhoe/grader scrape ☐ Other: ....
☐ Formed track   ☐ Animals   ☐ Water course/drainage line   ....

GROUND COVER:

PERCENTAGE GROUND COVER ON EXPOSURE: ☐ %

Within exposure(s)
☐ Leaf litter/bark/twigs/wood
☐ Grass/vegetation
☐ Moss/lichen
☐ Rubble/gravel
☐ Water
☐ Redeposited sediments (e.g. slumping) .
☐ Other: ....

Off exposure(s)
☐ Leaf litter/bark/twigs/wood
☐ Grass/vegetation
☐ Moss/lichen
☐ Rubble/gravel
☐ Water
☐ Redeposited sediments (e.g. slumping)
☐ Other: ....

PERCENTAGE GROUND COVER OFF EXPOSURE: ☐ %

ROCK OUTCROP:
☐ No rock outcrop (No bedrock exposed)   ☐ Rocky (10-20% bedrock exposed)
☐ Very slightly rocky (<2% bedrock exposed) ☐ Very rocky (>20% bedrock exposed)
☐ Slightly rocky (2-10% bedrock exposed)

COARSE FRAGMENTS (in situ aggregates):
☐ 2-6mm (Small pebbles or fine gravel)   ☐ 200-600mm (Stones)
☐ 6-20mm (Medium pebbles or gravel)   ☐ 600mm-2m (Boulders)
☐ 20-60mm (Large pebbles or coarse gravel)   ☐ >2m (Large boulders)
☐ 60-200mm (Cobbles)

BACKGROUND NOISE:
☐ Leaf litter/bark having same color/sheen/shape of artifacts
☐ In situ aggregates (coarse fragments from parent outcrops - see above)
☐ Imported aggregates (e.g. road gravel/sand/shell/etc.)
☐ Other: ....

PERCENTAGE BACKGROUND NOISE: ☐ %

OTHER DETECTION LIMITING FACTORS:
☐ Deep excavation/erosion (i.e. below archaeological horizon)
☐ Burning effects mimicking artifacts
☐ Other: ....

LANDFORM:

Slope:
☐ >30° (>56%) Very Steep
☐ 18-30° (33-56%) Steep
☐ 6-17° (11-32%) Moderately Inclined
☐ 2-5° (2-10%) Gently Inclined
☐ 1° (1%) Level

Relief:
☐ Very high
☐ High
☐ Low
☐ Very low

Pattern:
>300m
90-300m
30-90m
9-30m
<9m

☐ Hillcrest/ridge   ☐ Creekline/bank
☐ Upper slope   ☐ River terrace
☐ Mid slope   ☐ Swamp
☐ Lower slope   ☐ Lake edge
☐ Flat/plain   ☐ Dune
                     ☐ Other: ....

Page 2

EXISTING VEGETATION: ☐ Grassland ☐ Rainforest ☐ Swampy ☐ Desert/Xeric
☐ Open woodland ☐ Forest ☐ Shrubland ☐ Other: ....

Tallest stratum:	Species noted:	Height:	Crown separation:
☐ Trees	....	☐ >20m	☐ Touching to overlapping
☐ Trees/Thicket	....	☐ 13-20m	☐ Touching or slightly separated
☐ Shrubs	....	☐ 7-12m	☐ Clearly separated
☐ Other	....	☐ 4-6m	☐ Well separated
	....	☐ 1-3m	☐ Trees ~100+m apart/shrubs ~25+m apart
	....	☐ <1m	☐ Clumps of 2-5 trees/shrubs 200+m apart

Understorey:		Height:	Crown separation:
☐ None	....	☐ >12m	☐ Touching to overlapping
☐ Trees	....	☐ 7-12m	☐ Touching or slightly separated
☐ Trees/Thicket	....	☐ 4-6m	☐ Clearly separated
☐ Shrubs	....	☐ 1-3m	☐ Well separated
☐ Other	....	☐ 0.5-1m	☐ Trees ~100+m apart/shrubs ~25+m apart
		☐ 0.25-0.5m	☐ Clumps of 2-5 trees/shrubs 200+m apart
		☐ <0.25m	

Ground Layer:		Height:
☐ Tussock grass	....	☐ 1-3m
☐ Sod grass	....	☐ 0.5-1m
☐ Ferns	....	☐ 0.25-0.5m
☐ Moss	....	☐ <0.25m
☐ Vines	....	

LAND USE: ☐ Undeveloped ☐ Grazed ☐ Built-up area ☐ Quarry/extraction
☐ Forested ☐ Plowed ☐ Road verge ☐ Mining
☐ Cleared ☐ Cultivated ☐ Other: ....

**SITES/ISOLATED ARTIFACTS
LOCATED (see separate forms):**

NOTES:

PHOTOGRAPHS:

SURVEY: OPEN SITES

OPEN SITE/ISOLATED ARTIFACT RECORDING FORM		Page 1

SITE NAME/ NUMBER: _____

RECORDER/S: _____   DATE: _____

DIMENSIONS: LENGTH: _____ m   WIDTH: _____ m   ☐ Measured   ☐ Approximation

STRUCTURE/ POTENTIAL: ☐ Surface only   ☐ Possible sub-surface deposits   ☐ Possibly stratified   DEPTH: _____ cm/m

LOCATION DETAILS:

☐ UTM   EASTING: _____   IF NON-TOPO MAP, WHAT MAP?: _____

☐ GPS   NORTHING: _____   1:24K QUAD NAME: _____

☐ LEGAL   TOWNSHIP _____ RANGE _____ SECTION _____ ☐ ¼ of the ☐ ¼ of the ☐ ¼

DESCRIPTION OF SITE AND LOCATION: ....

....

....

SITE BOUNDARY DEFINITION CRITERIA:

☐ Natural boundary   ☐ Oral tradition
☐ Decline in artifact density   ☐ Limit of survey area/impact area
☐ Decline in visibility   ☐ Arbitrary
☐ Other: ....

VISIBILITY ON SITE: _____ % ☐

decreasing to _____ % _____ m away from site

EXPOSURE DIMENSIONS: WIDTH:
LENGTH: _____ mm / cm   _____ mm / cm

SLOPE: _____ °

☐ Measured   ☐ Approximation

ASPECT: N   NE   E   SE   S   SW   W   NW

CONDITION OF SITE: ☐ Good (in situ/ largely in situ)   ☐ Fair (some sections disturbed)   ☐ Poor (heavily disturbed)   ☐ Destroyed

DISTURBANCE FACTORS: ....

....

SITE CONTENTS: ☐ Clustered/clumped   ☐ Scattered   **STONE ARTIFACT RAW MATERIALS:**

☐ Stone   ☐ Metal   ☐ Chert   ☐ Quartzite
☐ Bone   ☐ Glass   ☐ Silcrete   ☐ Volcanic
☐ Shell   ☐ Ceramics   ☐ Mudstone   ☐ Sandstone
☐ Wood   ☐ Charcoal   ☐ Quartz   ☐ Other: ....
☐ Plant material   ☐ Other: ....

No. OF ARTIFACTS: _____   ☐ Estimate   ☐ Absolute count   MAXIMUM DENSITY: _____ artifacts per _____ cm / m

STONE ARTIFACT TYPES: ☐ Flaked   ☐ Ground   ☐ Quarried

☐ Whole flake   ☐ Broken flake   ☐ Core   ☐ Grindstone   ☐ Blade   ☐ Unifacial point
☐ Retouched flake   ☐ Flaked piece   ☐ Axe   ☐ Hammerstone   ☐ Backed blade   ☐ Bifacial point   ☐ Other: ....

WATER SOURCES IN PROXIMITY (Code nearest source as '1' and tick others within 1.5km radius):

☐ Waterhole   ☐ Gully   ☐ Other: ....
☐ River   ☐ Lake/lagoon
☐ Creek   ☐ Swamp   DISTANCE TO NEAREST WATER SOURCE: _____ metres   ☐ Measured   ☐ Estimate only
☐ Spring/soak   ☐ Claypan

Page 2

STATUS OF WATER SUPPLY: ☐ Permanent ☐ Temporary ☐ Unknown

TYPE OF WATER: ☐ Fresh ☐ Brackish ☐ Unknown

WATER MOVEMENT: ☐ Still ☐ Flowing

PHOTOGRAPHS: ☐ No ☐ Yes   Roll No.: _____   Exposure No.: _____

SKETCH PLAN OF SITE:

SURVEY: QUARRIES

QUARRY/QUARRIED OUTCROP RECORDING FORM: Page 1

SITE NAME:

RECORDER/S: _____   DATE: _____

LOCATION DETAILS:

☐ UTM   EASTING: _____   IF NON-TOPO MAP, WHAT MAP?: _____

☐ GPS   NORTHING: _____   1:24K QUAD NAME: _____

☐ LEGAL TOWNSHIP _____ RANGE _____ SECTION _____ ¼ of the _____ ¼ of the _____ ¼

☐ Hill top or ridge line   ☐ Creek/river
☐ Slope   ☐ Other: ....

FORM: ☐ Isolated outcrop   ☐ Pebble beach   ☐ Other: ....
        ☐ Series of outcrops   ☐ River cobbles

ASSOCIATED   ☐ Flake removal scars   ☐ Imported raw materials
FEATURES: ☐ Knapping floors   ☐ Other: ....

DIMENSIONS OF SITE:

LENGTH: WIDTH: If outcrop, average height: _____   Number of pits/flake scars: _____

_____ mm cm   _____ mm cm   If series of outcrops number: _____

☐ Measured   ☐ Approximation   Average length of pits: _____

PIT   ☐ Circular   ☐ Rectangular   ☐ Other: ....   Average width of pits: _____
SHAPE: ☐ Oval   ☐ Lenticular   ....   Average depth of pits: _____

RAW MATERIAL:

☐ Chert   ☐ Quartzite   ☐ Mudstone   ☐ Unknown
☐ Silcrete   ☐ Volcanic   ☐ Quartz   ☐ Other: ....

No. OF ARTIFACTS: _____   ☐ Estimate   MAXIMUM DENSITY: _____   artifacts per _____ cm m
                             ☐ Absolute count

% of flakes on site with cortex: _____   % of available stone worked: _____

ARTIFACT TYPES:

☐ None   ☐ Trimmed blanks   ☐ Modified cores   ☐ Flakes/blades   ☐ Decortication flakes
☐ Untrimmed blanks   ☐ Unmodified (unused) cores   ☐ Hammerstones   ☐ Other: ....

CONDITION OF SITE: ☐ Good (in situ/largely in situ)   ☐ Fair (some sections disturbed)   ☐ Poor (heavily disturbed)   ☐ Destroyed

DISTURBANCE FACTORS: ....
....

WATER SOURCES IN PROXIMITY (Code nearest source as '1' and tick others within 1.5km radius):

☐ Waterhole   ☐ Gully   ☐ Other: ....
☐ River   ☐ Lake/lagoon
☐ Creek   ☐ Swamp   DISTANCE TO NEAREST WATER SOURCE: _____ meters   ☐ Measured   ☐ Estimate only
☐ Spring/soak   ☐ Claypan

Page 2

STATUS OF WATER SUPPLY: ☐ Permanent ☐ Temporary ☐ Unknown

TYPE OF WATER: ☐ Fresh ☐ Brackish ☐ Unknown

WATER MOVEMENT: ☐ Still ☐ Flowing

PHOTOGRAPHS: ☐ No   Roll No.: _____   Exposure No.: _____
☐ Yes

SKETCH PLAN OF SITE:

SURVEY: STONE ARTIFACTS

STONE ARTIFACT RECORDING FORM

SITE: _____

RECORDER: _____

Area/Unit: _____

☐ Surface scatter   ☐ Excavation: _____

DATE: _____

Spit/Level: _____

FLAKES (FOR CORES SEE REVERSE)

Artifact No.	Raw Material (if known)	Typology F = Flake BF = Broken flake FP = Flaked piece	Length (mm)	Width (mm)	Thickness (mm)	Platform width (mm)	Platform thickness (mm)	PFA to ridge relationship H = None B = Behind S = To one side TW = Between I = Indeterminate	Platform Focalization B = Broad F = Focal	Over-hang removal (Y/N)	% Dorsal cortex	Dorsal scar count	Dorsal scar terminations F = Feather H = Hinge S = Step	Core rotation (Y/N)	Termination F = Feather H = Hinge S = Step I = Indeterminate	Breakage N = None P = Proximal M = Medial D = Distal L = Lateral	Comments

CORES (FOR FLAKES SEE REVERSE)

RECORDER: _____   SITE: _____   DATE: _____

Area/Trench: _____   Surface scatter ☐   Excavation ☐   Spit/Level: _____

Artifact No.	Raw Material (if known)	Typo-logy S = Single platform M = Multi platform	Length (mm)	Width (mm)	Thickness (mm)	Platform count (number)	Platform preparation (Y/N)	% Cortex	Cortical surface count (number)	Core body P = Pebble O = Outcrop F = Flake I = Indeterminate	Feather termination count (number)	Step/hinge termination count (number)	Weathering (Y/N)	Comments

SURVEY: CEMETERIES

CEMETERY RECORDING FORM

SITE/LOCATION:

RECORDER/S:

DATE:

DENOMINATION:
- [ ] Catholic
- [ ] Anglican
- [ ] Presbyt.
- [ ] Baptist
- [ ] Methodist
- [ ] 7th Day Ad
- [ ] Jewish
- [ ] Unknown
- [ ] Other: ....

GRAVE No (or REF No.):

SURNAME OR FAMILY NAME:

GRAVE TYPE:
- [ ] Individual
- [ ] Double plot
- [ ] Group plot

↓

Number of interments:

BASIC FORM:
- [ ] Tablet (upright slab)
- [ ] Horizontal slab
- [ ] Block
- [ ] Obelisk/pillar
- [ ] Statue/sculpture
- [ ] Cross
- [ ] Combination
- [ ] Other: ....
....

SPECIFIC SHAPE:

OTHER ASSOC PLOTS?: [ ] No [ ] Yes   Name/No:

ORIENTATION:
- [ ] North
- [ ] Northeast
- [ ] East
- [ ] Southeast
- [ ] South
- [ ] Southwest
- [ ] West
- [ ] Northwest

SIZE OF HEADSTONE: LENGTH _____ cm / m   WIDTH _____ cm / m   HEIGHT _____ cm / m

MATERIAL:
- [ ] Slate
- [ ] Marble
- [ ] Granite
- [ ] Cast iron
- [ ] Timber
- [ ] Tile
- [ ] Other: ....
....
- [ ] Sandstone
- [ ] Concrete/ Cement

FENCE/BORDER:
- [ ] NONE
- [ ] Cast iron picket
- [ ] Timber picket
- [ ] Brick border
- [ ] Stone border
- [ ] Tile border
- [ ] Other: ....
....

FENCE/BORDER HEIGHT: _____ cm / m

LETTERING:
- [ ] Engraved
- [ ] Engraved & Painted
- [ ] NONE

OTHER ITEMS ASSOCIATED WITH GRAVE:
- [ ] NONE
- [ ] Vase
- [ ] Glass covered display
- [ ] Personal items

- [ ] Lead
- [ ] Painted only
- [ ] Photos
- [ ] Statues
- [ ] Tiles
- [ ] Shells

INCLUDES FOOTSTONE: [ ] Yes [ ] No

- [ ] Other: ....
....
- [ ] Plantings
- [ ] Other: ....
....

MOTIFS:
- [ ] NONE
- [ ] Angel
- [ ] Wreath
- [ ] Ribbon
- [ ] Dove
- [ ] Flowers
- [ ] Foliage
- [ ] Book
- [ ] Cross
- [ ] Masonic
- [ ] War service
- [ ] Pillar/urn
- [ ] Other (please list): ....
....
....

INSCRIPTION (Please record exactly as it reads on stone, i.e. line by line and in same spatial order:

MASON:

TOWN:

EXCAVATION 1

SITE:		TRENCH/ SQUARE	
QUADRAT/ AREA:	SPIT/LEVEL/ CONTEXT:	DATE:	RECORDER/S:

Start Heights: End Heights:

WEIGHTS

Quadrat/ Area	Total	Coarse	Fine

Soil pH:

Soil Color:

Quadrat/ Area	Comments/Description	Please describe aspects of deposits in this order:
		Compaction Composition/ Particle size Inclusions Thickness & extent Other comments Method & conditions
		FINDS: ☐ None ☐ Stone ☐ Wood ☐ Seeds ☐ Ceramic ☐ Glass ☐ Bone ☐ Metal ☐ Plastic ☐ Other: ....
		PHOTOS: ☐ Yes ☐ No
		SAMPLES: ☐ None ☐ Bulk ☐ Soil ☐ Material for dating (please specify) ☐ Other: ....

EXCAVATION 2

SITE:

TRENCH/
SQUARE

QUADRAT/
AREA::

SPIT/LEVEL/
CONTEXT:

DATE:

RECORDER/S:

CONTEXT TYPE:

DEPOSIT ☐

CUT ☐

1. Compaction
2. Color
3. Composition/
   Particle size
4. Inclusions
5. Thickness & extent
6. Other comments
7. Method & conditions

1. Shape in plan
2. Dimensions
3. Depth
4. Orientation
5. Truncated
6. Other comments

Stratigraphic Matrix:

This context is: It correlates with:

Your interpretation: Internal External Structural Other

Your description of it:

Why do you think this?:

FINDS: ☐ None ☐ Seeds ☐ Bone ☐ Other:
☐ Stone ☐ Ceramic ☐ Metal
☐ Wood ☐ Glass ☐ Plastic

PHOTOS:
☐ Yes
☐ No

WEIGHTS:

Total Coarse Fine

SAMPLES:
☐ None ☐ Bulk
☐ Soil
☐ Material for dating
   (please specify)
☐ Other:

SKETCH PLAN (REMEMBER TO LABEL ALL CONTEXTS AND TO INCLUDE SCALE, NORTH AND DIMENSIONS):

LEVEL RECORDING

LEVEL RECORDING FORM

SITE:

SURVEYOR(S):

DATE:

Height of site datum:

☐ Height asl
☐ Arbitrary

Page ____ of ____

1. Level Position	2. Backsight	3. Inter-sight	4. Upper cross-hair	5. Lower cross-hair	6. Foresight	7. Height of Instrument (HOI) (Line of Collimation) [= RL + Backsight]	8. Reduced Level [= HOI - Inter-sight]	9. Upper cross-hair minus lower cross-hair	10. Distance in meters [= upper x-hair - lower x-hair x100]	11. Bearing (º)	12. Description

PHOTOGRAPHY

PHOTOGRAPHIC RECORDING FORM		

SITE: _____   DATE: _____

PHOTOGRAPHER: _____   CAMERA: _____

☐ Digital or   FILM TYPE: _____   FILM SPEED: _____   FILM No: _____

FRAME No.	DESCRIPTION	DIRECTION

RIM DIAMETER CHART

Note: The chart on page 396 must be enlarged by at least 206% to be accurate.

Rim/base diameter chart for ceramics

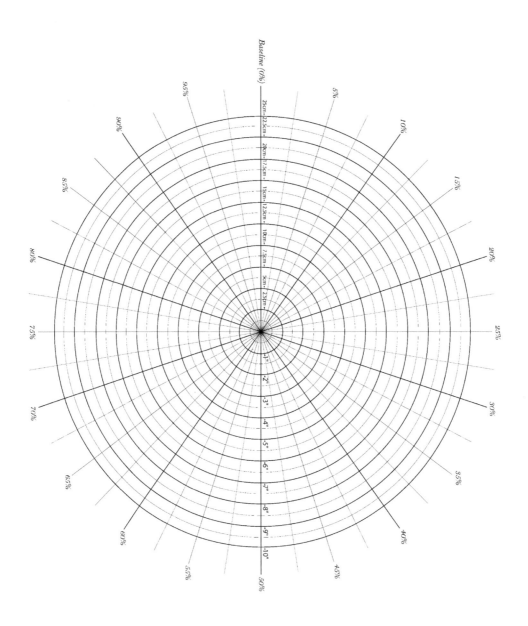

Rim/base diameter chart for ceramics

SAMPLE PRESS RELEASE

June 1, 2005
For Immediate Release

For more information contact:
Diane Brown, 317-274-7711
habrown@iupui.edu

IUPUI Anthropology Students Uncovering Remains of the Past

INDIANAPOLIS—Anthropology students are once again uncovering the buried past as the 2005 IUPUI Archaeology Field School runs through June 22. So far the dig site near the IUPUI campus has unearthed a diverse collection of household items, along with what is believed to be a pet burial site.

Students enrolled in the for-credit summer school class, offered by the School of Liberal Arts at IUPUI, are excavating three empty lots once occupied by homes at 903–913 California Street. Built in the 1870s, the homes were razed sometime between 1985 and the 1990s.

Students have begun digging excavation units in the backyards of the homes where a series of outbuildings, such as outhouses and stables, once stood, according to old insurance maps. These structures were typically used by residents to discard household trash.

This summer's dig is the sixth session of excavations conducted as part of the Ransom Place Archaeology program, a cooperative project between IUPUI, the Ransom Place Neighborhood Association, and the Indianapolis Urban League. The project uses archaeological excavations, oral historical research, and public interpretation to probe the complex confluence of African American culture, business and consumption, and race and racism in Indiana's capital city.

Artifacts uncovered so far this summer include a small porcelain doll, a Vaseline bottle, and a tin box that may have held makeup or cigarettes.

An excavation pit at the rear of 907–909 California Street has yielded a pocket of animal bones in what is believed to be a pet burial site. Further digging may yield a tag on the dog's collar or other buried clues to date the dog's demise.

"If an animal carcass was left exposed on the surface it would quickly be dismembered by a variety of neighborhood scavengers, so this was clearly an intentional pet burial," field anthropology professor and field school director Paul Mullins wrote May 30 in the online journal of field school activities.

"A series of small nails laying in lines directly alongside the body suggests the dog was either placed within a small box or had wood lining the sides of the burial shaft (though no wood survives in the burial or left a clear stain, which would typically happen)."

Visit the website www.iupui.edu/~anthpm/fieldschool2005.html to follow the escapades of Mullins and his class of modern-day Indiana Joneses.

Or stop by the site. Dig hours are 8:30 a.m. to 3 p.m., with a lunch break from noon to 1 p.m., Mondays through Fridays. Visitors are welcome to come observe or join in as volunteers.

APPENDIX D
INTERPRETATION PROJECT PLANNER

STORY OUTLINE

Use this table to indicate an outline for your interpretation. **Themes/messages** are the general elements of the overall story that you think are important and want to convey. Although they could just as easily be told at more than one place, the **story elements** are the ways in which you would illustrate these themes/messages at this *particular* place. **Physical elements/remains** asks you to note down the physical (archaeological) features of the place that could be used effectively to tell particular parts of the story.

Table D.1: Story outline

Place or element of place	Possible stories	Themes/messages	Story elements	Sites/physical remains
EXAMPLE ONLY	**Landscape:** Human interaction Changes	**Humans are constantly interacting with the landscape**	**Indigenous use of resources and meanings of landscape elements**	**Sources of food/water/materials Medicinal plant species Camping places**
	Ecological relationships: Between people and plants Between people and animals			

INTERPRETATION PROJECT PLANNER

Program/Project (title):

Site/Place:

Intended audience [type(s) of people and their age range]:

Is there any information about who visits this site now and why?

Visitor Analysis (if Possible)

Estimate of visitor numbers:

What are their needs?

What are their expectations?

What are their movements (i.e., from where have they come and to where are they going)?

Linked interpretation opportunities (are there any complementary sites?):

General objectives for audience to obtain (the aims of your interpretation):

Specific objectives for audience to obtain:

Knowledge/appreciation of:

Skills of:

Attitudes/values of:

Theme(s) of your interpretation:

Chosen technique(s):

Essential equipment (if any):

Content outline:

CHECKLISTS FOR TABLES, FIGURES, REFERENCES, AND LITERATURE REVIEWS

Checklist for Tables and Figures

❏ Does the table or figure contribute to the presentation?
❏ Have the data/accuracy been checked?
❏ Does the table or figure follow its mention in the text?
❏ Should the table or figure be included in the text or an appendix?
❏ Are the tables and figures numbered consecutively?
❏ Are sufficient details given to interpret the table or figure? Is it self-explanatory?
❏ Is the caption sufficiently detailed?
❏ Are the captions in the text consistent with the List of Tables or List of Figures?
❏ Has a consistent format been used for all tables or figures?
❏ Are units of measurement clearly stated?
❏ Are abbreviations explained in the table or figure?
❏ Could the table or figure be presented more simply?
❏ Are column entries in tables correctly aligned?
❏ In figures, are vertical and horizontal axes of graphs labeled?
❏ In figures, is the zero position on the vertical axis shown?
❏ In figures, are units of measurements indicated and clearly shown on axes?
❏ In figures, are the separate observations comprising the graph marked?
❏ Can the figure or table be easily read?
❏ Is the table correctly positioned on the page?

Checklist for References

❏ Has each page of the references been numbered?
❏ Has every work cited in the text been included in the bibliography/references cited?
❏ Have the rules for alphabetical and chronological ordering of references been consistently followed?
❏ Have institutional requirements for referencing format been met?
❏ Does each book reference include:

❏ —author(s)?
❏ —date of publication?
❏ —title of book?
❏ —publisher?
❏ —place of publication?

❏ Does each journal reference include:

❏ —author(s)
❏ —date of publication?
❏ —title of paper?
❏ —title of journal?
❏ —issue and volume number?
❏ —inclusive page numbers?

❏ Have the rules for spacing, capitalization, and underlining been followed consistently?

Checklist for Literature Reviews

❏ Have you synthesized the known archaeology of the region and identified the limits of this in relation to the study area?

❏ Have you synthesized the known archaeology of the study area, including all sites previously found within or near the study area?

❏ Have you assessed the results of earlier studies in light of current knowledge and of what you propose to do?

❏ Have you synthesized the ethnographic information available for the study area and its surrounding region?

❏ Have you identified the range of archaeological evidence that is likely to be expected in the study area?

❏ From this information, have you identified the main archaeological issues and questions that you will address within your study?

❏ From this information, have you presented potential models for past human use of the landscape that are relevant to your research problem?

DETAILED CHECKLIST FOR CHM/CONSULTANCY REPORTS

CHECKLIST FOR CHM/CONSULTANCY REPORTS

This is only one suggested format for a standard consultancy report, and not all categories will apply in every circumstance. Particular states, provinces, or agencies may have specific reporting standards. Check with them before writing your report.

Title Page
- ❏ Title of report
- ❏ Client or group for whom it is prepared
- ❏ Date
- ❏ Author's name and address

❏ Acknowledgments

Summary/Abstract
- ❏ Overview of project
- ❏ Overview of results
- ❏ Overview of significance
- ❏ Overview of recommendations
- ❏ Any restrictions on the use of the report or on the information contained within the report

❏ **(Table of) Contents**
❏ **(Table of) Figures**
❏ **(Table of) Tables**

Introduction

❏ Brief description of project
❏ Where the project is located (e.g., brief statement of nearest town or important geographical feature, state or area of state, borders of study area) and why the project was commissioned/carried out
❏ Who commissioned/funded the project
❏ Aims and scope of the study (include any formal briefs or informal instructions issued as part of the project)
❏ Types of investigation conducted (e.g., field survey, Indigenous consultation, excavation, document searches, oral histories)
❏ When fieldwork, analysis, and report writing took place
❏ Who undertook fieldwork, analysis, and report writing
❏ Any constraints or limitations imposed on the project (e.g., bad weather, limited time, attitudes of landowners, particular instructions that limited the survey in any way, such as instructions from tribal elders to stay away from areas)
❏ Any constraints or limitations of the data (including documentary sources) collected during the project (e.g., lack of suitable oral history informants, loss of data, inability to find certain information)

Background Information

❏ General description of study area (e.g., size, present land use, access)
❏ General description of environment (e.g., geology/geomorphology, topography, water courses, flora and fauna, relevant raw material sources)
❏ Previous impacts on the study area (e.g., past logging, clearing, plowing, mining, erosion)
❏ Description of proposed development and associated works, including what activities could be expected to have an impact on the archaeology

Previous Research

❏ Relevant ethnographic studies and findings within the region and the study area
❏ Relevant historical studies and findings within the region and the study area
❏ Relevant archaeological studies and findings within the region and the study area
❏ Relevant oral histories and findings within the region and the study area

Methods

❏ Research strategy and aims
❏ Detailed description of fieldwork methods for all stages of fieldwork; outline clearly the equipment and techniques used to implement the research strategy (e.g., choice and location of sample areas, recording methods, collection methods, storage of artifacts/information, methods of analysis)
❏ Discussion of any problems that arose during fieldwork, analysis, or report writing
❏ Detail of the constraints on archaeological visibility during the survey
❏ Description of any decisions made in the field or the laboratory that changed the scope of the study
❏ Details of personnel involved
❏ Details about the curation of artifacts, records, field notes, and photographs

Results

❏ Summary of what was found or achieved (e.g., quantities, types, distribution)
❏ Description of findings based on field notes and recording forms
❏ Relevant tabulations of data, photographs, and illustrations

Discussion

❏ Summary of points of interest or major research problems emerging from the study
❏ Discussion of the evidence in regional and local perspective
❏ Implications of the findings and areas for future research

Assessment of Significance

❏ General statements of significance for the study area
❏ Specific statements of significance for individual sites/areas (including whether further research is necessary to adequately determine significance)

Statement of Impacts

❏ Implications of the probable effects of development on the study area and the findings (including both direct and indirect impacts)

Recommendations

❏ General management recommendations, including alternatives where possible (e.g., dealing with the study area in general or with particular zones or areas within it)

❑ Specific management recommendations, including alternatives where possible (e.g., dealing with individual sites or artifacts)

❑ Discussion of any issues or problems attached to these recommendations (e.g., client's preferences, difficulties, attitudes, compromises)

❑ Identification of any legal requirements or processes that must be followed

References

Appendixes

❑ Relevant additional information, including information that needs to be kept restricted

❑ A glossary of any technical terms or definitions used in the report (including definitions of artifact types, attributes, measurements)

❑ Copy of the project brief and any other relevant information from the client outlining the scope of work

❑ Letters of advice outlining management recommendations/opinions from community groups (e.g., tribal councils)

INDEX

ABOUT THE AUTHORS

Heather Burke is senior lecturer in the Department of Archaeology at Flinders University in Adelaide, Australia, and has many years' experience as a consultant archaeologist.

Claire Smith is president of the World Archaeological Congress and University and research professor in the Institute of the Advanced Study for Humanity at the University of Newcastle, Australia.

Larry J. Zimmerman is professor of anthropology and museum studies and Public Scholar of Native American Representation at Indiana University–Purdue University Indianapolis and Eiteljorg Museum.

CPSIA information can be obtained
at www.ICGtesting.com
Printed in the USA
LVHW062347100520
655330LV00014B/2071